2013

COACH OF THE YEAR CLINICS
FOOTBALL CLINIC NOTES

Lectures by Premier High School Coaches

Edited by Earl Browning

Telecoach, Inc.
www.nikecoyfootball.net

The More We Tell
The More We Sell

ISBN: 978-1-932540-05-5
ISSN: 1945-1202

Telecoach, Inc. Transcription: Kent Browning, Emmerson Browning, and Tom Cheaney
Diagrams: Travis Rose
Book layout and cover design: Emmerson Browning - Telecoach Inc.

Cover photo: (front) John T. Curtis High School, LA
Cover photo: (back) John T. Curtis High School, LA
Cover photo: (back) Mount Carmel High School, IL

Special Thanks to the Nike Clinic Managers for having the lectures taped.

Telecoach, Inc.
3512 Foxglove Lane
Louisville, KY 40241
www.nikecoyfootball.net

Table of Contents

John Beck

Drills Used To Develop Linebackers

Crater High School, Oregon

The Oregon High School Coaches Association does a fantastic job of putting on a first class football clinic. We can all go to the clinic and hear great speakers and I am delighted to be a part of it. I have seen many of my coaching buddies this week.

I was talking to some of the coaches earlier in the day and they asked about my background. I started in Hermiston, Oregon and was there for six years. I moved from there to Barlow High School for eight years. That was a fun time and a great learning experience. From there I went to North Medford, which is one of the best places there is to coach football. That was a great opportunity. I went to Crater High School after that, which is an interesting story in itself.

Crater High School is in a low social-economic area. It had always been the little brother and in some cases little sister, to Medford High School. My entire staff came from North Medford to Crater High School. It has been a great experience to build the program at Crater. We have the best community support, great parents, and great players. The boosters are phenomenal and it is a great situation.

I coach the linebackers. I added up all the years and I have played or coached linebackers for a total of 39 years. I am not telling you I have all the answers but I have done it for a long time. I have a system to develop players as freshmen all the way to their senior year. I like how things have developed and played out over the years. I hope you get something from this lecture.

I have coached several years in different places. Very rarely do you have a player come through your program that is a Division-I player. That is especially true in Southern Oregon because the population base centers in the metro areas of Salem, Eugene, and Portland. The last couple of years, I have had a player that fits the fantasy mold for Division-I players. I had a Samoan linebacker this year that is 6-2, 251 pounds, and he ran an 11.1 hundred yard dash. He is the real deal. He got a full ride to the University of Arizona. If he stays healthy, he will play at the next level. However, most of my linebackers fall into the 5-11 to six foot, and 175-190 pound category. That is the reality of coaching in Southern Oregon.

We look for certain qualities in a linebacker.

DEVELOPING LINEBACKERS

Qualities we look for in a Linebacker

- **Play maker**
- **Wants to play defense**
- **Has a desire to learn the game of football**
- **Coachable**
- **Great work ethic**
- **Loves to hit**
- **Physical size does not matter; size of heart does**

When you go down to watch kids in the middle school or Pop Warner Leagues you can see these qualities in those players. We want to find the players that can make plays. They may not be playing linebacker but we want to find the players that are making plays. If they have good motor skills and move well and hustle, they are the players I am looking for to play linebacker. We can teach them the techniques.

I want players that want to play defense. They may not look the role but they want to play linebacker. If you have to ask a player to move from a defensive back position to linebacker, it may not work out so well. The player that verbalizes about being a good tackler is the one I want playing linebacker.

They must have a desire to learn the game of football. They must be willing to put time in to watch films with other coaches. They must attend more summer camps. I want to know if they are spending the extra time on Hudl and other football media sources to learn football and get to the next level?

I want to know if they are coachable. Are they a "yes sir and no sir" type of player? If their attention moves in and out, they are not the type of player I am looking for to play this position. I need their full attention.

I want a player that has a great work ethic. I want him to be the first player in the weight room and the last one to leave it. I want them to be the first on the football field and last to leave. I want them doing all the extra things it takes to play the position.

Above all qualities for a linebacker they must love to hit. They must be physical players. With all the talk today about concussions, I have to be careful with that quality. I need to know if they like the physicality of playing linebacker and the collisions that go along with it. It is not the size of the player that counts bit it is the size of his **heart**.

Linebacker Fundamentals

- **Being able to Communicate is essential!**
  - Teach them how (In all Drills)
- **Let the player know your expectations:**
  - Attitude in practice – games
  - Speed – Quality of practice drills
  - Alignment – Rules – Responsibilities
  - If you think you are wrong
  - It is OK to be mad
  - Be willing to listen to your player as a coach

Everyone has coached linebackers that were the quietest players on the field. I coached a couple at North Medford High School who ended up being first team All-State linebackers. In our system, our linebackers are the quarterbacks of our defense. We had to teach these players to be the communicators on the defense. We teach them how to do that in our drills.

As a Coach, you must have a variety of drills that fit your scheme. You need to divide the drills by days. On Monday, we practice on the run. On Tuesday, we work on defending the passing game. On Wednesday, we work on the tendencies of the opponent. We have a variety of drills that fit what our opponent is showing offensively. We want to coach technique in every drill! It is important to keep a variety of drills for each phase of the game.

The first thing you do in the development of a linebacker is to work stance and footwork. You can coach stance while you are doing your footwork drills. The movement drills we use are:

- **Buzz – Go**
- **Buzz – Wave – Go**
- **Big Wave**
- **Shuffle over the bags – Scoop and Score**
- **High Knees over the bags – Strip and Score**
- **Box Drill**

When I do a drill, I do not like to use more than four linebackers at one time. (Diagram #1) When we do the "buzz and go", the coach stands five yards in front of them. I like to put them in our schematic for linebackers. We play with a Ram, Backer, Mike, and Whip linebackers. In the drill, the first thing they do is align in a good stance where their feet are parallel. I want their butts down, knees bent and on the balls of their feet with the heels off the ground a small bit. If they are an inside linebacker, we want the hands inside the knee. If they are an outside linebacker, we want them outside the knees.

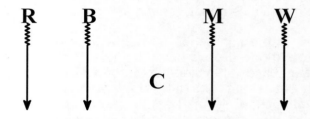

Diagram #1. Buzz and Go

When we scout teams, we want to know the cadence they use in games. We introduce that cadence in this drill. We want our players to hear the opponent's cadence and get uses to it. The coach gives a start movement and the linebackers buzz their feet staying in a good fundamental position. We do not want to take any false steps in this drill. He gives them the motion to come downhill and they attack forward without false stepping or going backward. We check their stance and footwork in this drill.

The next progression is the "buzz, wave, and go." (Diagram #2) The coach uses the cadence and starts the drill with movement. They buzz their feet and the coach gives them a shuffle direction with the football. He moves them right and left with the ball. He checks their stance and their footwork to make sure they do not take big steps or crossing their feet. We want small choppy steps within the framework of their body. The coach gives them a go motion and they repeat the first drill and come forward without false stepping.

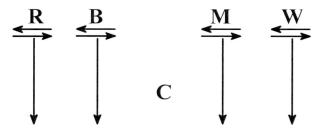

Diagram #2. Buzz, Wave, and Go

One of the drills I use for movement is an NFL linebacker drill. (Diagram #3) The coach told me if you want to find out how athletic they are, run them in a wave drill over half round bags. Place the bags in lines and have them wave run over them. It allows you to see which players can get over the bags efficiently and which ones cannot. We do not do this drill too much, but we use it periodically. It tells you who needs the work. We want them to step over and not to cross their feet.

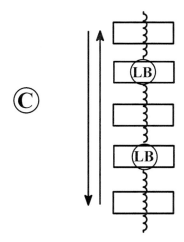

Diagram #3. Big Wave

The next drill is "club shuffle over the bags." (Diagram #4) This is a good drill especially on pass rush days. The linebacker starts the drill with a club to pin the outside shoulder. He goes over the bags in a lateral direction. Over the last bag is another pop-up dummy. He clubs with the opposite arm at the first dummy. At the end of the drill, the coach rolls out a ball, he scoops the ball, and scores with the fumble. To change the drill you can put a form tackle at the end instead of the scoop and score. This drill works on the club and rip as well as the tackling and scooping skills.

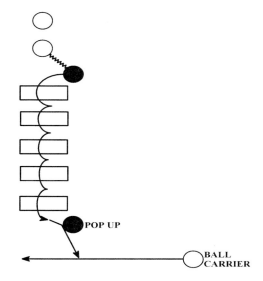

Diagram #4. Club Shuffle

We use the next drill in our turnover circuit. (Diagram #5) It is similar to the previous drill without the clubbing movement. This works on movement and pad level. They shuffle over the bags getting their hands down on the bags as they go over them. They keep their pad levels down and move laterally across the bags. You can run any type of finish to the drill you want. We work scoop and score on the end of this one.

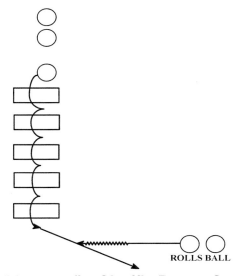

Diagram #5. Shuffle Bags - Score

Anytime you do a drill, make sure you have a finish to the drill. Have a combination skill at the end of the drill. You can tackle, scoop and score, intercept a pass, or anything you can think to do.

Another drill we do in the turnover circuit is the "high knee strip." (Diagram #6) We have been statistically 1st or 2nd in turnover margin in our league eight out of the last nine years. I believe it is because we work on creating turnovers all the time. The linebacker runs over the bags running forward. We look for the pad level down as he goes over the bags.

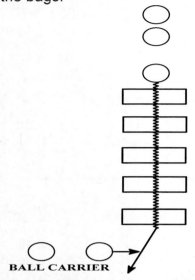

Diagram #6. High Knee Strip

As the ball comes out, he wants to scoop it and score. At the end of the bags is a ball carrier with the ball in the arm toward the tackler. The linebacker plants his foot, secures the back shoulder of the ball carrier, and wenches the ball free with his inside hand.

One of my favorite drills is the "box" drill. (Diagram #7) The drill is set up in a 10 X 10 yard box. We put two players in the box and give them directions of movement. We give them lateral wave, pass drop right and left, forward run, up/downs, and move backward. It is a movement drill with two players in the box.

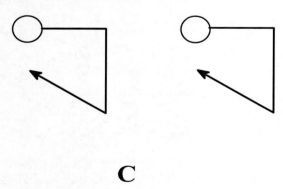

Diagram #7. Box Drill

We also do this drill as a conditioning drill and we want to do it when they are tired.

The next part of playing linebacker is taking on the blocker and separating from the block. The linebacker has to strike and separate from the block and run to the ball. We have a teaching progression we use. The first thing you must teach is the strike. In the beginning, we do that on a one-man sled. They want to attack the blocker, put our toes on his toes, and attack half the man. We play gap control defense and use the half man technique.

We want to get our toes on his toes, strike with the hands to the breastplate, and extend the arms up into the throat area. The feet must be in motion the entire time. We want to move the blocker backward, disengage, and get to the ball. We accomplish that three different ways in our drills.

- **Strike – Separate and Shuffle (R-L)**
- **Strike – Separate – Shuffle – Tackle (R-L)**
- **Strike – Separate – Read the Ball Carrier**

We use the Popsicle sled (one-man sled) to do this drill. (Diagram #8) In the first progression, we use the strike, separate, and shuffle off the sled. They strike the sled and extend their arms, drive the sled back and release, and then shuffle right or left. We watch their feet to make sure they do not step back before they strike the sled. We incorporate the second part of the drill and add a ball carrier moving to one side or the other. They perform the first part of the drill and attack into a form tackle on the ball carrier.

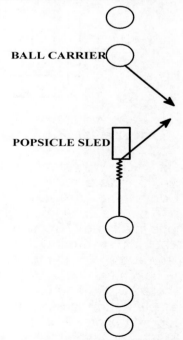

Diagram #8. Strike, Separate, and Tackle

The third part of the drill is to react to the movement with the ball carrier. (Diagram #9) When the linebacker attacks the sled, he is attacking half the dummy. If the ball carrier moves to the other side of the dummy, the linebacker has to redirect his separation and get across the face of the dummy. He has to react to the ball carrier in either direction. They do not separate until they see which way the ball carrier is going.

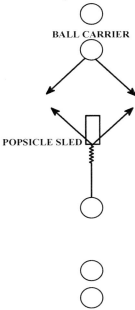

Diagram #9. Strike, Separate and Read

After we work the drills on the sled, we go work against people. The first drill is the "triangle strike" drill. (Diagram #10) This is a padded drill. We have three blockers and a linebacker. The linebacker aligns in the middle of the three blockers. There is one head up the linebacker and one to each side in a three-point stance angled in toward the linebacker.

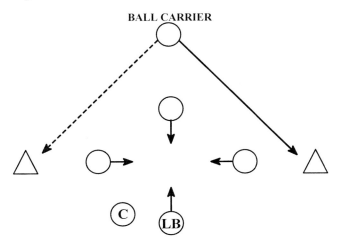

Diagram #10. Triangle Strike

It is a reaction strike and recoil action by the linebacker. The coach stands behind the linebacker and directs the blockers. He calls them one at a time by pointing to them. The linebacker reacts to each blocker and recoils back into his position. On the last blocker, he separates and performs a form tackle to the outside on a cone.

The next drill is an "angle strike" and get over the top drill. (Diagram #11) This drill teaches the linebacker how to play across an outside crack block or down block from the outside. He has to club and get over the top of the blocker. He cannot go under the blocker. If he goes under the block, he better make the tackle. In the drill, we have two blockers and one linebacker. The linebacker starts in the middle of the two blockers who are three yards inside and outside of him. If the outside blocker comes first, the linebacker has to strike him and fight over the top of his block to the outside. Once he gets to that position, the second blocker attacks him from the opposite direction. He repeats the drill, separates and attacks the ball carrier at the end of the drill in a form tackle.

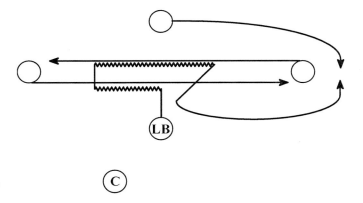

Diagram #11. Angle Strike

When the linebacker plays the outside block, he punches to the breastplate and grabs the outside shoulder. He extends his arms, pulls with the outside shoulder, and rips with the inside hand to the outside.

The zone drill has two blockers and a linebacker. (Diagram #12) This is a read and react drill. We read pass or run from the two blockers. The linebacker aligns on the center in the group but reacts to the two outside blockers. If he gets run action, the linebacker wants to get underneath the blocker. He buzzes his feet, tilts his torso, and runs underneath the blocker to make a form tackle on the ball carrier. He turns his shoulder and rolls off the blocker. The move is not a rip. It is a shoulder roll off movement. If the blocker shows pass, the linebacker drops into his pass responsible.

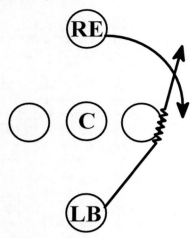

Diagram #12. Zone Drill

The "skate drill" is an upfield defeat the block drill. (Diagram #12) There are three parts to the drill. The linebacker defeats a block at the line of scrimmage. He works up the field and defeats a perimeter block. He continues up the field and makes a form tackle on the ball carrier. This is a great drill with option teams. When we play option teams, we run the drill daily. We run it periodically during the other weeks.

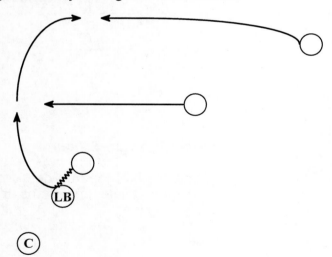

Diagram #13. Skate Drill

We like to put the linebacker at a disadvantage. We can block him high or low. I know cut blocking is illegal, but we want the linebacker to attack playing with his hands on the blocker at whatever level that may be. We also give the perimeter blocker an advantage so the linebacker has to work to get outside leverage on his block.

Tackling is the most important skill in playing defense. This goes to our defensive philosophy. Tackling is the most visible attribute a defensive player can display. It does not matter how fast you run, how hard you hit, how great a pass rusher or pass defender you are, without the ability to tackle with confidence and control you will not be considered a great player. Conversely, be known and respected as a force on the defensive unit.

What makes a great tackler? To a tackler outstanding physical ability is not essential. What is essential is an intense burning desire and determination to get to the ball carrier and bring him down to the ground in the most advantageous manner for the defense. We can teach the other techniques. You cannot teach heart.

The coach is so important in teaching the defense to run to the ball. If you coach the linebackers get behind them in drills and run to the ball with them. Encourage them and let them see you participating with them in running to the ball. Be the leader and they will follow. Our linebacker coaches run to the ball with our players.

TACKLING AXIOMS:

There are certain physical constants in outstanding tackling that we must always emphasize.

- **Chest and eyes up**
- **Low pad level**
- **Z in the knees "good bent knee position"**
- **Eyes across the bow**
- **Strike on the rise**
- **Explode the hips and eyes on contact**
- **When you are ready to tackle, take one more step**
- **Wrap arms and dig fingers into cloth**
- **Drive feet and square hips**

When you get to the tackle, you tackle through the man and not to him. The form tackle is primarily the same thing as tackling techniques.

The Form Tackle:

- **Close on the ball carrier with proper attack angle**
- **Break down in the open field with low pad level**
- **If not on the open field, attack on the rise with low pad level**
- **Eyes are up and across the bow**

- Explode eyes on contact
- Wrap up and lock fingers, dig into cloth
- Drive hips and keep driving until ball carrier is down

One of the things we pride ourselves on is getting people to the football. In our films, we consistently have 8, 9, 10, and 11 defenders around the football. The first defender makes the tackle and drives the ball carrier up the field.

Second – Third – Fourth Man:

Whatever your angle or position, the other players involved in any tackle must put their whole effort into the following:

- **Insure tackle and polish off ball carrier**
- **Make everything go backwards**
- **Strip the ball**
- **Carrier swarm to the football, we want 11 hats on the ball.**

We have five tackling drill we use. I am sure most of you do these drill. We have an **angle tackling** drill, which is a form tackling drill to teach head, hand, shoulder, and leg position. They align in pairs with a ball carrier and tackler. The tackler starts one man behind the ball carrier. Do not start them off in an even position. If you do that, the ball carrier plants, breaks backside, and the defender arm tackles. They are one yard apart and go at a 45 degree angle toward the coach. The tacklers apply his tackling technique in the above statements. Make sure you go both directions so they tackle with both shoulders.

We do the same thing in the **down the line tackling**. It is a hip movement drill. It forces the tackler to get into position to tackle any time the runner turns up. The ball carrier changes speed three times during the rep. We want a walk speed, a jog speed, and a run speed. This teaches the linebacker to keep the same relationship of one man behind the ball carrier. He has to learn to turn the hips and run while keeping his shoulders square to the line. We run the drill from the sideline to the hash mark. At the end, the ball carrier turns up and we do an angle form tackle at this point.

The sideline tackle is at a close distance (5 yards apart) close to the sideline. (Diagram #14) The ball carrier has two moves. He can cut back on the tackler or try to beat the tackler up the sidelines. The ball carrier goes at 50 percent speed and the tackler is at 70 percent speed.

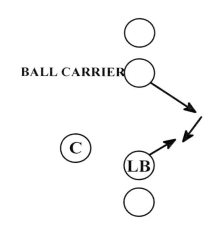

Diagram #14. Sideline Tackle

The "Arbuckle" open field tackling drill starts at ten yards apart. The tackler is on one side and the ball carrier is on the other. They run toward each other. Immediately before five yards, the ball carrier has to make an inside or outside move. When the running back comes to balance to avoid the tackle, the linebacker does the same thing and applies his angle tackling techniques. The coaching point is to focus on the belt and not on the shoulders. This is not a full speed drill. We run this at 70 percent of full speed.

You can run the "eye opener" drill a million ways. The one I am going to show you is one we like. (Diagram #15) We try to hold the distance down and work on the technique of the drill. The runner has three ways to go. He can go straight ahead, right, or left. The tackler uses his tackling technique in the tackle wherever it is made.

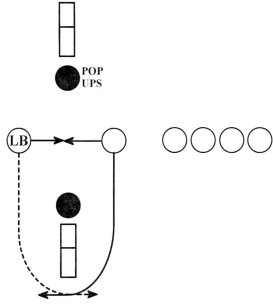

Diagram #15. Eye Opener

The phrase we use with the tackler is to "get your eyes up and bite the football."

With all the teams playing spread schemes, we have to teach the linebackers pass drops. On the snap of the ball, the linebackers drops at a 45 degree angle to their drop area and plays inside out on receivers. We check the nearest threat to the receiver to the quarterback. That is our triangle read. The linebacker tilts at a 45 degree angle and retreats until the quarterback sets up. At that point, the linebacker begins to backpedal and gain depth. If we use a cone drop drill, we are teaching the linebacker to take his 45 degree angle and get to a spot in his zone.

The "Palamar" drill is a break flat drill. (Diagram #16) The linebacker backpedals straight back from the coach. When the coach cocks his arm, the linebacker breaks on the throw and intercepts the ball. There are two receivers in the drill. The coach throws to one or the other. The entire objective of the drill is to get to the ball. If they round their corners or run bananas to the ball they will not get there.

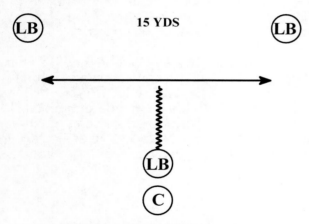

Diagram #16. Palamar Drill

The next drill is the combination of the zone drop and the Palamar drill. The linebacker uses his 45 degree angle drop and breaks flat to intercept the ball. The linebacker tilts, drops, backpedals, and breaks flat in this drill.

The "quick neck" drill is a by-product of modern football. (Diagram #17) It is a zone drop with a speed turn technique. The linebacker zone drops by using a 45 degree angle drop. If he gets a crossing pattern and tries to zone turn back the other way, he loses the receiver. He does not plant and open his hips the opposite way, he flips his head and neck around and speed turns into the receiver.

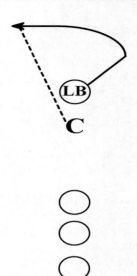

Diagram #17. Quick Neck

The linebackers have a read progression. They read the line, to the near back, and to the quarterback. We have four linebackers focusing on reading the quarterback. The quarterback can take a 3-step, 5-step, sprint out, naked, and boot action. The linebackers must react to each of those movements. The inside playside linebacker is the secondary contain man if the quarterback leaves the tackle box to his side.

The Ram linebacker covers the deep flat on that action. The backside inside linebacker mirrors the quarterback. The backside outside linebacker drops and tries to get under the post dig from the backside receivers.

You have to drill the linebacker on what to do if he takes the bait on a play action pass. We teach them to forget about everything but getting to his drop spot. He turns his back on the quarterback and gets back as quickly as he can to his responsibility. When he gets there, he can square up and look to the quarterback.

Thanks for your attention and good luck next year.

Brian Blackmon

Power Running Game "Truck Series"

Opelika High School, Alabama

It is a pleasure to be here. I am going to talk about the "Truck Play" because that is something in which we believe. I want to use this platform to share a couple of things I believe about coaching. I want to tell you why I coach. My background was not in coaching. My degree was in accounting. I was going to school to be an accountant. I saw dollar signs and all I wanted to do was make money.

While I was getting my master degree, I got an opportunity to go back to my home school and coach football for my old high school coach. I fell in love with coaching and decided that was going to be my calling. There are some startling statistics in society today. I think it directly gives a reason of why we need coaches.

The job description of a football coach is bigger now than it has ever been. One day you must be a counselor. The next day you are a chauffeur. You have to be a teacher and father figure to some of your players. The job description for coaches will not fit on one side of a sheet of paper on your resume.

We live in a country where 65 percent of youth suicides come from fatherless homes. Eighty-five percent of children with behavioral disorders come from fatherless homes. Seventy-one percent of high school dropouts come from fatherless home. The most startling statistic says that 70 percent of the youth in state institutions today come from fatherless homes. The job that coaches have today is unbelievable. There are 13.7 million single parents in our society. There are 22 million children raised in single parent homes. That is 25 percent of all the children in the United States. Eighty-two percent of those single parents are moms.

Sometimes the only male figure the player has in his life is his coach. I am that coach that is trying to discipline them for the first time. I am the first male that is telling them what they are going to do. You will find out that can lead to rebellion.

If you have rules without relationships, that will equals rebellion. That statement goes for your household and your own children. If you try to discipline your children and do not establish a relationship with them, they will rebel.

We are going through a culture change. In 1960, 17 percent of the children in this country went to bed at night without a father figure in the home. That figure is up to 25 percent today. That is why I believe coaching is so important.

Coaching is a fraternity. We do not have any secrets. We try to do what we do to the very best of our ability. I like to play games against my friends. If you coach with a grudge against another coach, you will never be the coach you want to be. On Friday night, as coaches, we are going to coach and compete as hard as we can, shake hands at the end of the game, and walk off the field. We are not supposed to treat each other with disrespect off the field or let our players hear us talk about other coaches with disrespect.

If we have a player thrown out of a game for swinging at another player, it all starts with us. Everything starts from the top and I believe that. My best friends are coaches. Banker, lawyers, or accountants cannot help me when my best player is acting like a butt hole in school. If I am trying to run behind a 200 pound tackle against a 300 pound defender, there is no doctor I can call that will give me help with that problem.

That is why what I do for a living is so important to me. In this profession, you need to be able to separate "who you are" from "what you do." That is huge and it took me a long time to figure it out. I am still working through that. I hope I will eventually get there. Who I am is a child of God. Who I am is a husband. Who I am is a father to my children. What I do is coach football. Actually what I do is coach kids to play football.

Today we are going to talk about our "truck play" and the things we do off it.

OUR PHILOSOPHY

- **Spread to RUN!**
  - **Tough mentality**
- **Use Multiple formations and motions.**
- **Run to Equated Numbers.**
- **Gap Schemes and Zone Schemes.**
- **Spread the Ball around. Make them defend all skill players.**
- **Play Fast! Mentally and Physically.**
  - **Tempo**
  - **Knowledge**

We are a running team. We did average 17 throws a game. We do not spread the offense to throw the ball all over the place. We are a run first play action team. We want to create a tough mentality. When the Air Raid offense came out, I felt it had some merit but I felt it was a finesse offense. If you were a spread team, you were a finesse team. I do not believe in that.

I met with Tony Franklin and talked about the offense he runs. The only thing I think about that offense was it did not have a solid ground game. I believe that playing great defense and running the ball is how you win football games.

We use multiple formations, motion, and we try to run to equated numbers. We use zone and gap schemes. The "truck" play is our number one gap scheme play. This play is where we hang our hats. If you play wing-T football, the "truck" is akin to the buck sweep. My personal philosophy is to run the zone scheme against odd fronts and gap schemes at even fronts.

We want to spread the ball around and make the defense defend all our skilled players. We do that in the pass and run games. We run the "truck" play with slot receivers, wide receiver, the quarterback, and running back. We try to move the ball around and give different looks. We try to play fast both mentally and physically.

In high school, we have to figure out who we have on our team and try to win with them. That is the fun part of coaching. The teams from year to year change with what the players can do and what they cannot do. We need to understand our players and the players have to know what we want. If we set a standard and hold them to it, I believe they will accomplish what we want.

That is a little about who we are. I believe you need a base play. For the last 6 or 7 years that play has been the "truck" play for us. It sets the tone for our offense. Everybody that plays us knows we run this play. They still have to defend the play. We run the play any time on any down. If everything else goes haywire, we can go to this play and run it. We have confidence in it and feel comfortable with it. Our players believe in it because we believe in it.

BASICS OF THE TRUCK

- **Must always have a down blocker on the edge; Either a Wing or a flex Tight End**
- **Better play to trips**
- **Can run with any skill player (versatile)**
- **Great play vs. Squeezing Defensive End**
- **If overload to trips check counter or shuffle**
- **Can pull guards, center, or tackles**
- **Vs. 3 man front use TE or Double 4 to PSLB**

This play is a better play to the trips set. We love to set our trips look into the boundary and run it into the short side of the field. It is a great play because most coaches will not load up into the boundary. They would rather defender the field than the boundary.

We like to run the play against a squeezing defensive end. We want to see how the defensive end is playing. Does he play up the field or squeeze down? We play games with him. We can read him, block him, kick him out, trap him, and try to stretch him. If he is trying to play a hard squeeze, this is a great play to run against him.

If you run this play along with the power play, it becomes better. You kick him out on the power. He squeezes inside and starts to wrong shoulder the block and we down block on him.

You can pull your guards, center, or tackles. We base the play on the personnel we have. If you have a center that is athletic enough to pull, do it. When you run this play against a three-man front you need to use a tight end or double the 4-technique with the wingback and offensive tackle to the playside linebacker.

Our basic alignment is a trips set with a wingback outside the tackle to the three receiver side. (Diagram #1) The wingback could be your tight end. He sets in 2 X 2 feet set outside the tackle's hip in a square stance. He has no stagger in his feet so he can step with either foot in any direction. The offensive linemen have a two-foot split between each lineman.

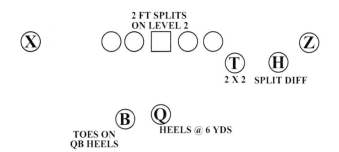

2 FT SPLITS
ON LEVEL 2

2 X 2   SPLIT DIFF

TOES ON
QB HEELS

HEELS @ 6 YDS

Diagram #1. Base Alignment

We say our linemen are on a level two depth off the line of scrimmage. That means they are in a three-point stance with their hands on the center's toes. You must coach your guards to be in a balanced stance and not tip the defense as to when they pull.

If the ball is in the middle of the field, the wide outs are around the top of the numbers. If the ball is on the hash, the receiver to the boundary is at the bottom of the numbers. The field receiver is two yards outside the hash mark.

The H-back or slot receiver splits the difference between the tight end and wide receiver. We have different kinds of players in that spot. We prefer to have a bigger player at the slot so he can crack on the playside linebacker. The defender that makes the tackle on this play is the frontside linebacker.

Trying to wrap the guard to the frontside linebacker is hard. If you can crack with the slot on the frontside linebacker, it becomes a better play. The quarterback aligns in the shotgun with his heels at six yards. The running back has his toes on the heels of the quarterback. We try to keep that alignment standard regardless of the play.

We base our offensive line rules on the Wing-t offense. I came from a Wing-t background and played in that offense.

Offensive Line Rules

- **PST:** Down, Zero linebacker, BSLB (vs. 4 tech. Combo W/ Wing)
- **PSG:** Pull (if 1st puller out kick force, if not turn up & check inside out) Listen for Uno call from the back
- **C:** PS A gap to BS A gap (vs. double A's make "stay" call to BS guard)

- **BSG:** Pull turn up. Look inside out. Stay call, Scoop BS A gap.
- **BST:** Secure B-gap; Cut BS 3 Tech

The playside tackle's rule is down. That means he blocks down on anything aligned between him and the offensive guard. If he has a 4i, 3, or 2-technique, he blocks down. If there is a 0-technique linebacker and the tackle has no defender in a down block situation, he blocks the 0-technique linebacker.

If he has a 4-technique defender aligned on him and a 0-linebacker, he blocks the 0-linebacker. However, he cannot simply step inside on the way to the linebacker. The 4-technique defender is a hard slant defender most of the time. If he tries to release inside, the slanting defender will cave him down the line of scrimmage. He takes an inside step and parks the 4-technique until the wing comes down on him. If the 4-technique slants, the tackle gets his outside hand on the slant tackle and drives him down. The wing takes his block on the 0-technique linebacker.

The front side guard has a pull rule and he pulls every time. If the guard has an inside-shade on the center, the center reaches the shade and the guard pulls. If he is the first puller out, he kicks out on the force player.

If he is not the first puller out, he turns up and blocks from the inside out. We do not marry him to a linebacker. If the inside linebacker tries to run through, we catch him in the wash of the down block. The guard pulls through and looks for the first color inside to outside. We give them areas to look for and tell them never pass up a color.

If the playside guard gets a "Uno" call from the back, he turns, wraps, and turns up on the first color to show. "Uno" means a back in the backfield will kick out the support player. The defense will move and things change. We give them an area and tell them to block what shows. The play is a video and not a still snapshot.

That "Uno" calls comes from a particular formation. When you play from multiple formations, you must communicate when the blocking is going to change. You must have an offense line that is flexible enough to understand that.

The center's rule is playside A-gap to backside A-gap. If he has a double A-gap alignment, he has to make a stay call to the backside guard. He blocks the playside A-gap and the backside guard scoops the backside A-gap. If it is a four-man front, the center blocks the playside A-gap. If there is a shade in that gap, he reaches him. If there is a 3-technique on the guard and a 1-technique to the backside, he blocks back.

We expect him to make the reach block on a shade nose. When the alignment is a "G" or 2i-technique, it is tougher. The center has to get a piece of the defender. He reaches flat to that side and gets on the block. We do not expect him to get his hat to the outside and reach the defender. What we expect to happen is for him to make contact, prevent penetration, and drive on the 2i-technique defender. If the tackle and wingback do a good on their down block on the 5-technique, the center runs the 2i-defender into that pile and seals his block.

If the guard knows he is going to get that technique, he can tighten his split to bring the defender closer to the center. If your center is exceptional, he can run the nose into the 5-technique, continue around, and become an extra puller on the play.

The backside guard is the second puller to the playside. He turns up outside the down block and blocks the first color in that area. If he gets a "stay" call, he scoops the backside A-gap. The backside tackle scoops the backside B-gap. If there is a backside 2-technique, he has to come down hard inside.

Skill Rules:

- **Wing:** Down, Zero LB, BS LB (if defender jumps outside, run him out)
- **B:** Open, crossover and receive handoff. Stay high 3 steps past the mesh reading the block of the 1st puller out. If he kicks put outside foot in the ground and get north. Work off 2nd pullers block.
- **H:** backside – Cutoff Safety, #2 in trips – Crack to FS safety
- **Q:** Secure snap. Take short cheat step play side, hand off & carry out fake.
- **X / Z:** Stalk or Push Crack Safety

The wingback has the exact same rules as the playside tackle. If you have a tackle that is not very smart, the wingback can tell him what to do. He has a down block rule, but we qualify his rule. Once he makes contact, it does not matter the reaction of the defender. If the defender jumps outside, the wingback blocks him. He does not release him and go to some other defender. Once he makes contact, he tries to wall him inside.

If the 5-technique is a hard loop defender, the wingback stays on his track to the inside and we kick him. However, if the wingback makes contact on him he becomes his man. If we have a 4-technique defender, the tackle and wing double him to the backside linebacker.

The B-back opens and takes a cross over step. He receives the football on the third step. He must stay high for three steps past the mesh area. On the third step, he sticks his foot in the ground and turns north and south. We want to run the ball one yard outside the hip of the playside tackle. He sticks his foot in the ground and bangs the ball into the off-tackle lane or bounces the ball outside. We do not bend this play. If he does not stay high, he will run into the backside guard.

He is under control until he plants. At that point, he becomes a bulldog. He reads the block of the first puller. In his three-step movement past the mesh, he has to find the first puller. If the puller logs the defender, the ball bounces outside. If the puller has inside leverage and kicks out on the play, the back goes up inside.

The problem we run into is the defender cutting down the first puller with a wrong arm technique. We coach the second puller to get his inside hip aligned to the outside hip of the first puller. We want him deeper on the pull so he is on the outside of the first man pulling. If the first puller goes down, the second puller can get around the pile to the outside and still be a blocker. If the guard pulls directly behind the first puller and the first puller is cut, the second puller falls over him and the defense has free runners to the ball. They take two blockers out with one defender. We never want that.

The running back and second puller should be going to the same place. If the first puller logs the support defender, the second puller and the running back go outside that block. If he kicks out the support, the second guard and back turns up inside the kick out.

The slot or H-back has a cutoff rule to the backside and a crack rule to the playside. He goes inside and cracks on the strong safety or the first color. It could be a linebacker. If he cannot get the crack, he climbs to the next level and blocks the free safety.

The second thing we can do to slow down the backside pursuit is to throw a bubble screen to the backside. The quarterback reads the backside linebacker. If the backside linebacker chases the ball inside and the quarterback like his numbers to the outside, he throws the bubble screen to the backside.

The X and Z receivers stalk or push the corner off. That is a game plan situation depending on how the secondary plays their defenders. If the team is a quarter-coverage team, we want the receiver pushing the safeties off with vertical routes. We love situation where the corner has to become a force player. If they are a cover-2 team that rolls their corners, we like guards on corners.

The first defense is a "4-3" defense. (Diagram #2) We like to run to the 3 and 5-technique defenders. That means the center does not need to make the reach to the A-gap. The H-back cracks the Mike linebacker if he can. If the Mike runs through, he climbs to the free safety.

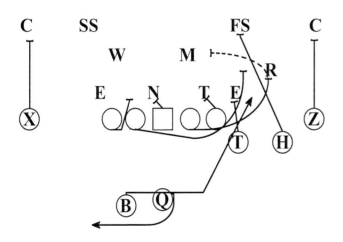

Diagram #2. Truck vs. 4-3

The second puller is going to wrap up on the playside Mike linebacker. That is a hard block for him. If you have a center that is more athletic, you can scoop the 1-technique, pull the center, and block the Mike linebacker. The backside guard has to find the playside linebacker as he pulls to preventing him from running through the playside A-gap.

Against an eight-man front or "4-2-5" defense, we see the safeties creeping down into the box. (Diagram #3) That is especially true with a trips set.

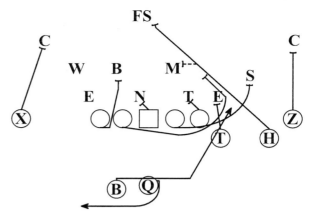

Diagram #3. Eight-Man Front

When we run this play, the H-back does a crack-block on the Mike linebacker. If the Mike linebacker disappears, he climbs to the free safety. We may have to develop something to the backside to hold the backside linebacker out of the play. However, if the slot can get a crack on the Mike linebacker our numbers against the defender work out in our favor.

In the "3-4" front, we have two 4-technique defenders on the offensive tackles. (Diagram #4) You need to analyze your opponent. You must know if they are a one or two-gap scheme. You need to know if they shade the tackle if you put the tight end into the game with his hand on the ground outside the offensive tackle. Against the 4-technique defender, we want to double with the tackle and wingback to the backside linebacker. The slot wants to crack the playside linebacker.

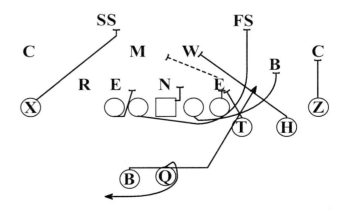

Diagram #4. Truck vs. 3-4

The playside guard pulls, kicks out on the outside linebacker, and the second guard comes through for the free safety. He is probably running the alley. He is the extra fit defender for the defense.

We used to see the "3-3" defense a lot but now most of the time it is the "4-3" adjustment to the trips set. (Diagram #5) It is the same play. The rules tell the offensive tackle and wingback they double the 4-technique to the 0-linebacker. If the 0-linebacker disappeared to the backside A-gap, we continue for the next linebacker.

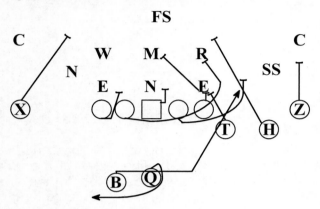

Diagram #5. Truck vs. 3-3

That is the way we block the play with our base rules. We teach the base rules from the first day and apply them against every defense.

Sometimes the blocks do not have to be picture perfect blocks. We have some little players trying to block some big players. It is hard for the defenders to make tackles when someone is in their path. That is what we tell our blockers. If you cannot get him blocked, at least get in his path. If they do that, the defenders ends up trying to arm tackle the backs. Our backs will make at least five more yards with someone trying to arm tackle them.

People are teaching their 3-technique a different technique to combat the down block. They take one-step at the guard. When they read the pull, they want to play a cross-face technique of the tackle coming down on the down block. With a defender trying to play cross face, we teach the tackle to get their head up field.

When he steps he does not put his head across as he did on a penetrating defender. He punches hard with the inside hand to the breastplate and keeps his head up field. His outside hand is on the backside of the defender. When the defender tries to work across his face, the blocker plays heavy with the outside hand and rips his hips around to keep him inside.

When our small blockers have to block on bigger personnel, we coach them to block the bottom half of he defender. We tell him all we need is a stalemate. He has to stop the feet of the defender. We want them to get their leverage under his leverage and stop his bottom half. If we can stop their feet from moving our guards and back can usually get outside of them. On the crack block, we do not coach them to try to knock the linebacker out. If he is not looking, he can take his shot. However, if the linebacker sees him coming, he wants to get a wide base and make it tough to be run over.

I want to show you some different ways we can run the same play. (Diagram #6) We align in a 2 X 2 set with the H-back in the wide slot. The running back aligns to the playside and uses the "Uno" block on the support. When he give the "Uno" call the playside guard knows he will turn up inside the B-back's block. He turns up and blocks the first color to show. Nothing changes for anyone else. On the "Uno" call, you get an extra puller on the play.

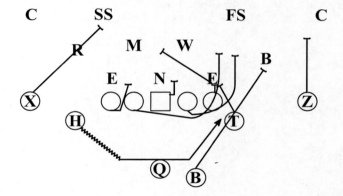

Diagram #6. H Truck

We can run it with the running back into the trips side of the formation. (Diagram #7)

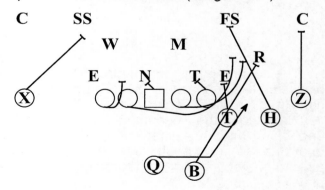

Diagram #7. Q Truck

He uses his "Uno" blocking scheme and the quarterback runs the ball. There is no fake to the running back, he leads the play and kicks out the support player. The blocking is the same as the regular truck play.

The thing that hurts the play some times is the backside linebacker running through the front side A-gap. If we have a stalemate on the playside 3-technique and do not get movement, it exposes the playside A-gap. When the weak side linebacker sees the guard pull, he runs through the A-gap. If we get movement, we close that gap and there is nowhere to run. If the linebacker runs through, he does one of two things. He knocks the pulling guard down or comes off his hip and hits the running back.

You must have an answer for that kind of play. (Diagram #8) What we do is to release the center up on the backside linebacker and read the backside nose. When the center steps into the playside A-gap, the nose sees the pull of the guard and the running back. He runs like crazy in the back pocket of the pulling guard. The backside tackle turns out on the 5-technique defender. The quarterback rides the running back, pulls the ball, and runs the backside B-gap.

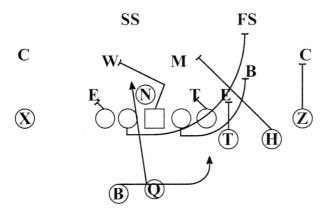

Diagram #8. Truck Read Nose

We ran the same thing against the 4-2 look with the Will linebacker in the box. (Diagram #9) We still read the nose, but we do not pull the backside guard. The center stepped into the A-gap and blocked the Mike linebacker. The backside guard blocked the Will linebacker. The backside tackle turned out on the 5-technique defender and we turn the nose loose. The quarterback reads the nose. If the nose chases the running back, the quarterback pulls the ball and runs into the B-gap.

The philosophy on that play is "if you cannot block them, you read them."

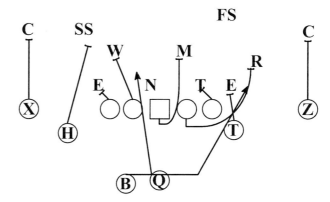

Diagram #9. Truck Read vs. 4-2

You can do many things with the play. You can tie the bubble screen with it. You can use the truck blocking and run a quarterback speed option. Instead of kicking out the support, you option him and pitch off him. You can run many players on the play. The play is limitless as to what you can do. If you are creative, you can do many things. If teams scheme to stop the play we have answers to what they do.

We have tried to run the play from the pistol set. It is the same blocking and we use the following rules for the quarterback and running back.

Pistol

- **RB:** Open step and aim 1 yard outside yard outside the Tight Ends alignment.
- **QB:** Open to RB handoff and reverse out with naked fake
- **Not as good of a play for us from this set**

The truck play from the pistol was not very good but the naked bootleg was a great play.

The truck is a versatile play and one we believe in. We do many different things from it. The only thing that limits you is your imagination. Do what is best for the players and what fits their skills.

Thank you coaches! I appreciate you attention.

Gene Bowen

Skill Progressions For The Offensive Line

Rogers High School, Washington

Thank you for those kind words. I appreciate the introduction. My objective here is to break things down and to be real simple. I approached my lecture today on the time when I started out going to clinics years and years ago. I wanted to hear someone that could break down the techniques so I could have an active progression to work through, rather than just trying to figure things out on my own. So I have approached this lecture with that in mind.

There are more coaches here that have far more experience and expertise than I do. I want to keep it simple and show you some things that work for us. I hope you can gain a few ideas that will work for you.

As an offensive back I always appreciated the guys up front. I realize nothing good was going to happen for me if the guys up front did not do a good job. Over the years I have worked my way from an Eighth Grade Coach, to the JV level, and then to the Varsity. I worked with the offensive line under a couple of good head coaches. I was fortunate to be an assistant at Rogers High School before I became a head coach. It has been a lot of fun and I have been fortunate to have worked with a lot of great people. This is what makes this game so great.

"Most battles are won before they are fought." Sun Tzu

It is important to give you a background for the foundation for success. Obvious the right mind-set is a huge factor.

I want to give you our foundation for power. When we talk about power, we are talking about being explosive. We want to be strong and quick both in the run game and the pass game. That is where I am headed with some techniques and some drills that we have put in our system.

I am like most of you, in that I steal ideas where ever I can. I have taken ideas from all of the coaches I have worked with. I do believe young people need models and not critics. I feel that is our job. We want to win and we want to be competitive but the game is also about building good young men. I feel I have been very fortunate to have worked with our young guys.

"Young people need models, not critics."
John Wooden

I can name you several quality coaches and colleagues. They include the following.

Mike Huard
Jeff Gardner
Bill Wernofsky
Dave Williams
Chris Van Sligtenhorst
Coach Picha @ CWU
Coach Morton @ UW
Coach Best @ EWU
Coach Hodkinson @ WWU

I can give you a list of books that cover the subject very well. I am listing these as good reading material.

- *Make The Big Time Where You Are*
  - Frosty Westering
- *Faith In The Game* - Tom Osborne
- *Winning Every Day* - Lou Holtz
- *They Call Me Coach* - John Wooden
- *Season Of Life* - Jeffrey Marx
- *Teaching Character Through Sports*
  - Bruce Brown
- *Championship Team Building*
  - Jeff Janssen, M.S.
- Man's Search For Meaning
  - Viktor E. Frankl

One of these books is a little cerebral that tells the story of the power of the mind, and the power to make choices, is the book by **Viktor E. Frankl**. It was recommended by a Sports Psychologist.

In all of the horrors of the holocaust, here was a man watching people die all around him basically because these people had given up on life. His mind-set was to survive one-day-at-a-time.

This is what we are teaching our players. We want them to survive one-play-at-a-time. Then they can worry about the next play. The idea of the power of the mind-set was explained very well in that book.

Like a lot of programs we have a Mission Statement that is our guiding principle. It does cover athletics and competition, but it is really about the value outside of the game of football.

OUR MISSION

Rogers Rams Football will be focused on the Pursuit of Excellence. Our duty is to instill the courage and values in our athletes that will allow them to compete at the highest levels on the field and, more importantly, throughout their lives.

I tell our parents this from the beginning at our spring meeting, and again at our fall meeting. It is not popular to talk about it being OK if you do not win kind of thing. Ultimately we want our players to be great sons, husbands, and later fathers, and good citizens. Hopefully, they will be responsible adults. They will have to take care of us when we are at an old age. Our job is to teach them how to be responsible and to be able to make good choices.

We define SUCCESS for them. This is difficult in a world that tells you that you need to have all of the money and all of the power. Some of our kids today get this in their head. For those of us that know we are not going to be rich need to focus on something else to consider being a success. We try to get our guys in that mind-set to be all they can be.

SUCCESS

"Success is peace of mind which is a direct result of Self-satisfaction in knowing you did your best to become the Best that you are capable of becoming." --- Coach **John Wooden**

As I said before I steal ideas and then try to figure out where they fit. I have read a lot of John Wooden material. This is my take on the Wooden Pyramid. Everyone has a different angle on his

model. Here I tried to insert confidence that would not just apply to sports, but to any area the athletes pick.

WIN EVERY DAY

"The 'final score' is not the final score. My final score is how prepared you were to execute near your own particular level of competence, both individually and as a team." - John Wooden

Everyone has a view on this subject. I can talk about any subject from this chart. Everyone can put their own slant on the chart.

COMPETE - Total Release			
FOCUS - W.I.N.		CONFIDENCE - Play Fast	
CARE - Respect All	COMMIT - to Excellence		TRUST - Integrity
DISCI-PLINE - Do Right	ATTI-TUDE - The Blue Line	SACRI-FICE - Servant Warrior	HABITS - Choices

I can talk about anything the players want to talk about on this chart. If they want to talk about relationships with their parents, I can talk about that subject on the chart. I tried to put areas that covered more than just winning games.

The terms Discipline, Attitude, Sacrifice and Habits cover a lot of subjects. There is a poem called the *"Dash"* about a person when he dies they put the birth date and the date of death on his tombstone. They also put a dash between those dates. (1940 – 2013) What happened between those dates cover a great deal more than just a dash. How you live your life is the story that needs to be told.

We stress the point of making good choices along the way in life. Our kids today are bombarded daily with decisions. Our job is to help them learn to make good decisions on and off the field. If they do not make good decisions off the field, they are not going to be on the field.

Next I have a few points that come from Lou Holtz on *"Character and Trust"*. He asks three questions in talking about this subject. The first question: *"Can I trust you?"*

The second question: **_Are you committed to excellence?_**

The third question: **_Do you care about me?_**

If you have those three things going on, you will have a solid foundation. You have to make choices, you have to commit to something that is bigger than yourself, and you must be trusted. You can talk about the upside of this topic where you can talk about focus on the play, to play fast, and eventually the team.

Also, the players will have to compete for jobs in life. If we can build a firm foundation with the players, we feel like we have done our job.

We think these things will make them a better football team. If they make good choices it will carry over from their personal life to their football life. Those are big concepts for us.

We try to focus on the offensive line and try to paint the picture for them. We talk to them about the realities of the offensive lineman.

THE REALITIES OF THE OFFENSIVE LINE

"Commitment to the team - there is no such thing as in-between, you are either in or out." - Pat Riley

- **No Credit - ALL BLAME**
- **No Name – NO INK**
- **No Pain - OTHERS PAY**
- **Never get to touch the ball!**

We want them to understand it is a different world they live in. For those of you that were offensive linemen, my hat is off to you. I was not a lineman, but I know enough about the game to say it all starts there.

The offensive linemen are the ultimate commitment to the team. They never get credit for anything good they do. The players that score get all the credit. The linemen take all the blame. The first thing that goes wrong we hear the coaches yelling at the linemen to block the play. "The line is not making a hole!" Even as we know the reality of the facts we are still blaming the line for the problems. They get no credit, and they take all the blame. We have told our guys the facts so they know what they are getting into.

Not many players come into high school as natural linemen. They have to learn how to play in the offensive line. We are a three year high school so we only get them for those three years. We do have five Junior High Schools that feed into us. I cannot tell the coaches of those schools to do certain things because the players are at such a young age. Those schools run their own plays and system. We have to paint a picture for them to get them ready.

We never have a reporter come up to us after a game and ask us permission to talk to our offensive guard. They want to talk to the running back and the quarterback.

Other people may say "No Pain" for the offensive linemen. That is not true. There is pain and there is blood, and it can get ugly out there. They must realize that others must pay for their mistakes.

Linemen never get to touch the ball. The only time they get to touch the ball is when we break things up and play street football. They can throw the ball and catch the ball in that type of game. They probably do the hardest work in the program, but they never get credit for the work. Some of the players are fine with this. You have the foundation on how to work the linemen where they are rewarded for their hard work.

COACHES MIND-SET

"The coach's most powerful tool is love." JW

"ENTHUSIASM is the fire in our furnace; it is the spark that keeps us going in high gear.

Enthusiasm brings on Excitement

- **Excitement then produces Energy**
- **Energy generates Extra Effort**
- **Extra Effort develops Excellence."**
  Frosty Westering

"THE BLUE LINE" - Flip the switch

Coaches must sell the team on ideas, and we must sell the linemen on our concepts. As coaches we must bring out mind-set when we deal with the offensive linemen. Most coaches have to teach all day, and stay up preparing for the next game. By the time they get to practice they are really tired. The coach must generate enthusiasm before they take the field. Whatever it takes to get them to practice, they you must get there.

We actually painted a Blue Line on the sidewalk where our players crossover from the locker room area over to the practice field. When our players cross that Blue Line, they have to flip the switch. I challenge my coaches to be ready to go when we cross the Blue Line as well. That is a very important concept. The energy you bring, and the enthusiasm you bring to practice will be infectious. You players will rise to the way you present yourself.

If you are flat and never tell the kids they are doing a good job, or telling them you love them, then they are going to be flat You would be amazed at the power of positive thoughts and the positive attitude and enthusiasm. It is huge.

Next we move to the Offensive Line and their Mind-set. We talk to the offensive line about things they can control.

OFFENSIVE LINE MIND-SET

"Nobody who ever gave their best effort ever regretted it."

George Halas

WE CAN CONTROL:

- **Attitude**
- **Effort**
- **Choices**
- **Toughness**
- **Unity**

We talk about the things as a team that we can control. For the offensive line this is even more important. We cannot control how big the other defensive man is, or none of that stuff. You can control your attitude and your effort. In thinking back, I cannot think of any scholarship lineman we have had in the number of years I have been at Rogers High School. We have had some receivers and other players receive scholarships, but perhaps only one lineman has received a scholarship.

We have had to make do with players that were not great players, but they buy into the fundamentals and what we are trying to teach them. They get good at fundamentals. They control those things they can control. The choices they make each day are the same choices all of our players make day-to-day.

The key is to get the six or seven guys on the offensive line to buy into the system. We do not have names on the back of the jerseys. We do not give stickers or decals for great plays. We concentrate on team, team, and team. We did decide to do special T-shirts for the offensive line. If other players what to get T-shirts that is fine. However, I have no sympathy for backs and receivers that do not have a lot of respect for the offensive linemen.

BE THE CAR

"You need more than a coat of paint."

- **Wheels / Tires - RB / WR**
- **Driver - QB**
- **Brakes / Body - Defense**
- **ENGINE - OL**

Those who really know cars want to know what is under the hood.

The people want to know about the Engine of the car. We sell our guys on the idea the offensive line is the engine of the car. The team cannot go anywhere without the engine. We hype on this constantly. It is true. "You do need more than a coat of paint to drive on the road."

OFFENSIVE LINE CONSIDERATIONS

"Adversity causes some men to break, and others to break records."
...Unknown

- **Balanced Run / Pass**
- **Attack right and left**
- **Run and pass from same look**
- **Spread the Field; wide splits**
- **Put players in position for success**
- **Simplify + rep it = confidence**

The first thing our line must be able to do is to have a balanced run and pass play with the same exact look. We cannot tip the plays. Coaches are always watching film looking for the things players do to tip plays off to the defense.

We must be able to attack both right and left. We must be able to move in both directions. We must spread the field. We like to take wide splits. We take up to four foot splits with our offensive linemen. All of the things I am going to show you are about putting players into position for success.

It may be the scheme we run. We thing the spread offensive system fits our kids. It may be the individual techniques that give us the edge. The players must have some success. We start out building that success slowly. The last point is to simplify the plays and rep those plays until the players are confident they can run the play successful.

We have narrowed our offense down to two basic concepts. We run the Inside and Outside Zone, and we do run the Counter play. It was a good play for us last year. We took the big splits and ran the Counter and it worked well for us.

We have a couple of pass protections schemes. After that, our linemen do not have to think. They find out what is lined up in front of them and then they must work their techniques.

CORE PRINCIPLES

"The difference between the possible and impossible lies in the man's determination."
- Tommy Lasorda

- **Start with great feet**
- **Get our eyes on target**
- **Low man wins**
- **Inside man wins**
- **Be violent with our hands**
- **Hit and Run**
- **FINISH! FINISH!! FINISH!!!**

I want to take you through a progression here. We start with great feet. You must start with a great foundation. After that you must know where your eyes are going. You can go over on the defense and coach the offense so you can see where the offensive players' eyes are going.

The next point is "low man wins." This is a concept that goes way back in time. When I was a young coach I would demonstrate this technique, but now I get the players to do the demonstrating. Inside, low man wins.

We want to be violent with our hands. We put shields on the defensive dummies so we can punch the heck out of them. If you punch your own players in the chest over and over a lot, you are going to hurt players. We do not want to hurt our players because we want them ready on game day.

We talk about hit and run in football. We may brush block the defender and go downfield looking to block another defender. The past phase is to finish the drill.

BUILDING A FOUNDATION

"You can't fire the cannon from a canoe."

- **Feet**
  - Balanced and downfield
  - "Air in socks" not balls of feet
  - "Ladder" not a pole
  - Squat technique

- **Knees**
  - Aligned over toes
  - Wide not knock-kneed
  - Not pointing at the ground

- **Back**
  - **"Hermanized"**
  - **Hips back and locked in**

- **Eyes**
  - "Through top bar"

- **Hands**
  - **Just inside stagger thigh pad = Balance/square**

I do not know how many of you have players that come to you that are ready to get off the football. When the ninth graders come to us this spring they are rough. It is not a natural thing like going out and throwing the football. You can learn those things because that is a natural thing. You do not see kids going out to practice blocking. They do not do that. We have to teach them how to block and take advantage of their skills.

We may have the young players come down to the weight room to see what a blocking technique looks like. That is where you must start. He has to learn what balance is in a stance.

Once we get them into their basic stance, we go to the basic steps. They have to take at the most, three steps.

STEP PROGRESSION

Everybody is looking for instant success, but it doesn't' work that way. You build a successful life one day at a time. - Lou Holtz

- **"JAB"**
  - **First Step = tie 6 inch step (straight/angle/flat)**
  - **"Load the guns"**
- **"STICK"**

- ○ **Second Step = Win "Punch" inside /target and stick on**
- **"MOVE"**
  - ○ Roll hips – Duck walk

DRILL PROGRESSION

""The Six W's: Work Will Win When Wishing Won't." - Todd Blackledge

We want to work on maximum reps. We line up four guys across in a line. (Diagram #1) It does not matter on the numbers, I do not care. We line them up and call out "Ready – Set – Go." We do the front line. Then we do the second line and then the third line. We are correcting the stance, and correcting the different steps for the line. We are doing all of the fundamentals on the line.

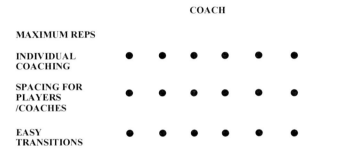

COACH

MAXIMUM REPS

INDIVIDUAL COACHING

SPACING FOR PLAYERS /COACHES

EASY TRANSITIONS

Diagram #1. Drill Progression

We are working on fundamentals on the first two days. We are working on those first two steps starting out in our practice. We stress the stance, first step, and second step concepts.

STANCE & START

Coaching Points:
- **Must work both sides**
- **Keep it tight**
- **Don't show numbers**
- **Drive out - not up**
- **Full foot in the ground**
- **Inside edges**
- **"Graze the grass" not stomp**
- **"Ladder" not a pole - stay wide**
- **Finish with acceleration**

LEVERAGE DRILL

Coaching Points:
- **Hands inside**
- **Thumbs up**

- **Lock into chest plate / keep it tight**
- **Eyes target under numbers**
- **Flat back**
- **Sink hips**
- **"Ladder" not a pole - stay wide**
- **"Drive for five" NOT "push the car"**
- **Progress to weave to feel pressure**

In our initial teaching we go in this mode and rep the heck out of the drills. We work on the drills and rep it a bunch. Hopefully, come game time we will have some muscle memory when things go astray in the game, right. You can see how the perfect technique has been rehearsed over and over but it still is not simple. We want the blocking techniques to become a habit. We work against the defense where the man is moving a little that makes it more difficult to block him. (Diagram #2)

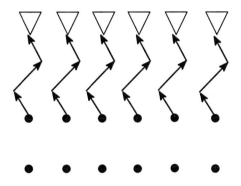

Diagram #2. Moving Leverage Drill

Next I want to cover the Second Level Drill. It is a lot like a form tackling drill. We do have players working in combos, with 2 X 2 drills where you have to replace a backside tackle. The tackle is going to be working up to the second level immediately. We have to coach him on techniques on how to get to second level.

SECOND LEVEL DRILL

Coaching Points: (Diagram #3)
- **Great stance and start**
- **Accelerate off LOS**
- **See LB and project collision point**
- **"Shimmy down" to hit position**
- **(same as form tackle drill)**
  - ○ **Load**
  - ○ **Strike on the run**
  - ○ **Gain leverage**
- **Cover numbers "judo block"**

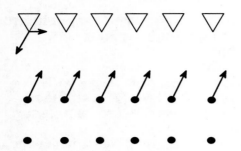

Diagram 3. Second Level Dill

We teach the drill very similar to the way we teach a tackling drill. "Eyes level, break down, head up." These drills are not full speed. They are slow drills. They are teaching type drills. We can tell the players to turn and take three steps. We tell him to take three steps and pin the defender up. We want to make sure they are in the correct spot.

SLED PROGRESSION

6-point strike drill
3-point stance /starts

Coaching Points:
- **Off-set for proper reach / trail steps**
- **Weight back**
- **Elbows tight**
- **"Holster guns" --- hands load to hips**
- **"Punch his lungs out" –violent hands**
- **Extend / hips in**
- **Drive and elevate NOT "push the car"**

We are getting a new sled this year. We have been working on one of the old Gilman Sleds. We are getting a new 5-Man-Sled, because that is mostly what we do now. If the tight end has to come inside to block, we can work him in to the drill somewhere.

We do a lot of the 3-Point Stance and Start Drills. We are off-set on almost everything. We want to get the feel for being off-set from the defender. We can beat the heck out of the sled without beating up our defensive line.

Back in the old days the coaches would get on the sleds and stand up on them. In those days the coaches would make the offensive line drive the sled down the field before they blew the whistle to release them on the blocks. That may be a drill that is for conditioning and it may have made them tougher, but it did not simulate what we wanted. We only go for three or four steps on the sled.

After we go the first time, we can re-set and go again on the sled. It is re-set, go. We get off three times and this is what we want. First, it makes the drill closer for the linemen instead of just grinding the sled where they just end up pushing the sled at the end. Second, it stimulates the type of block we are trying to instill in our offense. We want to be as quick and fast as the Oregon Ducks with the up tempo on offense.

Last year we were not perfect on the up tempo, but we became very efficient. We were snapping the ball within five seconds after the referee marked the ball ready for play, He marked it with 25 seconds, and we were snapping the ball with 20 seconds left on the play clock. By the middle of the season we had to slow things down, because we had to learn how to burn the play clock at times. One thing this did for us was the fact we got rid of our snap count. I will talk about that later if you want to know more of what we do.

CHUTE PROGRESSION

- **Stance and Starts**
- **Leverage**
- **Second Level**
- **242**

Coaching Points:
- **Start position under chute**
- **Not duck under the chute**
- **Work with shields**

We have an old Oklahoma type chute. We could not go very far in the chute. Now we are going to have a "trap" type chute where the players can work on their trap steps and all of the other plays. We can do all of the drills we discussed on Stance and Starts. We can do all of the leverage drills as well.

The one point I want to stress on the chute drills is to make sure you get the guys in line to be successful on the drills. We want the players up under the chutes where they do not have to run a mile to block a defender. We do not want to beat up our defense on the drill so we do use shields on the guys.

OFFENSIVE LINE APPROACH - RUN GAME

- **Alignment = Know the technique of the defense. (covered or uncovered).**
- **Assignment = Know where the play is going (play side or backside).**

- **Snap Count = Get off the ball (listen for check at LOS).**
- **Fit = Target for initial contact (hit and stick).**
- **Finish = Feel the defender and cut off pursuit (move feet and compete).**

This is the check list our guys are going through every single play up on the football. It comes out fast. They must know all of the information covered as they approach the line of scrimmage.

We got rid of our snap count. We only had a couple of off-sides all year. We put the snap count on our center. We did not mess around with "hand down," or any other signal. Our line got down and took a check. The quarterback called "Set-Go; Ready; Check;" and we could add a color in there if we wanted. Then the quarterback called "Blue 90 – Set." Then the center snaps the ball when he is ready.

Some coaches think the defense can get off the ball the same times as the offense. Not really! We did change up our cadence a little, but we became efficient at drawing the defense off side. We do not motion on offense. I am a simple coach. When we did try to use motion, we screwed up the quarterbacks initial read, especially on the short passing game. The quarterback was reading leverage, and when we went in motion the leverage changed. So we decided to run our offense. We run the inside and outside zone plays and a quick passing game. We run the bubble from the outside. We did mess around with the Dart and Counter plays. We use a couple of trick plays here and there and that is about it.

Our rules on alignment concerning a lineman being covered or uncovered are very simple. If the down offensive lineman has any shade on him, he is considered covered. (Diagram #4)

UNCOVERED = NOT SHADED
1ST STEP MUST GET YOU IN POSITION

Diagram #4. Covered / Uncovered

We tell our lineman the first step must get them in position to block the covered man. The man on the left is not covered, and the man on the right is covered.

After our offensive linemen understand the covered and uncovered concept, we work on the "Me!-You!" Concept. If the linebacker comes up in the hole we go single blocking and pick him up. (Diagram #5) But if we can double the down lineman, we will.

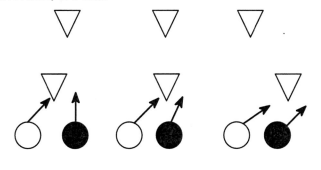

COVERED = "DRIVE-REACH"
UNCOVERED = "TRAIL"

Diagram #5. "242" Me-You!

We want to drive the down lineman back into the linebacker. We want to drive them back to the second level.

If the defensive man is outside on our down man, the inside man must think linebacker. He comes off the ball looking for the down man to come inside, and then he looks for the linebacker. (Diagram #6)

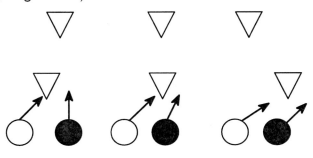

COVERED = TARGET PLAYSIDE # / PIT
UNCOVERED = GET TO HIP; NEAR #

Diagram #6. "242" Concept (Double)

We let the players come up with their own codes each year on the Me-You blocking. They have fun with it and they make up names with it. (Diagram #7) They give the calls and stay with their blocks.

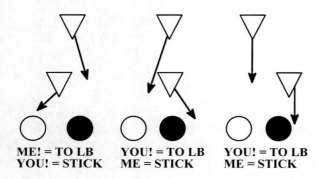

ME! = TO LB YOU! = TO LB YOU! = TO LB
YOU! = STICK ME = STICK ME = STICK

Diagram #7. Finish "242" Me!-You! Level 2

PASS PROTECTION - POST SET

Priority = Close inside gap
- **Step lateral with inside foot**
- **Gain leverage inside half man**
- **Punch inside**

"POUND THE POST" / HOLD THE LOS / FLATTEN

Coaching Points:
- **Sit in the chair" - wider stagger**
- **"PEZ Dispencer" – head back**
- **"Look through the window "hands up**
- **"6-inch pop" – punch not lean**

I want to talk for a minute about our Pass Protection. We work two basic sets just to get our feet right. We work a Post Step. We use the same type of stance we used before. We come up to the line, and after we get the "Ready – Go" we Post Step. We are aggressive as we step up in the line of scrimmage.

In our 90 Pass Game we are a lot more aggressive and we block much as we do in our run game. We do not sit back on the line of scrimmage.

PASS PROTECTION KICK SET

Priority = Cut off outside / speed rush
- **1ˢᵗ step quick drop step outside foot**
- **Stay square to LOS (not turn hips)**
- **Maintain leverage**

"KICK-SLIDE" - GIVE A LITTLE TO WIDEN" - "RUN HIM HIGH AND WIDE"

Coaching Points:
- **"Sit in chair"/"PEZ"/"Window"**
- **Must be prepared for inside or outside**
- **Inside = "pound up" flatten**
- **Outside = "kick it out" widen**

Gaining inside leverage is a big deal. You have to stay inside your man. We have to take away the shortest path to our quarterback.

PASS PROTECTION POST SET

Priority = Close inside gap
- **1ˢᵗ step lateral with inside foot**
- **gain leverage inside half man**
- **punch inside**

"POUND THE POST" - HOLD THE LOS / FLATTEN

Coaching Points:
- **"Sit in the chair" - wider stagger**
- **"PEZ dispencer" – head back**
- **"Look through the window "--- hands up**
- **"6-Inch Pop" – punch not lean**

I want to talk about the idea of "sitting in a chair." We do not have a big stagger. When we open in our Post Set to slide outside, we want to increase the stagger. One foot is on the front leg of the chair, and the other foot is going to be on the back leg of the chair. We exaggerate the heck out of this in practice. "Sitting in the Chair." We have our hands up to form the window and I am ready to punch straight out. We want the head back on the set. We want to punch the defender so we hit him at the last six inches of the extension.

PASS PROTECTION KICK SET

Priority = Cut off outside - speed rush
- **1ˢᵗ step quick drop step outside foot**
- **stay square to LOS (not turn hips)**
- **Maintain leverage**

"KICK-SLIDE" - GIVE A LITTLE TO WIDEN. "RUN HIM HIGH AND WIDE."

Coaching Points:
- **"Sit in chair" / "PEZ" / "window"**
- **Must be prepared for inside or outside**
- **Inside = "pound up" flatten**
- **Outside = "kick it out" widen**

PASS SET PROGRESSION *INSIDE RUSH*

Coaching Points: (Diagram #8)
- **Work rt/lt stance in drill**
- **Sit in the chair/wider stagger**
- **Shoulders/hips square to LOS**
- **Time the pound and punch**
- **Target inside shoulder**

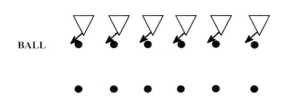

Diagram #8. Inside Pass Rush Drill

PASS SET PROGRESSION OUTSIDE RUSH

Coaching Points: (Diagram #9)
- Work rt/lt stance in drill
- Sit in the chair-wider stagger
- Shoulders/hips square to LOS
- Kick to widen/not turn and face
- Target outside shoulder/near hip

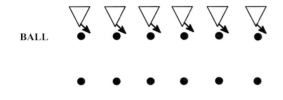

Diagram #9. Outside Pass Rush Drill

Next we have an Outside and Spin In drill. (Diagram #10) We work both sides in the drill.

Coaching Points:
- Work rt/lt stance in drill
- "Sit in the chair" -- wider stagger
- Shoulders/hips square to LOS
- Feel pressure release
- Hand check to pound up into LOS

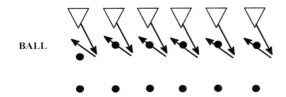

Diagram #10. Outside and Spin In

Coaching Points:
- Work rt/lt stance in drill
- "Sit in the chair"- wider stagger
- Shoulders/hips square to LOS
- Feel pressure release
- "Hand check" to pound up into LOS

"POUND THE POST" - "KICK – SLIDE"

Coaching Points: (Diagram #11)
- Sit in the chair-wider stagger
- Shoulders/hips square to LOS
- Keep foot in the ground as slide

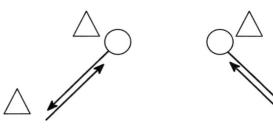

Diagram #11. Kick-Slide

MIRROR DRILL (NO HANDS, FRAMED UP, STEP IN)

Coaching Points: (Diagram #12)
- Maintain inside leverage
- Quick, short steps "ladder not pole"
- Shoulders/hips square to LOS
- Keep feet in the ground

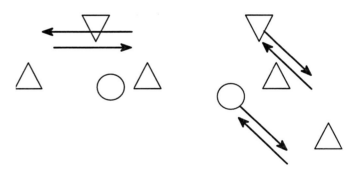

Diagram #12. Mirror Drill

SPEED RUSH DRILL

Coaching Points: (Diagram #13)
- Kick back to cut off path
- Hips square to LOS (able to catch spin)
- Keep foot in the ground as slide
- Prepared for inside move

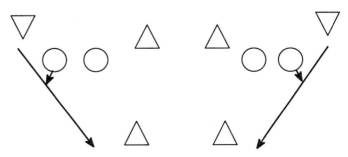

Diagram #13. Speed Rush Drill

Here is an old standard. It is called "Hat on a Dummy Drill." (Diagram #14) I think you have to define the rush lane for the defender. Otherwise, those guys will cheat. They should not run outside of their rush lane.

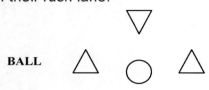

Diagram #14. Hat on a Dummy Drill

Coaching Points:
- **Snap count for offense**
- **Keep drill to realistic timing - 4 count**
- **Identify position of ball**
- **Move "QB" launch point**

OFFENSIVE LINE APPROACH - PASS GAME

- **Alignment = Know the technique of the defense --- see first threat for stunt**
- **Assignment = Know where the QB is going are you play side or backside?**
- **Snap Count = Get off the ball (listen for check at LOS).**
- **Fit = Target for initial contact (punch and recoil).**
- **Finish = MAKE IT PERSONAL (no one touches our QB)!**

We repeat the same things in the Run Game. We set up the same type of 242 Drills. (Diagram #15) instead of Passing Game it is the Running Game.

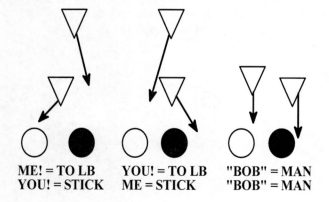

ME! = TO LB   YOU! = TO LB   "BOB" = MAN
YOU! = STICK   ME = STICK   "BOB" = MAN

Diagram #15. "242" – Me – You - Bob!

REVIEW

- **Fundamentals**
- **Mental Approach**
- **Foundation**
- **Two Steps**
- **Punch Placement**
- **Low Man**
- **Inside Man**
- **Make it Personal**

WHAT'S IMPORTANT NOW!

W.I.N. EVERY PLAY

- **Alignment**
- **Assignment**
- **Snap Count**
- **Fit**
- **Finish**

Golfer mentality – What is important now? We stress it is important to do things on time and do them accurately. What is important now? Everything we do has an importance. Everything we do we have a choice. You either chose to go full speed or you chose to go half speed in a drill.

THE PURSUIT OF EXCELLENCE

"The quality of a person's life is in direct proportion to his commitment to excellence, regardless of his chosen field of endeavor."
Vince Lombardi

Thank you very much. If I can help you in any way, feel free to drop me a note. Thank you.

Gene Bowen
bowengs@puyallup.k12.wa.us

Ricky Bowers

Implementing the Outside Zone

Ensworth High School, Tennessee

When I was younger, I only coached basketball. I never wanted to come to Kentucky to play basketball because we always got the crap beat out of us. In recent years, we are playing football. I am at the Ensworth School, which started in 2002. I had the good fortune of being in on the beginning of the school. They wanted to offer something to the greater Nashville community. The people that built the school borrowed 52 million dollars to build a campus. They called me and one other guy to come over and help them do it. It was one of the great pleasures in my life.

I had an uncle that was an athletic director in college. At his hall of fame induction, I remember him saying, "What is important is that no one gets the credit." The truth is anyone could be successful at Ensworth because it is a fantastic place. If you are ever in Nashville, please feel welcome to drop by and see the campus. It is a beautiful 126 acre campus. We have a 10,000 square-foot indoor athletic facility. We have 426 students in the school. We have no Physical Education at our school. However, we have a fitness program at our school for everyone. We have this for a minimum of 180 minutes a week.

That means that all the members of the athletic teams are in weight training and fitness sessions for 180 minutes a week. As a football staff, we do not oversee their conditioning and weight training. Our time we spend with the team on the football field is our time just coaching them. The football stadium is a 20 million dollar facility. We started with 52 million for the school at the beginning and advanced that total to 118 million in our expansions.

I am the basketball coach, football coach, and athletic director. I was not sure what I wanted to do with this presentation. When we started the school, we had some fundamental principles we wanted to put in place. One of those principle was we were going to be a "family place." We wanted to spend 25 hours a week with academics in the classroom. We had 15 hours a week doing what we called extracurricular activities. That period included football. Of those 15 hours, three hours were fitness. That left us with 12 hours a week for us to institute all that we did athletically.

The 12 hours a week included the practice, game, and travel. If you are trying to produce a championship football team on 12 hours of training a week, you need great instructors. When we come to practice the time element is tight. We hustle every minute we are on the field. There is not a lot of chatting on the field. We went with the Hudl a long time ago. That has been a lifesaver for us. Every student that comes to the school gets a laptop.

We do not sit down and watch tape with our players. They do it on their own. In our practice sessions, the coaches do nothing but teach. When I hired our staff, I tried to get the best teachers and coaches in the country. Paul Wade is one of those people. He is a football person, knows the game, is great with players, and is a great tactician. Since he came, we won three straight state championships. Paul will talk about our offense.

PAUL WADE: ASSISTANT COACH

As coach said, in practice we do not have time to waste. I came from another school where if things went wrong we stopped and started all over again. We do not have that luxury at Ensworth. I am going to talk fast and move quicker than you normally see. I am going to talk about the outside zone. We run the traditional outside zone. We teach the rip, reach, pull, and overtake. You probably run the same scheme. We found out we had to be more complicated to run it in our league.

WHY?

- **Defensive linemen began holding the rip and reach blocker**

- **33 stacks started moving in tandem**
- **Our guards not athletic enough to pull &
  over take; but our center & tackles could**
- **the under defense**
- **We were big & strong and could angle
  block for the pin & pull**

The defensive coaches in our league were teaching their linemen to hold the first rip and reach players so they could not get through to the next level. The meant the second and trail players got caught up and the linebacker were running free.

The 33 stack teams started moving in tandem instead of moving in X-stunts. If we faced stack defenders both went in the same direction. If the down lineman could not rip through or reach to the second level, we had a linebacker running free. It would not have mattered if they crossed on their stunts.

This year we had young guards but they were big. The starters were 325 pounds and 285 pounds. The first substitute off the bench was 315 pounds. They could push people but they could not run. The center and tackles were experienced players and athletic enough to do something different. We had to figure out what we could do.

Most every team in our league ran some form of an odd front. When they stemmed the front most of them went to an "under" front. With the shade defender to the tight end side, we had problems on the inside and outside zone plays. We could run the ball to the weakside and account for everyone except a rolled down safety. We wanted to keep the play to the tight end side, but we had to account for the shade nose guard. We thought we were big and strong enough to angle block and that is where we came up with the "pin and pull."

With big and strong guards, we could use their angle blocking skills to block down on defenders. We could use the center and tackle as the primary pullers in the offense. We felt it gave us an advantage on the opponent. We utilized the personnel we had to the best of our ability.

The teams we saw each week were multiple five-man fronts. We wanted to build formations and be very simple. With the time element in our drills, we got no more than 2 hours a week. We get 57 minutes a day with our offense. We

wanted to run the same play and use some trickery to give them different looks.

GAME BY GAME BREAK DOWN:

		NP / OZP
•	MUS	60 / 10
•	LEX CATH	65 / 20
•	McCALLIE	58 / 15
•	RALEIGH	41 / 5
•	BAYLOR	66 / 31
•	BGA	57 / 16
•	JP2	50 / 20
•	MBA	51 / 14
•	BA	64 / 28
•	RYAN	46 / 14
•	McCALLIE	57 / 18
•	MBA	47 / 15
•	MUS	59 / 23
	TOTAL	721 / 229 / 32%

This is a game-by-game break down of our season. The left hand number is the total number of plays we ran in the game. The number to the right is the number of times we ran some version of the outside zone play. I do not know if that is many plays or not. We are an I-based team that plays out of a huddle. We play fast, hurry-up in practice to get accomplished what we need to cover. However, in the games we play at a slower pace.

In the last two years, in our big games and against Baylor Prep, which we played in the last two state championship games, almost 50 percent of our offense came from the outside zone concept. One of our big games was against Brentwood Academy. You can see we ran almost 50 percent of our plays from the outside zone concept. We ran one simple play but did it in a multitude of different ways. It accounted for 32 percent of our offense for the year.

In our offense, we also run the ice, power, counter, and a little of zone read. In our offense our fullback, who is a glorified guard, is making room for our best player. The outside zone and the frequency of which we ran the play helped open up our play-action passing game. Every play we have we try to have an option and a play action play off running play.

DEVELOPED DIFFERENT BLOCKING SCHEMES:

- **Multiple formations, motions, flips –
  window dressing**

- **Each week we looked at how to block zone and which boots would be good**
- **Both strong and weak**
- **Offensive line calls, sideline call, check with me's**
- **Set up drills in Indy period to simulate play.**

We were running so many variations of the zone play it became our best play action passing plays. The zone boot and half boot (naked) became our best pass play. We wanted to develop different blocking schemes. We used multiple formations, motions, and flips as window dressing. We have motion in our play calling almost 100 percent of the time. Sometimes it means something that is significant and sometimes it means absolutely nothing.

Each week we looked at how to block the zone play and which of the boot plays would be good. Each week the defense may be different which required an adjustment in the blocking scheme. We wanted to run it both strong and weak. In one week, we may run the play action to only the strong side or the zone to only the weak side. We planned for the opponent and ran the scheme according to what they did.

We want to call the plays a variety of different ways. We could call it in the huddle or at the line of scrimmage. He had a check-with-me system the quarterback used in the audible system. We gave all our plays animal names. If there was not too much crowd noise, he simply yelled the play at the line of scrimmage. Our offensive line had the opportunity to change the blocking scheme at the line of scrimmage.

If we called "outside zone", when we got to the line of scrimmage, the center or playside tackle called what the blocking scheme should be. In order to make this work we had to set up some kind of drill in practice. We set up drills in Indy period to simulate play. I called the play and they went to the line and called the schemes that fit the defense.

The first defense is a simple 50-front. The techniques we use are ripping, reach, pull, and replace. Our scheme dictates our steps depending on what the defense does. We do a drill with the offensive line for five-minutes called "first step." They absolutely hate it. We do this drill from the first day we start practice to the very last Thursday before the state championship game.

I simply call a play, and call "set-hike." They must take the first step that goes with the play. It could be a drop, angle, power, or whatever the step might be. When we watched the film, I might circle one of the offensive linemen's feet. He knew exactly what that meant.

In our regular blocking for the outside zone, the playside guard and tackle work against the 5-technique tackle and Mike linebacker. (Diagram #1) The center and backside guard run the scheme for the nose guard and backside linebacker. The tight end reaches for the Sam linebacker. The fullback is the lead blocker on the play. The techniques for the linemen are the rip, reach, pull, and overtake.

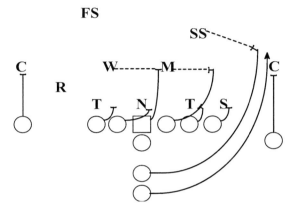

Diagram #1. Regular vs. 50

If we can get the running back to the safety in a one-on-one match up, we have won in the blocking of the front. The fullback is responsible for the first outside support defender.

We installed this scheme for teams that ran a read technique. The power and ice play were working so well the 5-technique defender and Sam linebacker squeezed the B and C-gaps. We came up with the "GT-scheme." (Diagram #2)

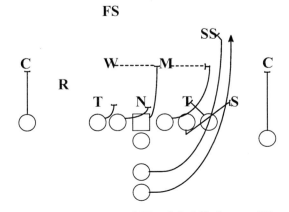

Diagram #2. GT with Kick vs. 50

From the playside guard to the backside, everyone runs the regular zone blocking. We use a simple X-block on the 5-technique defender and Sam linebacker. The tight end blocks down, the tackle pulls outside, and traps the Sam linebacker.

We tell the playside guard he is responsible for the Mike linebacker. In the diagram, he is pulling around the tackle and up on the linebacker. We wanted the guard to be smart about how he blocked the Mike linebacker. You cannot angle block down on the 5-technique and zone block on the linebacker the same way. If you do, they will run into each other. On one week, he may zone the A-gap and in other weeks, he would drop and pull around for the scraping Mike linebacker.

The tackles rule on the cross block is to pull and kick out the Sam linebacker. (Diagram #3) If the Sam linebacker squeezes to the inside, he logs him inside. The center and fullback go outside the log block by the tackle. The center looks for the Mike linebacker scraping from the inside and the fullback leads on the support player.

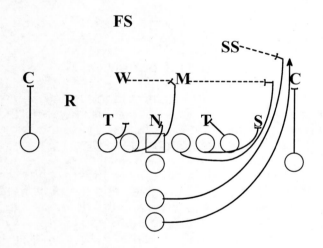

Diagram #3. GT/Log

We use the "pin and pull" technique to take advantage of the mobility of the center and the strength of the guard. (Diagram #4) In the diagram, we use a kick on the 5-technique and Sam linebacker. The playside guard angle blocks down on the shade nose to the tight end side. The center pulls as the guard did on the GT scheme. He blocks the Mike linebacker. The backside guard and tackle wall off the backside defenders. The center must not move before he snaps the football. The fullback leads inside and the running back follows him.

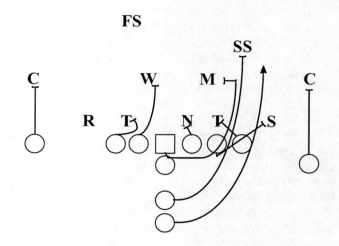

Diagram #4. Pin & Pen/Kick Vs. Under

Against a 33-stack defense we run the true rip, reach, pull, and overtake on the stack defense. (Diagram #5) The reason we do that is because of the X-stunts most 33-stack teams run. Teams in our league began to move the tandem stack in the same direction. The tackle reached for the 4-technique defender, which slanted to the outside. The Sam stepped to the outside instead of filling the B-gap. When our guard pulled for Sam, he ended up humping on the tackle's hip because he could not get over the top.

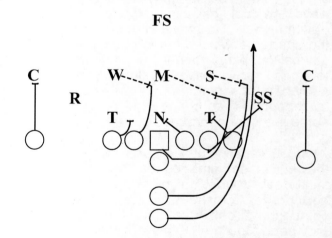

Diagram #5. Pin and Pull/Kick vs. 33

We used the "pin and pull" scheme. The tight end pinned the 4-technique defender and the tackle pulled out side for the strong safety playing the force. The nose was the A-gap player to the playside and the Mike linebacker played the B-gap. We pinned the nose with the playside guard and pulled the center for the Mike linebacker. He eyeballed him and blocked him the smart way. If the Mike linebacker blitzed the

B-gap, he blocked him there. If he continued to run, the center turned up around the down block of the tight end. The fullback led through the C-gap on the Sam linebacker.

One thing I want to mention is the importance of the backside-blocking scheme. We want to build a wall on the backside to give the running back a seam. We call it high-lowing the backside. When we run, the outside zones that play could be a play that hits in the A-gap. We run the play so much the pursuit of the defense is extremely hard to the playside. There is a distinct tendency for the defense to overrun the play. It gives us great cutback opportunities. The backside has to block effectively because the ball can cut back to them.

Each week when we plan for the upcoming game, we consider three scenarios. If we play an odd front team, we want to see how they adjust to an X-over, twins, and two tight ends. We want to know how they adjust their front in each one of those situations. We can get the X-over by stepping the flanker on the line of scrimmage and the X-receiver off the line. (Diagram #6) We motion him to the flanker's side and run the zone back into the short side of the formation. The motion gives us an unbalanced formation. Most 50 teams roll the strong safety down and the free safety over with the motion.

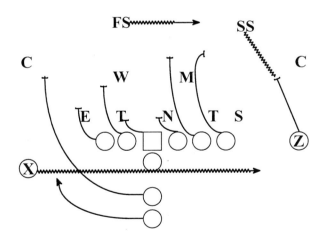

Diagram #6. X-Over Motion

This puts the corner as the support defender to the backside. We run the zone play to the short side and have an effective play.

I make the line calls on most plays. The offensive linemen have the opportunity to change the call. However, it had better be the right call. If they change the call and it is the wrong call, they

will have some sideline time or a butt chewing from the coach.

We had special rules for the guard in a twin formation scenario. Normally 33-stack teams play their defenders in a 4i-technique on the offensive tackle. (Diagram #7) With the twin set to his side, the 4i-technique moves to an outside shade on the tackle. That becomes a hard overtake block for the guard. We tell the playside guard to take his first step and decide where the 5-technique is going. If he is going outside, we tell the guard to turn back on the Mike linebacker.

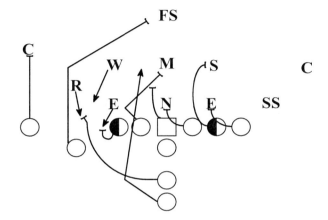

Diagram #7. Twins

Since the 5-technique stepped to the outside, the Will linebacker is going that way also. They also have the over-hang player in the C-gap. That gives them three defenders in the C-gap. The offensive tackle reaches for the 5-technique defender and the fullback aims off the tackles rear to block the support. He ends up blocking the Will linebacker coming outside. The running back sees there are two defenders in the C-gap and cuts the ball into the B-gap.

When we align the fullback, we do not give him a set depth from the quarterback. We tell him to align for success. He knows the play and he has to adjust his depth to block the overhang to the outside or the Will linebacker. He aims for the outside of the playside tackle's hip. In most cases he wants to stay tight on the hip.

When we coach our offensive line, we tell them they do not need to pancake defenders to have an affective block. We must get the defenders running and then get in their way. I heard a defensive coach the other day talking about his linemen. He said he wanted them to run to the ball. We do to. If they are running to the ball, we are blocking decent.

We can use the "pin and pull" scheme against 33-stack teams. In this diagram, we use a special blocking adjustment with the tackle and fullback. (Diagram #8) We pin the nose guard with the playside guard. The tight end pins the 4-technique tackle. The playside tackle, instead of kicking out the strong safety, pulls up on the Sam linebacker. The fullback aims at the tackle's butt and kicks out the strong safety. The tackle and fullback exchanged blocking assignment.

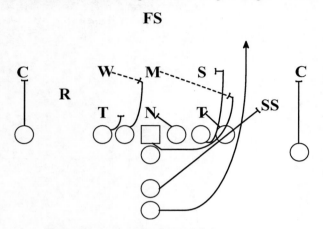

Diagram #8. Pin & Pull Special

We used the concepts from the zone scheme to help us with our power scheme. Our backside guard was not athletic enough to get to the strong side to turn up on the Mike linebacker. We decided to use the GT scheme or the "pin and pull" scheme to get to the edge. We kicked out with the fullback and used the guard and tackle pulls off the GT scheme. The tackle pulled around the down block of the tight end for the Sam linebacker. The guard pulled and blocked the Mike linebacker.

We also ran the "pin and pull" scheme, blocked down with the guard on the shade nose, and pulled the center and tackle. The tackle pulled around the down block for the Sam linebacker. The center pulled around the down block for the Mike linebacker.

When we pulled the center and tackle, they were our athletic linemen. The guards were big but not very mobile. To the backside of the power play, we ran a full zone-blocking scheme.

We have a good scheme to the weakside of the defense. When the under front covers all the linemen to the strong side. (Diagram #9) The defense aligns in a 2, 5, and 9-technique to the tight end side. To the backside, there is a 1-technique tackle and 5-technique end. We run

the play to the weak side. The playside guard pins the 1-technique to the inside. The offensive tackle reaches the 5-technique defender. The center pulls for the Will linebacker. The fullback comes outside the tackle's block and has the free safety.

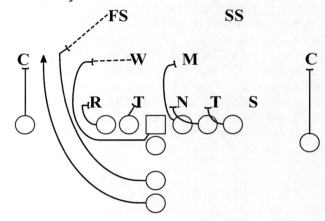

Diagram #9. Pin and Pull Weak Vs. Under Solid

We played a team that was a 50 front team however, on the goal line they went to a "6-5" defense. Because they had two A-gap players in the gaps we could not run the outside zone play, but we could use the "pin and pull" scheme. The guard pinned the A-gap defender inside and we pulled the center for the 0-technique Mike linebacker.

The tight end pinned the defensive tackle and the tackle logged the outside linebacker. We aligned in a three-back set. When teams see three backs in the backfield they think the play will be off tackle or double isolation. We used the "pin and pull" scheme and blocked the safety and corner with the blocking backs.

We tell the running back to key the fullback's numbers. If the fullback is turning up field, the running back should see only one number. If the fullback gets into a kick-out position, the running back should see his inside number only.

This was a simple way we took a true version of the rip, reach, pull, and overtake and made it a viable scheme. With the time restraints, we were not able to do many different things. We took our best play and changed it up from week to week. It helped us gain an advantage over our opponent. Thanks for your time.

Rocco Casullo

Odd Man Front Blitz Package

St. Thomas Aquinas High School, Florida

Thank you very much. My topic today is defensive football. We feel that is the way to win football games. We have a number of goals for our defensive team. We want to win the game. Our goal is to force field goals and prevents touchdowns. It is our job to take the ball away from the opponent's offense. We want to set up good field position for our offense. We must control the momentum of the game and win our first series of the game. That is extremely important to our defense.

Our number one objective for the defense is not allowing big plays. On first and second down we want to stop the run. We must defend the middle of the field first. We defend the field from the inside/out. On third down, we mix in some zone blitzes against the passing game. We want the ball thrown short and outside in that situation. We let the speed take over and let the safeties get to the corners.

We want to play gap sound on every situation that presents itself. We want to execute the defense successfully. To do that you must have good communication and teamwork. The defense must be mentally tough to deal with "sudden change" in the game. Those situations happen very quickly. Our motto on defense is, "If you think you stink." We want them to shut their mouths and hit people. We want to get players in position and get them going fast and forward.

The first thing I want to talk about is what we refer to as a "max-set." That involves "one and no back" sets. We name the offensive formations by city names. We try to make it easy for our players to identify formations. The first set is a "Destin" set. That formation is a spread 2 X 2 formation with a tight in the set. We want two blitzes for each formation. It is like a vocabulary test. You try to memorize as much as you can. That keeps it simple.

In this set, we have a "Destin X-call." (Diagram #1) We are a "3-4" defense. The inside linebackers are Mike and Will. The outside linebackers are Sam and Rush. The Sam linebacker is the strong side linebacker and the Rush is the open side linebacker. We play with Mike to the call side and Will to the away side. The X-call, involves the Mike, Will, and nose guard. The nose has a "NOB" technique. That means on the snap of the ball the nose is going outside into the B-gap. We identify the direction by the alignment of the one-back in the backfield.

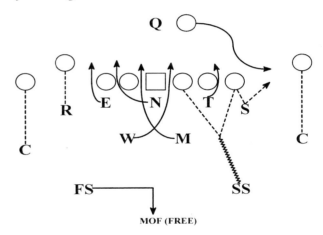

Diagram #1. Destin X-Call

The Mike linebacker aligns on the two-receiver side and blitzes the A-gap to the tight end side. It is an X-stunt in the middle, and the Mike linebacker is the first blitzer. The nose guard plays across the guard's face and gets into the B-gap to the two-receiver side. The Will linebacker is the second blitzer. He crosses behind the Mike linebacker into the A-gap to the two-receiver side.

Our Rush linebacker is our hybrid linebacker. He can come off the edge, play good run support, and match the number 2 receiver in the twin set. In this front, he has the number 2 receiver. He could have a "banjo" switch call with the corner to his side. We try to disguise everything in the secondary as a cover-2 shell. The corners are up and the safeties align at 10 yards. At the last second before the snap, we adjust to what we are going to run.

On this play, the strong safety to the tight end side rolls down and becomes a box player. He is a robber player or a low-hole player. If the back releases he has him, or he can play the tight end. We have to play tough man coverage with the corners on the number 1 receivers to their side. The up-front rushers must get to the quarterback. This is a gamble for the defense. This is a five-man pressure scheme.

The Sam linebacker is a lock down defender on the tight end. He has to get his hands on him and control him. He has to limit the tight end from doing anything to beat us. This is the first blitz we use in the Destin formation. You can use these blitzes against any formation.

In the front, the open side end aligns in a 6-technique and has contain responsibility on the pass. The nose guard aligns in a 0-technique head up the center. To play this defense, the nose has to command a double team or at least hold his ground. The tackle plays a 5-technique on the outside shoulder of the offensive tackle; however, he is a B-gap defender on this stunt. The Sam linebacker aligns in a 9-technique. The Sam linebacker gets his hands on the tight end and plays the running back if he releases to the flat.

The free safety in Destin is the middle of the field player. He plays over the top of the number 1 and 2 receivers and has the post cuts from those receivers. He could also spy on the tight end in case he tries to get down the middle of the field.

The base defense is an "Okie" front. We are a one-gap defense. We want to keep all blockers off the linebackers.

We call the 2 X 2 spread-formation with no tight end "Detroit." From this set, we run "Smoke" and "War." (Diagram #2) We like to run this stunt to defeat the option play. If we run "Smoke", that is the Sam and Mike linebacker blitzing off the edge. We base the stunt off where the running back sets in the backfield. The tackle aligns in a 5-technique and long sticks all the way over into the A-gap to the side of the stunt. The nose guard is in a 0-technique and slants into the weakside A-gap. The defensive end aligns in a 6-technique and he is the contain players to the backside.

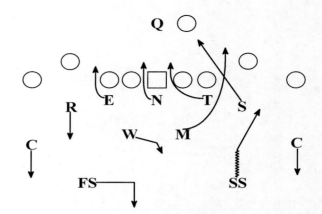

Diagram #2. Detroit Smoke

The Sam linebacker aligns two yards outside the offensive tackle and two yards off the line of scrimmage. He comes off the edge in a tight path to the running back in the set. The Mike linebacker aligns in a 20-technique on the guard and high blitzes off the edge outside the Sam linebacker. If it is a zone play, the Sam linebacker has the dive. The Mike linebacker comes off the edge and plays through the quarterback to the pitch if they run the inside zone read or option. The Will linebacker is the backside player.

The Rush linebacker is the seam player. The corners play cover-3. The free safety is the middle of the field player. The strong safety is the seam player to the stunt side of the formation. The Mike and Will linebackers, must key the back. If a back flares, they must take him.

This is a great call against the zone read play. The only way to defend the option is to attack it. You cannot sit back and play the option. Teams will find out what we are doing and move their set back at the last minute. When they do that, we check from the "smoke" call and run the "war" blitz, which is the same blitz to the other side. (Diagram #3)

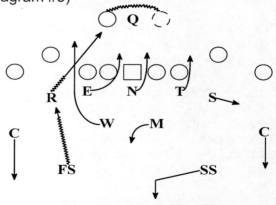

Diagram #3. Detroit War

We call the blitzes by the letters of the players. **SM**oke is Sam and Mike running the blitz. The **Wa**R is the Will and Rush.

The end runs the long stick into the A-gap and plays the dive. The nose goes into the strong A-gap. The Rush comes off the edge as the low blitz and the Will linebacker comes off the edge as the high blitz. The strong safety comes to the middle and the free safety rolls down into the weak flat.

If we have a balanced set, we run the blitz to the field side. We did not see any pistol sets this year, but if we do, we run the blitz to the field.

We play teams that run the 3 X 1 bunch-set. Against this set, we make a "**S**uga**r**" call. (Diagram #4) The 5-technique defensive end slants into the B-gap. The nose is a 0-technique defender and plays the A-gap. We want him to maul the center. The tackle is a 5-technique defender. We want the tackle to bull rush the offensive tackle but we want him to work to the inside. That is an important point. The Sam aligns on the point receiver in the bunch set and jams him. He is coming on a contain blitz.

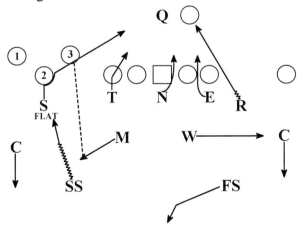

Diagram #4. Sugar

The Mike linebacker plugs the B-gap on runs and plays the hook/curl zone on a pass. The Rush linebacker aligns 3 yards outside and 2 yards back off the offensive tackle and blitzes off the edge. The Will linebacker plugs the A-gap on run.

On a pass, he wants to get under a slant pattern by the number 1 receiver. If there is no slant, he plays the curl/flat area. The strong safety rolls down and plays the flat area to the bunch side. The corners play cover-3 and the free safety rolls into the middle third.

When a team aligns in the bunch set, they try to create problems by crossing and rubbing defenders. The Mike linebacker has to be the wall player on the number 3 receiver in the bunch. The Sam linebacker aligns on the point receiver and beats him up. The patterns in the bunch depend on the point receiver releasing off the line. Any inside routes coming from the number 3 receiver, the Mike linebacker has to get his hands on him.

The strong safety stems down and replaces the Sam linebacker. The Sam linebacker blitzes off the edge and the strong safety works to the flat zone. The bunch package like to send the number 3 receiver up the seam deep. That is why it is important for the Mike linebacker to get his hands on him to slow him down. The free safety rotates back through the middle and picks up that pattern. The corners play cover-3.

The Will linebacker gets under the number 1 receiver. However, he has to see the back in the backfield. If he releases, the Rush linebacker should be home free on the quarterback. If something happens, the Will linebacker has to play the wheel or seam from the back in the backfield.

Toronto is a three-wide receiver set. The blitz is "**SW**im." (Diagram #5) The Sam and Will linebackers run the blitz. The defensive end slants into the B-gap. The nose slants into the weakside A-gap. The tackle slants into the weakside B-gap. The Rush linebacker takes away the slant by the number 1 receiver to his side and plays the running back to his side. The Mike linebacker plugs his gap on the run and plays the hook/curl to the strong side. If the number 3 receiver comes out of the backfield, he has to wall him to the outside.

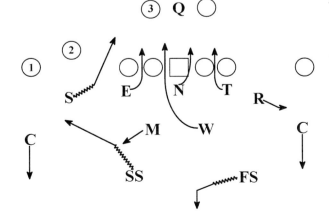

Diagram #5. Toronto Swim

The strong safety rolls down into the strong flat zone. The free safety is the middle of the field zone player and the corner play cover-3. We want the Rush linebacker to get into the offensive line and quarterback's head. He is an aggressive blitzer. When he is not coming, he has to make them think he is. He stems in and out and shows the blitz.

Our free and strong safeties are almost like linebackers. They are strong run supporter and must read the runs. If we get a run to the weakside, the Rush linebacker has to take on pulling guards and fullback. The free safety has to read those schemes and react up in support.

The Rush linebacker does not come late. He reads the play, get to his area and sits down. He is responsible for any screen that way. This defense puts a lot of pressure on the Rush linebacker.

When we align the linebacker on air, we put them in a quarter-turn to the inside. That points them at their keys and allows them to react quicker to where they need to go. Any formation we see we play the run read first. The Rush end reads the offensive tackle for his key. If he gets the high hat or pass set, he play pass.

When we blitz, we apply the motto. "If you think, you stink." If they are going to think, they must do it while they are rushing the quarterback. When we blitz, we must get home. You must react and go get the quarterback.

We call the empty sets, "Eagle." The call we like against the empty is "**RaM**". (Diagram #6)

The "ram" is the Rush and Mike linebacker. In this set, the Mike linebacker stacks behind the 5-technique tackle to the three-receiver side. The tackle slants inside to the B-gap. The nose is in the 0-technique on the center. The end aligns in a 5-technique and slants into the B-gap. The Rush linebacker is outside to the weakside.

The Mike and Rush linebackers are coming off the edge in this blitz. The Will linebacker aligns in a 0-stack behind the nose guard. He drops to the box and takes the number 3 receiver if he comes inside. The free safety drops down to the two-receiver side and plays man-to-man coverage on the number 2 receiver. The corner plays the number 1 receiver in man coverage. The free safety and corner play "banjo" coverage on the two receivers. That means they zone off and play man on the receiver that come toward them.

On the three-receiver side, we play box coverage. The Sam linebacker aligns on the number 3 receiver and plays the flat. The corner comes off and plays the deep third. The strong safety rolls down on the number 2 receiver and plays the hook/curl zone.

Any time a team goes to an empty set we expect to get a sack. The Rush linebacker comes off the edge and the defensive end slants inside. One of those players usually makes the sack. It put a tremendous amount of pressure on the offensive tackle and there is no back in the backfield.

We do many run blitzes. Against a two-back set, the main thing is to have all gaps covered. In this blitz we go to the "under" front. We call this blitz, "Under Wolf" cover-1. The Wolf call is the Will linebacker. (Diagram #7)

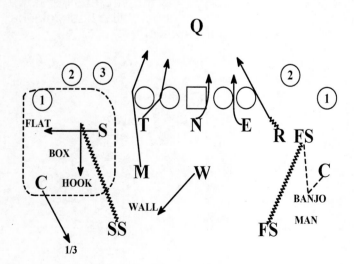

Diagram #6. Eagle Ram Box

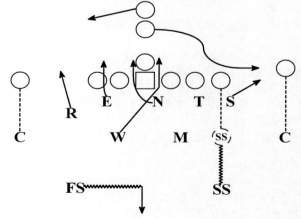

Diagram #7. Under Wolf Cover-1

The nose aligns to the field A-gap. The tackle is in a 5-technique and the Sam linebacker is in a 9-technique. To the weakside, the defensive end aligns in a 3-technique on the outside shoulder of the guard. The Rush linebacker is three yards outside and two yards deep from the offensive tackle. He is in a quarter tilt toward the tackle and reading the tackle to the back in the backfield.

The nose aligns in the strong A-gap and cross the centers face into the weakside A-gap. The Will linebacker blitzes through the strong side A-gap. The 5-technique defender is the B-gap defender. The strong safety rolls down and plays head up the tight end at linebacker depth. He is a C-gap defender from this position. We play cover-1 in the secondary. The corner locks up with the number 1 receivers and the free safety is the middle of the field safety. We lock the strong safety on the tight end. If the end blocks, the strong safety becomes an additional box player.

The coaching points go to the Sam and Rush linebacker. If any back comes out of the backfield into the flat zone, Sam and Rush must take them. It is hard for the Sam linebacker because he has to play his technique on the tight end. However, if the back releases, he has to go right now. The same thing is true with the Rush linebacker. His alignment allows him to have better vision on the back in the backfield. He can see the offensive tackle and the back. We are in man-coverage on the corners. If the back comes out and the outside linebackers miss him, the back can run forever.

If the inside linebackers are not good at reading their triangle reads, get them playing forward. Do not let them sit and catch blocks. The weakest link in this front is the defensive 5-technique tackle. If you do not have a tackle that can stay in his gap it makes it hard on the Mike linebacker and safety. If the blockers turn the tackle, and the tight end gets off on the Mike linebacker, it puts a lot of pressure on the safety to make the play in the C-gap.

If we do not have a tackle that can fight off the slip block, we run a **S**nake call. (Diagram #8) On the snake call, the strong safety times his move and rolls down into the box and blitzes the C-gap. The tackle slants inside into the B-gap. That makes it easier on the Mike linebacker and the strong safety. To run this blitz, we change the coverage to cover-0 and we bring the free safety to that side to play the tight end in man-to-man coverage.

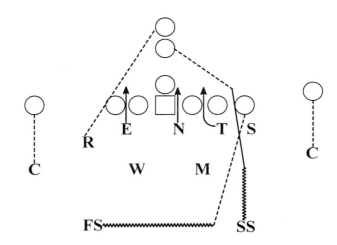

Diagram #8. Snake

If we run the Snake Blitz, the Mike linebacker does not blitz. In a pro-twins set, we can run "under/**M**ink." The front is an under front and the Mike linebacker blitzes the weak side A-gap. (Diagram #9) This is a simple blitz. The nose comes off his shade on the center and slants hard into the strong A-gap. The Mike linebacker cross the center and blitzes the weakside A-gap. If we play cover-1 as the coverage, we bring both corners to the same side and cover, the twins set.

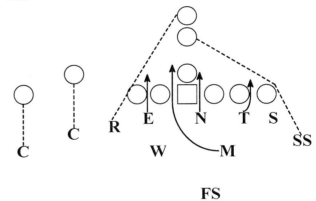

Diagram #9. Under Mink

We bring the corners over when teams bring their two split receivers to the same side. The corners are more adapt at playing coverage in man coverage and pattern switching. They are used to playing the banjo call and do it better. Banjo is an important concept with teams that tries to rub off our defenders. The concept combines zone and man principles. It allows your corner to switch receivers when they cross. The inside corner plays the inside breaking patterns and the outside corner plays the outside breaking patterns.

When we game plan each week, we have two blitzes for every formation. If they are one-back, two-backs, or no-backs, we have two blitzes for each formation. If the offense adjusts to the first set of blitzes, we make adjustments and go to plan B.

If you play teams that will let you bring the strong safety into the box, put him in there. That is the key to the blitzes. He can make 12-14 tackles a game from that position. If teams are in 21 and 22 personnel groupings, the strong safety should be down in the box.

The Sam linebacker is a C-gap defender. If the tight end blocks down, he gets his hands on him, and stays in the C-gap. If anything runs outside of him, the strong safety is the force player and he pursue from the inside/out. We put the Rush linebackers in a quarter tilt so they can see the tackle, pulling guard, and the back. They must use their peripheral vision to see all they need to see. They have to learn how to play in space.

We call the twins-open a "bomber set." (Diagram #10) We run a "RinSe" blitz. This blitz is the Rush and Sam linebackers on an inside blitz. This is good against a two-back zone read team. This confuses the blocking scheme for the guards. The defensive end and tackle align in a 4i-technique and long scoop to the outside. The nose plays down the head of the center. The Sam and Rush linebackers blitz the B-gaps through the offensive guards.

deepest receiver goes in the pattern. The corner to the single receiver side has him man-to-man.

Alabama runs this blitz many times. This is a good blitz to disrupt a zone read by the quarterback. The Sam and Rush linebackers on this stunt must go. There can be no hesitation. When the down defender long scoops outside, they must be right off their butts and attacking the guard. It is a great blitz against the run and the pass.

The technique of the nose playing in a 0-technique can be a two-gap technique. We tell him to maul the center and play football. He cannot let the center turn him. If the guard blocks down on him, he must hold his own. They cannot take him off the ball or turn him so they can slip to the backside linebacker.

When the Rush and Sam linebacker come from the outside, they key the guards. If the guard turns out on them, they know they must close into the A-gap. They must play through the guards. If the guard turns inside to double the nose, the linebacker plays his hip. He comes tight off the hip of the guard and plays football.

If they attempt to scoop on the nose, the linebacker blitzing through that gap will make the play. He will run it down before it can get to the other side. He has to be aware of the offensive lineman that will try to block him. The backside offensive tackle on plays away from him has to secure the B-gap. The blitzing linebacker has to know that block is coming and play through it.

If the offense has three-backs in the backfield, we call that a "Bone." (Diagram #11)

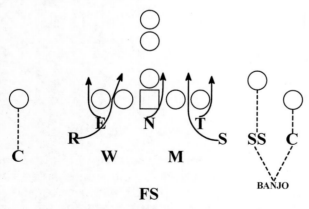

Diagram #10. Bomber Rinse

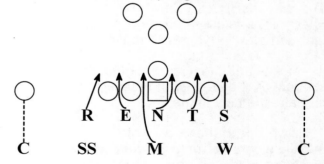

Diagram 11. Bone/Sink/Mink Cover-1

We can play cover-1 behind this blitz. The Mike and Will linebacker must take the backs coming out of the backfield. The strong safety and corner to the two-receiver side play a banjo technique with the twin receivers. The free safety is in the middle of the field playing as deep as the

When we play a team like this, it is complete gap control. This blitz is "sink/Mink/cover-1."

This is a Mike linebacker blitz to the field. The defensive end and tackle align in 3-techniques. The Sam and Rush linebacker are in quarter turn stance on the edges. The nose slants into the weakside A-gap. The Mike linebacker stacks behind the nose and blitzes through the strong side A-gap.

The Will linebacker is outside the Sam linebacker to the boundary. The strong safety is in the same position to the strong side of the field. We are in cover-1 in the secondary. The free safety is in the middle of the field and plays deep as the deepest. If anyone comes out of the backfield in motion, we must man-up with him. If the running back becomes the number 2 receiver to the boundary, the Will linebacker takes him. The strong safety rolls down into the box. If there is motion to his side, he covers it.

The Mike and Will linebackers are over the guards' 90 percent of the time. With the Mike linebacker in the middle, he has a triangle read. The strong safety and Will linebacker are outside and read the guards. The hardest thing to teach the safety is how to read in the box.

If you play the Okie front, you must have good coaches to put it together. The odd front puts pressure on the end, tackle, and nose. They need coaches that can help them play the variations of the techniques.

The only time we had any trouble with preparation was against Byrnes High School out of South Carolina. They were a good veteran team with a smart quarterback. We lined up to run the first blitz and the quarterback stepped back and called an audible. We checked the defense, to the second call. The quarterback called another audible. We did not have another blitz. We are all right most of the time unless you go deep into your playbook.

In the spring we install all the verbiage and calls. We can run any of the blitzes I just showed you with any formation.

I appreciate your time and attention. I will be around if you have questions. Thank you very much.

J. T. Curtis

Structures Within the 50-Defense

John T. Curtis Christian High School, Louisiana

We are here to share some ideas and learn together. The one thing I have learned in 44 years of coaching football is there is no one-way to do it. There are many different ways to make it work. What you want at the end is for it to taste good. There are numerous ways to get the job done. Regardless of how you make the gumbo, there are key ingredients you must use to make it good. Garlic, onions, celery, bell peppers, shrimp, crab meat, and crawfish, are just a few of the main ingredients.

Football is the exact same way. There are key ingredients you must have if you are going to be successful as a football "team." It is not what you line up in. It is what you can execute. What I am going to try to do today is go over some things that may be helpful to you. It is impossible for me to come up here for an hour and give you a scheme that will help you go home and win games.

If I can give you some thoughts and ideas that you may be able to implement into what you are doing, it has been a successful lecture. If it makes you become a better football team and a better coach, then it is a successful clinic. I can go home feeling good about what has happened.

There is one thing I think is paramount that you do if you are to be successful. You must be **organized** in everything you do. I have coached for 44 years and I have never gone to the practice field without a written practice schedule. I am talking about a minute-by-minute practice plan. Depending on the day, I will have a 2 hour to 2:15 minutes written out practice schedule available.

We are going to **coach everybody** that is on the field. I do not have dummy squads. I do not practice 11 players and the rest of them stand and watch. If they are out there, we are going to coach them. They are going to be involved in football drills. If a momma walks up to me and says, "You have not given Johnny a chance." I can say, "Yes I have." Every day he gets a chance.

Every minute of each day, he has the opportunity to show us what he is capable of doing.

This gives the coach an opportunity to teach them how to play the game. I do not know how many coaches you have on your staff, but I want to use the scout team coach as an example. Coaching the scout team is more than just lining players up in a position. It is more than just holding a dummy. The coach has to teach them when they are in the scout position how to play the game.

Those players have to play for you the next year. The more we can teach them when they are young freshmen and sophomores, the easier it will be to teach them when they are juniors and seniors. We want to teach every minute of every day on the practice field.

In our **pre-practice**, everyone is involved in one way or another although special teams have the priority. Punters, kickers, snappers, holders, and returners have the priority. However, everyone is going to work on something that will be beneficial for him during the regular practice. If we are going to work on a fold block in practice, we do it as part of the pre-practice session. During that time, we work on any difficulties the player may be having with his individual technique.

We want to do this before practice starts. That keeps us from standing in a drill and teaching a particular technique. Pre-practice is just as important as your regular practice. We organize the pre-practice so that special teams and specialist can get the work that they need to do on a consistent every day basis, in order to be an affective kicker.

How do we practice? We practice a little for a long period. You cannot teach tackling in one day. You cannot teach tackling in a week. If you do not teach tackling every day, you are not going to tackle very well. I want to tell you a few things about that before we go too much further.

You can say it how you want to say it. However, you will never here this come out of any coach at John Curtis Christian High School on the practice field. You will not hear them say, "All we want is to front up the tackle or just thud him up." "All we want to do is hit the ball carrier with a forearm shiver and break down around the ball and touch the ball carrier on his waist."

You can go back and watch the Super Bowl or any game you want to watch and look at the missed tackles. Defensive player hit the ball carrier with their shoulders and forearm, he bounces off them, and keeps running. The announcers talk about how good the running back is. It is not a great running back. It is a poor tackle. The reason for this is the fact coaches spend five minutes a day working a tackling drill and 1:55 minutes fronting up the ball carrier. **Repetition** is going to determine the product you get. If you tell them to front-up the ball, bump off, or butting up, that is what happens in the games.

We played in a state championship game this year against a great quarterback. He was a three-year starter. His two brothers before him were quarterbacks and his father was the quarterback coach. He was a great player. We beat them last year in the state championship and they came out on fire. He was 16-18, in the first two drives they had. However, they did not score. We caused a fumble and intercepted him on the second possession.

When he completed a pass, we tackled the receivers on the spot. There were no yards after the catch. We got that done by the way we practice. When we tackle in practice, the players put their chest up on the tackle. The tackler puts his chest and his arms on the ball carrier. In practice, we do everything you are supposed to do in a tackle except drive him to the ground. We do that in games because that is what we practice.

We talk about that every single time we snap the ball when we are on defense. It does not matter whether it is a perimeter drill or inside drill, that is how we talk.

When you teach a drill, **teach slowly**. Do not start at full speed. Expand the speed slowly. However, after the teaching, you must practice at game speed. If you do not **practice at game speed**, do not expect to play fast in the game. We do no conditioning after practice. The reason we do not is because I hated it when I played.

About half way through practice, I began to think about the sprinting at the end. I want my players thinking about practice instead of conditioning. I want them to practice the tempo that we play in the games. We get in shape to play football and get aggressive about football during practice. We run to the football in practice as if it were a game. We do it every day and it is an emphasis for everyone.

I know it is hot in south Florida but it is hot in Louisiana and we must consider that when we practice. I take care of it and get them off the field so they have a chance to get a little water and cool down a bit. However, when they are on the field, they turn and run to the football.

We teach that in a drill we do in our two-a-day practices and in spring training. (Diagram #1) We start the drill by placing cones on the sidelines. We space them at the line of scrimmage with the next one coming at two and half yards down the field. After that, the cones are spaced at five yards intervals down the field. We start the drill by putting the defense in the middle of the field. We start it there because we do not want them exhausted when we first teach the drill. We teach the drill slowly and expand the speed until we reach the far hash mark of the field.

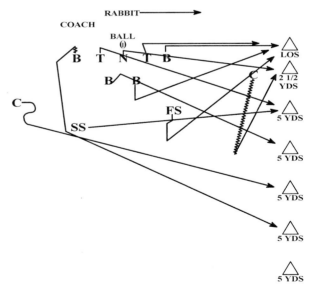

Diagram #1. Pursuit Drill

This is our pursuit drill. I know you think everyone does this drill. I am going to explain how we do it and why we do it this way. I want this drill to look exactly like the football game. I want all the defenders pursuing on the line of scrimmage or two and half yards off the line of scrimmage chasing the ball. We emphasize that we want to make tackles on their side of the line of scrimmage and not ours. The only thing I ask the rabbit to do is get width as quickly as he can. That gives the defense a direction. After the rabbit starts and gives them direction, he comes back.

Before I talk about the defense, I need to clarify one thing. If you are over 40 years of age, this position is a defensive end. If you are under 40, he is an outside linebacker. Old coaches understand that. We play a 50-defense. With the invention of the "3-4", that position became outside linebackers. If I say ends, I mean outside linebackers.

The outside linebacker takes his stance. When the rabbit starts, the outside linebacker has to take his steps to execute his technique. He does not start running as soon as the rabbit starts to move. He takes his steps, turns, and runs down the line of scrimmage as fast as he can run. He runs to the cone on the line of scrimmage. The defensive tackle does the same thing. He comes down the line and attacks the first cone.

The front side linebacker is on an angle downhill to the line of scrimmage. He starts at a depth of 5 yards, pursues outside, and gets to the two and half-yard cone. The nose, takes a stab step, runs down the line of scrimmage, to the two and half yard cone.

Some coaches will tell you their players cannot do that. I say, "Let's practice it until they can!" I say let us practice them and see what they can do instead of what they cannot do. The defensive tackle reads, throws his shoulder, and comes parallel down the line of scrimmage. He crosses the nose guard face and sprints to the sidelines at the first five-yard cone over the line of scrimmage. The strong safety reads, makes his movement up the field, and gets to the next cone. The other defenders should be in between his movement.

The backside outside linebacker is the last defender in the pursuit drill. He is the last man to make the tackle. He steps, jabs, and shuffles back. He is the last resort. The playside corner backpedals for two steps, plants, and comes up the field. It is important for you to check his angle. He cannot simply run straight up the field. He has to be the first or secondary contain player, or an alley runner depending on the strong safety. He has to run the angle he plays in the game.

The free safety makes his move depending on what the secondary coach called. If it is an option team, he comes down the line of scrimmage, reads the number 2 receiver, and becomes an alley player. If it is a passing situation, he shuffles, breaks into his coverage, plants and comes to the alley. You must create the angle you want the defender attacking the line of scrimmage based on who they are playing from week to week. I think the pursuit drill is the beginning of where you need to be in order for your team to be as effective as they should be.

You must coach responsibility. I do not have many pet peeves. However, one of my pet peeves is not coaching when you are on the field. If you are on the field with a hat on your head or a shirt on your chest that has "Coach" printed on it, I do not want you to shoot the breeze or talk to your fellow coach about what went on in school that day. We do that when we go into the office. Coach because that is what you are there to do. Coach every player you are responsible for every single day. If we are going to improve, the pictures they see must be accurate. That comes from the scout team coach doing his job.

If we have a punt drill, I want the players that are going to catch the ball in the future doing that job. I want them to run to catch the football and retrieve it. That way the next year when you tell him to catch the ball and not let it hit the ground, he knows what you are saying. Little things make the difference.

I have a couple of things I am going to go over that I think are good. I want to show you some of the things we do with practice organization. On Monday, in our defensive drills, we work on the "5-2" defense. We have a script of plays we work. We have 21 plays scripted. In those 21 plays, the entire second unit gets seven of the first 14 plays. If you think you need as many reps with the first unit as you can get, you should think about injury. If one of your first team athletes is lost for the season or a game, who do you substitute? Do you put the backup on the field and say, "Go out there and do a good job," or do you work with him to get him ready to play before the injury.

Give them the seven plays they need to be ready to play. The backup player needs to know the opponent's best plays, what they are good at, and how you plan to stop them. The last seven plays on the script are for the mix of players you think will play in the game. That is the first team players and second team players combined that you think are going to get playing time. You and I know that not everyone on the second team is going to get playing time. We do the exact same thing with the inside drill.

On Tuesday, we look at some kind of nickel front. On Wednesday, we mix the two together as part of the script. We work on the 5-2 and nickel package. The script on Wednesday is a unique script. We use game tape of the opponent to make our script. We take the longest drive against the best opponent or a game winning drive and make that the plays run in the script for Wednesday's practice. Those plays are the plays their coach is going to call when the game is on the line. Those plays are the plays the coach wants to run. Those plays reflect his personality.

To get the most out of your drills you must think about the scout teams that run the offense against them. My secondary coach came up with a great idea. If you have two or three scout group working against the first defense, he tries to get two good receivers with every group. The next three best receivers are in those groups. He takes his worst receiver and implements them into those groups. In the groups, he has good receiver, okay receivers, and bad receivers.

He goes into the groups and numbers the receivers 1-5. The routes he has to make sure are run correctly are numbers 1, 2, and 3. Those are the best receivers. The 4 and 5 receivers line up in places where it does not matter if the patterns are run correctly or not. Usually 4 and 5 end up at the running back's spot, if they are not coming out of the backfield. That way you work everyone in the drill and get the looks you need to see. None of the coaches are yelling at someone for not running the correct pattern.

If you spend some time and set up the scout teams and run them where you get the best looks, it will save you time and patients. The players do not need to know what you are doing. It lets everyone be a part of the team.

You play as you practice. As you go through your preparation, you need to think about things like this to make your practice more effective. Everyone is on the same page and trying to get the same things accomplished. The team hears one voice from seven or eight different coaches.

We are a 50-front defense. Everything we teach we base out of the 50-front. (Diagram #2) When we go to spring practice, we teach

everything out of that front. We play the front but we will be able to vary our defenses not based on the formations we face, but the techniques we are going to execute. The nose guard can play a nose or 3-technique because the technique is not going to change. We are an attack-read defense.

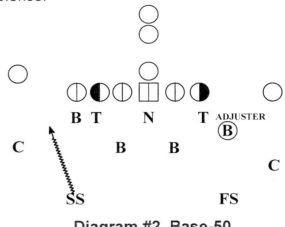

Diagram #2. Base-50

In the old days, we played a read defense. People got nervous and said that sounded too soft. What they did next was run everyone up the field. Doing that did not sit well with what we did on offense. We wanted to teach them how to attack, but also learn to read. We make the 9-call for the linebacker depending on the side we call. If it is a single 9-call, that is the weakside linebacker on the weakside of the defense. The 9-call is going to be the adjuster in the 50-defense.

Our outside linebackers are not going to be the biggest players. However, they will be players that can run, tackle, and can defend the pass, and can play the run. If you have a good athlete who is not quite fast enough to be a corner, make him an outside linebacker. We do not flip/flop our players. They play left and right sides of the defense.

The second thing you want to do is find out if the center can snap the ball to the quarterback and block someone at the same time. If you play an even front, you are not challenging the center. Snapping the ball in the shotgun with a defender on your nose is not an easy thing to do. The offense will try to help the center with a protection scheme some way. They must do it if the nose is a real player.

The good news is the nose does not have to be a big player. If he is, that is a bonus. He does not have to be fast, but if he is he become dangerous. If you can combine, "speed and size", you have a good nose. However, small and quick can be just as effective. If he is big but a step slow, you need to give him a direction to go. If he is moving, the center cannot block him because he is too big. They have to double him. When the offense starts putting two blockers on the nose, they open up lanes for blitzes.

If the offense has to double the nose, we can overload the back in the backfield. He can only block one at a time. When we bring linebackers, we play man-to-man in the secondary with a free safety. The nose tackle can put the offense in a dilemma. Last year we had two good nose guards. They were exact opposite types of players. We played them both. One of the nose tackles was a bigger and stronger player and the other was a smaller and quicker player. We interchanged them and opponents had fits trying to block them.

We played two different players but their technique never changes. I do not want the offense to know how I am going to play by the personnel I have on the field.

If we call "99", that is our variation of the double walk away for the outside linebackers. (Diagram #3) Both our outside linebacker are going to play like strong safeties. We will be in some form of a 4 man rush with the down three and one of the inside linebackers. We can play in a three-man rush scheme. If the nose guard can play and he has speed, there is nothing better than that twist stunt between the nose and a defensive tackle. The nose guard can loop to the outside, turn the corner, and attack to the inside.

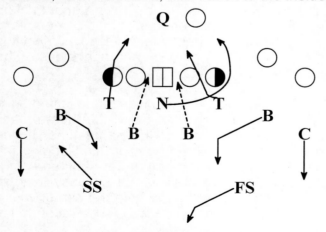

Diagram #3. 99-Front

If they do not coach the offensive guard to that side extremely well, we can get around the corner with the nose. The 5-technique tackle

comes inside on the guard. He is inside the tackle's block. If they try to switch the blocks with the guard taking the tackle and the offensive tackle coming outside on the nose, the tackle has the guard beat. He is on the edge of the guard's shoulder and inside his hip. He can release straight to the quarterback. You will have a three-man rush that will handle everything you need to handle and be able to keep all your outside linebackers in coverage and have yourself protected on the edge.

From the 99-front, we can rush three, four, or five defenders. When we blitz from this front we do it with the two inside linebackers. The outside linebackers play their coverages. We can bring one inside linebacker on a blitz and have four-man pressure or bring both linebackers and have five-man pressure. There are a number of ways you can use line movement and linebacker run through to pressure the quarterback.

People have played the 50-front since the famed football coach Bud Wilkerson was at Oklahoma. I have run this stuff since Oklahoma ran it in the 50's. This defense is still relevant today. This defense will give offenses fits. Centers do not like to deep snap and block no matter what they tell you.

From the 50-front we can slide into the "4-3" front. (Diagram #4) In that situation, we want to take our worst defensive lineman off the field at times. I go to my defensive line coach and ask him who is the best pass rusher on our team. I also want to know who is the weakest pass protector for our opponent is. I want that match-up. I am going to substitute so that my best rusher is on their worst blocker. I want to take our worst pass rusher off the field and replace him with a third linebacker that runs better.

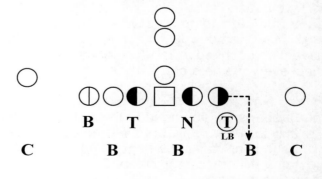

Diagram #4. 4-3 Front

In the championship game we lost our best linebackers. He signed at Tulane. Our other linebacker signed at LSU. It was a good year for linebackers. The one that signed at Tulane was a good linebacker but he was only 5-10. That will not make any difference and the big boys will wonder how they missed him. After the injury, the player we brought into the game was a backup strong safety. We trained him to play the linebacker position although he was a safety. All season long, he worked in that position. We told him it was like playing strong safety except we thought he was physical enough to play the run. He blitzed, sacked the quarterback, and separated the quarterback's shoulder early in the second half.

Using your personnel and putting them in a position that they can be successful is a key to winning games. To do that, you must think through the process of preparation. You do not know when one of your key players is going down and you must have their backups prepared to play. You are looking for that kind of flexibility in your backups.

From this alignment, we can go into our nickel front. (Diagram #5) This is what we would play on passing situations. We like to play the "4-2-5." The thing that will help you is teaching players where to align in relationship to the hash marks. We rarely play 3-techniques. We play tight 2-techniques because we want the linebackers to run and make plays. If the ball is on the hash, we play the field tackle in a wider 2-technique. He is still a two-gap player and does it by getting his hands and head into a position to control both gaps. He cannot get out of his rush lane.

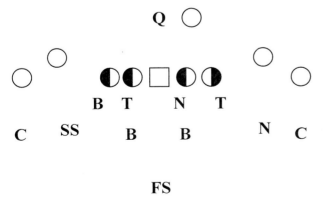

Diagram #5. Nickel Front

The boundary tackle is in a 2i-technique. He can get inside because he has only 17 yards to protect. The number one concern I have in the

three, four, or nickel front is that the linemen get back in the rush lanes when they rush the passer. The offense completes more passes because we get out of our pass lanes than anything else. When they get out of their rush lanes, they give the quarterback a passing window the size of this room.

They stay in their passing lanes because of practice. It is like the stunt in the three-man front between the nose and the tackle. If they wash the tackle coming inside down and the nose looping to the outside gets too wide, there is a tremendous passing lane.

The other thing we do from the nickel front that I think has merit is the "nickel over." (Diagram #6) We play the nickel to the trips set side. That keeps the offense from using the number 3 receiver to that side against an inside linebacker. This allows us to keep both inside linebackers in the box, play the running quarterback, and still have sound coverage to the trips side.

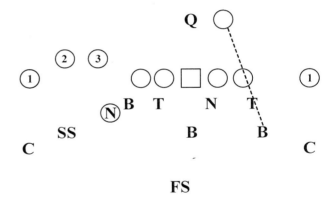

Diagram #6. Nickel Over

Teams get into some kind of trips formation or motion into that formation, to get single cover to the backside. (Diagram #7)

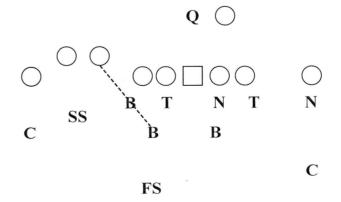

Diagram #7. Nickel Double

That is the opposite of what we want to do. We take the nickel and play him to the single receiver side. That tells the offense they will have to beat us with their fourth best receiver. We are not going to let them take their best receiver and get one-on-one with a corner. We are going to press him at the line and not let him get off the line of scrimmage.

We have two ways to play the number 3 receiver to the trips side with the nickel double on the number 1 receiver. The inside linebacker can play the number 3 receiver or the outside linebacker can match up on him.

The flexibility of the 4-5-2 comes from the 50-front concept as far as pass rush. The advantage you gain is the extra defender called the 9-end. We train him to play nickel back. If the offense brings the second tight end into the game, the nickel has to step up and play on the tight end. You have to coach him to step up and play the block of the tight end. It is a mismatch at times. We coach him how to play the mismatch and we ask him to stay on the line of scrimmage. He has to bite, fight, and claw not to be knocked off the line of scrimmage and create creases in the defense.

If the tight end blocks down, the nickel has to take on the fullback. All we want him to do is create a pile with his body and the body of the fullback. We do not ask him to make a play up the field. The offense does not want to play with two tight ends. That is something they do not want to do.

The last thing we do with our 50-concept is the "33." (Diagram #8)

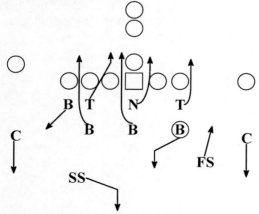

Diagram #8. 33-Front

Teams that want to throw the ball all have good players. They say they want to run the ball but they really do not. They think if you play three-deep, they can beat you with four verticals. We play three-deep against the best teams. It all depends on how you coach your defense.

We do not let receivers release off the line of scrimmage freely. We are going to hang in the seam long enough to give the free safety time to do what he needs to do. We line up in the "33" and bring the fifth rusher from where we want to bring him. The only thing the offense knows is the three down linemen are coming but that is all. They do not know where the fourth and fifth rushers are coming from.

If I rush five defenders, I still have six to defend the pass. I have not weakened myself defensively by rushing five defenders. Our ability to scout will determine where the rushers will come from. It depends on what they try to do to be successful against us.

All the things we do comes from our base 50-front. The nose guard's technique will not change whether he is playing head up the center or head up the tight end. His reads and techniques will not change.

Coaches I have enjoyed my time here and I hope I gave you something you can use. Thank you very much.

Chuck Donohue

Passing Game Off Zone Action

Southern Regional High School, New Jersey

I have been fortunate to have the opportunity to talk here a couple of times and I really enjoy it. I believe in football clinics. To me, the Nike Football Clinics kickoffs the winter season as far as figuring some football things out. It stirs my thinking about things I can work on during the spring and summer.

I want to throw some things at you that we run in our offense. We are not an Oregon type of football team. That is not our style. We read the edge defender on the tight end and split end side. We do it in a very simple way. We have experimented in reading the inside linebacker and I will go over that with you from a passing standpoint.

If you want to start to talk about the passing game, the first thing you have to do is have an honest evaluation about your personnel. What can your players actually do?

CHECK LIST FOR YOUR PASSING GAME

1. **Honest Evaluation of Personnel:**
   QB, OL, RB, WR, TE
   - **Ability to play multiple positions and take advantage of their skills.**
   - **Create formations that stress a defense.**

Make sure if you are going to utilize spread formations that you are able to handle any problems that could be coming from it. An example for us would be this. We are not going to run the zone read offense if we do not have a good tight end. I do not like to have short edges and the problems it presents. Our tackles have a difficult time in handling the speed guys on the edge. That is how we feel about it. You may not feel the same way. We want to give ourselves a decent chance in handling protection for our quarterback.

How many of your players can run multiple positions? Are they smart enough to handle it?

Are they physically capable of doing it? You want to be able to get into different formations in order to give the defense problems. We have an advantage in our league because there are only two teams that run the zone play. Everybody else is running the wing-T or a Navy type of offense. Our offense is not something our opponents face every week.

We need to create formations that stress the defense. The single most important thing we have done in the past few years is to add the wingback next to the tight end. It has been extremely good for us in causing problems for the defense when making adjustments.

2. **Teach and drill fundamentals in the off season**
   - **January to August**
   - **Coach the feet in your agility sessions**
   - **Power in the weight room**
   - **Coach where you can see their eyes**

In the off season our offensive linemen are working on their zone steps in their agility drills. The wide receivers are working on their releases. When we start up in August, we are not teaching techniques. We have refined the techniques we want to use in the off season. You need to control kid's feet. This is true especially with young kids. They run too fast and they let their feet get too wide. They get into really bad body positions. You do not want to coach through that in August and September when you really need to focus on your upcoming games.

If you are a zone team and a passing team, you need good footwork. We cut out the karaoke drill a few years ago because there were some other things we wanted to do. For instance we want a wide base shuffle. We want our linemen, receivers, and defensive backs to be able to shuffle to the right and left. We have incorporated the wide base shuffle into our agility drills because it is a skill we want to utilize in our basic defensive play.

If you sit down and go through the skills you want your offensive linemen to utilize and then incorporate that into your agility program, you are ahead of the game. We are constantly coaching feet. In the weight room with power cleans and dead lifts, we want to coach them to make sure their feet are underneath them. We coach them to leave the ground when they clean. The little things where you are breaking years of bad habits are important and this gives yourself a chance if you are working on it during the winter.

I believe strength and power come out of the weight room. I believe speed and quickness comes out of your agility program. That is how I look at it. We try to incorporate some of the same principles in both of them.

It is important to coach the offensive line, coach the quarterback, and coach the receivers from the defensive side of the ball instead of always from behind them. It is a big thing. Every chance I get to talk to young coaches I tell them this. I wish someone had told me this a long time ago. If you are an offensive line coach and practicing zone blocking, you can see exactly where their eyes are focused from the defensive side of the ball. You can see if they are on their eyes are on target and other aspects you need to see.

If you are coaching the quarterback in a zone concept, you should be standing at the angle behind the quarterback that he is making his read. Whatever read you have taught your quarterback you should be standing at an angle behind him so that you see the same thing that he sees.

I coach the receivers more than any other position. If you are coaching the receivers in 7- on-7 drills you should be standing in the secondary to see the eyes of the receivers and what they are doing when they are coming off of the line of scrimmage. You can see if a receiver has the bad habit of looking at the ground at the snap of the ball. Kids do that and it is a really bad habit. If you are a defensive secondary coach you know there is a reason why his eyes are down. If there is a defensive back in front of him and his eyes are down, there is something wrong there. If he is looking down, he is going to stop there and make a break. Coaching the eyes is extremely important.

3. **Have the Protections look like the run.**
   - **Quick Game**
   - **Naked/Bootleg**
   - **Down field throws**

As a coach, you have favorite routes and concepts in your head already. You can apply those to what I am talking about today. This is nothing earth shattering but at the same time, I can give you a concept that you can adapt to what you want to do.

I am not a big statistics guy because statistics can be deceptive. However, you cannot throw interceptions. In our first eleven games we threw five interceptions. We threw three in the last game. You cannot let your quarterback throw interceptions. He cannot throw them in 7 on 7 drills or any other drills you practice. If we are talking about the passing game, and I do not tell you that, then I am doing you a disservice. It is funny in that we are quick to pull the dude commits a fumble, yet we seem to give the quarterback a lot more freedom to be reckless with the football. If you throw 50 times per game you may be a little more lenient. If you throw ten times a game you have to make completions. If you are a run oriented team and you throw the ball just a few times, you cannot afford to miss any passes.

4. **Patterns that can be used against a defense with one or two high safeties, or in man coverage.**

When you put your patterns into your offense and when you put your patterns into the game plan, you are doing yourself a great service if they are friendly to these three types of coverage's. These are the three most common defensive coverage's seen in high school football. I am talking from a high school and not a college standpoint.

5. **Throw on first down, short yardage, and coming out.**

I think you have to throw on first down. I think you have to throw on short yardage situations. I think you have to throw the ball coming out of your end zone. I really believe some of your best opportunities to complete passes are in those three situations. The situation may not be right for a particular game but you have to go into a game prepared to throw the ball in those situations. If a team has you pinned down and you are not physical enough to run the ball when you are backed up, you cannot wait until third down to throw the ball. You have to take your opportunities on first down when it is a friendly situation to get your guy open.

6. **Box numbers affect the play.**

You have to decide if the box numbers are going to affect the play or not. Are you going to give the quarterback the opportunity to change the play from a run to a pass or a pass to a run? Is there going to be a signal in your offense that you give the quarterback where you run one certain play in a given situation?

We are a no huddle team. We are a no huddle team for one reason and one reason only. So they don't fight in the huddle. I am being perfectly honest with you. I got to a point after many years of coaching where I could not take it anymore. I knew it was happening on the field and it was not a battle I knew I could win. If you give them a signal from the sideline as to where they have to line up, you have eliminated that problem. I am not trying to be funny. That is why we run the no huddle.

Next I want to talk about the quick passing game.

QUICK GAME

1. **Protection – Inside Zone Rules**
   - **Don't go down field (91 – 99)**
   - **TE**: Lock or Release
     - In the Pattern
     - In the Hole
   - **RB**: 1 Back = Flash, 2 Back = Base or Boss

You need to have some sort of quick passing game to complement the zone run. If the numbers in the box are not advantageous, or a player is in the box that you do not want in the box, your best opportunity to get four yards is to throw the ball quickly. It may be a one route situation or a combination route, whatever you want.

Our protection in the quick passing game is inside zone protection. We do not go down the field in 91 or 99 protections. We want to come off the ball exactly like it is inside zone. We use a two point stance. We do not have big linemen. We have smaller athletic type players. They are very functional in the two point stance. We treat the protection with the exact same rules as our inside zone blocking. We keep it very simple. They only have to remember one type of blocking for this.

We can lock the tight end into our protection or we can release him in our 90 game. Most times we keep our tight end in the blocking scheme. We do this in order to give us the best

run look we can get. The term we use is "stay". Our quarterback can call out stay at any time and the tight end will stay in to block, even if he is live in a quick game pattern. We also dummy call it on a run so defenders cannot get a read.

Against two linebacker sets, we may split him out at six to seven yards to split the two inside linebackers. If we have an athletic tight end against a 4-3 defense, we may set up a linebacker with a basketball type move or back pick with our rear end and then step away from him. The ball does not go to the tight end very much in a one linebacker defense because I figure that cat is better than our guy. If we can split the linebackers, I figure we have a nice hole to sit in to catch the football.

We flash our running back in the protection. Our zone protection to the right is 91. To the left it is 99. It is a word call and not a number call. If we are in a tight end right (91), the running back is flashing to the left and the line will follow their zone rules to the right. The running back is responsible for the edge rusher on the backside. We do have a way to change that if the defender on the backside edge is too good. By flashing the running back across, we should hold the linebackers.

When we used to bring the back out to the front side, the backers were dropping out even though the line was coming off low because there wasn't a threat. We started using the term flash across the front. The ball fake does not matter and you do not have to ride the back. It is just enough to cause the linebackers to have to bite. A big thing in the quick passing game is to get the linebackers to step up and get the ball to who you want to on the outside without the linebackers being in the play. Again, we are talking at the high school level. The linebackers want to be in the box. We want to keep them in the box and throw the ball.

When we run the inside zone, we have a Base call and a Boss call. If we are in a two-back set on a Boss call, both backs go to the back side. The line is zone blocking to one side and the two running backs are going to the other side. We have good protection to the backside, especially if there is an edge rusher coming off the backside. We like to run the inside zone with a Boss block and have the fullback blocking off the tight end, and blocking support off the inside zone play. The linebacker does not know if the ball is coming inside or where it is hitting. We have complemented our protection for the quick game from our two back set.

If we are in a first down situations, or second and short or coming out from the goal line, we can put eight men in the protection and get a match up on the outside with our receivers that we like.

If we go Base the fullback seals to the backside. The halfback goes to the play side. Now we have the ability to take care of those edge rushers who have basketball abilities that we are starting to see and who drive you out of your mind.

2. Break point at 8 yards.
- **Conversions: Hard/Soft**
- **Combinations: 2 and 3 Man**
- **Mirror Patterns**
- **1 and 2 Safety Beaters (Double Slant)**

Our break point is at eight yards with reference to our patterns. Our stop, out, slant, and our high route all break at eight yards. You can stand behind your quarterback in practice and determine where your break point should be. We are an average speed type of team. We are going to snap the ball and catch it, and have a simple flash, and run a stop route. If the ball is not in the air at the stop, it is not right. You have to stand behind your quarterback during practice during 7 on 7 in order to see those things.

We are not worried about winning 7 on 7 competitions. We run the 7 on 7 to get the basics covered. We bring our center to 7 on 7 so he is snapping to the quarterback and not the second string quarterback. We want to get the little things covered.

We have a breakpoint that is consistent. The defense knows at eight yards one of four things is going to happen. He is going by me, break to his left or his right, or he is going back to the ball. This is what I expect to see on the film. I do not want to see receivers turning and waiting for the football. I want the ball launched and out of the quarterbacks hands or it is not a quick game. If it isn't, it is not going to complement your run game.

The quarterback has to have the mentality that we are hitting the quick passes. We are not missing the passes. We have to move the sticks. We have to force them out of the box. If we throw incomplete passes, the defense is going to stay in the box. On the quick passes the ball has to be in the air when the receiver turns around.

How many of your receivers hitch in the quick game? There is no hitch in the quick game. If he hitches, it is too late. It does not matter if the quarterback is under center or in the gun, it has to be catch and launch the ball for it to be the quick game.

A small drop play with a two man route takes a little longer and is a different type of play. We are looking for a player vacating space and we want to get the ball to our guy quickly at that spot. The ball has to come out and is that a very important coaching point.

3. Quarterback Under Center or Shotgun
- **Good Footwork in both situations.**
- **If and When You Check?**
- **No Hitch in the Quick Game!**
- **Summer 7-on-7.**

I love to have the quarterback under center. The problem with being under center is the defense is going to be coming in both the A-gap and B-gap, and you better get rid of the ball. We have been a shotgun team for eight or nine years so we do not get A-gap or B-gap blitzes. We just do not see it. We see all kinds of stuff coming off the edge. From the gun, we have plenty of time to see it and protect against A-gap and B-gap blitzes. I do feel you can generate a lot more power out of a three step drop. If you can protect it, then I think it is the way to go. With the gun, I do not have to spend time on Tuesday and Wednesday trying to protect against the blitzes inside. We are just like you guys, we have a time limit and need to maximize our time.

Make sure you are coaching your 7-on-7's. I like having tournaments because our guys can go against defenders that are really good. I do not put a lot of emphasis on winning the competition. The emphasis is on us getting better. We film our 7-on-7's. We use the tape in summer time to teach this because when school starts you do not have the time. If you want to implement something new, you should work it to death during the summertime. If you are thinking about changing a kid's position, work it to death during the summer.

We run two zone play schemes. We run zone away from the read key which we call Zone. We read the defender on the end of the line of scrimmage to the backside. (Diagram #1)

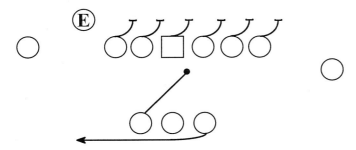

Diagram #1. Zone Read Open Side (Zone)

We also will run the zone and read the defender on the end line to the play side. We call that Veer. (Diagram #2)

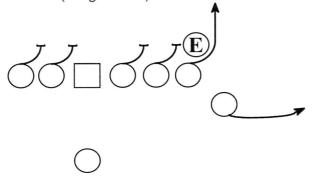

Diagram #2. Zone Read to Tight End Side (Veer)

We prefer two men to the outside when we line up. This is what our number one formation looks like. (Diagram #3)

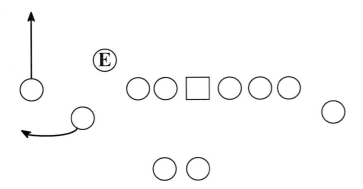

Diagram #3 Number One Formation

We need to have a passing play out of this formation and we like to use the bubble.

Zone Read Open Side

1. **Bubble**
   - **Block or Run Off**
   - **Bubble: Drop Open Step, #2 or #3**

The slot man drop steps and runs to the boundary. The number one receiver is stalk blocking the corner. If we have two-on-two with no alley player, our first read is to the bubble. The problem I have with the bubble is you are taking a really good athlete and running him into the boundary where he can get pinned. That means you need to have a really good stalk blocker on the outside. We stalk block with one hand because we do not want a holding penalty. We punch and slide. If the defender goes to the other side, the first hand goes down and the other hand comes up. I get all over them if they put two hands up. You do not block with your hands anyway, you block with your feet.

Sometimes we can just run the corner off instead of stalk blocking him. We can have the slot man back up a few steps and catch the ball. We can get a good receiver against a defensive back in open space. If you put a physical guy in the slot you can have a really good pickup. If you have some talented guys and like the bubble concept this is two different variations that you might use. It can give the defense problems. We even motion to it with a running back getting to the slot. You have a good match up if you throw it to him.

Zone Read Tight Side

1. **Inside or Veer Scheme**
   - **TE and Wing**
   - **Motion from Open Trips or the Backfield**
     - **TE:** Release to Safety
     - **WR:** Bubble
     - **QB:** Read Edge Defender

I like running the inside zone to the open side and the veer to the tight end side. (Diagram #4)

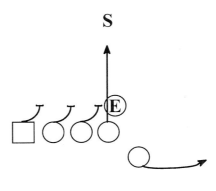

Diagram #4. Zone Read Tight End Release

We are involving both edge players but it keeps it simple. If we run the Veer to the tight end side that means we bring the zone TO the ride and TO the give key, the outside defender. We are reading the man over the tight end. We release our tight end. We bubble the wingback. If you are a tight end zone team try running the bubble off of it. It is a great play.

The running lane is favorable to the tight end and wing side. The safety is run off by the tight end. The wing takes the corner. Even if it is a boundary play, you will get six or seven yards. The defense has to decide how they want to play you. If they play you three-on-two to that side, they have to play you two-on two to the other side. This formation was really good for us.

2. Create 3 on 2 versus Slot

In our game plan we want to create a three-on-two versus the slot. We are going to execute bubbles and quick game until we get three over two. If we get three over two, we are going to take the ball to the tight end side. It may be with boot, naked, or the veer play and the read. Chances are they will only have six men in the box.

If we want to run inside zone to the tight end side we have a great match up versus six in the box. Those are good numbers for us. If you have a quarterback, a tight end, a running back and six linemen against six you should be effective using the inside zone to the tight end side.

Keep your offense as simple as you can. Our tendency is to fall in love with something we see during the season or at a clinic and want to included it in our offense. We do not have the personnel to run the new offense, nor the time to put the new plays in properly.

We have to ask ourselves what are we putting our time into for the passing game. Is the time we use for it in practice related to the time we are going to use it during a game? Are we running more routes at the end of the year or fewer routes at the end of the year? I think the right answer is to run fewer routes at the end of the year. I have read somewhere when the game is on the line go back to your first day. What was the first run or pass play you put in? You should mark it down somewhere so when it gets down and dirty you know what to go to.

Next we want to add a tight end and wingback combination. We want to implement combina-tions to beat the one high or two high defenders on the tight end and wing side. It may be a China route with the tight end going to the corner and the wing going to the flat. It may be the wing clearing and the tight end slamming flat. Use whatever you do in a tight end and wing situation in other parts of your offense. Study what tight end and wing teams do and put those passes in. You just need a couple of them.

One change up we have is on the zone read to the open side. We can run "Pacer" protection where we read the inside over the top linebacker. We block the offensive tackle which is the normal give key on the give. We show the bubble look on the outside and that is the first read. We put a receiver into his drop zone behind him. We can run it with the number one receive running a slant or the tight end running a drag from the other side. This works and we want to utilize it more this coming year.

We are reading the linebacker. If the line-backer runs over the top, we give the ball to the running back. If the inside linebacker fills, we throw the ball into his drop zone.

I believe the guys you want to attack in high school are the linebackers. You need to work the ball in front of them or behind them. Work the ball inside of them or outside. We want to drive the linebackers out of their minds. We run the ball so much the linebackers have to play the run. When those guys are in heat and attacking the ball like crazy, that is when we want to throw the ball.

As I said before on first down, second and short, and coming out of our end zone is a great time to throw the ball. You need to practice it to be good at it. Put the ball on the one yard line and practice it so the kid knows what it looks like. You have to set the situation up and run your two or three plays for that week.

We lost the championship game this year. I can tell you we passed ourselves out of bad positions, coming out from the five yard line or less, on three different occasions. We ran out of the hole a total of zero times. We had no other option. We had the linebackers up and we could throw the ball behind them. That was our answer and we had to do it.

Thank you men. I hope I gave you some things to think about.

Mike Dougherty

Special Teams Practice Planning

Stonewall Jackson High School, Virginia

I appreciate you coming in to hear this lecture. I was just telling a few coaches that Special Teams is a tough sell being last to speak on the clinic schedule. I know most clinic lectures are on quarterbacks and receivers or some phase of the offense or defense. I am going to talk about Special Teams Practice Planning.

I have been a head coach for 13 years now. For the first five or six years each spring I would find myself talking about finding a Special Teams Coach. In the back of my mind I was avoiding coaching the Special Teams myself. Some of the Special Teams we used to send out on the field then were not very special. About eight years ago I bought into the fact I could not find anyone to do the job the way I wanted it done, so I have coached the Special Teams since that time.

I am fortunate that I am in a situation where I have no responsibility on defense and I can devote my time to Special Teams. With other administrative details I have to do, coaching Special Teams is something I can do and enjoy.

We had a great year this past season. I want to share with you how we develop our players, talent wise, practice organization wise, attitude wise, and how we approach our Special Teams. I want to talk about the ways we tried to motivate a group of kids that did not know how to put their helmet on when we first got them. We are a very athletic school and we competed in the league with large schools that have 3000 students. We have a large number of kids as well. We are not as large as some of the schools we play so we have to take advantage of all of our players and their talents.

STONEWALL JACKSON SPECIAL FORCES

What are the Special Forces at Stonewall Jackson High School all about? First and foremost we want players with a good attitude. We want players that are proud to be on the Special Forces Teams. Do we send our quarterback down the field on the kickoff? No! We are smart enough to know better. We want players that have a great attitude about being in constant battle with the offense, defense, and Special Teams.

- **Attitude**
- **Playing Hard**
- **Being Tough**
- **Knowing Your Job**
- **Doing Your Job**
- **Caring about Special Forces**

The way to get the players to want to be on the Special Teams is by doing what we do on offense and defense. We give the Special Teams decals for their helmets. We pick a Special Teams Player of the Week. Each week one of the captains is selected from our Special Teams. This year for all of our games it was the same player. Hands down, he embodied what we wanted on our Special Teams.

We encourage all of our teams to play hard and to be tough. Knowing your job and doing your job is important. We do spend time here going over the scouting report and getting the players to buy into what we are planning on Special Teams for the week. We discuss the mismatch problems for our opponents and our mismatches as well. Special Team Players knowing their job is our job. And we want the players to care about the success of our Special Teams. We want players to be proud of our Special Team accomplishments.

STONEWALL JACKSON SPECIAL FORCES PHILOSOPHY

- **Do one thing and get good at it.**
- **Practice, Coach and Emphasize technique.**
- **Get the right player in spots to make plays.**
- **Educate your players.**
- **Know the strengths and weaknesses of your scheme.**
- **Know the strengths and weaknesses of your opponent's scheme.**

We are a Rugby Kick School. We want to do one thing and get good at it. A few years ago I did not have anyone that could punt. I got a kid off the soccer team and he could kick. We started using the Rugby kick then and have continued to use that type of punt. We want to continue to use the Rugby punt and we want to get good at it. I am not going to change to the spread punt in the middle of the season. We have other punt formations in our playbook, but from day one I tell the kids what we are going to do and we work on it.

We emphasize techniques in all of our drills and practices. When we get to the film portion of our Special Teams we find everything we do here are football fundamentals. It is not Kickoff Techniques, but football techniques. We are teaching the players to be football players. If they are good football players they should be able to run down the field and keep the return team inside the 30 yard line. That is one of our goals as you will see later.

We want to get the right players in the right spots to make plays. Everyone would love to have the six foot player that is 190 pounds that can run a 4.5 on the 40 yard sprint. If you had that kind of players you would win a lot of games. However, if you have players that are five foot eight, and 165 pounds, and he runs the 40 yards in 5.1, you have to get him down the field on the kickoff.

We are going to educate our players. We provide them with an electronic playbook, and we hold them accountable to study the playbook. We spend a lot of time with the kids on the Special Teams.

We want then to know our game plan, and we want them to know our strength and our weaknesses. At one time we were weak in all of the positions on the Special Teams. When our Punt Team would run out on the field I would cringe as they ran on the field. We don't have that problem anymore.

We definitely need to know the strengths of our opponents when we punt. We watched some teams that could not possible block our Rugby kick the way they line up against our formation. It was obvious they were not spending their time in practice working on the kicking game. You have to spend time to coach the players and the assistant coaches on the different phases of the Special Teams.

PRACTICE WHAT YOU PREACH

- **Practice Special Teams every day.**
- **Limit 1 Special Force per practice early on.**
- **Involve entire team in Special Forces practice.**
- **No Standing around - Players or Coaches.**
- **Run your Special Forces period at the beginning of practice.**
- **Immediately following "Special Period" or warm up.**
- **Insert Special Forces during team time DAILY!**

We are going to practice our Special Teams every day. We start every practice with it. We are an up tempo offense. We ran 96 plays in two games this year. We are running a play every eight to ten seconds. I insert the kicking game in the offense and defense and we can call on our Special Teams during either the offensive or defensive periods. We can call for the Punt team to come on the field and punt the ball. They must come on the field and punt the football, and be off the field in ten seconds. We concentrate on the speed of the few things we are going to do on Special Teams.

In our early fall practices when we are going two practices a day, we work on Special Teams in the morning and in the afternoon. We want to make sure we can become good at that one thing for that one day. The next morning we review the special play we worked on the day before, and then install the next phase of Special Teams.

In our two-a-day practices we spend one hour and a half on Special Teams each day, and still get all of the offense and defense covered. One thing that helps in this respect is the fact the up tempo offense is going a lot faster and we get more accomplished in a shorter time frame. We never huddle in practice.

We want to involve the entire team in our Special Teams. This year we had two players that were over 300 pounds on the Special Team. They loved playing on those teams. We want everyone involved in practice.

If you allow an assistant coach to stand around and goof off while you are working on Special Teams, it sends a message to the players that the drill is not important, and they will not be interested. Hold all the players and coaches accountable to make sure they are involved in the Special Teams practice. Give all coaches a part of the Special Teams and you will not have that problem.

We have two depth charts of teams on all Special Teams. If the first string player is not ready to go, we want to make sure the second string player is ready to step up and fill in on Special Teams.

SPECIALTY PERIOD – PRE-PRACTICE

- **Punter, Kickers, Snappers, Holders, Returners**
- **Limit the participants to maximize reps.**
- **Be organized – Have managers set up the filed daily.**
- **COACHES ON THE FIELD!!!**

We insert the Special Teams into the practice daily. The coordinators may not like it, but we can call for any of the Special Teams and they must be ready to go on the field and execute the Special Teams action. I think this is one of the reasons we are so successful on Friday night.

On Friday, our Special Teams eat first. They get off the bus first. They are a part of my "Crew." They want to be in my crew. Any intrinsic award you can give these players to get them fired up is worthwhile. We put our Team Logo on one side of our helmet, and our award logos on the other side of the helmet. Those tiny stars that cost me three dollars per sheet make their day when they are awarded logos for Special Teams play. Today the kids will question you if they think you missed a play that would give them a logo for the helmet.

I will be glad to share anything I do not have time to cover here today. If you will send me a note, I will send you a copy of the Drills we use in the Special Teams Circuits. In addition I will include our Two-Point PAT Chart, and our Grading Chart we use.

SPECIAL TEAMS CIRCUITS

- **Entire team participates in circuits.**
- **Entire coaching staff participates in circuits.**
- **Be organized. Have field set up ahead of time. Use managers for this.**
- **Skills taught in these circuits apply to all aspects of football.**
- **One third of the Friday night game is Special Forces. One fourth of practice should be devoted to Special Forces.** ·

We want everyone to participate in the Circuit phase. This includes the players and coaches. If you can't make it, we find someone that can make it, because we want everyone on the field when we do the circuits.

On a Friday night we average between 25 and 28 Special Team plays per game out of over 150 plays. That is the reason we figure we need to spend one fourth of our time on Special Teams. Our older players will tell the younger players they should not mess up with the Special Teams time periods.

KICKOFF CIRCUIT

- **Station 1: Split double team. Use the hand shields.**
- **Station 2: "Fit Drill." Fit – Push pull – get off block – Make tackle – Thud!**
- **Station 3: Tackle drill. Sprint 5 yards – Come to balance and form tackle. Straight on tackle and angle tackle to both sides.**
- **Station 4: Avoid Opposite drill. Dip and Rip, stay in your lane or get back to your lane immediately.**
- **Station 5: Sink – Fit Drill. Sink hips – Fit hands – drive 3 yards. Use hand shields.**

During the Kickoff Circuit you will see the five stations going on at the same time. We have a coach in charge of each station. We rotate every two minutes. There is a specific drill taught at each station that pertains to each specialty. We cover all points listed below.

KICKOFF CIRCUIT

- **Split Double Team**
- **Fit Drill**
- **Tackle Drill**
- **Avoid Opposite Drill**
- **Sink – Fit – Drive Drill**

On the Split Double Team Drill we take two players with hand shield dummies. We line up the players in one line five yards from the dummies. One at a time the player must split the two dummies as he would in splitting a double team on the Kickoff Coverage. After everyone goes through the dummies, we turn around and do the drill coming back the other way. The drill goes on for two and one half minutes.

We have a coach at the dummies to give the players feedback. I take the defensive coach and make him in charge of that drill. He needs to know the feedback he wants to give them before they start practice.

On the Fit Drill we have the defensive men on a line. We place a blocker with a hand shield dummy on the defenders nose. He must use his hands to stop the initial contact by the blocker, and then he must move inside and go five yards and fit in a tackling position on the ball carrier.

In our Tackle Drill we are about 10 yards apart and we have the defensive man run toward the back. As the defender approaches the back he must break down and get into a good football position to make the tackle.

In our Avoid Contact Drill we start from the sideline eight yards from a blocker with a big stand up bell bottom dummy. We want the defender to rip as he makes contact and drive past the block avoiding contact as much as possible.

Once we get to our first scrimmage in the season, we do not run the Circuit Drills as often. We may only do them once a week. When the season starts, if we have a bad night on Friday night Special Team wise, we may go back on Monday and review all of our techniques on the Special Teams.

The last point is Sink – Fit – Drive Drill. The defender is five yards from the offensive man with a shield dummy. They come down the line to the dummy and dip, hit on the rise, and Fit, and Drive the man back, and get to the ball carrier. They must extend the arms and drive the man back. They want to take choppy steps and to extend their base.

These are the drills we use on the Kickoff Return Circuit. When we kick the ball to our opponents we want to stop them behind the 30 yard line, which is the 29 yard line. When we receive, we want to return the ball to the 41 yard line.

KICKOFF RETURN CIRCUIT

- **Station 1: Wedge Drill. 2-on-2 block. 3rd man goes to play side double team.**
- **Station 2: Sprint 5 – Pedal, gather. Come out and attack.**
- **Station 3: Punch and Drive – Fit – Punch – Drive on an angle.**
- **Station 4: Steer Drill – Punch – Steer plus Press Downfield – Run with them.**

- **Station 5: Sprint – Pedal – Gather – Finish – Use Stand Up dummy as target for gunners.**

DRILLS FOR KICKOFF RETURN CIRCUIT

- **Wedge Drill**
- **Pedal and Gather Drill**
- **Punch and Drive Drill**
- **Steer Drill**
- **Sprint – Gather – Finish Drill**

PUNT RETURN CIRCUIT

- **Pad Level Drill**
- **Ball Get Off Drill**
- **Hoop Drill – Block Kick**
- **Drive – Come to Balance**
- **Trail Drill**

The players love the loop drill. We use a simple volleyball instead of a football in the drill. We line up a path for two players to rush the punter. We use a rope to indicate the path of each player. It is open at the bottom, but is pointed at the top of the area where the punter is located. It is not like a U or a V, but a combination in that it points toward the punter. They rush the punter and block the kick. We can put some big bags in the drill and allow the players to lay out for the aiming point to block the kick. Everyone on our team learns how to block a punt.

We blocked two kicks this year and it was the big guys on the punt return team that blocked the punts. Blocking a punt is a game changing moment. I have been told that you win a game 90 percent of the time if you block a punt. We practice blocking the kick in the individual phase and in the team phase as well.

SPECIAL TEAM GAME PLANNING

- **K.I.S.S./Keep It Simple Stupid.**
- **Use your best available players.**
- **Delegate "Special Forces" duties to your entire staff.**
- **Grade your Special Force film the same as you would grade the Offense and Defense.**
- **Make "Special Forces" a big deal every day.**

I am a firm believer in keeping things simple. When we punt we are going to Rugby kick. Most of the time, we punt to our right side. When we are on the right hash mark we kick to the right.

However, we are going to force the opponents to cover what we could do on the punt. That is one of the reasons my quarterback punts. He may not be a very good punter, but he is good at running and throwing the football.

If the opponents are not spending 20 minutes a day working against our Rugby punts, it is one of our best plays. We went for it on fourth down 32 times this past year. We were successful 13 times, with 10 on runs, and 3 via the pass, with one of those for a touchdown.

RUGBY PUNT

- **Unbalanced formation**
- **Trips formation**
- **Ability to run it right and left**
- **Must have an athlete at punter**
- **Fakes to strength, field, and short sides.**
- **Practice this every day!**

We list our Two-Deep Charts for our Special Teams. We have the copies laminated and everyone on the staff has a copy, including the coaches in the press box. The coaches and the players know if one of the players goes down, the next man must step up. You may say too many people know this, but if a player goes down we want to have the backup player ready.

This year we did not get a penalty for having too many players on the Special Teams or having too few players on the Special Teams. In our last meeting before we go on the field, I have the different Special Teams stand up. There has to be 11 players standing.

We have a standard Chart to decide when to go for two points or to kick the PAT. It is something you should have available on game nights. You may think you can remember when to go for two points, but it helps to have the chart available on game night.

We have a Grade Sheet for Special Teams. It is very detailed. We grade the film and post the grades before the players get to school on Monday morning. The players want to know how they graded on the film on Special Teams. I grade all of the Special Teams but I do not grade any of the Offensive or Defensive plays.

We do not spend a lot of time in group film discussions. On Monday before we go on the field we do a quick five minute film session on Special Teams. I will point out about eight plays that are good, and two plays that were bad from our previous game. We are transitioning to our Special Teams Period and we want to know what we need to work on.

It does not matter if we win by 60 points, or lose by 60 points. I am still going to grade the Special Team players. The players are putting in the time and they deserve to be graded just as the other phases of the game are graded.

We practice the Rugby punt every day. It is the last thing we do before we go into the locker room during pre-game. We do two Rugby kicks and then we go inside.

The key is to have a Rugby punter that has some ability. He can be a basketball type play with agility and some ability to run and throw the ball. He has to be a kid that is smart. Any time we have 4th down and three yards or less, he has the green light to run the ball. It does not matter where we are on the field, it is his choice. I have to trust that he can make the right decision on the calls.

The rule for the Rugby punter is this. Once he leaves the pocket, there is no such thing as roughing the kicker. So you need to know if you move the punter, there is no roughing the punter. Our linemen are in a two-point stance. They can move from this position and cover the Rugby punts.

We do install the regular punt formation but we did not use it one time this year. We like using the Rugby Punter because we can do a lot more with him. This year we were in punt formation about 32 times and we ran the ball or passed the ball about 50 percent of the time on 4th down.

We line the Rugby punter seven yards deep. We want him to punt the ball about four yards to his right side. We want him hitting the ball at the five yard depth from where he lined up on the pre-snap. At times he ended up kicking the ball at the line of scrimmage.

When we line up for the punt, our linemen call out the number of the defender they are responsible for on the punt protection. On the snap of the ball the offensive line fires out hard, makes contact, and then gets down field to cover the punt.

We only have a guard and end on the weak side of the formation. When the ball is snapped we send the center and both ends to cover the punt. We have a left halfback that blocks on the backside and prevented the backside from catching the punter.

We used a simple system to assist the punter on the plays were we wanted to go for the 1st down. If we call Green it was a run. If we called Red, it was a pass. If we call Black, Black, Black, it is an automatic punt. You have to trust the punter to make the right decisions on the punt.

The punter runs four yards to the right side, and either runs the ball or passes it, or kicks it. When he gets to four yards outside, if he is going to run the ball, he sticks the right foot in the turf and turns his shoulders up field.

MUDDLE POINT AFTER TOUCHDOWN

- **Forces Defense to defend muddle.**
- **Potential mismatches on field.**
- **Opponent must use practice time to defend our PAT.**
- **Holder makes reads, and then makes the call.**
- **Fakes to muddle and moves away from it.**

On the Muddle Huddle PAT we want to force the other team to have to move seven players to the side. We ran the ball eight times and we were successful on seven of those time for two points.

We have three plays off the Muddle PAT. They are the fade fake, a screen fake, and a speed option to the weak side of the formation. If defensive teams' line up correctly we bring our offensive line back over the ball and complete the PAT. It forces the opponents to use practice time to defend us. The holder makes the read. We have fakes to both sides. When we come over to the ball to get set, we do a shift with our line. It does cause some teams to jump off sides.

We can call for the PAT during practice at any time. We want our offensive linemen going down on the line at the same time. We use all verbal calls for the fakes. This is all I have today.

In the packet I passed out include some general philosophical points. I have not created a lot of this information. I picked it up along the way in my career. Hopefully, you will get something out of this today that will help you.

I have a Special Teams Handbook that I give out. It is about eight pages. This is part of the player's playbook. We are almost all electronic now. Everything I give them on paper, they have on a thumb drive for future reference.

Playing offense for us is like playing polo. You are not touching the bottom of the swimming pool. You are swimming all of the time. Our players may run by the water fountain during practice but the do it on the run. That is our philosophy to move, move, and move. We treat every phase of our program the same. We do not have to conditioning the players, because we are moving so fast, they have to be in condition to play for us.

We were 56 out of 57 on extra points this year. Until the last play of our season, we were 56 of 56. We had three kids hurt, but we tied the PAT on the last play of the game. Our season ended on a blocked extra point. Our opponent made the last play and we did not. Our wing man was out of the game and we had a sub taking his place. The defense rushed from the outside and the wing man stepped outside to block him. A defender came through the gap and blocked the kick. You never teach a wing man to step outside on an extra point.

I am going to list some of the things we have in our Special Teams Handout. If you are interested in the film of the drills, drop me a note and I will send this sheet along with the DVD of the drills.

SPECIAL TEAMS GOALS

- **Punt Average 33.0 Net Yards**
- **Punt Return Average –10 Yards**
- **Better Net Punt Average**
- **Kick Off Cover – Inside the 25 Yard Line**
- **Kick Off Returns Past Our 30 Yard Line**
- **Win the field position battle**
- **More Kicking Points**
- **Make at least 2 Big Plays**
- **Allow No Big Plays**
- **No Team Penalties**

SPECIAL TEAMS OBJECTIVES

Special Teams is the aspect of the game where the "HIDDEN YARDAGE" can have a great effect on the outcome of a football game. We will win the hidden yardage game weekly with an excellent return game and a Dominating Coverage Game and Penalty Free Special Teams Play. We will accomplish this through hard work, being well disciplined, being disciplined in our assignments and techniques, and in playing every play as a 100 percent player.

1. <u>BEAT OUR OPPONENT</u> - In the Special Teams battle weekly.

2. <u>PLAY PENALTY FREE</u> - We will be tough, but not cheap. No re-punts or re-kicks. We must especially play penalty free in our return game.

3. <u>ESTABLISH FIELD POSITION</u> - With our kickoff return and punt return phases we will help the offense. With our kickoff coverage and punt coverage we will help our defense, putting our opponents in the hole.

4. <u>PROTECTION OF THE FOOTBALL!</u> - Vital aspect for our returners... we will not have any turnovers; Punt Team - No blocked punts is also protecting the ball. Field Goal Team - No blocked Field Goals or P.A.T.'s

5. <u>CREATE TURNOVERS</u> - Take the ball away by gang tackling and striping the ball away from returners, and blocking punts and field goals will create a big change in field position.

6. <u>EVERYONE IS INCLUDED IN OUR SPECIAL TEAMS -</u> No One is excluded!

Teams win 90 percent of the games in which they block a punt. That is 90 percent of the time! It doesn't take a genius to figure out that blocking a punt is something that we should spend time on in practice!

TIMING

For the best results and for reasons of safety, there are certain time requirements, which serve as performance guides for the three basic types of kicks in the game. These are outlined below:

I. <u>Punts</u>

- Snap (13 yards) 0.8 seconds
- Punter (13 yards) 1.4 seconds
- Total get away time 2.2 seconds (or better)
- Hang time (acceptable) 3.5 seconds (35 yard punt)

II. <u>PAT and Field Goal</u>

- 1.40 (or better)

III. <u>Kickoff</u>

- 3.5 seconds (or better) inside the 15 yard line

Here is a Chart that shows the odds of scoring a touchdown from the different positions on the file. Field Position is very important as you can see by the chart.

Offense Field Starting Position	Score
Inside Own 20 Yard Line	3.0 %
Between Own 20 & 40 Yard Line	12.5 %
Between Own 40 & 50 Yard Line	20.0 %
Between Opponents 50 & 40 Yd Line	33.0 %
Inside Opponents 40 Yard Line	50.0 %
Inside Opponents 20 Yard Line	66.0 %

SPECIAL TEAMS CHECKLIST

KICKOFF RETURN

1. Squib Kick
2. Onside Kick Mayday
3. Regular-Hash-Middle-Hash
4. Shift
5. After a Safety
6. Reverse
7. Recover
8. Lob (Sky) Kick

KICKOFF

1. Onside-Regular
2. Shift-Onside
3. Maximum Onside
4. Hash-Middle-Hash
5. Recovery
6. After a Safety
7. Reserve

P. A. T. / FIELD GOAL

1. <u>Hash-Middle-Hash</u>
2. <u>Swinging Gate</u>
3. <u>Bad Snap</u>
4. <u>Fake</u>
5. <u>Fast Field Goal</u>
6. <u>Long Count</u>
7. <u>2-Point Play</u>

P. A. T. / FIELD GOAL BLOCK

1. <u>Hash-Middle-Hash</u>

2. <u>Swinging Gate</u>
3. <u>Fake</u>
4. <u>Bad Snap</u>
5. <u>Fast Field Goal</u>
6. <u>Long Field Goal</u>
7. 2-Point Play

PUNT RETURN

1. Safe
2. Fake
3. Offensive Play
4. Quick Kick
5. Tight Punt
6. Blocking the Punt
7. Returns
8. Reaction-block Punt

PUNT

1. Pooch
2. Backed up
3. Taking a Safety
4. Fake, Run or Pass
5. Quick Kick
6. Blocked Punt
7. Long Count

SPECIAL SITUATIONS TO PRACTICE

1. Punting from hash marks
2. Punting from out of the end zone (tight punt)
3. Punting from the +40 or +45 yard line (sky punt)
4. Punting from bad snap situations
5. Covering the fair catch
6. Reaction to a blocked kick
7. Reaction to a partially blocked kick
8. Quick kick
9. Receiving punts deep in our own territory
10. Receiving punts at mid-field
11. Rushing punts near opponent's goal line
12. Punt safe defense
13. Reacting to safe punts
14. Onside kick
15. Expected onside kick
16. Surprise onside kick
17. Squib kick-offs
18. Returning Squib kickoffs
19. Bad snap on PAT-FG
20. FG Prevent (long field goals)
21. Defending fake field goals
22. Field goal returns
23. Unbalanced line for FG
24. Defending unbalanced line for FG
25. Field goal attempt after a fair catch
26. Taking a safety
27. Clock safety
28. Kick-off after a safety
29. Receiving after a safety
30. Fast Field Goal
31. Defending a Fast Field Goal
32. Swinging Gate
33. Defending Swinging Gate
34. Defending 2 point play
35. Kick from bad snap situations
36. Kick in wet field conditions

Drop me a note or give me a call if you are interested in what we do with the Special Teams. My information is listed below. Thank you for your attention.

Mike Dougherty
Stonewall Jackson Football
doughemj@pwcs.edu
Cell - 703-728-8393
Office – 703-365-2970

Paul Ellis

Counter Trey Package Versus The 3-5 Defense

Fort Payne High School, Alabama

I want to say it is an honor to be here. Fort Payne is located in the northeastern corner of Alabama. We are about 45 minutes away from Chattanooga, Tennessee. We have made strides in our program over the past few years. My first two years as head coach, we started 11-10. Since that time, we are 80-23. We have made great strides. I have a great staff that works hard.

In 2005, we went 4-6. We played everyone tough but could not win games. At that time, we were running the I-Option scheme with a wing-T offense. Our returning players were more suited to the spread offense. We went to the spread and it has taken off for us.

I am going to talk about our Counter Trey play against the "3-3" front. We live and die by that play. We pull the guard, and tackle, and we do not bring the extra blocker into the box area.

We are a 5A school, which is the second largest in Alabama. We have over 800 students in grades 9-12. In the last two years, we graduated 53 seniors. We had 28 this year and 25 the year before. That helped us by playing 18 year old kids instead of 15 and 16 year old players.

SECRETS TO OUR SUCCESS

- **"Team" concept – Unselfish "All In"**
- **Team camp**
- **Weight room – nobody out works us**
- **7 on 7 competitions – compete**
- **Practice tempo**

Everyone in football today talks about the team concept. I believe our players have totally bought into what we are doing. Because our coaches have an open and honest relationship with our players, it helps them to be committed to what we do. Our players enjoy football but bigger than that, they really like and love each other.

Our team camp is a big thing for our players. We go to a different places for camp each year and this year we spent about six thousand dollars for three days in camp. We want to get close as a team. In 2006, after coming off the "4-6" season, we went to team camp. The second day there we had our coaches meetings with our players by classes. After we were finished one of the seniors requested to have a separate team meeting for players only. I was reluctant to have the meeting but we let them have it.

The next morning was our last day in camp. The line coach always went around in the gator cart blowing the horn to get all the players up. That next morning no one came out of the cabins. We looked around and all the cabins were empty. We finally found a note in one of the cabins that said, "**Gone To Win Ten**, see you at the field." The night before in our team meeting, we had talked about winning ten games for the season.

The sun was about to come up as we went to the practice field. Before we got to the field we could hear the team. When we got there 68 players were aligned in perfect rolls clapping. That year we won 11 games.

Since then that is what our team camp is all about. We have that sheet of paper that was posted on the door, "Gone To Win Ten" framed along with a picture of that team in our field house. We still tell our players that story every year.

In our weight-training program, we want our players to believe that no one outworks them. We tell them they may work as hard as we do but they will not outwork us. Our weight room is huge. By 3:00 p.m. each day during our training sessions, you will not be able to see anything in our mirrors. There is so much heat and sweat in the room the mirrors fog up. They do a great job in the weight room and work extremely hard.

We compete in 7 on 7 competitions in the state of Alabama. The number of competitions used to be seven and now it is four. It does not matter to me as long as everyone is doing the same thing.

In our practice tempo, we try to practice super fast. That allows us to delete condition as much at the end of practice. I am an old school coach and I believe everyone is supposed to run at the end of practice. We run a little but not like, we used to run.

We are a no-huddle spread offense. We play mainly from a 2 X 2 (balanced) set. We would like to have a 50/50 run to pass ratio. We are here today to talk about getting the ball to multiple receivers. The quarterback and running back will carry the ball. We have a motion game where we use the H-back Y-receiver, and the Z-receiver in motion and hand the ball to them. We have to find ways to control the backside linebackers in the 3-3 stack defense. We have to account for the defenders in the box.

In our running game, we run the Counter Trey, which we call the double-trap scheme. The sister play, of the counter is the speed sweep. We also run the old trap play and zone plays. We will run some influence type of plays but that comes from my wing-T background. We used to play with a tight end in the offense. When we took that position out of the offense, it solved many of our problems. We run the Counter Trey from every formation and every motion pattern we can use.

I am going to show you this play, then I am going to bring my offensive line coach up here and let him talk about it some more. This is our "F" Counter Trey. (Diagram #1) We do something different with our F-back. We line him up behind the quarterback slightly behind his left shoulder. He is in a position so he can reach out and touch his shoulder with his right hand. Some people think we are running the pistol. When he runs the play, we want him to hit the play almost vertical. We want him to go right at the center. That is where the crease is most of the time.

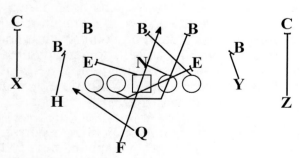

Diagram #1. F-Counter Trey

We do not want the back to bounce the ball. We are not athletic enough to bounce the ball. We are a "hurry up" offense but we get the play from a wristband on this play, the band reads as follows:

- **Left Tackle:** Pull - wrap PSB
- **Left Guard:** Pull - kick DE
- **Center:** Block Left
- **Right Guard:** Down/deuce - BSB
- **Right Tackle:** Deuce/BSB

When we talk about the pulling linemen, we always talk about one to <u>kick</u> and one to <u>wrap</u>. When we run this play, the playside guard blocks the nose guard in the middle stack. The playside tackle blocks the middle linebacker in the middle stack. The nose guard blocks left. We pull for the defensive end and wrap for the playside linebacker in the outside stack. The only defender not accounted for is the backside linebacker in the outside stack. We need to come up with schemes to keep him out of the play.

Coach Shankles will talk about our line. He has been my offensive line coach for nine years.

COACH SCOTT SHANKLES

First I am going to talk about our stance. Most of the time we are in a three-point stance, but can align in a two-point stance. Our splits are one-foot splits. Some people split their linemen more but as much as we throw the ball, I want them tighter. With the one-foot splits, the guards can get down on the nose guard quicker. Our depth off the ball is as far back as we can get. We align the guard's toes on the heels of the center. The tackles align with their toes on the guards toes.

BLOCKING RULES

Leave One to Kick, One to Wrap

- **BST:** Pull Wrap PSB
- **BSG:** Pull Kick DE
- **C:** Block Left
- **PSG:** Down/Deuce/BSB
- **PST:** Deuce/BSB

I love teams to play three-men fronts against us. The angles against those techniques are super. We have problems with the four man fronts. The big 3-technique gives us fits. Our base rules on the Counter-Trey have the backside tackle and guard pulling. There is one kick and one wrap on this play.

We describe the kick out block as the first defender outside of the playside tackle. The wrap block is the backside tackle. We tell him to turn up and block the outside linebacker in the outside stack in the 3-3 stack defense. The center's rule says to block left. That means he is to block the first defender he sees to the backside of the play.

The playside guard's rules are down/deuce/BSB. The down call is "down" block on the first defender inside of him. The "deuce" call is a call for a four man front team. I will talk about that later. The third rule is backside linebacker. The playside tackle's rules are deuce/BSB. The deuce rule is the combination block with the playside guard on a 3-technique defender.

We do drills for this particular play. We call the drills "DT Kick/Wrap, DT down, Dip rip LB, and Deuce block." When I do these drills, I try to give everyone repetitions. Our good players get more reps than the younger players do. They play JV football and get many reps doing that.

I want to start with the down block. When we do these reps in practice, I make sure they work on both side of the line. The play is the same going either way so I have them work on both side of the ball. The linemen on the right side of the ball are in a right-handed stance. Their right hand is down on the ground.

If they are on the left side of the ball, they align in a left-handed stance. The stance is different and the footwork is slightly different from the left to the right. If a player can handle both sides, we work him both ways. That includes pulling as well as down blocking.

We use the down block for the center, guards, and tackles. If the playside guard down blocks on the nose guard on the counter play, he has to step flat to the line of scrimmage and get his head across the nose guard. As he gets his head across the defender, he jams his outside hand into the ribs of the defender. If the nose is not attacking and the nose is reading, the guard can step more at the nose man instead of down the line.

The problem is the defender playing across the guard's face and getting back to the outside. When the guard feels the nose try to play across the top of his block, he has to work his butt up the field and move his feet. If the defender is going to get across the top, the technique forces the defender to give ground and get deeper up the

field. We do not have to hold the block as long with this scheme because it hits so quickly.

When we teach the trap, we do not teach a speed pull. When we drill the pull in practice, we do it down a board. (Diagram #2) We place the board at the angle we want and line the guard up. If the left guard pulls right, he steps with his inside foot. He steps and loses a little ground off the line of scrimmage. With his inside foot, he steps off the line of scrimmage and across the board. He rips the inside elbow to open his hips in the direction he is pulling. His second step hits on the upfield side of the board. He runs down the board to the target at the end of the board.

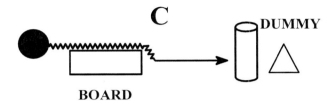

Diagram #2. Board Pull

As he approaches the target, he gathers and prepares to deliver a blow. I stand near the target and hold out my hand. They should be low enough in their run to fit below my hand. I do not want them running and have to dip to get under the hand. When we hit the target, I want the head in the hole. He puts his head inside the defender. We do this drill every day.

Sometimes the end plays so far up the field; he cannot be an effective part of the play. We tell the guard, if the defender has run himself out of the play to turn up and be the extra blocker down field.

When we teach the wrap technique to the backside tackle, the footwork is tremendously important. (Diagram #3)

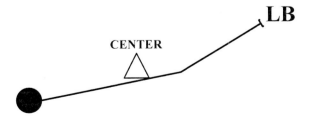

Diagram #3. Wrap Technique

He knows he is going to block the stack linebacker in the outside stack. As he aligns, he can see the linebacker with his peripheral vision. His first step is with his inside foot and is almost straight back off the line of scrimmage. He does not turn his foot to the inside. His toe is almost straight down the field as it was in his stance. The second step is almost a carioca step like we use in our warm up drills. The first step gets him off the line of scrimmage and the second step aligns him for his wrap technique.

With one-foot splits between the guard and center, and the guard and tackle, he is not far from the center. His angle puts him through the heels of his offensive guard's alignment. He picks up the target and adjusts his track as to the technique the linebacker plays. If the linebacker comes straight ahead, he wraps up and gives the running back a two-way-go. If the linebacker works to the outside, the pulling tackle blocks him that way. If the linebacker comes inside hard, the tackle pins him to the inside.

The playside tackle has to learn how to get inside and block the middle stack linebacker. (Diagram #4)

Diagram #4. Dip and Rip Linebacker

The defensive end in the 3-3 defense generally plays a heavy technique on the offensive tackle. The tackle has to learn how to drop his outside shoulder and reduce the shoulder surface as he comes inside the defender. He has to dip and rip through as a pass rusher would rip through a pass blocker. He wants to squeeze inside and make his shoulders small. His aiming point on the linebacker is one-yard in front of him.

If he goes straight at the linebacker, he will not block him. If linebacker scraps hard, the tackle wants to get his head across him and block him like a down block. If the linebacker reads the play and does not scrap, the tackle pins him and the back runs behind his block.

The deuce block is a double team block between the playside guard and tackle. (Diagram #5) We use this technique against a four-man front. The guard steps out with his outside foot and the tackle steps in with his inside foot to

where they are foot-to-foot in their position on the 3-technique defender. They are working the double team to the backside linebacker. They want to drive the defender back off the line of scrimmage but not so inside. They drive the 3-technique until the backside linebacker tries to pursue the football. We want the linebacker to have to bubble over the top of the double team to get to the outside.

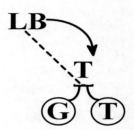

Diagram #5. Deuce Block

Whichever way he attacks the playside of the defense will determine which lineman comes off the double team. If he tries to come over the top, the guard takes over the 3-technique and the tackle comes off to block the linebacker. If he tries to run under the double team block, the guard releases the 3-technique and drops off to block him.

If the guard has a shade technique to his inside and a 3-technique on his outside shoulder, he gives a "back" call to the tackle. (Diagram #6) That tells the tackle, he has a down block on the 3-technique because the guard is going to down block on the shade defender. The tackle has the 3-technique defender by himself.

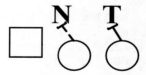

Diagram #6. Back

If the defensive end aligns in a 4i-technique on the offensive tackle, he will not be able to get under the 4i-defender to block the middle linebacker. He gives a "short" call to the backside tackle. (Diagram #7) The playside tackle steps with his outside foot around the 4i-defender and up on the stacked linebacker. When the wrap tackle hears the "short" call, he knows he will exchange blocks with the playside tackle. He wraps the playside guard's block and comes up on the middle linebacker.

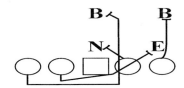

Diagram #7. Short Call

I am going to turn the program back over to Coach Ellis.

COACH PAUL ELLIS

That was a good explanation of what we do with our line. The first thing I want to talk about is how we handle the backside stack linebacker. If the F-back carries the ball, the quarterback has to hold the backside linebacker with his fake to that side. If the F-back is not carrying the ball he goes straight through and blocks the linebacker. We can use two different type of motion at him to influence what he does. We can use speed motion, which comes in front of the quarterback. We ride the motion back to hold the linebacker.

We can use orbit motion, which goes behind the quarterback. We can also run a wing-T crisscross motion to hold him. We can run the "speed sweep and read" and block him with the playside tackle. There are many ways to control the unblocked linebacker.

We run the "Quarterback" Counter Trey. (Diagram 8) On this play, we block the backside linebacker with the F-back. He aligns to the playside of the play. The quarterback turns and fakes the ball to the F-back who runs into the backside A-gap. He seals the backside linebacker. The quarterback, after the fake runs the ball in the playside A-gap. The play runs more up the center's butt than the gap. The offensive line blocking is the same as for all counters.

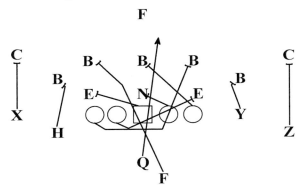

Diagram #8. "Q" Counter Trey

We bring the Z-receiver in orbit motion to hold the backside linebacker and run "Fullback" Counter Trey. (Diagram #9)

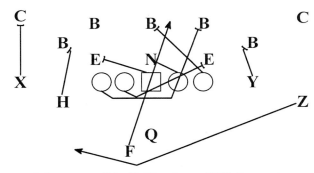

Diagram #9. Z Motion, "F" Counter

People ask if we run motion to hold the linebackers, why do the linebacker not blitz. When we run the motion schemes we run jailbreak screens away from the motion. People that play us know we do that and they very seldom blitz.

The next play is the "Halfback" Counter Trey. (Diagram #10) The line blocking is the same. We set the F-back to the playside and block the backside linebacker with him. The quarterback action is to fake the F-back, give the ball to the H-back, and carry out his bootleg fake. The H-back comes to the quarterback, plants, and takes the ball into the playside A-gap.

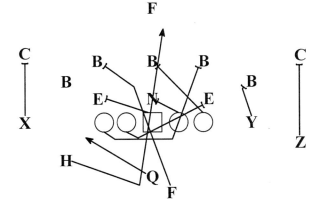

Diagram #10. "H" Counter Trey

We run the speed sweep read off the double trap (counter) blocking. (Diagram #11) Because of the way the middle linebacker reacts, we send the playside tackle to the backside linebacker. The backside tackle wraps to the middle linebacker. We crack on the outside linebacker and strong safety with the Y and Z receivers. We read the play side defensive end. If he squeezes to the inside, we give the ball to the H-back on the speed sweep. The H-back comes in motion running hard on the speed sweep. If the defensive does anything but squeeze, the quarterback pulls the ball and works vertical on the Counter Trey.

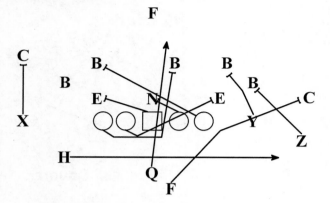

Diagram #11. Speed Sweep Read

On the speed sweep, the middle and playside linebacker usually move out of their stacks and toward the motion. The reason we adjusted the blocking was the playside tackle's angle to the middle linebacker. Because of the linebacker's movement, he was chasing the middle linebacker outside instead of pinning him inside. We decided to let the wrap tackle block him and send the playside tackle to the backside linebacker. That gave him a better angle on a linebacker. Since the wrap tackle comes from the inside, he could seal the middle linebacker outside, which was the direction he was going. The outside stack linebacker in most cases goes outside playing the speed sweep. The wrap tackle can see what he is doing as he pulls.

The companion play we use with the speed sweep is the "Halfback" Crisscross. (Diagram #12)

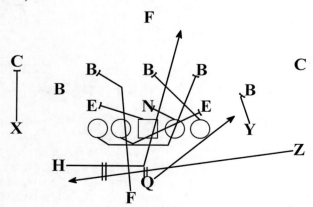

Diagram #12. "H" Crisscross

On this play, we block the counter to the right. The Z-receiver comes in speed motion toward the left. The quarterback hands the ball to the Z-receiver on the speed sweep. The H-back comes inside the Z-receiver and takes the handoff from him on a reverse. He gets into the plant area in front of the quarterbacks position and breaks into the playside A-gap. The F-back goes through the line of scrimmage and blocks the backside linebacker.

The quarterback hands the ball off and carries out his fake to the playside. He tries to draw the defense to him. In practice, we play around with this play. The "H" back carries the ball and pitches it back to the quarterback on a flea-flicker. The quarterback then throws it down the field.

I know we went fast on the lecture to get finished. If you have any questions, we will be up here for a while. This is no stroke of genius.

The question was, "what do you do if the middle stack stunts to the backside of the play." When our linemen block, they are blocking area. If the nose goes to the playside and the linebacker stunts to the backside, the F-back picks him up instead of going to the backside linebacker. The playside guard will block the nose because he has a down block rule. If the middle linebacker stunts backside, the playside tackle sees him go and keeps coming for the backside linebacker.

If the defense hurts us with that type of stunting, we run the naked bootleg or the crisscross. We can change up our scheme to handle stunts from the defense.

When we bring the Z-receiver in motion to that side, we usually get the backside stack linebacker coming out of the stack to support to the motion side. Even if he stays in the stack and we do not block him, he seldom makes the play on the F-back because it gets vertical so quickly.

Any more questions? I appreciate your attention.

Darrel Gorham

Start Of The Season Staff Procedures

Highlands Ranch High School, Colorado

I appreciate you coaches being here. I know there are many distractions in Las Vegas. Highlands Ranch High School is a large school in classification in the Denver area. We are a 5A school. We have 1600 students in our school.

Today I want to talk about the preseason meetings with the coaching staff. It is important for all the coaches on the staff to be on the same page to start the season. We have 15 coaches on the staff. I take them up in the mountains to a resort called Breckenridge for our retreat. We go up on a Thursday and meet as a staff for two days. On Saturday, the wives come up. We can wine and dine them and they are not so mad about their husbands being on retreat.

The reason I do that is to avoid all the conflicts that occur during the course of family living. When I have meetings at the school, something always pulls the coaches away. Some of them miss the meetings. When we go to Breckenridge, there are no distractions. We have productive meetings because they are all there.

Once we get there, we discuss everything. We start with special teams and go through all facets of our program. We discuss the schemes in addition to the personnel. After the general meeting, we separate into offense, defense, and freshmen coaches. We talk about schemes, personnel, and the program.

Toward the end, I have the freshmen coaches play football with checkers. Our freshmen staff is not always together at every practice. This is a neat thing for them. We separate the offense from the defense and give them different colored checkers. The offensive coaches go first and set up their checkers in an offensive formation. The defensive coaches set up their defense against the offensive formation. That lets them know where their alignments should be on defense.

Some of our young coaches do not know how to align to trips, twin overloads, or unbalanced sets. After the defense aligns, the offensive coach runs his play and has to block it correctly. If the coaches do not know whom to block, how would you ever expect the players to know? That is just an example of the things we do at our meeting and I think it makes a big difference.

This presentation today is similar to the first thing I do with all the coaches and I do the same thing every time we go up there. Coaches that have been with me before have heard it before. However, I think it is important that they hear it each year. Every year I add more to it because different things come up during the season.

I have expectations for all three teams. (Varsity, JV, freshman) I want all three teams on the same page. I want them all running the same numbering system. I want them running the same offense and defense. However, each level coach can vary a little if he needs to change it up some. They can deploy their personnel to fit what they do. If they want to put their best athlete at wide receiver and throw him the fade route, I do not have a problem with that. As long as the number system is the same and the schemes are the same, I do not care. I want them to learn how to block, tackle, and stay within the system.

We want our players to be physical on the field and in the weight room. Toughness is something we talk about many times. We want them to be both mentally and physically tough and we call that "Falcon Tough." When a player is acting as if he is hurt, rather than calling him a wuss or a little girl, we say be Falcon tough.

If a coach calls a player a sissy or some other term that fits the situation, I have a parent meeting the next day to explain what the coach meant. Rather than going through the confrontation, I want the coaches to avoid using those terms.

We talk to our players all the time about work ethics. We want them to have good work ethics on the field, in the weight room, and in the classroom. The school changed their procedure about in-school football lifting programs, which means we must lift after school. The school went to an alternating block schedule, which means we do not see our athletes much in school. We get them two days a week and that is not enough time. We could not get our weight training done in two days a week. That pushed our weight training to after school.

We want the players to be fundamentally sound and dedicated. Even if we have a down year, the players come every day and they need and deserved to be coached every day. The players need to be fundamentally sound even if they are getting their butt kicked. They will get older, mature, but need the fundamentals to be taught to them. It could be you have a bunch of young players or maybe you do not have the talent to compete with the teams you play, but they need to be prepared.

FALCON PHILOSOPHY

Offense
- **Run the ball to set up play action passing**
- **Use multiple formations and motions**

Defense
- **We want to stop the run, play with enthusiasm and create turnovers**

Special Teams
- **Set up special teams to score or set up great field position**

We are a running team. We are not a passing team. I tell our players and coaches that. We are unbalanced in our run to pass percentages. We run the ball 75 percent of the time. It is nice to throw the ball in July and August. It can be an awesome offense. However, when you get to November and December, which is playoff time, it is tough to throw the ball. Throwing the ball takes a different kind of player.

When I am going through this with all the coaches, many of them know and understand it. If the freshmen team is throwing the ball every down, that is not our philosophy. All that does is create dissension when they get to the JV level the next year if they are not doing those things. If the JV team is not stopping the run, creating enthusiasm, or creating turnovers, we need to set down and talk about what we are doing.

One thing I changed with our special teams is our punting game. In our punt game, I no longer have a punt return. I go for the punt block every

time. Normally when you work on punt return, you have a great punt returner. The opponent does not punt the ball to them. They kick it out of bounds or to a different area of the field. We work on punt blocks every day and try to develop the talent for that. There are players with a talent for blocking kicks.

We had a great punt return man two years ago. We did not change our punt block scheme. We tried to block every punt. If the punt team screwed up and punted the ball to him, he could elude everyone and still score without the blocking. Coming after the punt every time has a negative effect on the punter. It leads to bad punts and miss-kicked balls. It makes the center snap that much more important. If the snap is not perfect and the timing of the punt is off, we can get the block.

We want to work hard within the staff and parent groups. Working hard works with parents that are always asking questions about your program and what you are doing philosophy wise. Parents like that, attack the assistant coaches. They do not come to me. They want to go directly to the position coaches. I always instruct my coaches to answer with a single answer. Their answer is, "The players are working hard and the coaches are working hard." If they need more explanation they need to see Coach Gorham. The parent needs to hear only one explanation and that needs to come from me.

If they want to have a meeting with you, the tension will not be as great as it was at that particular time. When parents come to me and ask me "beside the players working hard and the coaches working hard, what are you going to do this year?" I simply tell them we are going to work hard. They do not need to know any more than that.

At the coach's retreat, we talk about that situation and who are the possible problem parents we have on our team. One coach, told me about a set of parents that talked to him after every game. Right away, we can target that situation and get on the same page. We keep using working hard as the answer. That attitude spreads throughout the team. The players will start to use that expression, especially when someone interviews them.

I always talk to the players about not getting on the bus until they know their role. We do not talk about playing time but we will talk about their role on the team. Everyone on the team has a different role. The same thing is true with the coaches. The coaches have a role.

Freshmen coaches are awesome people. I think we should pay the freshmen coaches the most of all the assistants. They must deal with the eighth graders coming up to the Freshman Team. To begin with, they are squirrely and cannot dress themselves. Their hormones are bouncing off the wall. You also have players coming into the program after being coached by the fathers for three years in the peewee league. They never lost a game and the father wants to know why we are not playing his son somewhere where he can run the ball every play.

Why do we have a 250 pound running back playing on the defensive line? We get those questions from parents. There has never been an objective parent when it comes to their son's talent. I appreciate what freshmen coaches do.

The next groups I want to address are the scout team coaches. Those coaches stand there holding up the cards and trying to motivate their players to keep going against the first team all the time. It is tough to do that and you must have a coach that understands it. You must know your role on the staff. If you do not know, you need to sit down with your head coach and figure out what your role is. Where do you belong on your staff? I think it is important for everyone to understand that.

ASSISTANT COACH

- **Dependable**
  - He will be on time for every practice session, help as requested and meet all of his responsibilities. (Game plans, practice plans.)
- **Loyal**
  - It is OK to offer suggestions or debate philosophical issues in private, but an assistant must be totally supportive during practice sessions, games, and public arenas. This also means when talking with parents.
- **Understanding**
  - It is not good enough to merely have knowledge and experience. High school coaches need to teach, nurture, and motivate their athletes.
- **Enthusiastic**
  - Being excited and bringing energy to practice every day is encouraged. It is easy to get excited for a game but it takes a special coach to be motivated every day during practice.
- **Positive**
  - Negative individuals do not inspire, motivate, and provide leadership, which is necessary for a team to be successful.

Dependability is an easy word to discuss. However, it is tough to depend on coaches who are not in your building. I do not know your situation, but we have some coaches in the building and some that are not. I must be flexible with the coaches and players. Not every situation is the same.

If I have a coach call and tell me he cannot be at practice because he has a sick child or has to work extra at his other position, I am not going to get down on him. I am not going to get crazy over that situation but at the same time, you want a person that is reliable and one that can be at every practice session. I am not a type of coach that is not flexible and wants everything done exactly as I want it. It does not always work out for an assistant coach. It is the same way with the players.

Loyalty is a big issue in any coaching situation. It is fine to offer suggestions and changes within in the staff situations. You can debate issues and differences of opinion in private. However, you cannot do that with parents or other coaches.

What we say in our meeting and what we talk about has to stay within that meeting. In that meeting, we talk about every player. We discuss his role on the team, talk about whether he is going to get playing time, and things of that nature. If that gets outside the meeting room, that is information people do not need to have. It is hard sometimes to bite your tongue but you must do it.

It is not good enough for a football coach to just understand football. He has to **teach, nurture, and motivate the athletes**. My coaching career spans 28 years of coaching. Things have changed dramatically in those years. When I was at the other school it seemed to me that the players there were hard working and tough. Now my players want to have personal trainers. We have sandwiches for the players but I have parents that want to bring in their own special sandwich for their sons. They feel they need that type of sandwich. It is hard to deal with that sort of behavior.

On the other side of the coin, are players from single parent homes. The coach cannot just be the coach. He has to be the father figure and role model for those players. You must be a counselor and sometimes you just have to be a friend. Some of my best friends are former players. They graduated, moved on, and now have families of their own. If I had the attitude of just coaching the player, I would not have established those lasting relationship with my former players.

Enthusiasm is something that sounds easy but it is not. Teachers do not have good days every day. Sometimes the coach has had a bad day teaching, or he is simply tired. If the coach is tired, he should not show that when he comes on the field. He has to get the energy from somewhere or the players will notice that immediately. If you allow players to walk at practice, they will walk. If the coach is not enthusiastic and not motivated, the player will play the same way.

If the coach has the players in a classroom situation going over a topic, he has to maintain decorum in the room. He cannot allow them to slump and layover in the chairs. If he allows that it is what he is going to get in coaching. If he does a technique wrong in practice and you do not correct it, you are coaching it. The coaches on your staff that do not teach for a living must bring their enthusiasm to practice every day.

The coach has to be a **positive** influence on his players. Negative individuals do not inspire or motivate anyone. Being positive is an easy term to understand but it is probably one of my biggest weaknesses. I get on the players too much. It is not good to do that all the time. It is easier to be positive than it is to be negative. The players will come to resent it. Find some terms that express an air of positive motivation. Everything that some coaches say is negative. Teaching does not have to be negative. The coach can always spin constructive criticism in a positive way. The coach has to figure out what motivates the player and use it.

The motivation for some players is a kick in the pants. For other players the kick in the pants destroys him. Know your players and use the motivation it takes for each of them. Positive coaching is better than negative coaching.

When we have the coach's meeting it is not just me talking. The coaches participate and give me feedback. Some coaches bring great ideas to the meetings. We share it with everyone in the room. By saying what a coach feels may help someone else in the room.

Coaches have different points of view and that is great. However, they must be able to **adapt** to learning new techniques and ideas to benefit the program. You can go to all the clinics you want. If you bring back things from those clinics that do not fit within the philosophy of your program, it will not work.

We are a program that will not have Division-I athletes every year. There are years when you have several good players and years when you have none. We do not have a Division-I player in our program next year. You must adapt to the players you have within your program. This past season we ran a "3 X 1" formation and had a quarterback that could make the reads that went with that scheme. This upcoming year we do not have that type of quarterback. We will play more of a wing-T attack. The offense has to change to fit the players you have at quarterback.

We do not get to recruit players. We must play the players we have and we want them to be successful. If you are a coach with some great ideas, bring them to the table. However, you must prepare to have that idea shot down if it does not fit the philosophy or the players within the system.

We have a **weight-training program** and we do go to **summer camps**. I think it is important that you not have only one coach in the weight room every day. I teach weight training during the day and I have some of my athletes in the class. We have a coach that does the weight room after school. However, I want every coach on my staff to pick one day a week to be in the weight room.

When they go to the weight room it helps build relationships with the players and they can see how hard they are working. Some of the coaches actually lift with the players. It is a bonus for them. They get to work out and see the player. If you pick one coach to run the program that is the only coach the players see and know. Make sure you get all your coaches involved with the weight room "IF" that is an important part of your program. I feel it is a tremendous part of our program and all the coaches participate.

Position coaching watching game film, and game planning are all part of taking pride in coaching. The position coach has to **watch the**

film before the players do. If you play the game on Friday night and bring the players in Saturday morning to watch the film, you need to watch the film before they see it. Do not watch the film with the players as your first time to see it. If you do you will not have any idea what to say when you see mistakes.

If you are like me the first time you see a film you will say things that will follow some of the things of which I just talked about. Your frustrations come out the first time you see it. Your comments may not be positive or reflect the way you need the players to understand. If you know, the mistakes you can spin criticism the way you need to. If you understand that before you get into the room, you can put the spin on it you want. Sometimes, you will have to get on the player in front of his peers. Being called out in front of his peers may be the type of motivation he needs. At least the coach knows what is going on before he gets in the film session. You have to watch the film the night before or before the players come in on Saturday morning.

Every coach should have a **goal** he wants to reach while coaching. They should have "Short and Long term Goals." They should often be evaluated so adjustments can be made. The assistant coaches need to sit down with the head coach and talk to him about those goals. If you want to be a head coach, the head coach needs to know that so he can help you along. If your main goal is to help fill up your time, he needs to know so he can put you in that role. I have 15 different coaches on my staff. I need to know what their aspirations are. My job as head coach is to help the assistant coaches reach their goal. If an assistant coach wants to be a head coach, I will try to show him what is involved. I will take him to the booster meetings, the parent meetings, and league meetings so he sees what is going on outside the practice field.

Are you a winner on and off the field? Winning is not a sometime thing it should happen all the time. I told the players about our championship team in 2004. They barely got into the state playoffs. We were the fourth seed in the tournament and everything clicked in the playoffs. We won the championship not with the best players, but the best team. I was involved with teams that were better than that team, but they could not get over the hump.

I keep in touch with most of the players on that state championship team. Most of them are highly successful people. There is a correlation there because the players learned how to be a winner. That is your job to teach them how to be a winner and be competitive every day. It is hard to do, but you have to talk about it all the time.

PRACTICE AND MEETINGS

- **Do not be late**
- **2:50 p.m. - 6:30 p.m. daily**
- **Meeting after every practice**
- **Have a daily practice plan**
- **Coaches will have a position meeting with their kids once a week. Always work on knowledge of football and building relationships with the kids.**

The meeting after every practice is informal. The meeting can be as simple as walking off the practice field and talking about things to do. It does not have to be a meeting in the coach's office. They need to get home and spend time with their families. It is simple communication of what we need to do.

The assistant coaches needs to have a daily practice plan written down. You need to plan more than the allotted time in case the head coach wants to run over on a drill. Make use of every second you are on the field and always know what you are doing.

Coaches need to build their relationships with the players. That does not mean only during the season. They need to work on it out of season also. Get to know the players. It will help you in the end.

GAME PLAN

- **Coaches will meet on Saturday to get the game plan ready.**
- **Coaches meeting on Sunday 7:00 p.m..**
- **Players watch Film daily.**
- **Freshman coaches meet and give their plans to Coach Gorham.**
- **Game plan will be 90 percent completed on Sunday.**

I do not want one coach working longer than the other coaches do. If the JV coaches are coaching on Saturday, then the varsity coaches do their game plan at the same time. They should finish about the same time. That way everyone is working the same. I want my assistant to understand I am trying to make it equal for everyone.

With the technology we have now the players can watch the game the same night and scouting films daily at home. All it takes is a DVD and they are in business. Players walk about with their i-Pad and can watch anytime they chose.

I do not want to tax the freshmen coaches any more than I have to. If they do not do a good job, it hurts all the way up the program. They have special problem they must deal with because of the age of the players they work with.

The game plan is 90 percent down on Sunday. It cannot be a 100 percent until we practice it. Always, someone does not understand. If not everyone can execute the game plan, we must simplify it or take something out of the plan.

We expect coaches to get a live scouting report when needed. They need to show up for pre-game and take notes on personnel. They need to see the players. I would rather they get there early and leave at the end of the first quarter, than come late and see the second half. You probably already know their scheme. You want to evaluate their personnel.

We have team dinners the night before the games. We expect all the coaches to be there. The reason for that is to make sure all the players are eating the night before the game. Without every coach showing up, the players will find ways out of coming.

As far as the discipline, the coach needs to handle his own during drills. He needs to remember that running only wastes practice time. Do the disciplining during the drill and make them understand it is discipline. If you would like to remove a player for a game or practice, please discuss this with Coach Gorham. Never say, "You will never play for me!" You never know what is going on in that kid's life.

What you see on film is what you coach. Do not tell me how terrible someone is. Coach him up because he is what we have. "Talking is not Reps!" Worry about the kids we have, not the ones we do not have. If they are doing it in the game, that is what you are teaching in practice. Do not be afraid to tell the players when you made a mistake.

We have a procedure of conduct we give to every player that goes through the entire year. We give them that at the first meeting and reinforce it almost daily.

"THE DO RIGHT RULE"

- **Don't embarrass yourself, your family, your school or your community.**
- **Corporate Expectations.**
- **"Gentlemen, citizens and students" before football.**
- **"No back talk" but coach., I just....**
- **"Listen don't talk."**
- **"Do not whisper, do not smirk."**
- **"Address faculty and staff with respect" Sir, Ma'am, Mr., Coach, Ms.**
- **"Positive public image" - the way we talk, dress and act in public. Our corporate image is our corporate expectations.**
- **Falcons football!**
-

These are rules they live by during the school year. It is a direct reflection on our team if he does not adhere to the rules. He represents football the entire year and not just football season.

SELF IMPOSED DISCIPLINE

We cannot control -
- **Ability and size of opponents**
- **Weather and conditions**
- **Game officials**
- **Opponent tactics**

We can control -
- **Our preparation**
- **Our performance**
- **Our treatment of our -**
  - Teammates, coaches, etc.
- **Our work ethic**
- **"Fix the problem not the blame**

I talk about these things daily. We place particular emphasis on things the players can control and things they cannot control. The things they cannot control are obvious. The game officials are one thing I have to emphasize with our coaches more than I do the players. They are part of the game whether they are good or bad, we have no control over that aspect. The coaches get so upset with the referees they forget to coach their players. The important things are what the players can control. They must have a clear understand of that aspect.

Coaches I enjoyed myself today. I hope all of you are winners on the tables. If there is anything I can do for you drop me an E-mail. Thank you.

Brian Hales

The No-Huddle Hurry-Up Offense

Butler High School, North Carolina

It is a pleasure to come here from North Carolina and see all the coaches here. There is a reason you have the reputation that you do down here. You have great talent, but it is obvious you work very hard at what you do.

During our season this year, one word started to upset me. It really started at the end of the season when we started into our playoffs. When people started talking about our football team, they talked about all the talent we had. I started to resent the word talent in a certain way. They talk about talent as if the player had something to do with it. They are hard working players and work at developing the talent they have, but their parents are the reason they have talent.

When you talk about a player, you need to talk about how hard working he is. When you talk about a team, talk about how well they execute. I do not let the media or others get away with talking about how talented we are. They may think that is a compliment, but I take is as a slight sometimes.

What I want to talk about is how we take the types of offenses we run and put it into a No-Huddle System. We are not a no-huddle team. We huddle 90 percent of the time. We use the no-huddle as a change up in a game. I relate that as a pitcher with a 98 mile an hour fast ball. He has the hard fast one, but he can throw the 91 mile an hour change up. The change up pitch makes him much more effective.

Our players wear wristband. If you want to make a lineman happy, give him a wristband.

We are on a very successful run at our school. The senior class that will graduate this sprint won 57 out of 59 games. In winning those games, we put up a bunch of points.

WHO IS DOG BITE?

- **Any personnel groupings that you chose**

- **Blue (1 rb, 1 te, 1 wr, 2 hb)**
- **Green (2 rb, 1 te, 1 wr, 1 hb)**
- **Orange (1 rb, 2 wr, 2 hb)**
- **White (1 rb, 2 te, 2 hb)**

When I put together a presentation, I do it from a journalistic point of view by telling who, what, when, where, and why. The first part of the presentation is "who" it is. We do this with every personnel group we have. We go into every week with 10 and 11 personnel groups. The third personnel group will depend on what team we play. In some weeks, it could be 12 or 20 personnel. When we set up our personnel groupings, we color code them on the wristbands and in our practice schedule. Our eleven personnel group is blue. Another one is orange, white, brown, and so forth.

WHAT IS DOG BITE?

- **Hurry-up, flurry style of offense**
- **4 plays determined by game plan**
- **Quick snap count**
- **An opportunity to catch a defense unprepared**

When we use the hurry-up, no-huddle scheme we refer to it as our "dog bite series." The "what" is a "Hurry-Up" style of offense? It is four plays that goes on our wristband. It has a quick snap count. It is an opportunity to catch the defense unprepared. It is an opportunity to take advantage of a defense that is not in very good condition. We feel good about the strength and conditioning of our team. We think we can take advantage of that with our Hurry-Up offense.

WHERE DO WE USE DOG BITE?

- **Should be able to run the first play from the M.O.F.**
- **Should be able to run the first play from either hash mark.**
- **Subsequent plays determined by likely end of previous play.**

The "where" has to do with the development of our game plan and our package? The first thing we must decide is can we run the play from the right hash, middle of the field, and the left hash mark. If the play is a 3 X 1 we may not want to put three receivers into the boundary. That could not be the first play in that series. The second play in the series is where we think the first play will end. The formation for play three will be where we think play two will end. The sequential plays will come with that thinking in mind.

WHEN DO WE USE DOG BITE?

There is a list of the "when" we use it. We find the most effective time to use the no-huddle.

- **After a big play.**
- **If our offense is lethargic.**
- **If our defense is on its heels.**

If you hit a big four vertical play or run a draw for a 20-25 yard gain, that is a good time to run the no-huddle hurry-up offense. You have a defense on the field that is looking at each other and trying not to blame someone. The sidelines may be in disarray and the coaches are overly excited about giving up the big play. That is when we want to jump on them with another play.

If the offense is getting lethargic and lazy, this is a good time to use the no-huddle. If the offense is getting sloppy and not getting into and out of the huddle, we want to stir things up and get them to concentrate. This picks up the tempo and forces them to align quickly.

If we have scored two possessions in a row, we may use it. We have the defense down and we want to go for the knockout punch. If their confidence dips that is a time to jump on them. It is a flurry style of offense. It is like a boxing match on TV. If one of the boxers stuns the other, they move in, start throwing haymakers, and try to knock the other fighter out.

WHY DOG BITE?

- **Create your own "sudden change" effect**
- **Take advantage of a defensive personnel package**
- **Take advantage of a poorly conditioned team**
- **Mayday!**

It creates a sudden change effect. If there is turnover by the offense, the defense coming on the field has to be ready for a quick attempt at a score. It could be a trick play or play action pass. If we have been running off tackle continually, we jump into it to speed things up and get the focus back on track. It gives your offense a greater sense of urgency.

If the defense brings a heavy defense on the field to stop the run, we may want to speed the game up and make them run. We can take advantage of a particular personnel package they have. If they have a nickel package on the field, we can jump into the hurry-up and not give them the chance to change personnel. If we put our power package in the game, it is to our advantage. Now you have defensive backs taking on pulling guards and fullbacks.

It gives us the opportunity to catch the defense with 12 players on the field if they try to change personnel. It lets you take advantage of a poorly conditioned team or a team that is not in as good of shape as you are. In North Carolina early in the season, there are extremely hot weather conditions. We feel we are in better shape than most of the teams we play early. If we go to the no-huddle two or three times in a half, it wears the other team down.

The last "why" occurs in a short yardage situation? If we have a third or fourth down and short yardage situation, we may go into a one play "dog bite." We call "May Day", and we do not huddle, and we run the play quickly. This is not a series or two series; it is a one play down. We line up quickly, run a wedge-blocking scheme, and run the ball to pick up the first down. It is a another way attack a defense that is not ready.

We do this in our JV program. We use the same four plays the entire season. In our JV games we do not exchange film and no one scouts those games. It allows us to train the younger players in the system. We use it as part of our conditioning program. We run through our "dog bite" series repeatedly. It helps them learn the plays. We get some physical benefit out of it.

Nine years ago, we only used one or two personnel groupings a game. Our offense over those years has evolved in to what we do today. The evolution occurred because of mistakes we made previously. We played Independence High School five years ago. They had a 97 game winning streak going. We kicked off to them and they fumbled the ball on the first play of the game at their four-yard line.

At that time, we did not have a 21 personnel group in our offense. We ran the ball three times in a row out of a one-back no tight end set and they stuffed us all three time. On the third down play the quarterback got a penalty for trying to push the running back into the end zone. They took the penalty and we threw the ball on the repeated third down play. They picked it off and ran 99 yards for the touchdown. We felt we were better than they were, but that deflated us, and we lost the game.

On Monday, we installed a three back goal line set on offense. That failed goal line situation taught us a lesson. That was something we added to our toolbox.

POTENTIAL SNAFUS

- **They are kids, they make mistakes (do not read it right, skip plays)**
- **Wrong Cards (See changes, collect old ones)**
- **Chain Gang (slooooow)**
- **War Zone**

This is not a perfect system. Your players are kids and make mistakes. You might be in a "blue" personnel group and they read the red personnel grouping call. Sometimes they read the wrong cards on the sideline calls. In one game, a receiver kept aligning in the wrong formation. We took him out of the game, checked his card in his wristband, and he was running the card from the previous week. We corrected that the next week by not laminating the cards until game day. They used paper cards all week and we replaced them on game night with laminated cards.

You must make sure your chain crew has someone on the downs marker that can get up and down the field. The year before, we had an older teacher on the downs marker. We constantly had to wait for him to set the downs marker in the games. We called for the "dog bite" series and had to wait on him to get the downs marker set.

Luckily, he got a pacemaker this year and did a much better job of getting the marker set. You do not want the referee or downs marker slowing you down. If you play on the road, the chain crew may be slow on purpose to give the defense a chance to catch their breath or substitute.

If you give an offensive lineman a wristband, it makes his day. We had one player the team nicknamed "War Zone." He took his "dog bite" card and on the backside he drew pictures of tanks, planes, and war zone stuff. That became his nickname. It is silly stuff but that is the fun things about working with high school players.

The following is an example of what the dog bite card looks like. The first thing on the card is the Dog Bite vs. (Opponent) the name of the team we play. It is a safe guard to make sure we have the proper card. We list the personnel groups we will use against the opponent for that week. In this particular example, we are using the Orange personnel grouping, which is one running back, two-wide receivers and two H-backs, using Green personnel and Blue personnel.

DOG BITE VS._____

ORANGE	GREEN	BLUE
1. Left Trips 49-Zone	Right Pro 35-Inside	LTP 39-Option
2. Left Trips Slant-spacing	Right Pro 56 X CTN	LTP 39-Inside
3. Left Trips 36-H CTN	Right Pro 438-Boot	LTP 435 89-Out
4. Left Trips Cali	Right Pro 435-Cali	Ripple Cali Spec Left

When you develop your plan you do not want your players running from one side of the field to the other to get into the proper formation. In the first example, the formation was "left trips" for all four plays. You do not want to go from left trips to right trips in your sequence. You wear your own players out with too many formation changes.

In the case of a play to the wide side, we may simply put trips out with no direction designation on the card. If we want to run the bubble screen from the trips set, we want it run into the wide side of the field. After your players become experienced at running the dog bite, they know the bubble screen goes into the wide side. If the ball is on the left hash mark, the offense knows we are going to be in right trips. The fun thing about coaching is when the players start to think as you do. That is when you know they have a good grasp of what you are trying to do with the dog bite series. You can be flexible in a given week. You may not want to use three personnel groups in the dog bite.

The personnel grouping are something that we use. It is not a rule that you need three personnel groups. It is something that we did to be as versatile as we can. The only thing that limits what you want to do is your own creativity.

MECHANICS

- **Call for "dog bite!" It comes in from the sideline.**
- **Formation is on the card or can be signaled in (ex. trips) (slide 11 vs. man press)**
- **Immediately when you get lined up**
- **Ball is snapped on a quick count (first sound)**

At the end of a play, the dog bite call comes from the sidelines. The coaches start to yell at the players on the field. We make the color call. In this example, we yell "Orange-1." Everyone looks at their card and sees the play we run. When the play is over, we come back to the line of scrimmage immediately and run Orange-2 from the card.

The first thing we must do before we run each play is align. We need to do that as quickly as possible. Once we get into the formation, we look at the card to see what the play is. It is important to align quickly because the other version of this package is our "mad dog" package. The dog bite series always goes on the first sound. If we call "man dog", we look for the free 5 yard penalty for the defense jumping off sides. It is a dummy call, which we do not snap on the first sound.

We have our staff meetings on Sunday night. In that meeting, we establish what the dog bite series is going to be. The plays on the card are predetermined plays, which come from our Sunday staff meeting. We type it up, put it on the game sheet, and work on it during the week. It does not change. If we have confidence to run this series, we know where the defense will align on these sets. However, they do not always end up where we think they will be. It does not matter where the defense aligns you still have to block them. If they do not align where we tell our players where the defense will be, they have to adept and apply their rules.

That is one reason you need simple line blocking assignment. We feel we can block any blocking scheme. Some plays in the grouping are predictable as to where they will end. However, some other plays could end up somewhere else particular if it is a pass play. That is the reason for some of the open formations directions. If we

run trips left into the wide side of the field and run a running play to the right, we know the play will end up into the boundary. We call left trips again and know the formation will be to the wide side of the field.

When you run this type of scheme, you would not think you would want to motion or have the ability to motion. Four years ago, we started to use motion with this series. When we did it, the offensive line jumped off side quite a bit. The offensive line was not patient enough. They knew it was the dog bite. They wanted to get into their stances and get off the line of scrimmage. One of the best things you can do in the dog bite is run an unbalanced formation.

The other system we use is the "Mad Dog" system. In this system, we can use it as a two-minute offense. We want to continue to get to the line of scrimmage quickly. We signal the formation from the sidelines.

When we go to the "mad dog" system, we hustle to the line and get set. The quarterback goes to a dummy cadence. The first sound that comes out of the quarterback's mouth is going to be loud and forceful. We try to get the defense to jump. However, it serves another purpose. We run the "dog bite" enough so that it draws a reaction from the defense. Even if they do not jump off sides, they will tip what they are going to do. The secondary will move and if they plan to blitz, it will show. You get a great read for what you want to run.

This year we ran for over 3000 yards and threw for 3500 yards. Our percentage of run to pass was 60-40 percent run to pass. We have done that without a seasoned quarterback. We had a veteran quarterback this year but he broke his hand half way through the season.

I told our quarterback this year before he broke his hand, in the "mad dog" system that I was going to let him call the plays. If you have a quarterback that has run the system, that is the way to go. If he understands the offense and knows what you are trying to do, it is the best way to do it. If you want to build confidence in your quarterback, let him call the plays. He wants to do it right and will work hard to make sure he does it right. If you trust the quarterback to make the right calls, the rest of the team will trust him. They think if the coach trusts him to run the offense, then I am going to trust him. That gives your offense a big shot in the arm.

When we get into the "mad dog" mood, we call our offense with a one-word cue or signal. Our curl/flat combination is "New York." If the quarterback calls "New York", the outside receiver runs the curl route and the number 2 receiver runs the bench route. It could be a flat or out cut. We call all of our formations with hand signals. Carolina is curls/corners pass. Instead of calling Carolina, we could use Tar Heels or Wolf Pack. Instead of calling New York, we could Jets or Giants. Tennessee is our toss sweep. If we called Tennessee, we run the play to our sidelines. If we called Tennessee opposite, we run it to the opponent's sidelines.

If we run the sprint out series, we run companion patterns depending on the second number in our sixty series. If we call "64", the second number is the pattern for the outside receiver. The wide receiver run the 4 route and the inside receiver runs the companion route. We try to match a high/low read for the quarterback. The 4 route is the inside curl and the companion route is a flat pattern. If we run "69", the outside receiver runs the 9 pattern, which is a takeoff, and the inside receiver runs a low breaking pattern, which is a bench or out route.

We pick small things that are easy to remember and make use of them. We rep them during the week, hit it hard on Wednesday, Thursday, and try to do it on Friday. There will be games where we do not use dog bite or mad dog one time. There will be weeks where we do it a couple of times. We do it that way and the players like it. I am sure there will come a time when we feel like we have too much for the players to comprehend. When that happens, we start subtracting.

In a no-huddle or two-minute offense at the end of a half, you do not need too many plays. We have three to four things that we can run. We have the wide play with Tennessee, the inside zone, and a draw. The defense is not going to play eight players in the box. You do not need a complicated pass blocking protection schemes. Our protection scheme is the same with the exception of the sprint out pass protection. If you put too much offense in these situations, you end up with more blocking schemes than you need.

We rep the four plays in the dog bite in practice every day. We have three formations and four plays in each formation. It takes us about 45 seconds to run one four-play series. We do not spend a lot of practice time running plays.

When you are a multiple formation offense, it is easy to add a lot of formations. For us to add a formation, we have to be able to do four things from the formation. You must run your base run and counter run from the formation. You must be able to play action pass and drop back pass from the formation. If you can do that from the formation, we can consider adding it.

We do not have freshman football at Butler. We have JV and varsity football. After the game on Friday, we do not meet with the team until Monday. We give them the entire weekend off. We ask a lot of them during the week and they deserve the weekends to do whatever they want. On Monday, the offensive players come to my classroom and we watch the game film. The defensive players go to the defensive coordinator's classroom and watch the game film. On Monday, the JV team goes out and has a scrimmage. That is a heavy and physical workday for them.

The staff has from Friday night after the game until Sunday night at the staff meeting to do the things that is required of them. They have to watch the game tape and grade their position groups. We meet as a staff on Sunday and make all the preparation for the upcoming week.

On Monday, the varsity goes to the practice field around 3:45. We work for about an hour to an hour and fifteen minutes. We go over the next opponent, put in our installs, and go over the formations we will use. The normal weekly practice begins at 3:00 and we are off the field at 5:15. That includes stretch time and conditioning.

I want to talk to the assistant coaches. Some of you think you are ready to be a head coach. You have done all your work and accomplished a bunch of things. My advice to you is to be patient. You are always going to have time to take a bad job. I was at Butler for 6 years. The head coach took another job down the road and I got the opportunity to be the head coach. A job may look good on the outside, but those situations are rarely good situations to take on.

It has been a pleasure to talk football with you. I appreciate it and I am overwhelmed and impressed by the turnout today. When I tell my staff about the reception I got here, they will understand why the football is so good in Florida. If there is anything else you want to talk about I will be around all week-end. Thank you.

Tom Harmon

The Wing-T Offense: An Update

Wayne High School, West Virginia

It is quite an honor to speak at a Nike Clinic like this one. I am not sure I will enjoy it because I like to be where you are sitting instead of being up here giving the lecture. Today I am going to talk about the wing-T. I am not an expert on that offense. I am not a Delaware follower, but I do know what is has done for us at Wayne High School. There are three divisions in West Virginia and Wayne we are in Class AA. We have an enrollment of around 650 students. Wayne is the kind of town where people leave their doors unlocked at night. The reason for that is they may get the opportunity to shoot someone.

If you watch us play, you would say we play hard. You cannot talk a great deal about what we do in our offense in fifty minutes. The backbone of our program is blocking. That is the one thing we spend time on and teach to the best of our ability.

We have a certain way we do things and a program we go through. The players are in the weight room busting their butts trying to get ready for next season. This time of year is when you create your toughness. I do not believe you can wait until next fall to figure out the type of character your players have. You want to know before the year starts that you can depend on and who are the tough players. We want to know who can handle the adversity that goes with any program. You create those things in the off-season and carry them over into the fall.

We have a sign posted in our weight room, which reads, *"Look at a stone cutter hammering away at his rock perhaps a hundred times without as much as a crack showing in it. Yet at the hundred and first blow it will split in two and I know it was not the last blow that did it but all that had gone before." Jacob A. Riss*

We talk about hitting the rock every day. If you hit it hard enough and hit it enough times, it will finally come true.

PROGRAM THOUGHTS

- **Concentrate on your average or below average players.**
- **If your players are even, play them all.**
- **Write off no young players.**
- **Chemistry is a daily job.**
- **Selling begins when they are young.**
- **Physically and mentally, attend JV and Middle School games.**
- **When adversity hits, rededicate to your basics.**
- **Avoid highs and lows in your approach to games.**
- **Hitters play, find them early and then back off.**
- **In critical times think of players and not plays.**

We do not spend a lot of time working with our good football players. I like to spend my time with players that are going to be difference maker for you. The players in the middle with their talent levels are the one that will make the difference in your program. Your real good players are going to be just that. As the coach you do not want to screw them up. Get them in the right places and let them play.

If you have many players in your program that are relatively even in talent and ability, play them all. The more players you can get involved in your program the better off you will be.

Do not write off any of the young players that come out for the team. Often you have players that can barely walk but after four years in a weight program, they become contributors.

Chemistry is a daily job. I am not saying you need to know their girlfriends and things like that, but you need to be aware of the things that go on within their lives. I do not think you should have big text discussions with them but you should be aware of things so you can head off something that could be a big problem.

Selling begins when the players are young. I have an 11-year-old son who has been running the same football plays since he was six years old. He will run those same plays when he is a senior in high school. When you have former players coaching the youth league teams, it can be a big help to your program. When we finish practice, I go down, watch, and listen to the things going on with our youth programs. Their plays and terminology is the same as what we use. At Wayne High School the system stays the same.

That allows us to branch out and do more when we get them in our program. We do not need to spend all our time working on base plays and things of that nature.

The head coach should attend the JV and middle school games. In addition to being there, he should be into the games mentally. I want to be on the sidelines. I want to look into those facemasks and see what kind of attitude they have. I want to see how they handle the adversities of the game and the physicality of it. I want to see those things when they are 12 years old. You can learn many things in those situations.

When adversities hit, you must go back to your basics. The basics are what will get you through tough times. In games, there will always be times when adversity strikes. When that happens, go back to the things you do well. They need to go back to what they did when they were six years old.

You want to avoid the highs and lows in game preparation. If we play Poca High School or Mingo Central, I try personally not to make too big a deal out of any one opponent. I think you need to keep your emotions even so you do not ride the emotional roll-a-coaster throughout the year. The players will do that enough without you adding to it.

Hitters will play. We want to find out who the hitters are early in the year. After that we do not hit much in practice. We play physical in the games but we do not hit that much when we practice. We find out who is tough and who will hit during weight training, in the off-season, and in early practice. I do not believe in running off soft young players with tough physical practices. That player you did not run off as a freshman may end up being a hitter as a junior. We do enough to know who is tough and then back off on them.

At a critical time in the game, think of players and not plays. I learned this the hard way. You have players on your team that you want to have the ball in their hands when the game is on the line. You know who you want to have the ball when the game is on the line. If it is fourth and two, you are going to give the ball to your playmaker. If it does not work, you can live with it.

OFFENSIVE THOUGHTS

- **Formation galore**
- **Balance right and left**
- **Be known for something**
- **Impression of simplicity but complex reality**
- **Stains on the front**
- **Everybody blocks**
- **Style points do not count**
- **A confused player is a slow player**
- **Do not be married to the game plan**
- **Fool the kids and not the coach**
- **Bag of trick**
- **Call what you see**
- **It is better to be wrong than indecisive**
- **Go fast with momentum**
- **Have the ability to change pace**
- **Double teams create confidence**
- **Hands do not hurt**
- **Find the worst player at each defensive level**
- **If it works, wear it out**

We run many formations. We are not a team that will stay in one formation throughout a game. We run very few plays but we run them from many formations. We want to have balance in our plays. Everything we run to the right we should be able to run to the left. If you run a middle trap to one side, you need to run it to the other side. We flip-flop our offensive line. We have certain players that pull and certain players that block down.

If you want to run your tailback to the left side you should be able to line up on the right side and run it to the left side. You need to be known for something. As the head coach, you need to answer that question. What is your signature play? What is your bread and butter play? What do you run when the game is on the line? If someone watched us play, what would they say we do? If you are any good, coaches should know what your offense is. They may be able to stop it but if they do not know what it is, the chances are you do not either.

Many things we do, look simple. However, there is more to it behind the scenes. It may look like a tailback running off tackle to the left but it is the tailback running off tackle five different ways. The adjustments we make at the line of scrimmage change from game to game and week to week.

"Stains on the front" is a phase we use to develop the mind-set of moving forward. We do not want the stains on the seats of our pants or on our backs. At the end of plays, we do not want the stains on the rear end of the uniforms. That is not a good thing. We want to finish and fall forward.

In our offense, everybody blocks. That includes the quarterback and everyone on the offense. I do not know if it takes a whole lot of talent to block. However, it takes a lot of effort. Effort should not be a problem for anyone.

Style points do not count with me. I do not care if we go into a game and only run two plays, and win. The object is to win the game. If the off-tackle trap works and you cannot stop it that is all we will run. To me there is nothing more demoralizing to the defense than to run the same play repeatedly. That creates doubt in the defensive teams mind.

A confused player is a slow player. I think this point is so important. Bobby Bowden said, "People muddy the water to make it look deeper." I think that sometimes we make the game of football excessively complicated. You must remember you are working with kids and some of them are still watching cartoons. When you teach you start very slow from a standpoint that will allow aggression. If they are confused, the less aggressive they play.

Some of our best game plans are not that good. You work on them all week in practice, but on the first series, they look like crap. I have found over the years, I am better if I just wing it out there on the field. That is a personal thing. You know your offense and you have a feel for what will work. Before the state championship game, I do not know what will be the first play. I do not know until they kick the ball and I start thinking about it a bit. When you cloud your mind you end up playing backwards.

When you coach a football game, you do not need to fool the other coach. You need to fool the players on the field. In your film study, find that player you can fool. If there is one player on the other team that is the player you go after.

You must have a bag of tricks available. You do not need to run them but you must have them ready to use. You need to call what you see and not what you think you see. Know your offense well enough to do that.

It is better to be wrong than indecisive. If you call time out with a fourth and two, when you walk out on the field to talk to the players, you must be confident. Even if you do not know what to call you must project that air of confidence that the next play will work.

When you have the momentum, you need to go fast. Get the play in the game and push the tempo. You must have all the tempos available during the course of the game.

Double teams create confidence. This is not in a textbook anywhere, but I believe that two people should whip one. I believe that two players from our team should be able to block the 5-technique from the Pittsburgh Steelers if you really want to block him. We try to create that every time. I would rather double team the 5-technique and leave the Mike linebacker alone, than half block the 5-technique and have him make the tackle. Make the linebacker run around the pile to make the tackle.

Football is a physical game. Hands do not hurt the opponent. We use the forearms and shoulder pads to create a surface. That goes for offensive players as well as the defensive players.

When you scout a team find the worst player at each defensive level. I want to know the worst defensive linemen, linebacker, safety, or corner. I create schemes to attack those players.

Offensively we run three basic football running series. We have the trap series, rocket sweep, and counter series. In the trap series, we run the middle trap, tailback off tackle, and the quarterback on the boot.

We run the rocket sweep to make the 9-technique play looser and not squeeze the off-tackle play. We block the off-tackle three different ways. That is six of the running plays we run.

The first play I want to show you is from our middle trap. The play is "32-trap." (Diagram #1)

The "32" is the 3 back in the 2 hole. The 3 back is the fullback and the 2 back is the tailback. The rule for the trap is to trap the first defender past the hole. If the defender aligns in the hole, we block him down. The play is "32", which is a 2 hole trap play. The center fills backside for the pulling guard. The playside guard and tackle in this defense block the inside linebackers. The guard goes to the backside linebacker and the tackle goes to the playside linebacker.

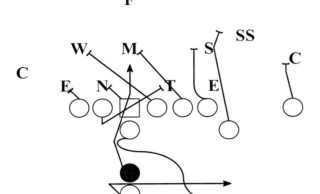

Diagram #1. 32-Trap

The fullback steps with his right foot toward the centers left foot. His next step is with the left foot, which squares his shoulder to the line of scrimmage. This puts him on the correct angle to the hole. He favors the centers down block and stays away from the trap block. As he comes through the line of scrimmage, he pick up the down blocks by the playside guard and tackle coming down on the inside linebackers. The play is a quick hitting trap play.

The trap 2 hole is to the right of the center. The fullback starts to the backside and bends the ball back behind the pulling guard. That is the reason he steps to the backside with his right foot. It puts him on his left foot for the second step heading into the hole.

The "26-trap" is the tailback running to the 6 hole. (Diagram #2) The 6 hole is between the right tackle and tight end. It is a wide trap play. The rules for the trap are the same. The left guard pulls and traps the first defender past the 6 hole. Everyone else blocks down. The center cuts off the backside for the pulling guard. The playside guard and tackle double-team the 3-technique defender to the backside linebacker. The tight end comes down on the playside linebacker. The wingback blocks the outside linebacker. We trap the 6-technique defensive end.

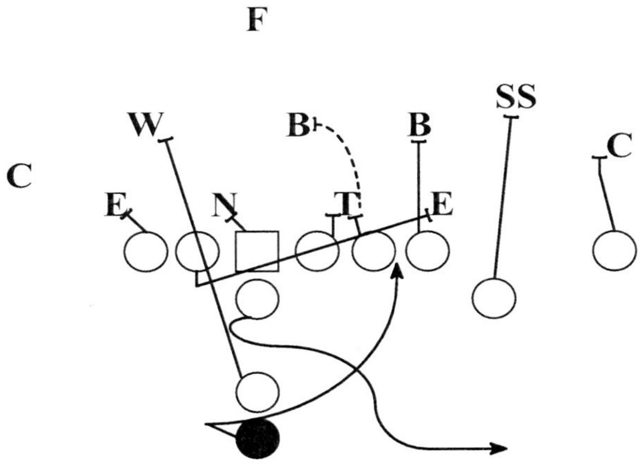

Diagram #2. 26-Trap

If the 6-technique squeezes across the tight end's face, he latches him and drives him to the inside. The trap blocker wraps up to the outside and looks for the linebacker. We tell the tailback when he breaks the line of scrimmage he looks for the cutback to the backside.

We do not always pull the backside guard and kick out. You work off the concept and not the play. If we pull both guards we call that the sweep. The trey call means the backside-guard and backside-tackle pulls to the playside. The guard kicks out and the tackle wraps up inside. If we run the blast play, the fullback is the kick out blocker. If we want the fullback to kick out and the backside guard to curl inside, we call that blast-curl. We can change the pull combinations with words. That tells everyone who pulls and what they do.

The next play is the boot run by the quarterback. (Diagram #3)

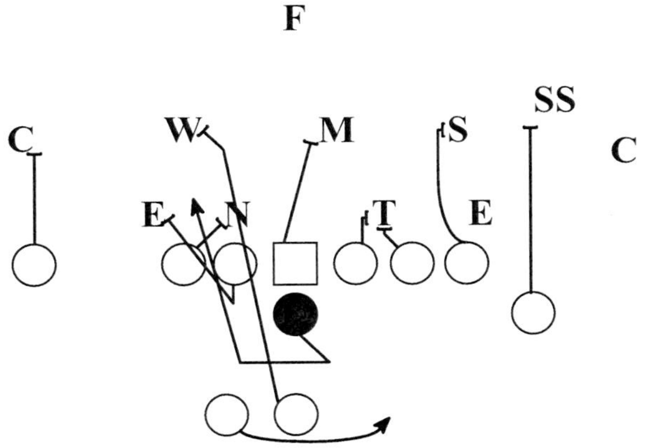

Diagram #3. Black Boot/Charlie

This play is a "Black-Boot Run." That means we run the play to the left or backside of the formation. The playside guard and tackle give a "yes or no" call for a "Charlie" block (cross block). If they give an "Andy" call, they are able to block their men in a base blocking scheme. They make the call as to the scheme they will apply. On the "Charlie" call, the fullback runs through the playside B-gap as an isolation blocker. The tailback runs his 26-trap fake. The quarterback fakes the trap and comes out the backside following the fullback isolation block.

If we wanted to run the same play but pull the backside guard and tackle, we call "Black Boot/ Trey." (Diagram #4) In that case, the fullback goes to the backside to cut off for the pulling linemen. The playside linemen use a gap scheme-blocking pattern. The blocking scheme depends on how the defense is reading what we do. If they key the fullback to take them to the play, they may not be right. On one block scheme, he is toward the boot. On another scheme, he is away from the boot. The more tendencies you can break the better you are.

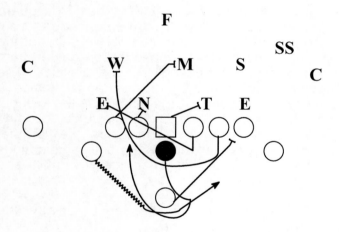

Diagram #4. Black-Boot Trey

We can run the "Boot-Pass" off the same sets. It is a stabilizing pass. We run standard patterns. The receiver to the boot side runs the corner and that is the first place we look. The tight end runs a drag across the field and the backside wide receiver runs the post in the middle of the field.

We run the "roll pass" with this series. The difference in the boot and the roll is the roll goes to the motion and the boot comes away from it. (Diagram #5) We run the 26-trap fake and roll to that side. The tight end runs a bench pattern at 10 yards. The wingback runs a wheel up the sideline and the fullback comes out of the backfield into the flat. It is a flood pattern.

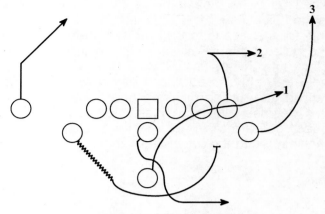

Diagram #5. Roll Pass

The "rocket" is our sweep. The set here is the unbalanced double wing set. (Diagram #6) Everyone to the playside reaches outside. We are not trying to turn the defender and hook him. We are trying to get to his outside and run. We want to work him up field as we go. We pull both guards to the outside and they try to get in front of the ball. If we ran this play from the I-formation, it would look like the toss sweep. All we are trying to do is get to the edge. The wingback comes in motion in the area behind the fullback. The quarterback snaps the ball as he passes the fullback position. He sprints to the outside looking to break up field.

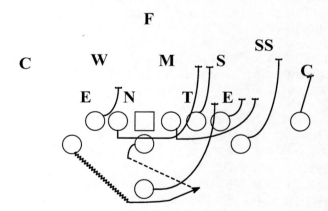

Diagram #6. Rocket Sweep

We try not to use the word reach. We refer to the technique as "gap-backing." The idea is they are stepping into the gap and pushing the defender up the field. I do not want them thinking they have to reach and hook the defender. We push up the field and outside.

The companion play for the rocket sweep is "34-gut." (Diagram #7) We design the play to look like the rocket play. The quarterback reverses out as if to pitch the ball to the motioning wingback. He instead leaves the ball with the fullback. The tight end and wingback to the playside make a call depending on what the 9-technique defender is doing. If he is tight to the line of scrimmage, the tight end takes him outside and the wing folds inside for the block on the linebacker. If the end steps outside the tight end, we reverse the assignments.

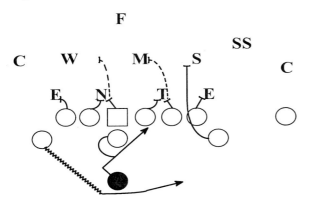

Diagram #7. 34-Gut

The playside guard and tackle work a double team on the 3-technique defender up to the Mike linebacker.

The fullback counter fakes away from the hole and comes back over the ball. The quarterback fakes the ball as if he were going to pitch it to the rocket motion and leaves it for the fullback who runs into the 4 hole.

We run a counter play from this set. We call this "45-counter." (Diagram #8)

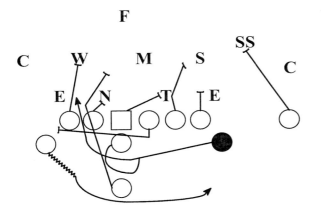

Diagram #8. 45-Counter

The 4 back is the right wingback. He comes underneath the quarterback, receivers the handoff, and runs to the 5 hole. The playside blocks the play like the Boot run. The backside guard pulls and kicks out at the 5 hole. The

quarterback reverses out and makes the play look like the rocket sweep. He rotates back to the line of scrimmage and hands the ball to the wingback coming underneath him. The fullback sifts through the line and blocks on the playside linebacker.

This is our version of the jet sweep. (Diagram #9) We call the play 49-fly. The right wingback comes in fly motion flat to the line of scrimmage as fast as he can. The quarterback takes the snap and reverses out. He wants to take the snap of the ball and hand it off as rapidly as he can. It has to be a bang-bang hand off. The quarterback is responsible for the timing of the handoff. As soon as the wingback receivers the ball he moves away from the line of scrimmage at a 45 degree angle, gaining depth to get around the corner. This is a stretch play and he wants to get to the sidelines.

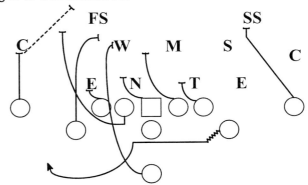

Diagram #9. 49-Fly

The offensive line reaches to the outside and we pull the on-side guard. In theory, the blocker can reach from a head up position to the next man to his outside. If we run it to a wide receiver, he has two ways to block it on this play. He can crack block or he can stalk block the deep back. We are not trying to reach, we are trying to get to the outside and run.

From the jet sweep, we run the "35-lead" play. (Diagram #10) The play looks like the 49-fly. The fullback carries the ball in the 5 hole. The wingback to that side folds inside and isolates the linebacker. The playside guard and tackle base the two down linemen to that side. Each play we run builds off the other play. When the fullback runs the play, we want him to go into the hole with his shoulders square. He wants to be under control so he can move. We do not want him out of control and running with reckless abandon. He must be patient because he has to see and move.

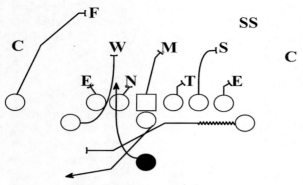

Diagram #10. 35-Lead

The "26-counter" is almost the same play as the 26-trap. (Diagram #11) It takes a little longer to run. It is the third play off the series. We run the 49-fly, the 35-lead, and 26-counter. The 2 back comes around behind the fullback, takes the handoff, and runs to the 6 hole. We pull the backside guard and kick out at the 6 hole. The blocking on the playside is gap blocking. We seal the play to the inside and kick out at the 6 hole.

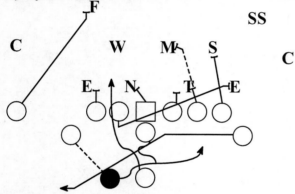

Diagram #11. 26-Counter

We can run the play out of the I-formation with trey blocking. (Diagram #12)

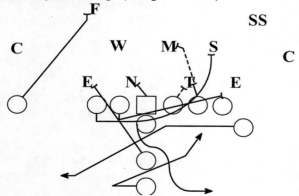

Diagram #12. 26-Counter/Trey

The fullback goes to the backside to cut off for the pulling guard and tackle. The 2 back takes a lead step to the backside and comes to the playside. The guard kicks out at the 6 hole and the tackle wraps inside for the linebacker.

We have a play action off this series called "Red Waggle." (Diagram #13) We fake the 49-fly, 35-lead, and throw the play action pass. The split end runs a post, the wingback runs a drag across the middle and the tight end runs a corner route. The 49-fake settles in the playside flat.

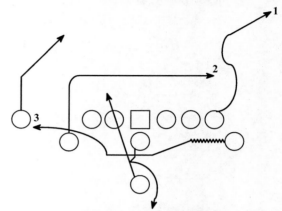

Diagram #13. Red Waggle

The last 8-10 years we have probably averaged 40 points a game. We have had fast tailbacks and quick ones. If you have great players, you are going to win no matter what you do. However, we have a system and if we have a great quarterback, you can have big numbers. What I covered today is only about 60 percent of our offense. That is our heart and soul. The players at Wayne High School know what our base offense is and how to run what we do best.

Sixty percent of our offense is our meat and potatoes. Some time we add rice and green beans to the menu and that is the way we look at games. I am a big fan of football and like good football. We like to think outside the box. I like good football plays but you do that after you take care of your scheme and you base offense.

I know this game is not rocket science. Our line splits are two feet, two feet, and three feet but can vary from game to game. On the jet motion, the quarterback is responsible for the handoff and timing of the play. If we move him as part of the cadence, the quarterback must make it work. If he uses his heel to start him, he has to snap the ball at the right time.

I appreciate your attention. Thank you for your time.

Jason Hawkins

Shotgun No-Huddle Fast Tempo Offense

Charlestown High School, Indiana

I want to thank the Nike Clinic Staff for inviting us to speak here today. I have my entire staff with me and I want to thank them for all they do for our program.

In the year 2010 after winning the first four games we ended up winning 3 and losing 3 for the rest of the season. I had a quarterback who was a sophomore that year. When he was a freshman he had started for the Varsity and we were 4-0 to start the season. We started out with our freshman quarterback and we were 4-0 and then he broke this collarbone. So the rest of the year we ended up at 3-3.

When we were 3-3 I knew I had to make a change in our offense to compete with the teams on our schedule. After the third game that we lost, I called the coach at New Albany High School to see if I could visit with them to talk about their offense. So after I met with our kids on Saturday morning, I went to meet with the offensive staff at New Albany. They were successful running the spread offense. I talked with them for almost three hours. They told me what they were doing, and what worked for them. I was luck in that I knew the New Albany coach and it helped me a great deal to visit with them.

Before we went to the Shotgun Offense we were an I-football team. Then we became an I-Spread Formation Team. We ran some Trip Sets to spread the defense out. But still we were an I-Formation Team. Later we ran with a tight end and wingback in our offensive look.

I knew what I wanted to do out of the shotgun offense. We were 3-3 for a reason. Our quarterback was running the ball only four times a game and he was our best player. He was our best football player and most of the game he was just a lead blocker for the running backs. That was not real smart at all. My answer to our problem was to get into the shotgun formation and utilize our talent better. I moved the quarterback to tailback.

We had a good receiver on the team. He had 67 catches and gained over 1,000 yards and 15 touchdowns. We still wanted to be able to throw the football. The answer was to go to the shotgun offense.

We are almost a full two-platoon football team. We are a 3-A team in Indiana which puts us in the middle of the classification for the state. We have close to 600 students in our school. We have from 60 to 80 kids on our football team, depending on the season.

Two years ago when we went to the shotgun offense we were 4-A and everyone played one position. After six games that year we told six players they were no longer on offense or defense. We have a great defensive coordinator and I feel comfortable with him running the defense and conducting practice. I am lucky in that area and I do not have to step on toes, and I do not have to be involved that much. When we changed to two platoon football we got double amount of time for six weeks to practice with just the offense.

This past season we had three kids playing both ways. That made practice planning a lot tougher. We had to go a little longer to get all of the practice sessions completed. Next year we are going to start 22 kids again. Planning practice will be a lot better.

I am not saying with a game on the line we would not use one of our better players to play both ways, particular in the last four minutes of the game. He is going to be in the game. He will have enough time to practice both offense and defense. However, for two hours and fifteen minutes we are going to practice one way with the players.

We are lucky that we have a coaching staff where each coach are able to coach a position. We have 12 coaches. We do not have all of the coaches in a paid position. We only have six coaches that are in a paid positions counting me. We are lucky to be able to find volunteer coaches. We try to do as much as we can for those volunteer coaches, but they are volunteers. They coach a position and we count them as a coach. Here are the coaches and the position they are involved with. I am the Offensive Coordinator and I coach quarterbacks.

COACHING STAFF

- **Jason Hawkins - Head Coach/Offensive**
- **Coordinator/Quarterbacks**
- **Denny Van - Offensive Line**
- **Chad Vincent - Receivers**
- **Jimmy Worley - Running Backs**
- **Chris Brafford - Defensive**
- **Coordinator/Safeties**
- **Eric May- Inside Linebackers**
- **Eric Fuston - Outside Linebackers**
- **Jake Cook - Corners**
- **David Daniel - Defensive Line**
- **Jaime Applegate - Defensive Line and Weight room**

Here are our records and stats for the last three years.

2010 BEFORE (3-3)
- **28.6 POINTS PER GAME**
- **338 YARDS PER GAME**
- **115 PASSING PER GAME**
- **223 RUSHING PER GAME**
- **6.0 YARDS PER PLAY**

2010 AFTER (5-1) SECTIONAL FINALIST
- **37.6 POINTS PER GAME**
- **409 YARDS PER GAME**
- **143.7 PASSING PER GAME**
- **265 RUSHING PER GAME**
- **8.15 YARDS PER PLAY**

2011 8-3
- **40.7 POINTS PER GAME**
- **434.8 YARDS PER GAME**
- **7.6 YARDS PER PLAY**
- **164.4 PASSING PER GAME**
- **264.5 RUSHING PER GAME**

2012 12-1
SECTIONAL & CONFERENCE CHAMPIONS
- **59.2 POINTS PER GAME (1st in State)**
- **490 YARDS PER GAME**
- **10.4 YARDS PER PLAY**
- **160 PASSING PER GAME**
- **329 RUSHING PER GAME**
- **18 PASS ATTEMPTS PER GAME**

- **37 RUSHING ATTEMPTS PER GAME**
- **QUARTERBACK RAN 14 TIMES PER GAME AND AVERAGED 11 YARDS PER CARRY**
- **RUNNING BACK RAN 16 TIMES PER GAME AND AVERAGED 8 YARDS PER CARRY**

We are a shotgun offense that looks to run the ball first. I do not believe you can throw the ball 40 times a game and be successful in high school. We want to average around 18 passes per game. As you can see we rushed the ball 37 times per game.

Our main offense is from the shotgun with a quarterback and one running back. We do run some plays utilizing two running backs. I will show that to you later. We do run some sets with five wide receivers and no running backs. Our main offense is with our quarterback and our running back next to him.

WHY WE LIKE THE SHOTGUN NO-HUDDLE

1. Kids love it!
2. We can always be in a good play.
3. We can dictate how fast we go.
4. It can make us balanced.
5. It gets more players involved.
6. We can attack the entire field.
7. Gets people out of the box.
8. I get the pen last.

NEGATIVES

1. Time of Possession.
2. Don't expect to have a top 10 defense.

Our Time of Possession is not very good. We are trying to go fast on offense. When you go fast you are not holding on to the ball very long. This is not helping the defense. Do not expect to have a top 10 Defense if you run a fast tempo offense. We only gave up nine points per game this year on defense. In our last game we lost by a score of 57 to 49. We were off the field on offense the entire second half. We could not hold on to the ball. We were ahead 49 to 21 at half time. We were beaten by the team that led the state in scoring.

I will be the first to admit that we did not do a good job of controlling the clock the second half. We continued to pass the ball play after play. I thought we should have used more time by going to a huddle. However, we were not a huddle team. We should have worked more to learn how to slow the game down. That is something we will work on next year.

WHAT WE NEED TO WORK ON

1. More "Check With Me"
2. Play Calling on 3rd and Long
3. Don't Be Stubborn

We know we must get better in our No-Huddle Offense. We need to do a better job of going to the line of scrimmage and making the correct call. The quarterback looks over to see if we want to change the play. If we have called a play that does not look good, I am going to change the call. We are going to work on calling the plays faster and make the "Check with Me" a better situation for our offense.

We all need to work on 3rd down and long situations. When it comes up 3rd and 8 for the first down, in high school you must have a few plays that you can hang your hat on. We need four or five plays we can depend on in those situations. We all need to know what we want to do in the crucial 3rd down situations.

The last point is not to be stubborn. The person that knows the most about our offense needs to be up in the press box. He is the coach that is going to be able to see a lot more than you can see from the sideline.

Here is the way we call plays. I call the play and the formation. Next I tell the coaches the call. My best man in the press box was my father who coached for several years and knows football. I may have called a counter play. He may suggest we run the sweep play. He can see the defense has loaded to one side and we can run the sweep to the other side. Because we had been very successful during the season, I would not change the play. I was stubborn. The play worked a lot of the time, but we were better than those teams we were playing. However, in the long run that did not help us, because later we were stopped by defenses as good as we were. The person in the box should call 40 to 50 percent of the plays. He is the man!

The one thing I want to know after every play is "Who made the tackle?" Does that make sense? We must be able to make adjustments depending on what the defense is doing to stop our offense. We should have something in our playbook to handle any situation the defense

runs against us. We have to be willing to call that play. Do not be stubborn.

When we first started out in 2010 we were a wristband team. We had a hard time communicating with the kids on the wristbands. However, it was an easy thing for us to get into the No-Huddle with the wristbands.

In 2011 we stayed in the wristbands. We used colors for the plays on the wristbands. We had plays that we wanted to run listed in Blue, White, Green, and Black. Also, we had Pass and Special on the wristbands. We had six plays on each of the sections.

I had to look on my play sheet and find a play in that color. I had a coach hold up the card for the color and I held up the play number to match the play on the wristband they were to run for that play. I spent most of my time looking at the play sheet instead of watching the game. It was difficult for us to continue that system. We changed to giving signals for the plays from the sideline.

WHY SIGNALS ARE BETTER THAN WRISTBANDS

- **Faster**
- **Not Limited On How Many Plays**
- **You Are Not Ever Looking Down**
- **Kids Cannot Misread A Signal**
- **You Don't Have To Worry About Making the Cards and Taking Care Of Wrist Bands**

Let me touch on the speed of our No-Huddle offense.

THE SPEEDS OF OUR NO-HUDDLE

- **Let's Go Fast**
- **Check With Me**
- **Slow Down**
- **How Do We Signal The Plays?**

The first point is to go fast. That is what we did all year long. We tried to go as quick as we could. We came to the line of scrimmage and we were gone.

This is how we signaled in the plays this year. I had three coaches standing in one area. In that group was our Receiver Coach, Running Backs Coach and me. I always gave the signal for the formation. I wanted to set the formation as quick as I could. We are a big 3 X 1 alignment team, or trips team. We ran some 2 X 2 sets.

When the ball is on the left hash mark, if we did not give a signal the players knew to go to a 3 X 1 formation. We had trips to the field and one receiver to the left.

If the ball was in the middle of the field we were in our 2 X 2 formation. If we are on the right hash mark we are going trips to the field side, and one receiver to the backside.

We may change that up from week to week. We like to use our tight end in the formation because some of the teams we play do not know how to cover the tight end. We can call Liz and we end up with a tight end, and two flankers outside of the end. The point is this. The kids know the formations we are going to be lined up in by the position of the ball in every part of the field. So if you want to change it, you can change it real quick.

We do need to work on slowing the pace with our offense. We need to look at the clock and kill more time before we snap the ball.

In the state of Indiana we can start practice as soon as school is out for the summer. We can practice in June. This past year we practiced two days a week in June. At the end of June we have a mandatory week off. So we had three weeks in June with two days a week practices. We had most of our offense in the system before July practice started.

We had six running plays and six passing plays in our offense before we started July practice. When we started out we wanted to be an Inside Zone team. We were not very good at running that play so we got rid of the zone play. Our signal for the Inside Zone play was for me to rub my fat belly. I thought that was going to be our "go to" play. If I rubbed my belly with my right hand it would be the Inside Zone to the right side. If I used the left hand it was the Inside Zone Left. The play just did not work out for us.

Our sweep play signal was as if you were sweeping with the old fashion broom in your hand. We could signal right or left on the plays. We added those two plays in our offense.

Our Quarterback Counter was probably our best play. Our counter was right and then left. I went to our faculty to get some help calling the plays. I went to see the teacher that worked with kids that could not speak and that used sign language to communicate. I asked the teacher what

the sign was for "Q." She went over all of the signals with me and we were able to come up with a system to assist us in calling plays. When I gave the deaf sign for "Q" our quarterback knew it was a run play for him.

We have plays we like to run at the 1-technique and plays we like to run at the 3-technique. We give a double signal when we call the plays. Our running back is looking at the 1 and 3 holes to see who is in those positions. The quarterback was coached to run the plays to the 1 or 3 techniques based on what we gave him that week.

We ran the Wrap play to the 1 hole, and we ran the Trap play to the 3 techniques hole. We ran the Quarterback Read play as well. So by using double signals we could run the plays we wanted to run. We could run the Counter and Sweep plays as we progressed in our signal calls.

WHY IS TRIPS OUR # 1 FORMATION?

- **Defense has to adjust to it**
- **Let's us attack every part of the field**
- **Gives us options running and passing**
- **We understand what we want and where to attack**
  - Sweep
  - Q Counter
  - Wraps
  - Jailbreak and bubble
  - Backside slant and rb swing
  - All-go

We were in Trips Formation close to 75 percent of the time last year. I am a big 3 X 1 coach. My dad coached for many years and he ran the I-Formation offense. He always ran trips with the I-Formation. I have always been a 3 X 1 coach since those days watching my dad teams play.

I feel the defense must adjust against the trips set. If the defense does not adjust to our trips set, that is fine. We have our jailbreak plays for out outside guys. We have our quick screens to the middle guy. Also, we have the bubble screens to the number 2 inside player. We can run the inside game with the tailback and quarterback. On the backside we run the slant play and the tailback runs the swing pass route. Our best pass plays are out of the trips formation look.

What coverage can we expect against our Trips Formation? We are going to see cover-3. They roll the strong safety down in the box. We have plays that we like to run against this defense. I am not saying we have all the answers against this adjustment but we have been successful against it.

One thing that is different in our trips set is the fact the running back is lined up on the opposite side of the three receivers. He is opposite the trips about 75 percent of the time. If we call REO it is our Trips to the right side. (Diagram #1)

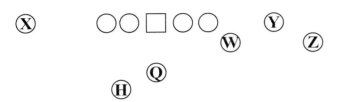

Diagram #1. Reo – Trips Right

If we want to run Trips to the left side we call Leo. (Diagram #2) It is just the opposite of Reo.

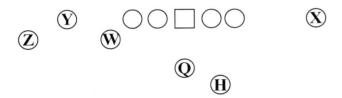

Diagram #2. Leo – Trips Left

The player in our offense that is our guy is the Wing man. He is not necessarily the player that is going to catch the ball, but he is the man that makes the plays work. The player in this position this past year was our defensive coordinators son. He is about 5'10" and 190 pounds. He runs a 5.2 forty.

He can catch the ball and he is a blocker. He is like a fullback and would be an H-back in the Pro set. He caught 9 bubble passes because he was so wide open in several games. He catches the pass and runs 20 yards downfield for a nice play.

He did everything we asked. He was our guy. He could have called the offense if something ever happened to me. He was the player that came to me to tell me what the defense was doing and what we needed to do. He was a tremendous player and he was our guy.

He has to be a good blocker. We want movement when we run our sweep play. We pull our guard outside to block the corner. (Diagram #3)

We block down on everyone else. If we can, we pull the offside guard and have him try to get in the alley and pick up anything that shows. The wing has to block down on the end. The tailback gets the ball and he tries to get outside as fast as he can.

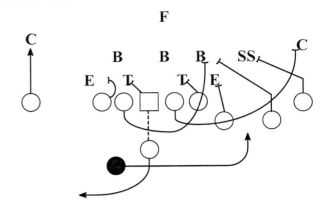

Diagram #3. Sweep Play

In every game we called the sweep as the first, second, or third play on the first series. This gets the defense on the move against this play. They see the tailback go wide on the sweep and are aware they must get outside to make the play. That is what we want them to do.

Our quarterback ran for 1800 yards this year. He threw the ball for 2000 yards. In the last two years our quarterback and running back have rushed for over 1000 yards each. I am going to show you our best play next.

It is our Quarterback Counter Play. Our wingback pulls and blocks on the linebacker either inside or outside. (Diagram #4) The left tackle comes inside and checks the 3-technique tackle and comes off on the middle linebacker. The center steps to the tackle and comes off on the linebacker on the backside.

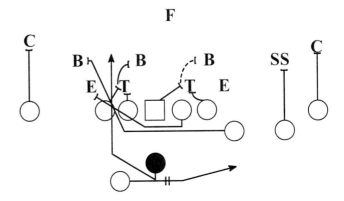

Diagram #4. Quarterback Counter

We try to cut the tackle off with our right tackle if possible. We fake the sweep play and the quarterback keeps the ball and runs behind the wingback pulling across the formation. This is where our quarterback made a lot of his yardage.

The Wrap Play was very simple. (Diagram #5) We pulled the guard to block the front side linebacker. It is a downhill run for the running back. Teams have to play our sweep play first. If the defense moves their linebacker too far over to stop the sweep, we are going to run the 2-counter. The Wrap Play gave us a play up the middle.

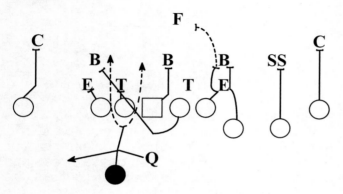

Diagram #5. Wrap

We are covering all areas of the field on three running plays. We run the sweep, counter, and wrap plays.

Real quick I want to talk about the passing game. The first pass I want to talk about is our Jailbreak Screen. (Diagram #6) This was our best play. Our Z-back is our fastest man. He is off the line of scrimmage. If he came in motion we would end up in a two-backs set. We can run the Jet Sweep with the Z-back. We can do a lot of different things with him. Our second best receiver is the X-end on the split end side.

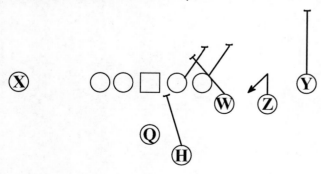

Diagram #6. Jailbreak Screen Pass

A lot of teams do not want to send their onside tackle down the field on the Jailbreak Screen. They want to run the end up the field and he never gets in the play. We do not teach that. We have five guys that are going to block someone.

We are throwing on our 5-step drop action. We want the Z-back to push off and start up field. He comes back and gets in the alley. The guard and tackle can lead the play downfield. The wingback seals inside. The center is cutting off on the backside.

We want to teach the wingback to catch the ball first and then run downfield. We do not want the receiver dancing around and trying to outrun everyone. We want him to pick up the blockers in front of him and run the ball down field.

Remember this: **<u>FTS - Feed The Stud!</u>** I got that from a former coach at Ohio State. Find a guy that can play football, and whatever you do, give the ball to the stud.

I will be here for the entire weekend. If you have questions I will be glad to talk with you.

Thank You!

Jason Hiser

Utilizing the 2-Technique in a 4-Man Front Defense

Pleasure Ridge Park High School, Kentucky

Thank you for coming to listen to a defensive coach. I am going to talk about our 2-technique in a 4-man front.

WHY USE 2-TECHNIQUES

- **Direct Attack "Hit The Man In Front Of You!"**
- **Center Mass On The Guard**
- **Mobility**
- **Create Confusion**
- **Makes The One Man Block More Complex**

We like the 2-technique because we can hit the man straight ahead of us. The kids like it as well. They like being head up on the guard. I feel like the best chance to get good center mass on the guard is with a 2-technique. We have put kids in a 1-technique and a 3-technique. The first thing the kids want to do is to swim over the guards to get into the backfield and they overrun the ball carrier. We tell our defensive tackles their job is to block the guards and keep them off the linebackers. The 2-technique provides us with some mobility. We line up head up but we can slant strong, slant weak, or play base.

It helps create some confusion to the offensive line. I know offensive linemen have rules to follow but they still have questions in their mind if the defender is going to slant to the A-gap or slant to the B-gap. It also makes the one man block on the tackle more complex.

Some of this may be redundant to some of you who are already defensive coordinators but for those of you who hope to become coordinators or are new to the concept, this is how we number our gaps and techniques. (Diagram #1)

Our players at PRP do a great job of learning our numbering systems and our techniques including our linebacker techniques. Our Shade is to the strong side of the center. Shadow is to the weak side. The 1-technique is on the inside eye of the guard. The 2-technique is heads up

the guard, and the 3-technique is outside of the guard. The 4i is inside eye of the tackle. Not sure why it is that way but that is the way we have used it over the years. It is how I was taught and I brought it with me to PRP. The 4-technique is head up on the tackle and the 5-technique is outside of the tackle. You can see the 6, 7, and 9-techniques. The 6-technique is head up on the tight end.

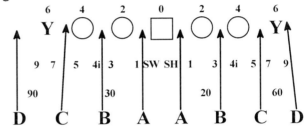

Diagram #1. GAP Numbering System

You can also see how we number the linebacker techniques. A 20-technique is head up on the guard. We just added the zero at the end on the linebacker calls.

Why is this important to us? If we see something in a game where we need to make an adjustment, we are able to communicate very easily and can make the adjustment very quickly. When your players know these techniques, it is so much easier to coach on the fly. If we tell a kid to go from a 4-technique to a 4i, we do not have to draw it up for him, he already knows where to line up.

On the offensive side of the ball, we number the techniques the same way. It is easier for them as well. An offensive lineman can come over to the bench and tell you what they are seeing and you know exactly where the man is. We are all on the same page. I know some coaches have a 2i technique, which we call a 1-technique.

It is important whenever you have a coaching change to make sure you communicate your system so everyone is on the same page and you do not create confusion with your players. Every player on our football team can label the players and their corresponding gaps including the linebacker techniques.

In the end it is still all about personnel. I know there are some defenses that utilize a 3-technique or a 1-technique and do an outstanding job. In my experience, we have not been successful using it. One reason for it in the past couple of years is because we have had to move a player from a slot receiver position to play Will linebacker. We have used a backup wide receiver playing as our inside linebacker. If we line up in a 1-technique type of look, the Will linebacker gets waylaid by the fullback. (Diagram #2)

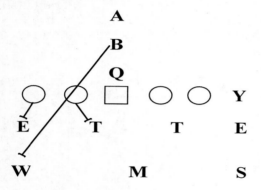

Diagram #2. 1-Technique Tackle

The same thing can happen to the Mike linebacker if the center blocks down on the tackle and the fullback blocks the Mike. An average offensive lineman with good feet can work his hips on the 1-technique easier than he can on a 2-technique. A lot of the teams on our schedule like to attack the B-gap on a weak side Iso play or on the strong side. I feel more comfortable in a 2-technique.

This helps us make the B-gap as narrow as possible. I want the running back to re-route in some form or fashion while in the backfield. I do not want him to have a clear window on the linebacker. We have put the tackle in a 3-technique in the past and they like to shoot the B-gap. We have had a very hard time getting them to center their mass on the guard. When we put them in a 2-technique, they do a much better job.

Let me talk about the guard and tackle combo block. When we have used a 3-technique, the offensive guards usually do a pretty good job of ripping underneath with their outside arm and coming off to the Mike linebacker. Nine times out of ten the 3-technique tackle is a B-gap player. It

gives the offensive tackle a free shot because he knows he is responsible for blocking down on the defensive tackle on the power play, for example.

What we ask our 2-technique player to do is to center their mass in the guard's chest. (Diagram #3) Do not let the guard rip under to the Mike. The 2-technique eliminates the "no brainer" down block from the offensive tackle. Our goal is to get a two-for-one. The tackle has to think for a split second about the tackle coming into the B-gap. We want to try to occupy the guard and tackle simultaneously, just long enough for the Mike linebacker to scrape over the top uncontested. We have done a pretty good job of doing it recently.

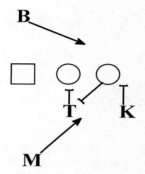

Diagram #3. Guard/Tackle Combo on a 2-Technique

This is how we coach the base technique of our defensive tackle.

BASE TECHNIQUE

- **Rise Up In Power Clean Type Form**
- **Center Mass Drill - Punch In The Guard's Chest**
- **Steer The Chest Of The Guard**
- **If His Right Side Shows / Influence the 2-Technique's Left Shoulder / Show Influence and Vice Versa.**

The first thing a defensive tackle wants to do when coming out of a three point stance is to stand up, and then attack the guard. We want them to come from the bottom up in a power clean type of movement. We drill punch the guard in the chest. We want to steer the chest of the guard. If he starts to swing his hips to turn us, we want to fight opposite and then rip through.

This is what our Base 62 and what we call "UK" defense looks like. "UK" means cover-2. It consists of two letters and it is a two deep look. (Diagram #4)

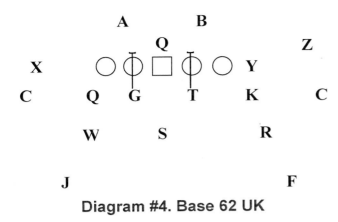

Diagram #4. Base 62 UK

The two tackles are in 2-techniques. We call our weak side 2-technique the guard. The strong side 2-technique is called the tackle. It helps us when we have twists or stunts if we have a designated strong side player and a designated weak side player. The Will is lined up in a 50-technique, our Sam is in a double zero technique. We designate the outside linebacker as Raven. Jack is the half safety who also plays some linebacker for us. We call the free safety Falcon.

When our 2-technique players get a call we want them to get center mass with one yard of penetration before they rip to the call side. When I draw up the plays for our players, I used to put arrows to indicate where they were to flow. The kids thought they were to shoot through the gap and penetrate deep into the backfield. Now I put a flat line, almost like a block, which indicates I want them to sit in the gap at one yard deep. I want to see them one yard deep in their gap in a linebacker stance with their feet and shoulders square to the line of scrimmage.

We harp on keeping their shoulder square throughout practice. This is probably the biggest point of emphasis we had throughout the year. It is not a slant for us. We do use the slant technique but we call it "62 Slant." If we call 62 Strong, we want one yard of penetration and to drive the guard into the backfield first, then rip to the strong side.

This is what it would look like if we called 62 Strong with strong flow. (Diagram #5) This shows flow and gap responsibility for an outside power play to the strong side. In cover-2 we know the cornerbacks have overall outside contain but our goal on sweeps is for the corner to pinch the outside hip of the runner. We want the Raven to pinch the inside hip of the runner. When we run our drills in practice, we tell them to put the cross

hairs on the runner's hips. That is where we want them to stay so they do not over pursue.

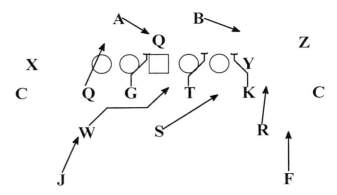

Diagram #5. 62 Strong UK - Strong Flow

The Sam linebacker is spilling over the top. The Will linebacker scrapes up to check the strong side A-gap. The Jack and Falcon have important tasks in cover-2. We are going to let the offense go 1, 2, and 3, off of the ball. Our eyes are to the backfield the whole time. In this case, Jack will wait for 1, 2, 3, and then look to fill the backside B-gap. It is tough to get high school defensive backs to do that all of the time but we worked hard on it during the season and got better at it.

If we call 62 Strong with weak flow the Jack is coming up in the alley. The corner is on the outside hip of the runner and the Will linebacker is on the inside hip of the runner. The Jack is in the alley straight up.

This is what it looks like from a 62 Weak with strong flow. (Diagram #6)

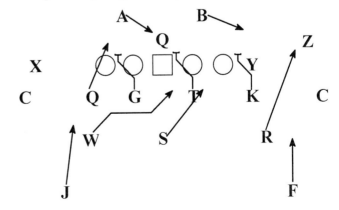

Diagram #6. 62 Weak UK Strong Flow

We ran two pass blitzes from the 62 flow this year. The first was Strangle where the defensive linemen angle movement is to the strong side and the blitz comes from the weak side. (Diagram #7)

We want the linemen to get one gap over and to the inside of the next offensive lineman.

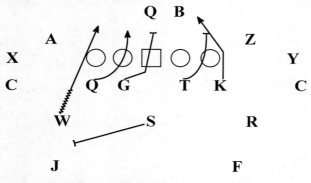

Diagram #7. 62 Strangle UK

We try to split the difference with the outside linebacker depending on who we are playing. The defensive lineman on the end opposite of the blitz has to know to rush at an angle expecting the quarterback to bail out to his side. The worst thing that can happen is to have a beautiful blitz to force the quarterback to scramble and then we lose contain away from the blitz side.

You will notice an arrow on the blitzing linebacker and the Quick end. They have full reign on their stunts. The two tackles still have to sit after one yard of penetration. We tell them they will get their sack when the quarterback moves up into the pocket trying to get away from the pressure off the edges.

This is a down and distance type of call. We are letting the Sam linebacker take a quick bail. He is trying to wall off the inside and get a re-route.

Wrangle means the defensive linemen are taking an angle movement to the weak side and the blitz is coming from the strong side. (Diagram #8) We can run this from our cover-3 look as well.

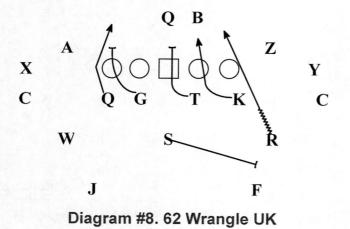

Diagram #8. 62 Wrangle UK

We have the same types of angles and responsibilities for the four linemen and the blitzing linebacker. I prefer to run it out of our "LSU" which means cover-3. Notice there are three letters for cover-3. That is how our kids remember it so it has stuck with them. (Diagram # 9)

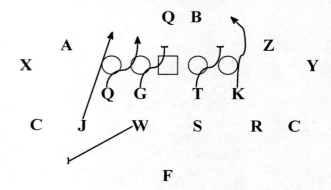

Diagram #9. 62 Strangle from LSU

I do not really like to bounce around from cover-2 to cover-3. Our kids have done a good job of learning both concepts however I would like to get to the point where we can run one of them very well, and leave the other one out.

Our kids know when we run the Strangle from 62 LSU, the Jack or weak side linebacker is coming on the blitz. Will does not have as far to go as Sam does to wall off the number 2 receiver. If it is third down and say 12, he may even cheat over to a 40-technique by the time the ball is snapped. Either one has to wall off the number 2 receiver but they have to keep their eyes on number one.

As he re-routes number 2, if number 1 is sitting in the flat for a bubble pass, he gets rid of number 2 and takes on number 1. If number 1 is not in the flat or is going vertical, he has to go vertical. Teams like to go four verticals if you run a lot of cover-3.

We run a couple of twisting stunts with our 3-techniques. If we call Texas, the tackle goes first. If we call Georgia, the guard goes first. You have to have the right personnel to run these twist. Some guys do a great job with the twist and with some guys you are just wasting your time.

We like to have some run blitzes out of 62 Strong or 62 Weak in our LSU or cover-3 look. We run these against two or more back sets. If there is only one back such as a 2 by 2 set, we call the blitz off. This is what it looks like. (Diagram #10)

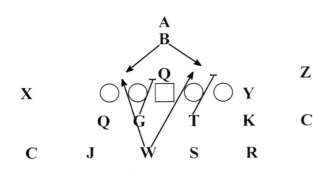

Diagram #10. 62 Strong LSU

We have been able to do this through hard work and learning our techniques. We are not as worried about statistics as much as we are about getting to the football.

If you guys need anything, let me know. I love to talk football. Thank you for coming.

The Will linebacker is reading the B-back or fullback and blitzing the gap to the side the fullback is going. This has been a good run blitz for us because it takes away the hesitation from the Will. The two tackles are slanting to their gaps to the strong side. If we run it as 62 Weak LSU, the Sam is going to blitz. Again he is reading the fullback. The backside guys have to be ready for a cutback if they run a counter.

From time to time we run 62-X-LSU. This time the 2-techniques take the B-gaps and the Will and Sam linebackers cross and blitz the A-gaps.

If a team goes unbalanced, we count the third man down on the line of scrimmage and he becomes the center for our alignment. If we run 62- Strong-LSU versus an unbalanced look we would line up like this. (Diagram #11)

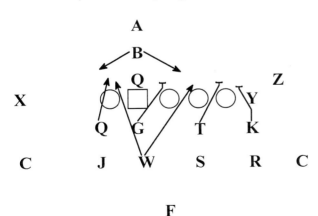

Diagram #11. 62 Strong LSU vs. Unbalanced

We put a big emphasis on scoring on defense. We scored on defense in seven of our games with nine defensive touchdowns. We constantly harp on getting to the football in an angry mood.

John Hodge

Basic 4-4 Defensive Adjustments and Stunts

Bourbon County High School, Kentucky

It is a privilege to be here. I cannot begin to tell you how humbled I am to speak at this clinic. Ever since the day Coach Browning called and asked me to speak, I have had two reoccurring nightmares. The first nightmare is at the beginning of the introduction after I am introduced. I keep looking up and there isn't anybody here in the lecture room. Thank goodness that has not occurred. Just in case, I did make a couple of my assistants come so I would not be the only one in the room.

The second reoccurring nightmare I have is I looking up and realizing that everyone in this room knows more football than I do. When I look up today, it looks like that nightmare has come true. Never the less, hopefully I can give you something you can take back home to make your players a better football team.

I spent ten years as an assistant coach at Boyle County High School. I was fortunate enough to have coached for three fantastic head football coaches at Boyle County and I learned a lot of football under Larry French, Chris Pardue and Chuck Smith.

I was able to bring two assistant coaches with me from Boyle County to Bourbon County High School. They have done a fantastic job along with the other assistants and their hard work is the reason for our success this year. Also, having several good players helps along the way as always.

We had a successful year and a lot of it had to do with our defense. We made it to the semifinals in the state playoffs this year and we played against a very good Belfry team who beat us pretty good. Our record was 13-1. It was the most wins for a single season in school history. It was the first district championship in school history and our first playoff win since 1998. We averaged giving up less than 100 yards rushing and less than 14 points per game. Our two top tacklers had over 140 tackles each.

When we got to Bourbon County we had a clean slate. We could run whatever we wanted to. In the end we decided on the 4-4 defense.

WHY THE 4-4? – IT JUST FITS!

- **Fits our personnel**
  - Kids in our program allow us to run our scheme
- **Fits our defensive philosophy**
  - Must first and foremost stop the run
  - Belief in fundamentals and team first approach
- **Fits overall philosophy on winning games**
  - Defense wins championships
  - Force the opposing team to do what it does not want to do

When we took over last February we had to look at the types of kids we had in our program. We had to determine their strengths and weaknesses and what we could do with them to be successful. The first thing that stood out to us was there were not very many big kids. We did not have any big strapping kids who could line up in a 0 technique and demand a double team every single play. We had to come up with a scheme that allowed us to draw some double teams so our linebackers could make plays.

The second thing the 4-4 does for us is it fits our defensive philosophy. We believe you must stop the run first. This is our number one concern when we come out to practice on defensive days. Our kids hear us tell them over and over and it really is a focus. All of our drills are set up to stop the run first. We believe if we can stop the run, we can dictate the situation to some degree.

The 4-4 defense forces us to be fundamentally sound. I know there are coaches who believe in shooting gaps and blitzing and it works for them. We believe in being fundamentally sound and playing great technique and focusing on a team defense approach. Part of the team approach is convincing the defensive linemen the best thing for the team is for them to get double teamed. It can be hard to teach at first but our kids slowly picked up on it and our early success helped.

Lastly, the 4-4 fits our overall philosophy on winning games. We believe defense wins championships and we believe in forcing the opponent in doing what it does not want to do. I think the best play in football is the dive play. If you can hand the ball off for a four yard gain why would you do anything else? If we can stop the dive and stop you from running the ball, to where you have to throw the ball about 30 to 40 times a game, we feel good about that.

We believe good defense starts with technique. Every day we work on techniques. In our individual periods we spend a lot of time to emphasize stepping with the correct foot, making sure our hand placement is correct, and reviewing blocking schemes we may see next week.

We also talk about getting 11 hats on the football. When you watch film on us you will notice we have 11 gold hats around the football. We want to make sure the quarterback, running back, or wide receiver is getting hit 11 times. We believe if we can hit those guys 11 times every time they carry the ball, they are not going to be running the ball as hard in the fourth quarter as they did in the first quarter.

We want to swarm to the ball. When we watch film with the kids we make it a point to count all 11 players in the picture frame at the tackle. They may not be in on the tackle, but they better be in the picture frame. If they are not in the picture we call that a loaf.

The 4-4 defense forces you to make sure you put your best players in a position to make plays. If you have great football players you can blitz and play games on defense but we do not have great players. We have to do a great job as coaches in teaching them to get in position to make plays. Are they always going to make big plays? No! They are just high school kids and some of them just make mistakes. We just have to give them the best chance to be in a position to make plays. How do you do that? It goes back to teaching technique. It goes back to teaching them how to get off blocks. It goes back to making sure there are not any false steps. It goes back to teaching and implementing our keys.

We spend the entire spring and most of the summer focused on getting 11 hats to the foot-

ball and on fundamentals. We do not do a lot of team defense in the spring. If you saw our spring game you could tell that was true. We focus on individual positions and may do some 7-on-7 but we do not go full team. Our focus is coaching our players up each and every day. This takes a lot of time and effort by our coaching staff but we believe that is the way you do it. In order to play this defense, you have to be fanatic in your fundamentals. Each player has to do a fantastic job in playing their role in the defense.

We teach fundamentals over plays. What I mean by that is when we go to team defense, we are not focusing as much on the plays the offense is running as we are on our own fundamentals. We believe if we are fundamentally sound it does not matter what plays are run against us. That is not to say we do not go over the plays you run, especially if it is something we have not seen before. We really focus on what we can control more than things we cannot control.

If you down block us, our defensive line is going to know what to do and how to handle it. Our defensive backs are going to know what to do if you are on the line or off the line, it does not matter what play it actually is. Our play is based on the fundamentals we teach. Our entire defensive practice is based around fundamentals.

We do not go team until the very end of practice. We may only run 15 plays of team defense on a defensive practice day. At the same time, our kids have seen every blocking scheme and every pass route they are going to face while in their individual groups, inside drills, or 7-on-7. We try to show how everything fits together when we finally go to our team period.

We do not ever want to see anybody lying on the ground. When we are practicing 7-on -7 we are coaching them to get to the football. If we are running the inside drill, we are teaching them to get to the football. Whatever drill we are doing, we are making sure we are coaching them to get to the football. It is a coaching point we stress in every drill every day. It isn't just something we coach one day a week.

There is not a day that goes by in spring and summer practices where we don't have a pursuit drill. We do not do pursuit drills necessarily like everybody else does pursuit drills. We do use it as part of our conditioning. One of the other things we focus on when we are watching film with our kids is loafs. We do not want a loaf. As you know, teenagers always want to know why and ask a lot of questions. We try to define everything we can so we define what a loaf is.

WHAT IS A LOAF?

- **Change Of Speed**
- **Not Turning And Going To The Ball**
- **Getting Passed By Another Player**
- **Laying On The Ground**
- **Turning Down A Hit**

A loaf is a change of speed. One thing that absolutely drives me nuts, whether it is defensively, offensively, or on special teams, no matter what you are doing, I hate change of speeds. I believe if you are going full speed, you cannot go any faster. There is no any reason why we should not go full speed. We watch for change of speed which indicates we were loafing.

We watch our linebackers and defensive backs to make sure they are turning and running to the ball. When the quarterback releases the football, we want people turning and running. Our defensive line is taught to turn and run to the football. They may not get to where the ball is thrown but we have to try to get everybody to the football. We implement this into our pursuit drills as well. Our guys compete against each other to get to the football. They do not want to hear in a film session that someone passed them up getting to the football. They do not want to get called out on a loaf. It creates competition.

If you are lying on the ground, you better need someone to come out to check on you. We never want to turn down a hit. If you have a chance to hit somebody you better take advantage of it. We believe we must be the most physical team. We want to hit people early and often.

We line up in a 1 and a 3-technique up front. We are in a 5 and a 6-technique with our defensive ends. We put our inside linebackers on the outside eye of the offensive guards. Depending on the look you give us, will determine the placement of our outside linebackers. Normally we line up on the outside shade of the tight end or ghost tight end if there is not an end. Our linebackers heels are at four and one half yards deep and we are trying to play downhill all the time. Our defense is designed to allow the linebackers to make a lot of plays.

This is our base 4-4 defensive alignment. (Diagram #1)

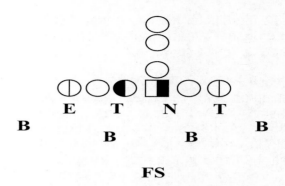

Diagram #1. 4-4 Base Alignment

Pre-snap reads are important to us. Every time the offense breaks the huddle or even against a no-huddle team, we look at these specific things.

PRE-SNAP AWARENESS

- **Formation/Backfield Set**
- **Down And Distance**
- **Field Position/Hash**
- **Stance**
- **Assignment**

We want to determine what formation the offense is in so we can get lined up properly. There are some offensive teams if you do not line up right are going to score a hundred points against you. Poor alignment can get you beat. Recognition starts in practice and we have specific recognition and alignment periods in our practices. We want to know what your backfield set is on each formation.

Down and distance is the next area of concern. Nothing is more frustrating than having a third down and eight and your defensive back lines up at seven yards, and at the snap of the ball he backs up four steps. Then he allows the receiver to catch the ball in front of him for a nine yard gain. Knowing the down and distance helps us determine what the offense is trying to do.

Field position and hash alignment have a lot to do with our defensive alignment. Offensive coaches do a great job with spacing. Formations have a lot to do with spacing but field position also comes into play. Through film study we may find a team likes to do certain things from specific field situations.

I do not believe you can play football standing straight up. Our defensive coaches get after our linebackers all the time about being in a proper stance. Sometimes a good stance is specific to a specific kid. We do not try to force a kid into a stance that is completely uncomfortable. We do want a fundamentally sound position so they can step and move efficiently in the direction they need to go. We want them ready to play.

The assignment part of it comes in the week of practice leading up to the game. It should become second nature to them by the time game day arrives. Each player should know beyond a shadow of a doubt what their assignment is according to the way the offense lines up. They should know what gap they are responsible for and should be running to the football trying to ruin some ones day.

Let me cover adjustments to the 4-4 we use.

FRONT ADJUSTMENTS

- **G-Technique**
- **7-Techniques**
- **Wide Technique (3 techniques)**
- **Odd Technique (3-4)**
- **Slant strong/weak**
- **Various schemes based upon opponent**

Our G-technique is where we line up our two inside guys in 2-techniques. Whenever we make adjustments to our base 4-4 defense, we do not want our fundamentals to change. We play it the exact same way. If the offense down blocks, we are squeezing and trying to get after the ball. If our fundamentals do change, we have to make sure we thoroughly cover these changes in practice. We still have to be fundamentally sound with what we do within the scheme.

Sometimes we line up in a 7-technique trying to take away what the offense does best. We might even combine some of these adjustments depending on what the offense is trying to do.

We have a wide technique where we line up in 3-techniques by our inside guys. If you are trying to blow us off the ball off tackle we might get into our 3-techniques and put a lot of pressure on your inside guys. We obviously have to look for the fullback trap if we line up this way. If they pull a guard, we want to get in his hip pocket and make a play. Our technique does not change. We still want to be stepping with our inside foot up front. At times we check to a 3-4 look with three down linemen and four linebackers.

We have our slant package where we can slant strong and weak based on tendencies the

offense may have. This goes back to what we see in film study for the upcoming week.

Each week we have various schemes based on what we see our opponents have previously shown in earlier games. We try to come up with some type of new wrinkle to give us some type of advantage. We especially like to give the offensive line a look they have not seen before and have not prepared for.

LINEBACKER ADJUSTMENTS

- **Walk**
- **Slide**
- **Overload**
- **Odd**
- **40**

Our walk adjustment is where we walk up our linebackers to look like defensive ends. In our slide adjustment we give more of a 4-3 defensive look. In our overload we are bringing some type of run blitz or pass blitz. We might be trying to overload one side or we might try to overload one player.

In our odd adjustment we check to a 3-4 look. We do not like to substitute much so we like to drop a lineman back to become a linebacker as long as we have somebody who can do it. This gives us our 3 man front. One of our inside linebackers will bounce out into the secondary.

Our 40 is a straight 4-3. We bring in a strong safety to back us up.

SECONDARY COVERAGE'S

- **Base: mostly play Cover 3, or Cover 1**
- **Odd fronts-various coverage's**
  - Cover 1/3/4/6
  - Disguise and confuse while making sure we are still in position to make plays

If we are in our base 4-4 defense we are going to play cover-3 or cover-1. If we are playing cover-1 we are feeling really good about life. We feel as if we can cover you and we are going to bring some pressure. We are not going to let the quarterback sit back there and complete passes. We are going to get some pressure on him.

In our odd man fronts, we try to vary the coverage's more. We run a variety of coverage's including cover-4 which is quarter's coverage and cover-6 which is quarter, quarter, and half coverage. When adjusting for trips, we like to use our cover-6 look.

The big thing is we try to disguise and confuse the quarterback but we still have to be sound and make sure we are in position to make plays. When I was the receivers coach at Boyle County I used to love when the defensive secondary would bounce around trying to disguise the coverage's. When the ball was snapped they were out of position more time than not and we would knock the goal post down.

We specifically work in practice on disguising with a purpose. We want to have a good reason for showing something because in the end, we have to still put our kids in the best position to make plays. We want to make sure they are in that position at the snap of the ball. Our primary focus is still stopping the run.

STUNTS AND BLITZES

- **Dictate the situation, allowing us to feel more comfortable with blitzing**
- **Finding mismatches through film**
  - **Our personnel vs. yours**
- **Use zone blitzes, which necessitates the need to get there fast, due to people being open**
- **Use overload blitzes**
  - **More defenders than you have protectors**
  - **Singling out one protector, forcing him to make a decision**

We try to dictate the situation all game long. We feel like if we can dictate the situation we feel comfortable in blitzing. I am not a big blitz guy because it makes me nervous. We try to find mismatches through film study. It is just our people versus your people. We all have the player we try to hide. We try to find him on your team. If we find him, we may do a little more blitzing than we normally would.

We use a lot of zone blitzes because we are trying to get to the quarterback very fast. We may overload your offense. We can bring more people to one side than you have available blockers. When we blitz, we are going to leave some openings. Offensive coaches today are good and they are going to find the opening. Unless we can get to the quarterback before he finds the opening, they are going to hurt you. From our scouting report we may try to single out one of

your weak pass protectors and try to make him have a bad night.

ADJUSTMENT TO AN ODD FRONT

- **Adjusting the 4-4 to an odd front defense**
- **Allows us to be more versatile**
- **Makes offense prepare more**
- **Allows for more coverage's and disguises**
- **Allows for more blitz options**
- **Similar technique taught**

We like to think we are a pretty simple base 4-4 defense. Making adjustments to an odd front is where we get creative. The odd front gives our opponent a different look to prepare for and allows us to be more versatile. If you play against us, this is where we try to do more as far as coverages and disguises. We are going to try to make you more nervous by walking linebackers up to the line of scrimmage.

The odd front allows us to have more blitz options. If we are in our odd front, it is likely we are bringing a defender. We try to make you make decisions that you normally do not have to make. Our kids love going to this front because it isn't the same old stuff we normally run. This is where we try to have a little bit of fun but the big key is it is modified by still using the same techniques we have already taught our players.

Teach the same techniques over and over again so they get better at them. At least for our front seven or eight we want them to do the same types of things each and every time the ball is snapped.

I think we have a great job even though we all complain about it sometimes. Being able to influence young people and to lead teenagers in the right direction is an awesome responsibility. I read something by John Maxwell earlier this week that I found interesting. He said, "**To lead is to influence. To influence is to add value to a person's life.**" That is what we do as coaches.

Thanks again for allowing me to visit with you. I try to learn something new about coaching football each day.

Good luck next season.

Blair Hubbard

Rocket Sweep From The Shotgun

Faith Christian High School, Colorado

What I want to do today is share some of my thoughts on the Rocket Sweep. Some schools around the country have adapted our flavor of the hybrid wing-T. That is especially true with the Rocket Sweep from the shotgun set. With that play we want to get the defense to flow to the play. We want to take advantage of that flow and run something counter to it.

I am going to break down the positions in the offense and get into the basics of the play. That way you will get a taste of what we do. The jet sweep or fly sweep has become very popular with spread offenses. We transitioned a few years ago to running the Rocket Sweep. When we were under the center, I loved what the Rocket did to defenses and how it got them to rotate. We finally transitioned the play into a shotgun set.

We had some running quarterbacks that came into our program. However, I did not want to get into the total option game. We took the Rocket Sweep and the rest of our wing-T offense and got into the shotgun set. In the Rocket Sweep, the quarterback uses a chest pass to the sweep runner instead of handing him the ball.

CASE FOR THE GUN-ROCKET OVER THE GUN-FLY / JET

- **It's simply faster than the fly / jet-sweep**
- **To perimeter-over 3 seasons**
- **Gun-fly 1.8 sec**
- **Gun-Rocket 1.4 sec**

We charted this over the course of three years and this is what we found. We charted high school teams, small college teams, and BCS teams. We consider the perimeter to be the outside edge of the tight end. We timed the jet or fly sweep. From the snap of the ball until it reaches the perimeter was 1.8 seconds. With the Rocket Sweep, you can get the ball to the perimeter in 1.4 seconds. Anything that gets you there .4 of a second faster, gives you an advantage.

HOW DOES THIS HAPPEN?

- **Proximity of ball carrier to the quarterback**
- **When the snap reaches the quarterback's hands**
- **Easier to handle at full speed**
- **Catch vs. hand-off**
- **Easier to recover from a bad snap**
- **No full speed mesh-point to time-up**
- **No new skill for ball carrier to learn**
- **Do not have to teach wide receiver handoff**
- **Enhances your misdirection game**
- **Forces the defense to decide faster**
- **Forces defenses to move pre-snap or play unsound defense**

If you run the fly sweep, when the ball hits the quarterback's hands, the sweeper is two to three steps opposite where the ball is going. On the Rocket Sweep, when the ball hits the quarterback's hands, the sweeper will be at worse behind the quarterback and at best, two to three steps past the quarterback. On the jet sweep, the quarterback catches the ball and hands the ball to the sweeper. On the Rocket Sweep, the quarterback catches the ball and tosses it to the sweeper. The catch is easier than a handoff.

If you run the fly sweep, there has to be a timed mesh area between the quarterback and ball carrier. You must spend time on the mesh area. On the Rocket Sweep, there is no mesh and we make the exchange at full speed. It is easier to recover from a bad snap. If the snap to the quarterback is high, he has to catch the ball, bring it down to the mesh area, and hope the timing is still there. You do not have that problem with the Rocket Sweep.

There are no new skills for the running backs to learn. It is a catch rather than a handoff. You do not need to teach a wide receiver to take a handoff. If you were handing the ball to the wide receiver, you would have to teach him how to take the handoff. On this play, he does what he does all day long. He catches the ball.

When we say it enhances the misdirection game, the enhancement comes in the time factor. The defense can see the ball but since it goes so fast, they must pursue faster than normally. Defenses have to run right away. If they do not we will beat them to the outside. They have to make the decision to move and run to the ball. It forces the defense to show their hand. It gives the quarterback a good pre-snap read. If they do not they will end up in an unsound defense.

The speed of the Rocket Sweep gets us to the edge immediately. If you have some speed in your program, you can do a good job with the Rocket Sweep. On this play, the defense has a tendency to over pursue the football. When they do that, we start to run the complimentary plays underneath them. Anything we run off tackle we tell our backs to look for the cut back. When teams setup to stop the Rocket Sweep we hurt them with inside traps and cutback plays.

In the play-action passing game we try to suck the safeties up with the Rocket motion and hit them over the top with the big play. If we run the Rocket motion away from the trips set, the defense has to leave enough defenders to that side or we will throw the bubble away from motion.

WHAT ARE THE ELEMENTS OF THE OFFENSE?

- **Multiple**
- **Shotgun**
- **wing-T**
- **Hybrid**
- **Spread**
- **Flex bone**
- **Power running**
- **Misdirection**
- **Option**
- **Play action**

If you would put our offense into some different terms, you could describe our offense as multiple and shotgun in nature. We are a hybrid wing-T offense with some elements of the spread. We have a power running strategy with a flex-bone game. We have enough options in our scheme that teams must prepare for that part of the game. We use misdirection as part of our steady diet and along with play action passing. We are in our no-huddle 100 percent of the time. We use wristbands, code words, and Oregon boards to mentions a few of the things we use. We try to push the pace offensively.

We have had a system progression since 1995. We started out as a double wing offense. From that scheme, we transitioned into a traditional wing-T offense. In 2003, we were still under the center and started to use the Jet Sweep because you did not have to block anyone from the 3-technique to the backside. In 2005, we ran the Jet Sweep out of the shotgun. We started to run the Rocket Sweep shortly thereafter. With the Rocket we do not block anyone from the 5-technique to the backside. We went to the no-huddle scheme in 2008. Now we are a no-huddle shotgun and Rocket Sweep scheme team.

The Rocket Sweep has enhanced our passing game. We are in the shotgun set but teams do not blitz us. They do not want to commit defenders to a blitz and give up the edges of the defense. The Rocket Sweep moves their coverage people and prevents them from running blitzes. We do not get hard rush ends coming off the edge because of the Rocket Sweep.

The Rocket Sweep puts the defense in some areas of conflict. The defenders directly affected by the Rocket motion are the defensive 9-technique, the inside and outside linebacker to the motion side, and the safety to that side. We are going to attack the defenders that are leaning to the outside and running out of the box to stop the Rocket Sweep. They have a conflict as to whether they play their responsible or do they try to stop the Rocket Sweep. We are going to attack them with our inside running game, the misdirection to the backside, and the passing game over the top.

We number our linemen. (Diagram #1) The even numbered linemen are to the right and the odd numbered linemen are to the left. The numbers of the linemen correspond to the holes of our play calls. We have holes 2, 4, 6, and 8 to the right and 1, 3, 5, and 9 to the left. The 8 and 9 numbers are the wide plays.

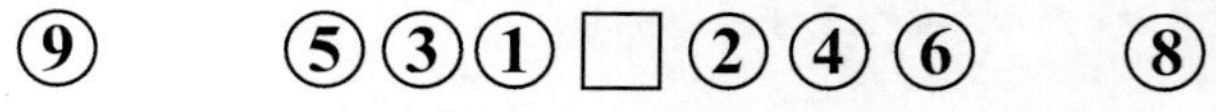

⑨   ⑤③① ☐ ②④⑥   ⑧

Diagram #1. Linemen / Hole Numbering

We use letters as well as numbers to describe our skill position players. (Diagram #2) The X-receiver is our left end. The Y-receiver is the tight end or wide receiver. The Q is the number 1 player and the quarterback. Number 2 is the F-back. The left wingback is the H-back and the right wingback is the Z-back. They are the number 3 and 4 players.

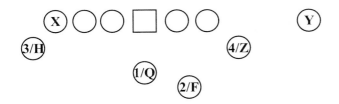

Diagram #2. Skill Position Numbering

We have a three-digit play calling system. (Diagram #3) The first digit indicates the lineman that is pulling. The second number is the player carrying the ball and the third digit is the hole the play is run. The word tells us the blocking scheme we use. The example is 136-Power. Lineman number 1 pulls to the right. The H-back carries the ball into the 6 hole. The word power means power scheme blocking.

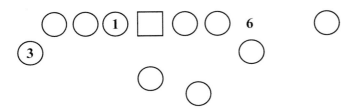

Diagram #3. Play Calling System

If we wanted to run a trap play, we call 221-trap. (Diagram #4) The lineman pulling is the right guard. The F-back carries the ball into the 1 hole. That is the first gap left of the center.

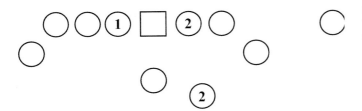

Diagram #4. 221-Trap

The Rocket play is 238-Rocket to the right and 149-Rocket to the left. We give our linemen wristbands with the rules written on them. This maybe the single best thing we have done to improve players learning and offensive efficiency. The wristband show what their base responsible for our base plays are. We use the wristband system from our freshman program to the varsity program.

GUARD	PLAYSIDE (Green)	BACKSIDE (Blue)
CTR	On-Gap-HLP-BKR	Pull Kick DE
DWN	On-Gap-HLP-BKR	Pull Kick DE
MISSL	On-Gap-HLP-BKR	Pull Up + In
PWR	On-Gap-HLP-BKR	Pull Up + In
RCKT	Pull-2-Pipe	1 Count/Scrn
SP-OP	On-Gap-HLP-BKR	Pull Up + In
TRP/ET	Gap-HLP-BKR	Pull Trap

We color code the cards. The playside rules are in green and the backside rules are in blue. The first play on the card is the counter. The playside guard's rule is "on." Anyone aligned on him is his "on" rule. He may get a double team from an adjacent lineman. If someone threatens his inside gap, he gives a gap call and blocks that gap. If he is in a double team with the tackle on a 3-technique defender and the linebacker runs through the A-gap, he comes off for the A-gap.

If he has no one on him or no one in the inside gap, his third rule is the "help" or HLP rule. That means the guard helps on a double team with an adjacent linemen. If there is no help block, he goes up on the linebacker inside of him or BKR. The initials on the wristband are HLP=help, BKR=backer, R2E=reach to engage, Pull=shove, kick, trap, up and in.

We use a cadence that requires discipline by the offensive players. The cadence is "Go-Ready-Set-Go, Down Set Hut." If we are not going in motion, we snap the ball on the second "Go." If we are going to put someone in motion, we call "go-ready-set-**GO**! Down-Set-**Hut**." We snap the ball on the "Hut." We do not put the back in motion with a signal. He comes in motion on the second go. The quarterback when he calls the second "go" gives a hard count and tries to get the defense to jump. He changes his voice inflection and at the same time, we have movement from the motion man. The defense hears the sound and sees the motion. That may influence them to jump off sides. If we hit a big play, we may come to the line quickly and snap the ball on the first sound, which is "go."

By using the cadence with the hard count, you can get a pre-snap look at what the defense is going to do. The cadence can lead to first downs each week.

I will go over the Rocket Sweep by position. We describe it as a "hyperactive outside zone play." Everything in the diagrams will be right sided plays. We can obvious run it in both directions. The Rocket play to the right is "238."

238 BLOCKING RULES

POSITION	RULE
Playside Tackle	Reach to Engage (R2E)
Playside Guard	R2E
Center	R2E
Backside Guard	R2E
Backside Tackle	R2E
Backside T-End	TD Block
Playside Y	Stalk Block
Playside Z	1st Man Outside

On the 238-Rocket, everyone pulls to the right. (Diagram #5) The number 2 and 4 linemen and the Z-back pull flat down the line of scrimmage. The center, backside guard, and backside tackle are using a wide scoop technique working up to the second level. The rules for everyone on the line of scrimmage with the exception of the backside tight end have the same rule. Their rule is to "reach to engage."

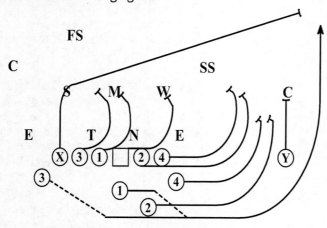

Diagram #5. 238 Rocket Sweep

That means they take a reach step to the right, open up and run to the outside. When he gets to the corner he plants and turns up. He is looking for a defender to engage. In most situations we will not block the 5-technique defender. We want to bypass everyone on the line of scrimmage and get to the second level of the defense.

If the 5-technique defender sprints to the outside, we would consider blocking him.

However, if he plays that technique on motion, we run inside of him with a conventional play. The number 4 lineman can get around the 5-technique and on occasion, the number 2 lineman can get around him also.

The offense blocker has to rip across the 5-technique, turn his shoulders, and run to the sidelines. The offensive tackle wants to do a pass rush rip technique on the 5-technique defender. We tell the blocker if they try to slow down to form block on the defender, they will lose him to the outside. If the defender is out in space and the blocker is trying to overtake them, he has to continue to run. Once they make contact on the defender, they need to keep running to the sidelines. It is the defender's job to cut off the backside. We want to rip, run, and keep the body between the defender and the ball carrier.

The center releases through the A-gap. We are not worried about someone blitzing the A-gap and making the tackle on the sweep runner. What I do not want to happen is someone coming through and hitting the quarterback. He does not block the A-gap. He wants to impede anyone coming through that gap. His job is to stay home and protect the playside A-gap.

The backside guard and tackle will never get in front of the Rocket Sweep to the right. We have them do something that will help us later. They can false pull to the outside. If the backside tackle has a hard charging 3-technique inside of him, he can cut him.

The best thing we can do is set up in a false screen set to the backside. That play can become a viable part of the offensive. (Diagram #6)

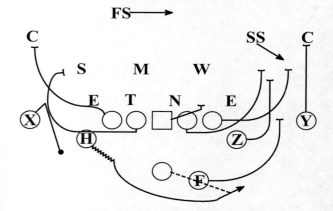

Diagram #6. Weakside Screen

If you have the X-receiver split that way, the backside tackle and guard can form a screen to the backside. That can become the alternative play to the Rocket Sweep. The quarterback can fake the pitch to the sweep back and throw the outside screen to the X-receiver.

You can also run the screen to the tight end on the backside. You must watch to see how the defense plays the backside. Do they honor the backside or disregard it?

The tight end to the backside of the Rocket play has a touchdown block. His job is to sprint across the field at the depth of ten to fifteen yards and tries to spring the running back for a touchdown. He wants to get the kick out block on the last defender in the pursuit wall.

You must convince your players the block is important. They do not believe they can make any difference coming from behind and across the field. It only takes one time for the blocker if he sees the results of his block leads to a TD.

The wingbacks are one yard outside the tackle and one yard off the line of scrimmage. We align him with his outside foot up and the inside foot back. He is in a square stance with his shoulders parallel to the line of scrimmage. If you tilt the wingback to the inside, he cannot make the reach block to the outside. If he is the motion back, he can drop step and get into Rocket motion. If he has a blocking assignment, he can open and get on his track to the outside.

The playside wide receiver has a stalk block on the corner unless he gets a crack call. When we run our stalk block drill, we do some things unique to our mechanic. We do this in two-a-day practices. We take the receiver and a defensive back and put them in a box. We form up the blocker and defender. The blocker is below the defender's eyes in his leverage. The blocker gets his hands on the defender's breastplate. His elbows are in and his thumbs up in his hand placement. The toes positioning is what makes this a unique technique. When the blocker locks up on the defender, we want his toes turned outside in his movement. This gives a duck walk type of posture. He sinks his hips and controls the defensive back.

The second part of the drill puts the blocker and defender 5 yards apart in the box. The coach gives the cadence and the receiver does the same thing as he did in the fitted up position. He moves into the defender and shoots his hands, locks out, and begins his duck walk stalk block.

When he puts his toes in an outside position on his drive, he can steer the defender and keep his body between the defender and the ball carrier. If the receiver can make contact and drive the defender back up the field ten yards, we will take that. The job of the stalk blocker is to stay in front of the defender and the back will make the cuts he needs to make.

The Z-back is the first man to the outside. He has to block the first color he sees. We do not assign him a player to block. He blocks the first defender he sees. The key to him getting outside is a fast and flat release. That is the key for everyone in the Rocket. They want to have a fast and flat release. Once he contacts the defender, he has to go flat and fast to the sidelines. If he tries to cut up field on the defender he will lose him. The ball carrier is going fast, the defenders are going fast, and for him to block anyone, he has to go fast.

If he cannot get to the outside shoulder, he runs him to the sidelines and the running back can cut back on him. The blockers running for perimeter blocks must block people that are threatening the play. They should never block anyone who is trailing the play.

I want to talk about the perimeter cut block. In Colorado, the rules say if the blocker engages the defender above the waist, he can slide down the frame of the defender to the ground as long as he does not lose contact. We teach this block to our wingbacks because they have to block larger defensive ends. We teach our wingback to put his inside shoulder on the outside toe of the defender and roll. This helps our wingbacks block the bigger players on the perimeter and slows down their charge.

The fullback scans the perimeter looking for someone on the edge that could be a threat to the sweep. He comes flat and fast and block the first thing off the edge. He takes care of any leakage that gets through the first wave of blockers.

The ball carrier is in near full speed motion. He is not full speed or out of control. (Diagram #7) He aims for a spot one yard behind the quarterback. He crosses the quarterback and wants to receive the ball two steps past the quarterback. The quarterback catches the ball and steps toward the H-back and delivers a two-handed chest pass with his thumbs down on the toss. We want the ball to go from the quarterback's chest to the H-back's chest. If the quarterback wants to deliver the ball one-handed and is comfortable doing that, we allow him to do it. If he wants to pitch the ball with the wrist action as if he were, shooting a basketball that is also fine.

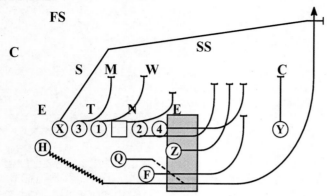

Diagram #7. Quarterback Pitch

There are situations on the corner that requires you to adjust the blocking. (Diagram #8) If the strong safety rolls down into a stacked coverage on the wide receiver, the fullback has to kick the safety out. The H-back has to cut up inside the kick out block of the fullback. The coaching point for the ball carrier is to cut up inside the kick out block, but get immediately back to the outside. If he cuts up vertically and stays on that path, the inside pursuit will run him down. He has to cut up and back outside to run away from the inside pursuit.

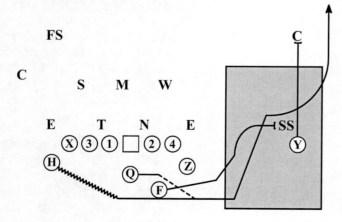

Diagram #8. Up and Out Path

The crack variation is something that we game plan during the week or it could be a game adjustment. (Diagram #9) If the safety cheats to the line of scrimmage and becomes dangerous with his alignment, we bring the wide receiver down and crack him. The fullback checks for anything immediately off the edge and gets on a path to the corner. He is going to kick out the

corner. The H-back has to remember if he cuts up, he wants to get back to the outside as quickly as he can.

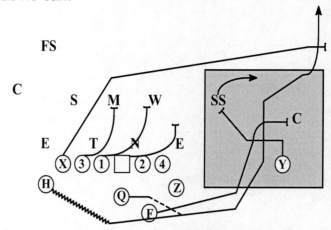

Diagram #9. Crack Variation

The wide receiver must take the path to get him to the block. If the safety is back in his alignment, he takes two steps down field and comes inside for the crack block. If the safety is creeping and in motion toward the line, the receiver has to come straight down the line of scrimmage and make the block. When the wide receiver comes down to crack on the safety, he wants to make sure he does not lose the block to the inside.

He wants to prevent the safety from getting off the block to the inside and attacking the ball carrier straight up the field. If the gets off the block we want him to fight over the top of the block. That keeps him from coming under the block and making the tackle for a one-yard loss. If he is going to make the tackle, we want him to run the hump over the top of the block and make the tackle for a five-yard gain.

If we game plan the crack block, we put it on the wristband-blocking scheme. We put it in "yellow." That tells everyone to be cautious on his blocks. The blockers sprinting to the outside do not want to collide with the blockers coming on the crack block. The blockers must know he is coming inside to crack and avoid him. We do not want a train wreck between our own blockers.

If we find corners playing press coverage, we run them off. Teams do not like to play us in man-to-man coverage for that reason. If they run with our receivers, they have no containment on the outside. Most teams that we play want to roll their corners down to contain or play hard corners.

We run a Rocket drill in practice. It is a perimeter drill. (Diagram #10) We set up the cones where the wings should be and run the play for timing and blocking scheme. The wings work both side. We work this drill every day during two-a-day practices and once a week when we start fall practice. In the two-a-day drills, the defense throws any number of secondary schemes at us. We want them to see different things and be able to adjust to the different secondary looks.

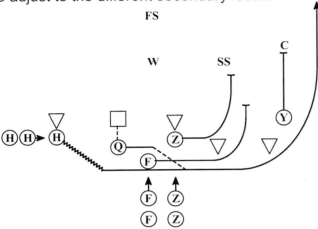

Diagram #10. Rocket Drill

We use spacer cones to make the H-back stay wide and not turn up too quickly. We have cones to make sure the fullback runs his arc outside the cones. When you do this drill, make sure you have a live snapper. Do not let the quarterback hold the ball and execute the toss. That does not help with the timing or mechanics of the play. It is still a timing play with the motion.

If there is a speed difference in the wingback motion, it is the wingback's job to time up the motion. It is not the quarterback's job to adjust the cadence to fit the speed of the wingback. He keeps the cadence the same and the wingbacks starts earlier or later to make the timing work.

If we run the Rocket to the tight end set, the tight end has to reach the defender and stay on the block. If he has a 9-technique defender on him, he has to reach him and stay on the block. You can turn the 4 or 5-technique defender loose, but the defender on the outside of the tight end must be blocked. The playside guard and tackle try to pull around the tight end's block if they can.

When you run the Rocket to the tight end side it is not as good a play. However, we have many big plays to that formation. When we call the Rocket we like to run it to the split end side. It is a shorter edge for the play. We run the play

to the tight end to keep the defenses honest. We run the Rocket to the tight end to set up our complimentary play. We want to run the play action passing game in that direction.

All kinds of websites out there deal with football and conversations between coaches. I put up a question on one of them. I asked, "**How do you react when watching film of a team and you see a false pull by a guard and you see it more than just once? What do you tell your Linebacker's?**"

When you play a hybrid or wing-T team, you tell your linebackers to key the guards. Here are the responses I got from other coaches.

RESPONSES FROM COACHES

- **It comes in stages**
- **Shock and Denial**
- **Pain and Guilt**
- **Anger and Bargaining**
- **Depression, Reflection, Loneliness**
- **Finally, Acceptance**
- **I show the LB's the film and go through the cycle again.**
- **False pulls makes me want to pull my hair out.**
- **JERKS!**

We have a way to "false pull" our linemen. We number our linemen. The right guard and tackle are 2 and 4. The left guard and tackle are 1 and 3. If we want to pull any of those linemen opposite the Playside, we use Spanish numbers. If we call 238-Rocket, Uno, we run the Rocket Sweep to the right and pull the left guard to the left. If we want to pull both guards to the left, we call "238-Rocket, Gorilla." If you play a two inside linebacker defense we can do that. If we do that, we still have blocking to the Rocket side. Pulling the guard opposite slows down the inside linebackers.

We run the Rocket Sweep in the red zone and as a goal line play. We tell the H-back to get his width and head for the pylon at the goal line. We try to seal the edge and use the speed to get to the end zone. Thank you for your attention.

Christian Hunnicutt

Incorporating Zone Blocking In The Offense

Lowndes High School, Georgia

Thank you very much. It is a pleasure for me to address you today. I am going to talk about "Incorporating Zone Blocking into your Offense." I think it is important to establish your "Non-Negotiable" or Culture immediately." That has to happen right away. I think you have to be proactive and work on pre-hab rather than rehab. You have to communicate your expectations and skills your players must be able to perform in order to get on the field. One of your biggest problems will often be seniors that are not playing.

When you build a high school offensive line, it has to be vertical and seamless. You have to expose the culture to all your players. The offensive line coach has to target the players he thinks can play in the offensive line. They do not grow up in the backyard blocking people. They grow up catching passes and throwing the football around. The fun of football to a young player is the throwing, catching, and running with the ball. If a kid is aggressive he may enjoy tackling, but he is not running around saying "I want to play offensive guard." He ends up playing defense.

The offensive line coach has to understand what he is dealing with as to the makeup of his players. There is a **Myriad of Problems** unique to being an Offensive Line Coach that you must face if you want to build a unit that is self-sustaining year after year

1. <u>Physically Difficult</u> – **Block a superior athlete consistently.**

2. <u>Mentally Difficult</u> - **The lineman must know whom to block, how to block a defender, and on a variety of different plays with the defense rarely in the same spot two plays in a row.**

3. <u>*Emotionally Difficult</u> – **Linemen are never allowed to fulfill the desires that were most fun as a youth (playing with the ball itself). They often receive much of the criticism if the offense does not move the ball, and receiving little recognition when the offense does move the ball down the field.**

The third challenge with an offensive lineman is the hardest to deal with. The offense line dwells in anonymity. No one knows his name and he will not get the face time he thinks he deserves. He gets the blame and none of the fame. That seems to be reserved for the quarterback, receivers, and running backs.

The dilemma of the offensive line coach is how to put an edge on the offensive line so they are mentally and physically tough without losing them. There are things the line coach can do.

MUSTS

- **Offensive Line Off-Season Drills and Practices.**
- **Teach, Preach and Repeat your Values.**
- **"What can they repeat back to you in an adverse situation?" Pavlovian Response is the End Result (Rigor, Not Ruthless; Competitive, Not Combative).**
- **PT Barnum**
- **4 Basic Needs all Players/Teams Share**
  - **Sense of Belonging**
  - **Sense of Worth**
  - **Sense of Competence**
  - **Clear Sense of Direction!**

If you start your drills for offensive linemen in May you are behind in your teaching. You must begin in January. You must start then instilling your culture and values. It is not enough to teach plays and techniques. You must teach your values. What the player can repeat back in an adverse situation will tell the coach how good his teaching methods are.

When you work your off-season drill, they should be rigor but not ruthless. You want the drills to be competitive but not combative. If you make it extremely tough on them in January and

February, what do you plan to do the remainder of the season?

The offensive line coach must have a P.T. Barnum type of skill. He has to sell his players on their importance when 99.9 percent of the people do not care. He has to do things to promote the offensive line within the school.

I teach psychology. I like it and I think there is a lot to it especially in coaching. There are four basic needs of all players. I listed them above. Those basic needs are especially important with offensive linemen.

The outside zone is incredible expensive. If you only wanted to run either the inside zone or the outside zone, I would chose the inside zone. The inside zone is less expensive. If you want to install the zone read offense, you should install the outside zone play first. You will need to spend more time installing the outside zone play than you will on the inside zone play. When you run the outside zone there is so many more things that can go wrong with the play.

OUTSIDE ZONE

If you are going to run the zone offense, you must commit to running option football. You cannot do just a little bit of the zone option. You must marry it.

PS: COVERED OR UNCOVERED – SPLITS AT 2 FEET

- **Covered Rule: (A) If you have Help – Drive your Inside Shoulder through the Sternum; Drive and Lift as you Ricochet to the Linebacker**
- **Covered Rule: (B) If you Do Not have Help (Man inside is covered), Drive through the Outside Number, and Drive your Inside Hand to the Near Armpit - Catch Arm**

- **Uncovered Rule: (A) Work to Take Over the Block from Day One.**
- **Uncovered Emphasis: (B) Protect your Gap First. You cannot slow down worrying about the linebacker undercutting you.**

You need to understand the rules for covered and uncovered offensive linemen. If the playside offensive tackle is covered and the playside guard is uncovered, the tackle has help to the inside.

The tackle drives his inside shoulder through the sternum of the defender covering him. He wants to drive, lift, and turn the defender's shoulder. The idea is for the guard overtaking the block. The tackle ricochets to the linebacker.

If the playside tackle is covered and the guard is covered, the tackle has no help to the inside. The tackle drives through the outside number of the defender. He has to work to get his inside hand into the near armpit of the defender and trap his inside elbow.

The uncovered rule is to work to take over the block. In covered rule A, the uncovered guard is working to take over the tackles block on the defender covering him. If the uncovered guard has a linebacker over him, he cannot worry about that linebacker undercutting or going back door on him with a run through. He has to protect his gap first. He steps into the B-gap and has to protect that gap and over take the defender aligned on the tackle. If the linebacker runs through, that is not as serious as turning the down defender loose.

GENERAL RULE: HELMET PLACEMENT FIRST, FEET SECOND

- **Our Approach - Coach and Hold the OL/TE Accountable for the Helmet First, because the feet will follow.**
- **Footwork – Gain Ground on the First Step. (No Drop/Bucket)**
- **Footwork – Defender determines your Footwork. The tighter the defender the tighter your steps and vice versa. The 1st step is in between 45 Degrees and Lateral.**
- **Footwork – the wider the defender, the wider the steps.**
- **Footwork – "Let's Run!"**

Our emphasis on the outside zone has been to place the helmet first and the feet will follow the head. We watch tape of practice every day. We grade the offensive linemen on first step and helmet placement. We hold our linemen accountable for their first step and helmet placement.

In our footwork we never want to bucket step or lose ground. We want to gain ground on the first step. The defender's width determines the length of the blockers first step. If the defender is playing in a 4-technique, the offensive tackle's first step is a tight step. If he is in a wide 5-technique his first step is longer. He has to get to the outside numbers or run his inside shoulder through the sternum of the defender.

Our offensive linemen do not look like offensive linemen. They look like linebackers and tight ends. They are not very big. However, they all can run, they are hard nose, and they have heart.

When you coach the uncovered lineman, there are four variable that you must rep each and every day.

GENERAL: UNCOVERED OFFENSIVE LINEMEN

Four Variables you must rep each day.

1. **From the beginning of the Off-Season Drills – Focus on One Look. (Covered OL – Reach, Uncovered – Overtake, your face on his face)**
2. **Progress to 3,5,9 - Does not Get Reached, Uncovered – Climb.**
3. **Progress to Linebacker <u>Run Through</u> with 3,5,9 not getting Reached – Sprint to the Onside Number of the linebacker.**
4. **3,5,9 Spike and Covered Offensive lineman Climbs to LB.**

The first thing we focus on in our drill work is the covered lineman reaching for a defender and the uncovered lineman hauling his tail trying to get face to face on the covered lineman's defender. The uncovered linemen's thought process is to overtake the block on the covered lineman. He takes the linebacker out of that thought process.

The second variable is the inability of the covered lineman to reach the 3, 5, or 9-technique defender. The uncovered lineman hauls all out and his key moves away from him. The key is how you coach him. If you say the hips moves away or the inside foot moves away, it does not matter. What the uncovered lineman sees is moving away from him. If the covered lineman cannot reach his defender, the inside gap gets wider and the linebacker running through becomes a threat. He has to climb through his gap to the second level.

The third thing we must coach daily is the uncovered lineman getting to the outside number of the linebacker. The fourth thing we must drill is the spike by the defender aligned on the covered lineman. When that happens the covered lineman has to climb to the second level.

When the uncovered offensive lineman is in his stance he locks his eyes on the linebacker. He wants to watch for any clues the linebacker may give away. When we run these types of plays the quarterback uses a hard cadence to try to get the linebackers to tip their hand. Once we snap the ball, his first move is to get face-to-face on the covered defender.

On his first step, he knows whether it is a run through or not. On the third step, he has to make his decision whether he can overtake the defender on the block. No one will get blow torched if the uncovered linemen are overtaking the defensive lineman and the linebacker "Back Doors" the uncovered lineman. We want to block the Big First. Defensive linemen make tackles for losses and linebackers make tackles for small gains.

UNCOVERED OFFENSIVE LINEMAN - OVERTAKE/RUB

- **Covered offensive linemen/tight end has to literally be Pushed Off.**
- **Uncovered Must Push with his outside Arm and be face to face.**

The covered offensive lineman reaches the defender aligned on him. He stays on that block until the uncovered lineman pushes him off the block. He does not leave that block until the overtake blocker has control of the defender. The uncovered lineman must be face-to-face with the defender and uses his outside arm to push the covered blocker off the block.

The backside scoop block is what we describe as an "Effort Block." This is the opportunity for the backside blockers to wear down the defenders. These are cut-blocks. The thing the backside linemen have to do is to know where the defender is going to be, not where he is. He cannot cut him on the first step. He will need to take two to three steps to the inside before he is in position to cut him.

We start our practice with a footwork circuit. In the drills we want to have a flat back, eyes up, gain ground with the first step, and play every run block as covered.

The first drill we do is an angle board drill for the uncovered lineman. In this drill we anticipate a spike from the outside and an overtake block from the uncovered lineman. He takes his first step and reads the inside foot. He drives through the outside number and drives his inside hand into the armpit of the defender.

The next board drill is for the covered lineman. He drives his inside shoulder through the sternum of the defender. He wants to lift, turn, and ricochet off to a linebacker. In all these drills, the players you must coach are the players holding the dummies or playing the scout techniques. We must get a good look at what we want to see.

The next part of this drill is the "catch arm" drill. This situation occurs when the covered lineman has no help and is blocking a defender by himself. The blocker works a single reach on the defender. He has no help and if the defender spikes or pinches inside, the blocker has to block him. He uses the inside arm as a catch arm for a slanting lineman. If the defender pinches, the offensive lineman stabs with his inside knee and works up to the defender. He wants to grab, the armpit, ribs, or inside elbow with his catch hand.

We do a drill called the "elephant drill." In this drill, we want to sort out the trash. That means movement from the defenders. The movement can be slants, pinches, linebacker fire stunts, and things of that nature. On the first step, the offensive linemen to the playside try to put their hands on the adjacent lineman's hip. They want to work their helmet onto the hip of the next linemen. It looks like a train of elephants. Once you get to the center, rip up and stop the nose guard's penetrations. Make him go back door.

The nest drill is a linebacker fit drill. The offensive lineman runs behind the feet of the next down linemen. His landmark is the far number of the linebacker. He wants to focus on hitting on the rise. We tell them it is not a sin for your hands to get wide. However, we do not keep them wide.

The backside cut drill is the next drill. The landmark is the far knee of the defender. As the offensive lineman comes down, he wants to throw his forearm across the defender and crawl through to the knee. It is not a sin to get your belly on the ground, however do not lie on the ground. We want him to get up as if he is on a hot stove. If he pushes off the ground, he keeps the defender blocked. If he lay there, the defender gets to his feet and pursues.

The next group of drills we use is a two-man pod of the covered and uncovered linemen. It is a two-on-two drill with two offensive linemen and

two defenders. There is a down defender and a linebacker. We work the three scenarios dealing with their reaction to the down defender.

The first scenario is the defender that we cannot reach. The uncovered lineman climbs to the linebacker and the covered lineman runs the defender outside.

The second scenario is the covered linemen overtaking the defender aligned on the covered lineman. The covered lineman climbs to the linebacker.

Scenario number three is the inside stunt by the defender. The uncovered lineman overtakes the stunt and the covered lineman climbs for the linebacker.

OUTSIDE ZONE RULES:

38/39 Outside Zone

- **PS Tackle**: Base reach C-gap, Possible catch arm, know if you have help.
- **PS Guard**: Base reach B-gap.
- **Center**: Base reach A-gap.
- **BS Guard**: Base reach BS A-gap.
- **BS Tackle**: Base reach BS B-gap.
- **Tight End**: Base reach D-gap.
- **Fullback**: Split flow; fill BS 4-technique to outside.
- **Tailback**: Drop step with BS foot, aiming point is butt of the tight end or ghost tight end, read widest Defensive Line playside. If he goes out, go in. If he goes in, go out.
- **Quarterback**: Open 4/8, Drive on course, extend ball with one hand. Execute hand off with depth, keeper action after hand off.

We can run the outside zone to the tight end or open side of the formation. (Diagram #1)

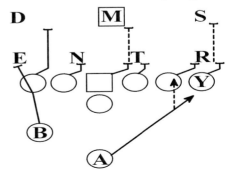

Diagram #1. Outside Zone Tight End

To the tight end side we have two pods working together. The center and playside guard work their rules for the 3-technique defender to the Mike linebacker. The playside tackle and tight end do the same thing for the 7-technique defender to the Sam linebacker.

If we run the play to the open side of the formation, we apply the blocking rules. (Diagram #2) The rules are the same for the playside guard and tackle and the backside guard and tackle. The difference is the fullback and tight end blocks. On the outside zone to the open side, the fullback blocks the force defender to the open side. The tight end base reaches into the backside C-gap. Against the odd front defense, the center and backside guard work the nose guard up to the Sam linebacker. The playside guard and tackle work for the 5-technique defender to the Mike linebacker. The fullback blocks the playside outside linebacker.

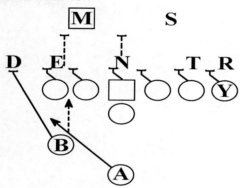

Diagram #2. Outside Zone Weak

We can change the fullback assignments and make him an extra blocker to the tight end side of the formation. (Diagram #3) We align him into the strong position to the tight end side and send him to the outside of the tight end to block the force defender.

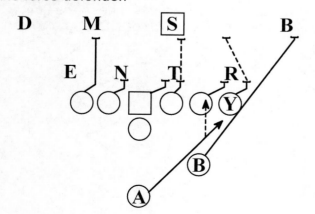

Diagram #3. Strong Force Block

We can also arc the tight end off the line of scrimmage and put him on the force defender. (Diagram #4) On that adjustment, the fullback blocks the second linebacker outside/in. He reads the block of the offensive tackle on the 6-technique defender. If the tackle reaches the 6-technique, he goes outside that block for the Sam linebacker. If the tackle cannot read the 6-technique, he drives him outside and the fullback goes inside that block for the Sam linebacker. The fullback reads the same thing the tailback sees. He is the lead blocker for the running back.

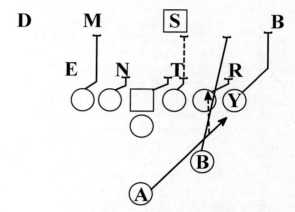

Diagram #4. Outside Zone Arc Block

We use these variations on the outside zone. The interior rules for the linemen do not change. The playside tackle must know the tight end is leaving and he is on a single reach block for the defender.

INSIDE ZONE

The inside zone is a vertical play. The inside offensive linemen (guards and center) are the key to the play. This is a less expensive play because there is less teaching involved. The splits for the offensive line are two-feet. The playside and backside use the covered or uncovered rules. On the covered rule, we must think getting about getting nose-to-nose with the defender and knocking off the blocker. We want to step with the gap side foot.

The uncovered rule is to step out at a 45 degree angle to the defender. We want to keep the shoulders and hips square to the line of scrimmage. We want to secure the block with the outside hand. They are thinking level two in their blocking scheme.

The covered lineman must prepare to drop and drive. If the 3, 5, or 9-technique defender spikes, he has to stay on track and not try to go back on that defender. We tell this rhyme to them. We say, "Stay on track and do not go back." The block ends up as a double team block with the covered linemen blocking half a man. The emphasis for the uncovered lineman is to work to keep his shoulders and hips square when the defender spikes into him. He wants to find the linebacker after his first step and secure his gap. If he turns his shoulders and hips, he ends up screwing up someone's block.

When we drive block, the stabilizers are the hands. That is what gets offensive linemen in trouble. In the drive block, we want to eliminate the stabilizers. When we get into the fit, we want to stay in it. The linemen have to keep their base wide and work with what we call a "steel spine."

When we drill the drive block we fit the offense and the defender into a block. The offense wants to drive, stay in the fit, keep the wide base, and keep the rigid spine. In this drill, we make the defender move one direction or the other. The blocker feels the movement and the pressure will tell him which way he should block the defender. We call that the "fit weave."

When we teach the drive base block, we want to adjust our pad level. We want to work with the eyes below the hands. We also use a drill called "half-man." We use the technique when the defender pinches and when the defender aligns in an inside position. (2i, 4i, 7-technique) The emphasis is to stay on track and do not go back, keep the shoulders and hips square, and pump the fist that is not engaged with the block. In that block, the lineman is trying to give his partner time to take over the block.

At some point in the block, the offensive player may stalemate with the defender. When that occurs, the lineman needs to drop his center of gravity and restart the block. He cannot give up on the block. He has to keep the feet active at all times. If the feet stop, the block is over.

INSIDE ZONE RULES

34/35 Strong

- **PS Tackle**: Base reach C-gap, Possible catch arm, know if you have help
- **PS Guard**: Base reach B-gap
- **Center**: Base reach A-gap
- **BS Guard**: Base reach BS A-gap
- **BS Tackle**: Base reach BS B-gap

- **Tight End**: Base reach D-gap
- **Fullback**: Split flow; fill BS 4-technique to outside.
- **Tailback**: Open cross over and chase the inside leg of the playside tackle, aiming point is inside leg of the tackle, read first down lineman.
- **Quarterback**: Open 5/7, drive on course, extend ball with one hand, extend ball with one hand, execute hand off with depth, keeper action, Running Back aiming point is inside leg of the tackle.

The rules for the interior linemen are the same as the outside zone rules. (Diagram #5) We use covered and uncovered rules. The tailback's footwork and rules change. He takes an open and cross over step aiming for the inside leg of the playside tackle instead of the butt of the tight end. He wants to get his shoulders square to the line of scrimmage running downhill. He bangs the ball into the hole or bends it to the backside. He reads the first down lineman for his cut.

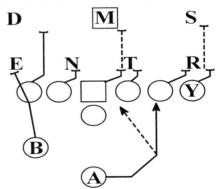

Diagram #5. Inside Zone Strong

I am going to have our offensive coordinator, **Todd Cooper**, come up and speak. He is the zone coach. He is tremendous with everything he does and is probably the best science teacher in the state of Georgia.

COACH TODD COOPER

I am going to talk about the passing game from the zone play. On our quick slant, our protection is the inside zone blocking scheme. The offensive line and backs run the inside zone play. Obviously, we do not go down field. The backside wide receiver runs a 5-step slant unless we tag a fade route. If we tag the route, the playside wide receiver runs the tag call.

The quarterback takes one good step with a flash fake gathers his feet and throws. If we get a blitz off the backside, the fullback picks it up. This is a good play if we get inside the 20 yard line.

The keeper comes off the outside zone fake. We can run it from multiple formations.

Keeper

- **Y Receiver:** Route – Protect/Slip
  Split = Tight End on end of the line. Depth = 1-2 yards
  Adjustment - Pin DE as long as you are winning release to flat after you lose against the DE.
  Hot / SA – Built
- **Z Receiver:** Route Deep Comeback
  Split = 12 Yards - Depth = 18 yards
  Adjust = Convert – Cloud
  Hot/SA = None
- **X Receiver:** Route = Beeline Post
  Split = 8 yards – Depth 15 yards in B-Gap vertical 5 yards. 45 degrees to far hash mark.
  Adjust = None – Hot/SA = None
- **B Receiver:** Route = Over – Split = split the difference. Depth = 10 – 12 yards over the playside Tight End. Adjust = None – Hot/ SA = None
- **A Receiver:** Route = Flake – 5 Yards Flat.
  Split = 7 BF – Depth = 5 Yards – Adjust = None – Hot/SA = None

We can align in a 2 X 2 set with the tight end to the side of the keeper. The quarterback fakes the outside zone to the twin side of the formation and boots to the tight end side. (Diagram #6)

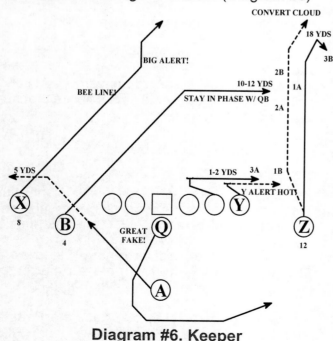

Diagram #6. Keeper

He wants to be nine yards deep and he reads from high to low in his progression. The Z-receiver runs an 18 yard comeback route. You can run a number of patterns with this receiver. This is a good place for a double move. In the base progression he is the number one choice. The rules for the backside receiver are simple. The receiver closest to the ball runs the over route. The next closest receiver, if there is one, runs a beeline post.

The over route by the B-receiver is 10-12 yards deep in the area of the tight end. As he runs the pattern he wants to stay in phase with the quarterback. He wants to be slightly in front of the quarterback running the boot and in his line of sight. We run the beeline post by the X-receiver as a slant to the depth of 15 yards in the backside B-gap. At 15 yards deep he breaks the pattern vertical for 5 yards. After the 5 yard vertical alteration he breaks at a 45 degree angle to the far hash mark. This is the "big alert" pattern.

The "big alert" is not in the quarterback's progression. It is a call-down from the press box. The tight end stays in to block. He wants to pin the defensive end to the inside. As long as he is winning the block on the defender, he stays on the block. If he loses the defender he releases to the flat. He is also the hot receiver on a blitz to his side.

The quarterback can anticipate breaking containment if there is an eagle alignment in the front to the side of the keeper. He has to alert hot routes verses a Sam linebacker fire or a secondary edge pressure to the keeper side of the play. We designate the base progression in the diagram as follows.

In the base progression it is:
- **1a. Comeback**
- **2a. Over**
- **3a. Flat**
- **4a. Run the ball**

The second progression is when the quarterback breaks containment.

- **1b. Pin Release Flat**
- **2b. Over route**
- **3b. Comeback pattern (It is a late read)**

On the diagram, it is (3b). The tailback makes a great fake and seals off the backside. If no one comes, he leaks out into a five-yard flat route.

We have many variations to this pattern. We can put the B-back in the backfield instead of the slot. (Diagram #7) He starts as the lead back on the outside zone. He comes behind the line of scrimmage and comes out the keeper side into the flat. He is the quarterback first choice if he breaks containment. We can align him in a wide out position, bring him in motion, and get him into the same area.

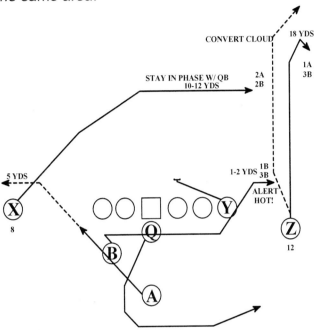

Diagram #7. Keeper Variation

I am going to turn it back over to Coach Hunnicutt.

COACH HUNNICUTT

I have been blessed to work with four great coaches. I am not very smart but I can write things down and learn from those things. I took things from the coaches that have made me a better coach. The first Coach was Dexter Wood. Coaches today do not take themselves serious in the classroom. Coach Wood was the opposite. He took teaching as serious as anyone did in the profession.

- **Dexter Wood** – cast a vision, discipline was consistent and pervasive personally and professionally, command presence, identify roles, great example of personal humility and professional will.
- **Jess Simpson** – insight and foresight, always on the cutting edge of player development, situational practice plan, sells "the plan" to everyone involved.

- **Chad Campbell** – others centered, daily accountability, can drop him off anywhere and he will fit, understands the basic needs (belonging, competence, direction, worth).
- **Mike Hodges** – listens with the intent of understanding, not replying. Has forgotten more about the offensive line than anyone knows. Oracle, but tells you "why".

Coaches I appreciate you being here.

Russ Jones

Organization in the Year Round Program

Syracuse High School, Utah

Thank you very much for that nice introduction. I want to start by telling you something about our school. Syracuse has an enrollment of 2000 students. We play in a league where the schools are in the 2000-2400 student population size. The powerhouse in our league is Bingham High School. Their enrollment is around 2350 students. We beat them on the way to the state championship game this year. We played Jordan High School in the finals and lost.

The players in our program are not big players. We have one or two players that are good size but for the most part our offensive linemen are in the 180-190 pound category. Our players feed off each other and play extremely hard. We try to develop those kinds of players at our school.

We opened as a school in 2007. In our first season we went 0-10. We played with only juniors and sophomores. We were small but we had many players in our program. Since the first season, we are 44-15. We have been to the state playoffs five times out of six years, the state semi-finals three times, and this year we made it to the championship game. Syracuse has an enrollment of 2000 students. We are proud of our players and the community. Syracuse is a football school. I have been at other school and they were not known for their football.

At Syracuse, we are known as a football school. We tried to make this into a football school but our players play other spots. We want our players to lift constantly. Our players lift in the morning and practice in the afternoon. That is what we base the philosophy on in our programs. It is one way we try to get our players to buy into the system.

We start in January and develop a calendar. We give each one of our players a packet and they take it to their parents. The program starts in January and goes all the way through December. We finished in November and we do not have much of an off-season. I am going to cover what

is in the packet and how we get the parents to buy into our system.

If we organize, know what is going on, and not try to work around the parents, the parents will get on our side. They will help us to get their sons involved in the sport. The first page of the packet gives a schedule of events we will participate in and the cost of each event. It also tells whether these events are mandatory or option for participation. Utah is a big 7-on-7 tournament state. The only tournament we participate in is the Weber State tournament held in June. It is a big tournament for our players.

The cost is $15, which all goes to Weber State. We may participate in one other tournament against a high school in our area. We have a summer camp at our school. The charge is $160 and it is a great fee. If you go to Utah State or another college in our area the cost is $300. After the camp, we start summer conditioning. There is a $50 fee for this program. We make sure we list each charge in the packet so the parents know exactly how much expense is involved. We also have general descriptions of what the fees are and how to pay them.

The second sheet of the packet is a copy of our 2013 schedule. It tells the parents when the athlete must report and a schedule of practice times. I also throw in a football schedule. It has our varsity, JV, and sophomore schedule. It also includes the dates for all the playoff games. That is basic information and time commitment for the players.

The third page is important to me and for our program. It is our "mission statement." We want the parents to buy into our program as the players do.

Mission Statement: *Welcome to the 2013 edition of Syracuse Football, home of the Syracuse Titans. The entire coaching staff is filled with excitement and enthusiasm* *heading into our 7ᵗʰ season. We cannot wait to work with the great young men of this community. In order for us to be successful our team must work extra hard in the weight room during the off-season and summer months. Additionally in August, we must have high intensity workouts during our two-a-day practices to kick off the 2013 season. To reach our full potential we need to have total dedication and commitment to our football program. We must realize this can only be accomplished through extraordinary commitment, positive attitude, and hard work and by taking one-step at a time.*

We are trying to tell the parents they need to plan their vacations around some of the things we are doing. In the mission statement we have an academic award given to players that achieve high academic standards. This award signifies we are students first and athletes second. We felt if we put this into our mission statement that it would get the school administration behind us. It also got some of the academic players in the school on board with our program.

These are the four criteria the players must meet.

- **Academics – 3.5 or higher**
- **Athletics – impact player (must meet the Athletic Lettering requirements)**
- **Leadership – Positive role model**
- **Citizenship – No "U's"**

This award is the most prestigious award we will hand out to our players. We also have general team requirements as a part of the Syracuse football team.

- **Maintain a 2.0 GPA throughout the year.**
- **No "U's" - Respect all administration, faculty and staff.**
- **Respect for yourself, players, managers, and coaches.**
- **No "sagging".**
- **Total dedication and commitment to the football program.**
- **Work to be a better player, individually and as a team.**
- **Be a positive role model.**

When we established our program in 2007, we had 85 sophomores and 70 juniors in our program. We had no seniors. The first year we went 0-10. I had just left a school that went 1-9. It was hard winning one game in a two-year period.

I began to question what I was doing. The first year we played with every team and battled to the end. There were no blowout games. One of the teams we lead at halftime played for the state championship. We knew we had some good things coming back for the next year. People in your program have to be good kids and role models in our community.

That is easy to say and hard to do. That summer we lost four players that got involved in some criminal activities. Those players left the program and the other players in our program stepped up. Our coaching staff went to a clinic two years ago and listened to a college coach talk about discipline. He said he had to eliminate 20 scholarship players out of his program because they were bad actors. He cut his losses and went on with his younger players. In high school you want to help the kids and give them the benefit of doubt but there comes a time you must cut your losses and go on with what you know is right.

I honestly believe that is how we got players to buy into our system and play together. It gives the players dedicated to the program the opportunity to step up and do the right thing. We had one player in six years that signed a Division-I scholarship. Nevertheless, our players play as a team, as a unit and they play tough together. We played teams in the playoffs this year that had five and six players going to Division-I programs. They were going to Utah State Utah, Auburn, and Alabama. We had two players sign with Dixie State College and one to Southern Utah. Those are small college programs.

They fight tough together and we develop that in the off-season. I believe that comes from our mission statement and our commitment to it. We have it posted on the bulletin board and they see it every day.

In our summer camp, we have other schools from our community that participate in it. In Utah, we have five days that we can practice. We have a three-hour session from 8:30 to 11:30. We start with defense and much of the session is chalk talk. In the afternoon, we go to offense. We work 1:30 to 4:30. After we have dinner that evening, we give them the rest of the evening off.

On Tuesday, we reverse the sessions. We go offense in the morning and defense in the afternoon. On Wednesday, we put the offense and defense together in the morning session. That afternoon we bring in four schools from the area and have what we call a "shoot out." About eight schools in the area have their camps at the same time. On this particular form I listed Layton, and Box Elder. We will have another school named Woodcroft join us.

The way the shoot out works is Syracuse plays defense first. We align at the 40 yard line. The first school runs a play, Layton runs a play, and Box Elder runs a play. We rotate through the three offensive teams against Syracuse's defense. We work three cycles and rotate the next defense on the field. Each defense plays nine plays in a series. We rotate the three offensive teams and the defense stays the same for nine plays.

This camp is something we do right at our school and the cost is cheap. We do not hire officials as we do it ourselves. On Thursday, we go defense in the morning and offense in the afternoon. That evening we take them to the Layton Surf and Swim Club. We have some fun with the players. We have a big Barbecue, they get to swim, and hang out together. All the coaches are there and we kind of come down to their level. The coaches bring their families and we all have a good time. It is a big get-together for our football program.

The next day is our scrimmage day. We all meet at Roy High School, which is very close to Syracuse. We do another tournament, which involves your varsity and JV programs. We have the varsity going on one field and the JV program on another. We also bring our sophomore team and they go later after the varsity and JV teams. This has been very beneficial for our program.

Every since I became the head coach we have participated in these scrimmage type arrangements. The coaches like it because it is at our school. They are not out of town. They get to sleep in their own beds and their routines remain the same. This is good for us. We have our five-day camp at our own school. It is probably similar to two-a-day practices but it becomes a fundraiser for us. We make close to 10 thousand dollars off the camp. We charge 160 dollars a player. If you have 100 players coming, that is 16 thousand dollars. The coaches make a little money and we have a good time doing it.

EXPECTATION FOR SYRACUSE FOOTBALL PLAYER

- **Attend all practices on time**

- **Parents, for any reason your son is going to miss practice you need to call the Men's Coaches Office before we practice and leave the following information**
  - Name
  - Phone number that you can be reached
  - Reason
  - Sick – Can your son attend practice? (even if it is to watch)

Missing practice without a valid reason

- **First time this happens, you sit out a game**
- **Second time it happens, you sit out another game**
- **Third time it happens, you are dismissed from the team**

Valid Reasons

- **Wedding**
- **Funeral**
- **Brother/sister leaving for mission**
- **Tardy to practice-extra running for the first two times, 3rd tardy miss next game**
- **Truancy from school, miss next game**
- **An "unexcused absence" on the day of the game you will sit out**
- **Any negative behavior can result in dismissal from the team**

If the player is going to miss practice, we want to know why. Some of the valid reasons are weddings, funerals, and missions. We are in a Mormon State and those things happen within families. There are other excuses but those are some examples. These are tough rules but you must give your players boundaries and they have to live within those boundaries.

On this sheet, we also have our requirements for getting a letter. They must attend all practices on time, maintain a 2.0 GPA, and play in 10 quarters. (Four plays in one quarter is a quarter) We put all these things on our web site.

We start our off-season program on January 2nd. The calendar is in their packet. We start with the varsity and map out what they will do for eight weeks. We have an eight-week cycle and in the ninth week, we go into a testing period. (Titan Challenge)

After we come back to school from the holiday break, we have sophomore orientation.

Our high school make up is grades 10, 11, and 12th graders. Our sophomore coaches go to the junior highs with fliers from our school. They want to enlist freshmen players to participate in our weight program.

We have a big orientation meeting for the sophomores on January 16th. We had 100 freshmen in that meeting this year. I spoke and the sophomore coaches speak. We show them a highlight film to get them excited about coming into the program. We give them their packet, which tells them everything they will do.

In the freshmen program, we lift on Monday, Tuesday, and Thursday. We lift from 3:30 to 4:30. We always give them Friday off because there are many holidays during that time. We go for eight weeks and have the "Titan Challenge." That takes us through the month of February.

Monday	Tuesday	Thursday
Freshman Workout 3:30-4:00	Freshman Workout 3:30-4:00	Freshman Workout 3:30-4:00

The first week of March, we start the eight-week cycle over. Our freshmen are still lifting Monday, Tuesday, and Thursday but they now lift at 6-7 am in the mornings. The reason we do that is the attendance factor. We did not have freshmen missing morning workouts. That allowed them to participate in other sports if they chose. We work two groups in the workouts. One group lifts and the other group goes through abilities in the gym. After 30 minutes, they switch.

Monday	Tuesday	Thursday
Freshman Workout 6:00-7:00 am	Freshman Workout 6:00-7:00 am	Freshman Workout 6:00-7:00 am

At the middle of the month we start team competition. With our varsity players we have a school curriculum that allows them to take a football class and other physical education classes, which deal with body training. We are lucky at our school because we get our players in a football class every other day. If their schedule works out, we could get them every day.

The team competitions start in March and include cone drills, pro agility, bag drills, and sumo wrestling. That fits in after we finish in the weight room. We take the top eight players in our program and they become the team captains. After we split up the top eight we try to equally divide the rest of the teams among players of like athletic ability. We want them to compete in everything they do. We keep track of the team competitions and have the finals at the end of the school year.

Our in-school football classes are part of our program. We get them early in the morning from 7:30-9:00 am. We divide the groups into lifting and agilities groups and alternate them. We are fortunate to have those types of programs at our school. I think if you are going to be in this sport for the long run, you have to sell your program to the administration so you can get these types of programs.

Our players work twice as hard as any other students do in those classes. We expect them to do it. We expect them to win and we expect them to work hard in those classes. We are going to be serious with them but we want to have the attitudes and environment very friendly. We give them boundaries that we want and they follow them.

When we get into April, we continue with our varsity players in the program. In April, we start the linemen and skilled-players lunches. We have the linemen one week and the skilled-players the next week. The coaches give up their lunchtime every Wednesday and meet with those groups in a classroom. The players get their lunch and go to the classroom. In that lunch period, we have an "Introduction" session with them.

We do not know the players very well at this point in the program. We want them to stand up one at a time and tell us about their family and where they live. Each player gets up and talks for a couple of minutes about his life away from school. You find out different things about your players during these talks. We do that with the linemen one week and the skilled-players the next week. The next time we meet, we talk about goals.

During the month, the workouts with the freshmen JV, and varsity continue as they did the month before. The second eight-week cycle comes up in May. That is our test week, which we call the "Titan Challenge." With our lunch program, the topic is still goals but as we approach May, the topic begins to focus on leadership. We want to know what they think makes a good leader. We want them to start thinking about the qualities of leaders and who they would like leading their team.

When we do our planning, we want to consider other sports that have events during this time of year. We do not want to conflict with the state tournaments in baseball, track, or any other sport. We do not do any team 7-on-7 work until after the other sports have had their finals. We work the 7-on-7 workouts until the end of school, which is June 7th this year.

On June 6th we are almost out of school. Our players come in and have our last 7-on-7 practice. We go from 10-12 in the morning. We do the final team competition from 12-1 and follow that with a big barbecue. We celebrate at the closing of those events. When we have the team competition, the winners at the finals get tee shirts.

The bottom line to me is this. The off-season has to be about competing and not just lifting. When we workout we spend 40 minutes in the weight room. They spend that time working and not hanging out and gabbing. They know the reps and percentage of weight with which they are maxing. After 40 minutes in the weight room, we put them through a tough ABS program, where they work on their ABS and oblique muscles. After that, they go to 30 minutes of running and agilities. One day may be form running and the next may be explosion and footwork.

During the third week of June, we run the football camp. After the camp, we give our players a bracelet. It says Titan Football and we put a theme word on it. This year we put "finish" on it. The year before that was "make no excuses." I want them to wear the bracelet after the final game on Saturday for the rest of the summer. After the camp, we give them a break until practice starts on July 15th.

We bring them back and start lifting in July. When we start back with the lifting program, we start our summer conditioning. During these sessions, we do not go long. We also mix in some chalk talks. Even though we do not go long, the players work extremely hard. We have the two-week acclimation period. The first week is weight training, conditioning, and chalk talks. The second week we are in helmets only.

In August, we continue with the weight training and conditioning. However, in the first part of the month we run a youth camp. Our players run the camp. It is mandatory that our seniors be there. It is good for senior leadership and it is good that the little kids in the camp know who they are.

After the youth camp, we take our seniors on a senior retreat. We pack them up and take an overnight trip. All these activities are in the packet we give the players on the first day. The parents see the packet and they know when the players are going to be involved with something in the program and can plan around what we do. This helps the parents to buy into what we have going on.

We have coaches meetings on Sunday. The offensive staff meets at my house and the defensive staff meets at Coach Faerber's (defensive coordinator) house. When we come to work, on Monday morning, there is a plan for everything and everyone knows what is going on with his group.

August 11th, is our first day of two-a-day practices.

On Monday morning we practice from 8:00 - 10:30 a.m. Our afternoon session is from 6:00 - 8:30 p.m. We follow this program until Friday. On Friday we have our Blue/White game at 9:30 a.m. In the evening practice we have the sophomores come in a 5 p.m., the Varsity comes in at 6 p.m. On Friday, we shorten the morning practice and have our inter-squad scrimmage. That afternoon when we come back for the evening practice it is a shorten practice because of the morning activities.

During the season, we bring our team in on Saturday after the game and do some lifting. We also watch the game film from the night before. With the advancement in technology, the players can see the game that night. We are a Hudl school and have the opportunity to see the film the same night. We download it on Friday night and the players can watch it. When they come in on Saturday morning, they know what we are going to point out. We point out what they are doing right and wrong.

Once schools starts we go with our Varsity and sophomores practice at 2:30 to 5:30 p.m. That is our routine until the next game on Friday night. We come in on Saturday morning and watch film and lift weights.

Everything I have talked about is in the packet and in detail. The calendar is complete and every event and date is on the calendar. If you have, everything written down the parents will jump on-board. Our first game is August 22nd and the last game of the season is October 25th. The next month is playoff month. If you get to the final game, the season will end November 25th. The following Monday and Tuesday is equipment collection day. The players should turn everything in washed and clean.

That gives us two weeks to prepare for the sophomore and varsity banquets. We make a big deal out of this. It is a fitting way to close your football season. We have our banquets in December. We have the sophomore banquet one week before the varsity banquet. They have the season off from the equipment turn in day until January 2$^{nd.}$ On January 2nd we start over again in preparation for the next season.

When we start our weight training program we have an A-Day and a B-Day. We run the program on an eight-week cycle. We go eight weeks before we test the players. We do circuit training and the first week the players get so sore they cannot stand it. It is all repetition work. We give them a percentage weight and they go for 45 seconds non-stop at each station.

The exercises we do on Monday and Tuesday are power cleans, military press, incline/bar, alternating straight leg dead lift/dumb-bells, box squats, step-ups and pull ups.

The first week is a circuit and the second, third, and fourth weeks the weight goes up and the reps come down. The fifth week, the reps go up and the weight comes down. The next two week we increase the weight and decrease the reps. The final week we increase reps and reduce weight, and then test. This is what works best for us. We do the same things with the other exercises in our workout.

The Wednesday and Thursday exercises are clean and press, straight leg dead lift/dumb-bells, bench press, shoulder circuit, back squats, bent over rows/dumb-bells, and dumb-bell explosion. We change the exercises so they do not get bored with lifting. Our Friday lifts are speed box squats, dumb-bell upright rows, dumb-ball bench and punches, box lunges/bar, alternate straight leg, chin-ups, and military press.

In the weight program, we have two testing periods. We test in March and May. In the testing period, we test 40-yard dash, pro agility,

bench, squat, and clean. We time the 40-yard dash electronically. We time the pro-agility with a stopwatch. When they do their weight testing, we are in direct supervision to make sure they do the lift correctly. We chart everything and put it on a sheet so they can see it.

Being a new school, we created all the boards that are on the walls. We have a record board in our weight room for lifting. It lists the testing criteria across the top of the board and the weight classifications of the players. We break our players down by weight. We have eight weight divisions.

We start at 90-120, 121-151, 152-182, 183-213, 214-244, 245-275, 276-306, 307+. On our board, we do not have anyone in the 307+ category or the 90-120 categories. To hold a record there must be more than four players competing in a weight class. We put the player's name, amount of weight they lift, and the month and year, they did it.

Next to our record board are our offensive, defensive, and special team's goal boards. These boards are on the wall and they see it every day they have class.

OFFENSIVE GOALS

- **Average 28 points per game**
- **Average 325 total yards per game**
- **Always score inside the opponents 20 yard line**
- **Average 4 yards on first down**
- **No turnovers on our side of the 50 yard line**
- **57 percent completion**
- **Average 55 plays per game**
- **Average 4 yards per run play**

DEFENSIVE GOALS

- **Hold opponents to less than 275 total yards**
- **No 100-yard rushers**
- **2 + turnover per game**
- **100 percent on 4th downs**
- **70 percent on 3rd downs**
- **Hold opponent to less than 10 points**
- **No points on the first drive of the half**
- **No points allowed/red zone**

SPECIAL TEAM GOALS

- **No penalties (all teams)**

- **No blocked kicks (PAT, FG, and Punt)**
- **Score 6 points or more**
- **Block a kick cause a turnover**
- **No opponent kickoff-return beyond the 25 yard line**
- **Kickoff beyond 30 yard line**
- **No opponent punt-return longer than 10 yards**
- **Our punt return average more than 8 yards**

We have the schedule of the teams we play across the top of the board and Titan marks in the categories that we reached our goal. When you fill up the board with accomplished goals you probably won the game. We want to post the goals so the players see them and remember them. When we come in on Saturday morning that is the first thing, they see because we lift on Saturday morning after games.

One thing you can do that adds value to your entire program is to put together a web site. If you do not have one I recommend you put together one. We put everything on the web site for students to see. You will be amazed what you will find on our web site. It is everything you would want to know about Syracuse Titan football. The biggest thing is the tab that deals with college recruitment.

We have a signing day ceremony for the players that sign scholarships. We make a big deal out of it. We hold it before school, and have highlight film of the individuals. It motivates the school and other players and it gives us a chance to visit with the parents. We invite all our younger players to the ceremony. We invite everyone to the signing party. You are honoring their achievement, getting kids excited, and it helps build your program, and promotes leadership.

We are having more eighth graders coming to our program that want to play up on the sophomore team now. They want to get involved in our weight program and participate in what we do. They want to come to our school. It is good because you get to know them and they get to know the coaches. They become familiar with everything that goes on within the program and the school. It builds confidence in them and promotes the things that we stand for in our program. It promotes physical and mental toughness.

Our sophomore record over the course of our program is 44-10. They learn how to win as sophomores. We get many players involved and had 60 players on the sophomore team last season. We have over 100 sign up this year. We try to play as many players as we possibly can at this level. If you do not involve them in some way, they will drift away from your program.

During the season, we continue to have lunch meeting with our players. We try to squeeze out every ounce of time we can with our players. We have film meetings at lunch with them during the season. They get their lunches and we sit and watch film together. It is team building. We want our players to invest time and not just spend time in our program.

Thank you very much for your time. I appreciate your attention.

Caleb King

The Multiple 3-4 Defense With Stunts

Havelock High School, North Carolina

Coaches I appreciate you being here today. I am going to talk about our defense. I want to show you what we do on defense and who we are. I want to show you how we get into our defense to set up the multiple blitzes and coverage's we use. One of the things we have is speed. We also have a good offense. If we can hold the opponent to under 13 points a game, we feel we will win most games.

We base everything in our defense on speed. We relentlessly attack the offense. We want to play fast. We want to be the most physical team on the field. We want to do our job first. The first major objective of defense is to stop the run. If you create turnovers and stop the run, you win most games. If you win on third down you get off the field. Our statistics on third down increased dramatically from 2011 to 2012. We doubled the amount of "three and outs" situations in 2012. We did a much better job on third down.

HAVELOCK DEFENSIVE GOALS

1. **STOP THE RUN**
2. **Cause 3 turnovers per game.**
3. **WIN 3RD DOWN**
4. **Block one kick per game.**
5. **Hold the other team to 13 or less points.**
6. **Hold the other team under 200 yards total.**
7. **Hold the other team under 100 yards rushing.**

We are a multiple "3-4" front. We divide our defense into halves. We have a <u>call</u> side and an <u>away</u> side. To the call side we have the end, nose, Mike linebacker, free safety and rover. The Sam linebacker, tackle, Spur safety and Jack linebacker goes away from the call.

The first front we play is our "Tiger" front. (Diagram #1) In the Tiger front, we play the end and tackle in 4i-techniques on the inside eye of the offensive tackles. The Jack and Rover linebackers play a 9-technique on the tight end if they have one. The Mike and Sam linebackers

align in a 30-technique on the outside eye of the offensive guards. The nose is a 0-technique head up the center.

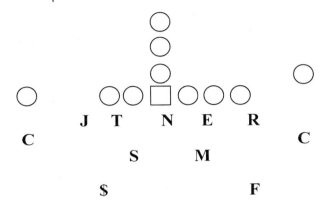

Diagram #1. Tiger Front

In our Tiger front, if the offense trades the tight end over, we play left and right positions and do not flip our defenders. In this front if the offense is strong right or strong left, we still have two 4i-techniques, two 9-techniques, and a 0-technique. The Mike and Sam are still in 30-techniques on the guards. We are an eight-man gap team. We play gap control the entire time. As in every defense, we have checks we go to for specific fronts or formations.

In our secondary our base look is the same every time. We do not want the offense to know the coverage before they snap the ball. The corners align at 4-6 yards off the wide receivers. They cock inward toward the ball with their outside foot on the inside foot of the receiver. We call the strong safety the "spur" and the free safety the "free." The "free" aligns two yards outside the end man on the line of scrimmage and eight yards deep. If the offense has one wide receiver to his side, the "spur" aligns two yards outside the end man on the line of scrimmage and eight yards deep. If there are two wide receivers to his side, he aligns 4-6 yards on the number 2 receiver. His alignment is the same as the corners on a two wide receiver side.

When we align in our secondary look, we could play 0-coverage, robber, cover-3, quarters, cover-2, and Tampa-2. We can play all of those coverages from this look and the offense will not know which one it is in their pre-snap read. We want the offense to guess and read the secondary in post-snap.

We use the "Tiger" front against offenses that have multiple offensive sets. The defense is flexible against many formations. We call the front to a number of keys. We can call the front to the tight end, multiple-receiver side, field, or boundary.

In our "Eagle" front, we are a basic "under" front. (Diagram #2) The end plays a 5-technique on the outside shoulder of offensive tackle to the tight end side. The nose moves to the tight end side and plays a strong side shade on the centers outside shoulder. The tackle reduces down into a 3-technique on the outside shoulder of the away side guard. The Jack linebacker plays a 7-technique if there is a tight end to his side and a loose 5-technique without a tight end.

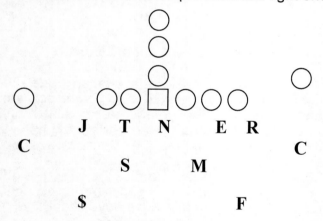

Diagram #2. Eagle Front

The Mike linebacker and Sam linebacker align in 30-techniques on the outside shoulders of the guards. The Rover plays a 9-technique on the tight end. If there is no tight end to his side, he plays a walk-away position on the wide receiver to that side. The alignment in the secondary is the same for the corners and safeties. The secondary is going to disguise what we are doing. We do not want to give the quarterback a pre-snap read.

We use the "Eagle" front against multiple set offenses. It is flexible against all formations. We slide the front to the tight end, multiple wide receivers, field, or boundary.

When we play spread teams, we bring in another defensive back and play our nickel package. We call that our "Base" front. (Diagram #3) We can substitute for a defensive lineman. Usually it is the Jack linebacker and we replace him with our next best defensive back. When we get in the "Base" front, we take on a 3-3 stack look. The end and tackle align in a 4-technique head up the offensive tackles. The nose plays head up the center in a 0-technique.

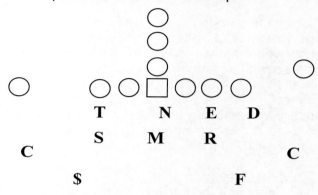

Diagram #3. Base Front

The Sam linebacker aligns in a 40-technique stacked behind the tackle. The Mike linebacker aligns in a 10-technique on the weakside shade of the center. The Rover linebacker stacks behind the end on the call side. The Nickel back aligns in a 9-technique if there is a tight end in the game. In most cases, with the nickel in the game there is no tight end.

The secondary alignment does not change when we go to the "Base" front but we have many more options. The nickel back gives us a multitude of things in the secondary. These three fronts show you how we develop from the "Tiger" front to the "Base" front.

In our arsenal of fronts, we play a bear front, which we call "Beast." (Diagram #4)

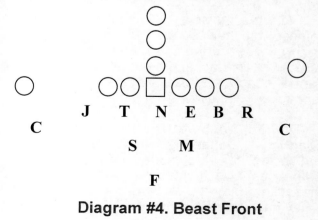

Diagram #4. Beast Front

The end and tackle align in 3-techniques on the outside shoulder of the guards. The nose is head up the center. The Jack and Rover linebackers align in 9-techniques on the tight ends.

The Mike and Sam linebackers stack behind the end and tackle in 30-techniques. If the "spur" is in the game, he plays a 7-technique on the tight end. We normally substitute for him and bring in a sub that plays linebacker in what we call the "Beast" position. The corners are in the "Beast" align at 4-6 yards off the line of scrimmage. They cock inward toward the ball with their outside foot on the inside foot of the wide receiver. The "free safety" is the middle of the field (MOF) player. This is our run stopping defense. You will not want to play this defense against a spread passing team.

END

Our End is the fastest of the three down lineman but must be physical enough to play inside the tackle. In the Tiger front he is a 4i-technique defender. In the Eagle front, he plays a 5-technique. In the Base front, he plays a 4-technique and in the Beast front he plays a 3-technique.

NOSE

The nose is the biggest and ugliest player you have. Our Nose is our biggest defensive lineman. He has to demand a double team and be the most dominant defensive lineman we have. This does not have to be the smartest player on your defense. He aligns in a 0-technique on three of the four fronts. The other alignment is a shade technique. If he aligns, head up the center he will probably be right with the calls. However, he must be a physical player.

TACKLE

Our Tackle will usually be smaller than our Nose but we ask him to be more of a technician than the Nose who is there just to cause chaos. He plays a 4i-technique in the Tiger front, a 4-technique in the Base front, and a 3-technique in the Beast and Eagles fronts. He has to play the down block and the reach block. He probably is the smallest of the three-down linemen. He does not need to be a big player but he must be a technician.

JACK LINEBACKER

Our Jack Linebacker is a hybrid player. He is either another fast defensive end or bigger linebacker type. If you have a linebacker that cannot read, play him at the Jack position. If he cannot read the guards, he will hurt you at the inside linebacker position. Put him at the Jack linebacker and let him play football. The player we played in that position went after everyone on every snap.

SAM LINEBACKER

Our Sam linebacker is our best tackling linebacker and has a nose for the ball. He is our ball hawk. We play him in a 30 or 40-techniques. We always protect him. We never let an offensive lineman touch him. He is a strong player and is always around the ball. He is our leading tackler. In 2009, we got 209 tackles from our Sam linebacker position. We expect him to make the most tackles on our defense.

MIKE LINEBACKER

Our Mike linebacker is our toughest most physical linebacker and the leader of our defense. I never ask the Mike linebacker to play in space and cover a receiver. The Sam and Rover linebackers can cover, but the Mike linebacker is a box player.

ROVER

We play the Rover position with our fastest linebacker but he must be physical enough to play a 9-technique on a tight end. This position is the hardest player to find. He has to play a 9-technique on a tight end and a linebacker position on the Base front. The last two years we were fortunate enough to have had a player that could play the Rover. If you do not have a player like this, you will have to substitute when you go to the Base front.

SPUR

The spur is the best player on the field. The player that played this position for us is going to South Carolina. Our Spur is a ball hawk that must also be the brains of the secondary. This is the position we roll down in coverage. He is the ball hawk when the ball is in the air.

FREE SAFETY

Our Free Safety is our hammer in the secondary. This is where we put our biggest hitter. He is more of a strong safety type than a free safety.

CORNERS

Our Corners are our fastest players and must be able to play man-to-man coverage. The last two years we were extraordinarily blessed. One of the corners is going to East Carolina. He is the only player that I know of that in back-to-back state championship games had fumble recovery's that went for 50 yards. The other corner was a 4 star running back.

When I draw up these fronts, I want to show different surfaces out of the same look. The offensive set is a spread formation with the tight end to the two-receiver side. (Diagram #5) The call we make is "Tiger-Strong-White." The first call tells us we are in the Tiger front. The second call tells us the line movement. The third call is the secondary coverage. The tight end aligns to the left with two receivers outside of him. The "Strong" call tells the defensive line we will slant to the left. The White call means we are in a cover-3 in the secondary.

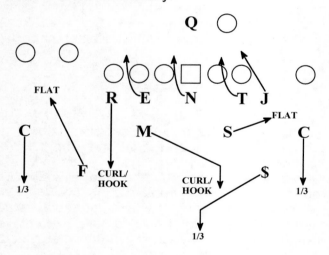

Diagram #5. Tiger-Strong-White (Sky)

The end, nose, tackle, and Jack linebacker slant one gap to their left. The coverage is cover-3. The Spur is going to drop down into the flat/curl coverage to the two-receiver side. With two receivers to the strong side, we roll the Spur down into the flat to stop the bubble screen. We call that "sky" coverage. If it is a pass, the Spur plays in the flat. The Rover linebacker drops for the hook/curl area. The Mike linebacker plays the hook/curl to the weakside, and the Sam linebacker runs to the flat zone. The corners and free safety play three-deep in the deep zones.

If the offense had only one detach receiver in the set the coverage call would be "cloud" instead of "sky." (Diagram #6) The threat of the bubble screen is gone. We roll the corner up into the flat area and he plays a hard corner on the wide receiver. The Spur plays over the top into the deep outside third.

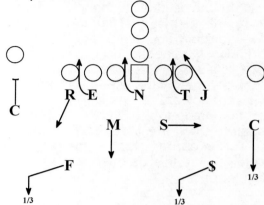

Diagram #6. Cover-3 Cloud

If the receiver takes an abnormal split of 18 yards or more, we go to a "rain" call. That means the corner locks up on the wide receiver man-to-man.

The next call is "Tiger-Red." (Diagram #7) The set is a 2 X 2 formation. Since there is no strength call the defensive line plays their techniques on run and pass. In the secondary, we play straight 0-coverage. We have a lock down man-to-man coverage on all receivers. The corners walk down and play "press bail" coverage on the wide receivers. They align in press position and bail out before the ball snaps. We have to play man-to-man for three seconds. When we bail, we do not want to get beat over the top. The safeties walk down and play lock man on the slot receivers. Since the running back is to the side of the Rover, he is responsible for him. The Jack linebacker is a blitzer on this call.

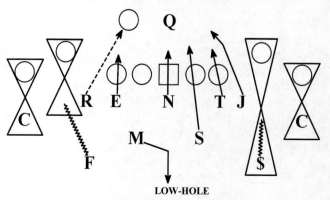

Diagram #7. Tiger Red

We lock the Rover linebacker on the running back. If the running back blocks, the Rover linebacker becomes an add-on blitzer and runs through the running back to the quarterback.

The Mike linebacker plays over the top of the Rover linebacker. In this situation, we would probably blitz the Sam linebacker and play the Mike linebacker in the low-hole as a free player in the middle. The reason we rush the Rover linebacker through the back is to protect against the screen pass. I want the running back on the ground, not releasing on a screen.

Everything we do with our defensive techniques is reading linemen. We are not looking into the backfield. The 4i-defenders align on the tackles inside eye but their eyes are on the guard. In his stance, his outside leg is back. When he steps, he steps with his inside leg into the tackle. If the guard pulls away from him, he follows the guard.

The backfield action will lie to you. The offensive linemen are like your momma. They tell you the truth every time. White is cover-3 and Red is cover-0.

If the offense motions from the 2 X 2 set into a 3 X 1, we check the coverage to a quarter-quarter-half coverage. (Diagram #8) The corner and free safety play quarter coverage on the number 1 and 2 receivers to the trips side. The Spur moves with the motion to the middle of the field. If the number 3 receiver is a threat on the vertical route, the free safety covers him. We will be man-to-man on the single receiver to the backside.

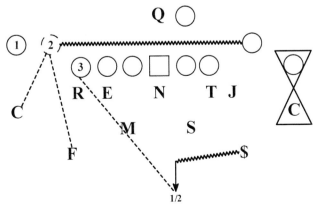

Diagram #8. Quarters Check

The Spur does not automatically take the number 3 receiver unless he is a ligament threat to get deep. Otherwise, he is playing free in the middle on all threats.

If we want to slant the defensive line to the weak side, we call "weak." (Diagram #9) The call is "Tiger-Weak-Orange." The front is a Tiger front slanting to the weakside of the formation. The Orange call is cover-2 in the secondary. The Rover linebacker, end, nose, and tackle slant to the left or weakside. The secondary is cover-2 corner roll coverage. The seam players in this coverage are the Jack and Mike linebackers. They wall the number 2 receivers to the outside. We do not want them running up the middle of the field.

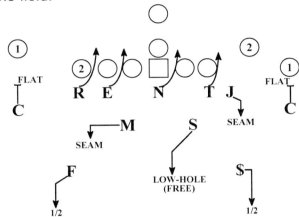

Diagram #9. Tiger Weak Orange

The Free and Spur play half field coverage down the hash marks. The corners roll up into the short flat zone to their side. The Sam linebacker drops into the middle of the field and is the low-hole player. He plays free in the middle of the field short. The holes in the cover-2 zones are in the middle over the linebackers and 18 yards on the sidelines. The 18 yard sideline area is hard for a high school quarterback to compete passes.

In this coverage, we can play Tampa-2 using the Sam linebacker. He is a strong safety-type playing linebacker and does not have trouble sinking into the deep middle. The problem we have in this coverage is the Mike linebacker playing a wall technique on the number 2 receiver. In some cases, that could be a slot receiver.

You can see we run multiple coverages out of the same look. We do not play multiple coverages on every other down in a football game. We do not play all the coverages in our package every week. We game plan what we play each week and the checks from each of those coverages.

The offensive coordinator run multiple formations and runs the same plays out of them. We do the same thing on defense. We show one front and one secondary look. However, we move on the snap of the ball and play multiple coverages. We do the same thing with our blitz package. We bring the same blitzes from multiple fronts.

We tie our stunts and blitzes into our multiple fronts, and disguise coverage system. We do both man and zone blitzing. Our blitzes are similar to any other teams. We bring field and boundary side pressures and bring the heat playing "0" coverage.

We have had success with our line by stemming into a blitz. Offenses today come to the line to see what you are in and check the play. This is difficult to do against us, because of all the movement, fronts, and pressures that we bring.

If the offense comes out in a no-back set, we may be in an "Eagle" front. (Diagram #10) With the three-receiver side to the right and the two-receiver side to the left. We align our strength to the three-receiver side. On the weakside, we walk the Sam linebacker out on the number 2 receiver to that side. The Rover linebacker walks out and splits the number 2 and 3 receivers.

To the trips side we play quarters with the free safety and corner. The Rover linebacker aligned between the number 2 and 3 receivers can play the bubble screen. He is the flat defender to that side.

The stunt that we like to run against the empty set is a five-man pressure stunt. We take the shade nose across the center's face into the weakside A-gap. The Mike linebacker fires the onside A-gap. The Jack linebacker comes off the edge. The offensive tackle has no help on his pass block. We feel our Jack linebacker can beat him almost every time.

The blitz we like to run is "Tiger-Pittsburgh." (Diagram #11) This is a three-deep fire zone blitz. The Rover linebacker is coming off the edge and the Mike linebacker is blitzing the A-gap. The nose crosses the centers face and gets into the weakside A-gap. The Jack linebacker drops into the flat and is the wall/flat player. The Sam linebacker drops into the low-hole in the middle and plays free. The free safety rolls down and becomes the flat/wall player to the strong side of the set. We play cover-3 in the secondary with the Spur dropping into the deep middle.

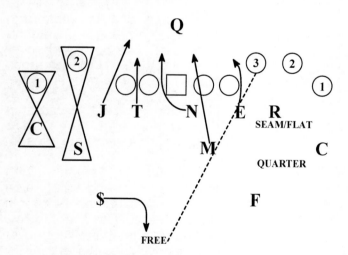

Diagram #10. Empty Set Blitz

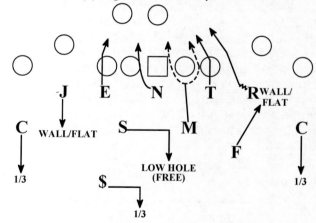

Diagram #11. Tiger Pittsburgh

We are making a wager that the wide receivers cannot cross the entire field before we get to the quarterback. On the two-receiver side, we lock up the number 1 and 2 receivers with the corner and Sam linebacker. The Spur is over the top of them reading the quarterback's eyes. He is free in the middle of the field and can see the number 3 receiver to the trips side. If they run the number 3 receiver vertical, he is in a position to handle him.

We give the Mike linebacker a two-way-go on the guard. We tell him to run through the open gap. We want to bring the blitz from the call side. We can call the side that we want to run the blitz. If we want to bring the blitz to the side of the running back, we have no problem making that the call side. If we want to bring the blitz away from the running back, we can do that also. The end to the Jack linebacker's side is the contain end on a pass rush.

We can stem our front by our game plan. In the game plan, we plan to stem from the

Tiger front to the Eagle front. (Diagram #12) With a subtle movement, we have changed the front and brought pressure to the offense. The offensive linemen have to be ready for blitzes from a stemmed front. The nose, end, and tackle, move from an 0-technique to a shade technique, from a 4i to a 5-technique and from a 4i to a 3-technique. The changes are minute but the offensive linemen have to alter their technique.

Diagram #12. Tiger to Eagle

The later the stem the more effective it can be. If you can time the cadence and move at the last second, you can gain a great advantage. I believe we do not stemming enough in our scheme. The Mike linebacker watches the quarterback. If he comes to the line and looks at the defense and calls check or something that may indicate an audible, we want to move when he gets back under the center. If he is in the shotgun, we move on the snap signal.

When the offense slows down to adjust to what you are doing on defense that means we are dictating to them.

We call the next stunt Eagle "Philly." (Diagram #13) The Jack linebacker is my wall/flat player to the backside. The free safety on the Philly stunt is the low-hole player. The nose guard is in a shade to the call side. He crosses the center's face into the weakside A-gap. The Mike linebacker fires through the call side A-gap. The Sam linebacker crosses behind the Mike linebacker into the call side B-gap.

This is a wide side stunt with crossfire between the A and B-gap. The free safety becomes the low-hole player. It goes back to the personnel. The Free is a hammer. He does not mind playing in the box. The Rover is the wall/flat player and plays in a loose 9-technique. In this scenario, we are trying to buy time until the pressure hits home.

Our linebackers do a lot of walking into and out of gaps. If you look at this from an offensive prospective, when the linebacker creeps up, the linemen is thinking the end is coming inside on a cross face move with the Mike blitzing outside of him. What does he think when the Mike linebacker creeps down into the gap? He thinks he has to protect that gap.

When we blitz, we want to disguise our stunts. We want to show when we are not coming and come from a distance on other stunts. I never want the offensive linemen knowing what is coming. If I can get an offensive tackle matched up on an outside linebacker, I will win that match up most of the time. The linebacker is more athletic and faster.

This year we felt we need to use more zone blitz schemes to counter some of the things offenses were doing to us. We came up with two fire zone blitzes that are simple to run.

The first one is "Dallas." (Diagram #14) The corner and Spur play a cover-2 read on the number 1 and 2 receivers to their side. The free safety and corner do the same thing to the other side. I know when I say this there are lots of holes in the coverage. They are not as big when we get into a 0-coverage.

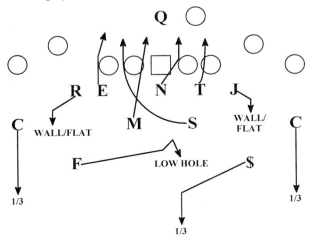

Diagram #13. Philly

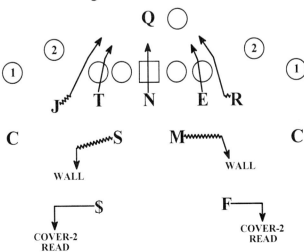

Diagram #14. Dallas

The Mike and Sam linebacker are the wall/flat players to their side. They have to keep everyone out of the middle of the field. If someone gets down the middle, we will pay dearly. We bring the Rover and Jack linebackers off the edge. We do this a lot with the running quarterback. They have a tendency to roll or scramble one way. I want him to go to the A-gap on the side he does not want to go. I want him turned up inside. If you watched Alabama in the national championship game, they were doing the same pressure. With four-man pressure the rush lanes are too wide.

The next blitz might be the simplest blitz of them all. The coverage is cover-3. On "Baltimore," We run these stunts because the offense has a tendency to fan protect with the 4i-defenders. (Diagram #15) The end aligns in a 4i-technique and rips to the outside across the face of the tackle. The Free safety cheats down and blows through the B-gap. The nose goes away into the weakside A-gap. The Sam linebacker is the low-hole player. The Mike linebacker is the wall player to the call side. We play three-deep in the secondary. The Spur rolls into the middle of the field.

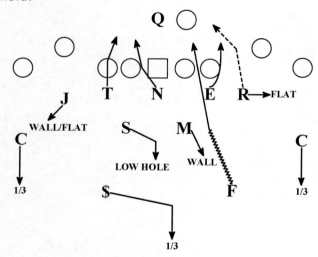

Diagram #15. Baltimore

I appreciate the opportunity to come and speak at this clinic. We have been successful at Havelock High School and hopefully we will continue to be successful. If there is anything I can do for you please contact me at Havelock High School. It has been a pleasure and thank you very much.

Glenn McNamee

Jet Sweep Series And Companion Plays

Central Dauphin High School, Pennsylvania

Today I want to talk to you about our Jet Sweep Series. I am going to share as much as possible about what we do. I am going to show you how we teach it and how we block it.

Through 2008, we were under the center. In 2009, we made the switch to the shotgun set. We went to the shotgun set almost exclusively. During the year in 2009, we put in the Jet Sweep. It was a complimentary play and it certainly was not the centerpiece of the offense. Since then the Jet Sweep Series has become most of our offense.

WHY THE JET SWEEP SERIES

- **Two-back running game from a one-back set**
- **Stretches the field horizontally**
- **Creates flow**
- **Takes advantage of defensive over pursuing**
- **Many good complimentary plays**
- **Skilled players in space – That gives them better and more opportunities to do their thing**

I want to talk about the advantages of running this series. While we were under the center, we were a two-back running team. We found that using the Jet Sweep gave us a two-back running game from a one-back set. Out of the one-back set, it gave us an opportunity to stretch the field both horizontally and vertically. When you put the back in motion, you have the two-back running game.

We know this from our experiences running the Jet Sweep so much the last two years. It creates flow from the defense. With the Jet Sweep you are actually going before we snap the ball. The defenses want to make sure they do not get beat on the perimeter. They want to fast flow to the ball, but you are gone. We pressurize the containment and force defenders to get there in a hurry.

Because they do not want to get beat outside, it creates the over pursuit in the defense. When they over pursue, it opens the door for some good complimentary plays to the Jet Sweep. I am going to share as many of those compliments today as I have time.

The only thing that limits the Jet Sweep is the imagination of the coaches. Most coaches want to know how to get their skilled players in space. I am impressed at all levels how coaches get the ball to their skilled players in space. The Jet Sweep Series gives them more opportunity to do their thing.

What I am going over today is our Jet Sweep Series and the options off that series. In the Jet Sweep Series we run the Jet Sweep, lead sweep, counter with pull and without, and play action passing. The other options to the series are the reverse, quarterback running plays, the shovel pass, motion across the formation, screens, and use of cadence.

I want to go over the Jet Sweep first. It is not the play we run the most. We run the lead sweep as our bread and butter play. It is a hybrid between a belly and a read-G. We run a counter with blockers pulling and without pulling. This series still has good play action passing.

When we get into our staff meetings, we talk about the defense. You never know what the defense will do to defend the sweep. We never know the adjustments the defensive coordinator has planned until you see them. We work hard at making sure we have a counter for anything the defense may do to stop the Jet Sweep. We want to make sure we have enough clubs in our bag to make the shot we need to make. I also want to talk about that today.

This is a play we try not to over coach. When we installed the Jet Sweep in 2009, I am a little embarrassed to say this but we did not study too hard on it. We did not go to clinics and talk to people about it. It became a trial and error process. It was more like back yard football. We give him the ball and let him do his thing. We try to coach up the rest of the plays in our offense. With this play we do not coach so much the techniques or details as we do the mentality of the play.

When we first put this play in we called it cyclone right and left. We wanted to emphasize the jet or speed of the play. We wanted the play to be fast and aggressive. Because of the speed of this play, it made us a more aggressive football team. It meant we did not need to hold the blocks as long to be successful. If you were on the backside of the play there was no way your defender had a chance to get in on the play. They could get down the field on a 45 degree track and block anyone.

The mentality of this play is to run and hit. The lead back wanted to emphasize the mentality of the play. He had to be aggressive on the play and lead the charge.

In our set we want the quarterback at four and half yards off the line of scrimmage. (Diagram #1) The running back aligns to the playside at five yards off the line of scrimmage. Normally he aligns a yard behind the quarterback's alignment and on the outside leg of the guard to his side. On this play, we want him closer to the line of scrimmage. He has to block the first thing off the edge. When the jet motion starts the hand off from the quarterback must be a bang-bang handoff.

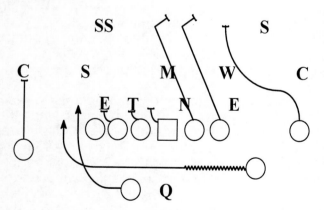

Diagram #1. Jet Sweep

We do not want the jet runners to have to be careful in his alignment. He wants to get as close to the line of scrimmage as he can. He cannot get too tight because he has to be a threat in the passing game as well as on the Jet Sweep.

He is a pass receiver in his alignment. When he leaves in jet motion, he has to gain depth in his motion to the quarterback so he can receive the hand off.

The lead back's aiming point is one-yard outside the tight end. He cannot get too tight so he does not become involved with the tight end. He has to get to the edge and out on the perimeter. His rule is simple. He blows up the first thing he sees. We do not tell him to block inside out or any other instructions.

The wide receivers to the playside use a stalk block technique unless it is man coverage. On some occasion we crack to the inside.

The offensive line is blocking similar to a zone-blocking concept. However, it is not the typical outside zone blocking concept. We are not going to hang on combo blocking as a true outside zone blocking package. If the linebacker scrapes to the C-gap, the lead blocker should see that as a threat and block him. If he blitzes the B or A-gaps, he will not affect the play. The jet runner should be past that gap if the exchange is on time.

We can run the Jet Sweep from any formation. You can use receiver as well as running backs to run this play. That allows you to run it to the tight end or split end. You can run it to a balanced set or an unbalanced set.

The Jet Sweep is an East-West play but we tell our back to make it a North-South play when the opportunity avails itself. We tell the jet runner as soon as he sees daylight to plant his foot and get upfield. We do not tell him to hit the play North and South, but when it is there, we want him to take it.

When we watch the tape of the game, we do not spend much time analyzing the jet runner's decision. We give them general reminders but we do not harp on what he should do on the play. We know the next time he runs the play he will make the right decision. We do not want to over coach it or get the runners thinking too much.

The tight end has to reach the defender aligned on him and stay on him. He is not so much worried about trying to hook him. He wants to make contact and keep running. He wants to stop the defender from penetrating up the field. We want all the offensive line running in contact with defenders.

I want to make a point about the fullback's read on his block. Blocking the perimeter is a huge aspect of the Jet Sweep. (Diagram #2) We want the receiver to block the first defender to his inside. If the receiver cannot block the defender because of his alignment or the speed that he attacks the line of scrimmage, he has to make his intension known right away. If he cannot block the first defender to the inside, he goes to the next defender, which is probably the free safety.

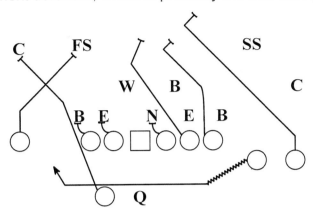

Diagram #2. Jet Crack

He cannot make a cloudy situation for the fullback coming out of the backfield. The receiver has to clear so the fullback knows he has to block the linebacker. The worst-case scenario is the fullback stuttering and hesitating about whom he should block.

The timing of the play is critical. Each player that runs the Jet Sweep has his own speed. The alignment of the jet runner changes because of the ball placement on the field. They cannot keep a consistent distance when they run the Jet Sweep because we want to stretch the field with our formations. We certainly do not want to tip the Jet Sweep by alignment. The wide receiver is responsible for the timing to the mesh. The quarterback cannot adjust the cadence for each player. They all must work hard at working on their timing from all areas of the field.

I do want to tell you that we do this at the JV level and the 8th grade team is experimenting with it at their level. You can be affective at any level running this play. You can teach it.

If the playside offensive guard has a 2i-technique defender on him and the Mike linebacker walks up into the B-gap, the guard has to reach for the Mike linebacker. The center has to get a piece of the 2i defender. However, if the 2i-technique is making a play on the jet

back, we have issues to deal with and it is not the blocking of the play.

If the linebacker comes late into the B-gap the guard will try to make a play on him. Nevertheless, if the exchange is good the linebacker blitzing the B-gap from a regular alignment will be no problem even if we let him blitz the gap.

If the defense wants to sprint to the sideline to keep the play from getting outside, we cut it up. If the tight end has a 7-technique and an overhanging linebacker, the tight end has to block down on the 7-technique and the fullback will block the overhang. The wide receiver will not be able to block him. However, I have seen the tight end block the overhang and the offensive tackle block the 7-technique. As I said before, the blocks do not need to be hook blocks.

If the linemen can get contact on the defender and run, we have a chance to have a good play. Even if the lineman makes contact he should not try to work to the outside. If he slows down he will lose the defender and lose his block. Keep contact and let the back make his move. If the back plants to cut up, the defender cannot stop because the lineman has contact and continues to push him to the sidelines.

If the defense wants to take away the Jet Sweep, they can. There has to be other clubs in the bag and other variations otherwise, you are in trouble.

The variation I am going to show you have been outstanding for us. It is a play we run more and with more success than the Jet Sweep. We call it a "lead sweep." It is a hybrid between a belly lead and lead-G.

The backside blocking is the same regardless of the front. (Diagram #3)

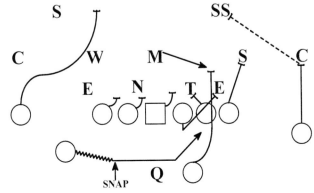

Diagram #3. Lead Sweep vs. Even

We zone the backside from the center to the backside tackle. The playside guard pulls and kicks out the defender over the tight end. The playside tackle has a down block on the man covering the guard. If there is no defender over the guard, he zones through the B-gap to the backside linebacker. The tight end blocks the first defender outside.

The alignment of the fullback in the base set aligns him in the B-gap at five and half yards. On the Jet Sweep, he aligns in the B-gap at five-yards. On this play he aligns on the inside leg of the guard at five and half yards. He is at normal depth but adjusts inside so he can read the pulling guard. If he is ahead of the pulling guard, it will be difficult for the fullback and the running back. He aims for the tight end's butt and reads the guard's block.

If the guard kicks out the 7-technique defender, the fullback hits underneath the guard's block and blows up the first thing he sees, which should be the Mike linebacker.

We want the jet motion to look like the Jet Sweep motion. The difference is the running back throttles his speed slightly. He wants to be behind the backside tackle when we snap the ball. The handoff is not the bang-bang play like the Jet Sweep. The nature of the play is a little different. The quarterback has to wait momentarily for the running back. The blocking scheme has to develop and we do not want the running back there too quick.

If the tight end has a 9-technique defender aligned on him, he blocks down to the inside and not outside. That is a "Toledo" call for us. (Diagram #4)

combination block on the 5-technique defender to the backside linebacker. Everything else on the play is the same. The playside guard pulls and kicks out or logs the 9-technique linebacker. The fullback still reads the guard's block on the 9-technique and turns up or goes outside on the log block.

The fullback has the same read. If we have a 4i-alignment, we give the "Toledo" call. (Diagram #5) With the 4i-defender favoring the inside gap, the tackle blocks him by himself and the tight end goes to the playside linebacker. The fullback comes through the hole and may get all the way to the safety. If the backside or middle stack linebacker did a good job of getting to the frontside, the fullback blocks him.

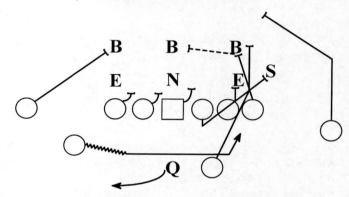

Diagram #5. Lead Sweep Stack

Sometimes in the huddle we call "56-Toledo." (Diagram #6) That means the tight end comes down regardless of the defensive front. If he has a 7-technique defender on his inside shoulder that is his block. He comes down on the inside defender and the guard pulls for the first defender outside the tight end. In most cases, it is the outside linebacker or overhang defender.

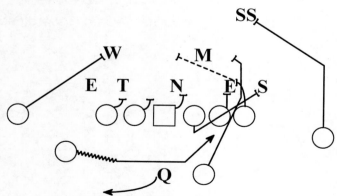

Diagram #4. Lead Sweep "Toledo"

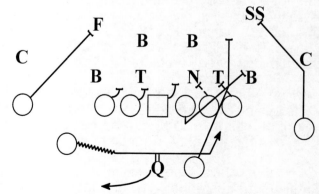

Diagram #6. 56-Toledo

The tight end and tackle have a combo block on the defender over the tackle. They execute a

The fullback knows that on a Toledo scheme against an even front the play hits one hole wider. He still reads the play but knows what to expect. On this play the running back alters his position to the quarterback. Since the play goes wider he wants to mesh sooner than later with the quarterback. Instead of being behind the tackle, he is in the B-gap when we snap the ball.

This play looks a lot like the Jet Sweep and that is by design. The running back throttles down at the mesh and starts to work downhill. What we look for is the outside linebacker playing up the field to stop the Jet Sweep. At times, he gets so wide we do not need to block him. The running back may read the guard's block differently than the fullback.

If the fullback turns up inside the guard's block, it does not mean the running back will. The guard's block may start out as a kick out block, but by the time the running back gets to the hole, the block could turn into a log block. In that case, he goes outside.

The backside blocks are important. The backside tackle scoops into the B-gap backside and continues to run for the backside linebacker. He stays after him even if he gets to the frontside of the play. We have actually cut the play back behind the backside tackle's block on the backside linebacker. The backside must stay after their blocks even though they think the play is gone. The backside linebacker is the most dangerous defender to the backside and makes most of the tackles on the front side of this play.

If the 9-technique defender closes hard to the inside, we must log block him. (Diagram #7)

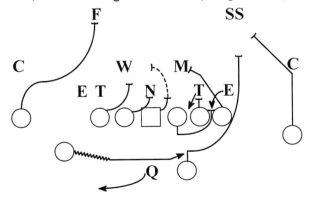

Diagram #7. Toledo Log

The guard pulls and cannot kick out the 9-technique defender because he is inside and down the line of scrimmage. He attacks his outside shoulder and knee and log blocks him to the inside. The fullback reads the block of the pulling guard and goes outside. He blocks the first threat whoever it may be.

We can change the blocking slightly and make the play a "lead-G" play. (Diagram #8) On this play everything is the same for everyone with the exception of the fullback and pulling guard. The fullback has the kick out block and the guard turns up or goes outside his block. Nothing changes for the running back. He still reads the kick out block and follows the guard. The pulling guard wraps up to the Mike linebacker.

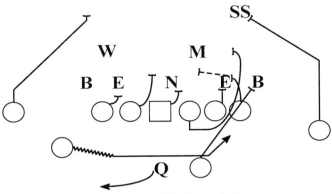

Diagram #8. Lead-G

The fullback has to beat the running back to the hole. On occasions he does not and it becomes a bad play.

The companion play to this play is the "counter" play. We run it with a pull and a no pull. I am not going to spend much time talking about this play because there are many ways to run it. You can pull one or two blockers off the backside. We pull according to the defensive scheme and scouting report. Sometimes we pull one and sometimes we pull two blockers.

The running back comes in jet motion. (Diagram #9)

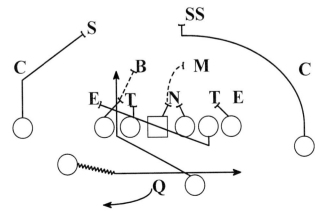

Diagram #9. Counter/Pull

We want him as close to the line of scrimmage in his alignment as possible. The jet motion is back to the bang-bang fake with the running back. We do not want the quarterback to wait on the jet motion. We want the running back to clear the mesh area immediately. If he is too wide and the quarterback has to wait, it throws off the timing of the entire play. It is a token fake by the quarterback and the running back. The fullback aligns in his normal position and comes off the butt of the running back.

The fullback aligns on the outside leg of the backside guard. His aiming point is the outside leg of the playside guard. He goes straight to that point. He cannot banana away from that line. If we pull both the guard and tackle, the guard kicks out and the tackle turns up inside. On this play only the backside tackle pulls and kicks out or logs the first defender past the playside tackle.

The playside linemen have a gap-blocking scheme. If the defensive alignment is a 35-technique set up, we kick out the 5-technique and combo the 3-technique to the playside linebacker. If the defense is a 1-technique and 5-technique, the playside guard blocks down on the shade defender and the playside tackle goes up on the linebacker.

If we run the play with "no pull", it becomes an isolation play to the playside. (Diagram #10) If the formation is a trips set, we motion the slot back as the jet motion. The backside combo blocks for the defenders to that side. The playside guard and tackle split blocks on the defenders to that side. The guard blocks down on the shade defender to his inside and the tackle blocks out on the 5-technique defender to his outside. The wingback folds inside the tackle's block and we isolate the linebacker.

We may leave an outside linebacker unblocked, but in most cases, it does not matter. We ran this play many times. When the running back comes through the mesh, the quarterback does not fake to him with the ball. The running back has to get low, make a good fake, and sell the Jet Sweep. As soon as the running back clears the mesh, the fullback has to go.

The motion moves the playside linebacker to the motion and makes the block an easier block. When the guard and tackle combo up to that backer, the tackle's angle improves because the linebacker moves away with the motion. When he sees the counter, the tackle has position on him. The same thing is true with the fold block from the outside. The nature of the play allows us to use smaller isolation blockers on the fold blocks. Their angle on the linebacker allows them to shield him rather the blow him up.

The variation of the play is to turn out on the 5-technique and turn inside that block with the pulling lineman, whoever it may be. That gives you a combination of the pull and isolation play. Nothing changes for anyone except the tackle and pulling lineman. We also run the counter-tray with the backside guard and tackle pulling. The guard pulls, kicks out, and the backside tackle turns up.

Another variation is to put the fullback to the same side as the jet motion. (Diagram #11) The defensive end sees the jet motion coming to him and gets up the field to stop the Jet Sweep. The play is the same except the defensive end opens the door by getting up the field.

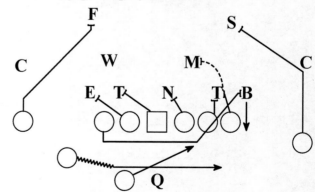

Diagram #11. Fullback to Motion

We can take advantage of the defensive end trying to come off the backside and run down the counter. (Diagram #12) We run a counter read play with the quarterback reading the backside end. If he pursues hard to the inside and tries to

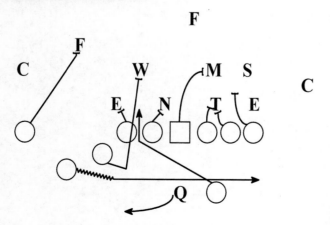

Diagram #10. Counter No Pull

run down the fullback, the quarterback can pull the ball and run out the backside on the play.

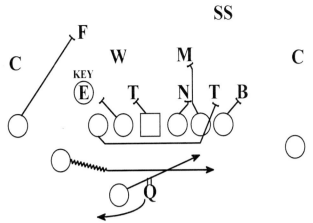

Diagram #12. Counter Read

Another thing we can do is run the counter to the same side of the motion without putting the fullback away from the playside. On the counters I showed you earlier, the fullback crosses the quarterback face to get the ball. (Diagram #13) We have the ability to run the same play without the fullback coming across the quarterbacks face. The fullback takes a two-step movement to the quarterback. On his third step he plants and goes back the other way. His alignment is on the playside and not away from it. When we run this variation, we call "same", which means the fullback aligns to the same side the play is going.

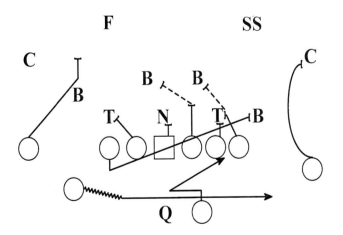

Diagram #13. Counter Read - Playside

We can run the counter with no pull and add the word "same" and run the play. (Diagram #14) Now the jet motion goes to the right. The fullback starts to the right, goes two steps, plants, and comes back the other way. The wide receiver folds back inside, isolates the linebacker, and we run the counter to the left.

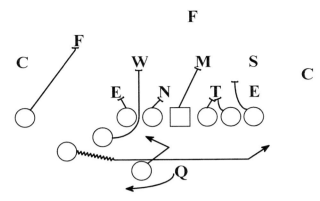

Diagram #14. Counter No Pull Same

I want to show you two play action passes off the jet motion. There are great opportunities for play action passes in this series. The first one comes off the counter play. (Diagram #15) We fake the Jet Sweep and fake the counter on this play. When we play action pass we want a receiver low, one in the middle, and one high. The jet motion is the low pattern coming out after the fake. The tight end goes down the field 10-yards and runs an out pattern to the sidelines. The wide receiver to that side runs the takeoff or streak pattern. The backside receiver runs a post.

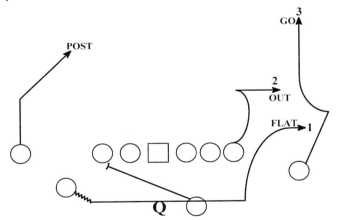

Diagram #15. Counter Pass

The quarterback's first read is the jet motion in the flat. If it is there, he takes it right away. If the flat pattern is not there, he looks for the tight end on the middle route. His last read is the deep patterns.

This series also fits into our quick series passing game. There are two things we can do off this pattern. (Diagram #16) We can throw the quick screen away from the jet motion or the quick slant to the side of the jet motion. This pass comes off the quick series. The quarterback does not fake to the jet motion. He catches the ball, finds the seams, and throws.

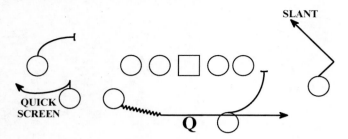

Diagram #16. Quick Series

The fake of the Jet Sweep is all in the hands of the running back. The quarterback does not fake the ball to the motion back. However, the action of the back and the proximity of the motion get the desired results. The outside linebacker is not dropping under the wide receiver. He is reacting to the motion. The same thing happens to the backside. The safety moves to the middle and everyone loosen their coverage.

We can use the jet motion and throw a simple out pattern to the wide receiver. We throw the ball off sprint out action to the side of the jet motion. The jet motion pulls all the underneath coverage and we have a pitch and catch to the wide receiver. It is a single one out pattern. What we get is single coverage on the wide receiver.

There are so many quarterback runs from this offense. I will show you one. The play comes off the lead sweep action. (Diagram #17) We pull the guard as we did on the lead sweep. We run jet motion and fake the lead sweep to the right. To the left we run the blocking scheme that goes with the counter with no pulling guard. We block down with the left guard and out with the left tackle. The slot back folds inside and isolates the linebacker. The quarterback fakes the lead sweep, pulls the ball, and runs into the isolation gap to the left.

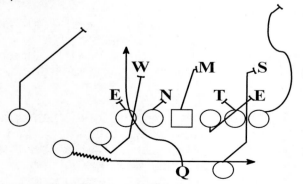

Diagram #17. Quarterback Isolation

The right offensive tackles down blocks on the lead sweep. However, on the quarterback isolation to the left, he wants to cut off the backside tackle. The 3-technique defender sees the guard in front of him pull to the outside. When the tackle comes down on him, he fights to the outside and the offensive tackle can let him move in that direction and cut him off.

We work hard on the fakes with our backs and quarterbacks. We refer to it as head, hands, and hips. We want to drop the head, and fold the hands into the body. We want the hips to roll with the ride of the ball. One other thing we do with the jet motion is to run our Wildcat formation. That puts our best running back at the quarterback position with the Jet Sweep motion coming. It can be a lethal offensive set. We can run the same offense with the Wildcat back.

The last option I want to show you is the reverse off the Jet Sweep. (Diagram 18) We fake the Jet Sweep to the left and run the reverse to the right. The playside tackle runs a technique we call a tight wheel. He releases downfield and wheels back to the outside for a kill shot on the defensive end. The quarterback gives the ball to the running back on the Jet Sweep and becomes the lead back out the backside. The running back runs the Jet Sweep to the outside and flips the ball to the wide receiver on the reverse. The tackle wheels and blocks the defensive end. He wants to get on the upfield shoulder of the defensive end. The quarterback leads the wide receiver around the corner.

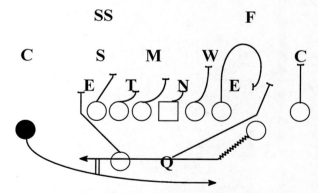

Diagram #18. Flanker Reverse

We want to run the reverse to the tight end side as well as the split side. If we run to the tight end, the tackle still runs the wheel technique. The tight end chips on the defender on his way out and gets downfield.

I hope this helps. Thank you for your attention.

Dan McSurley

Wishbone To Flex-Bone Offensive Concepts

Clinton-Massie High School, Ohio

In 1987 our team went 0-10. That was probably the most significant thing that has happened in my coaching career. After the season, the Superintendent called me into his office. He was a former offensive line coach. He was a tough administrator. He simply said, "Get you act together or do not plan on coaching and teaching here next year." I was the offensive and defensive line coach at the time.

I had a baby on the way and was living in a trailer at that time. I went to the head coach and told him I needed this job and if they were going to fire me, I wanted to call the plays. He gave me the opportunity to coordinate the offense. I took the opportunity and ran with it. I did not know where I was going with it. I picked up from the library an instructional video by Darrell Royal on running the wishbone offense. I took that film home, set up the projector on the kitchen table, and used the refrigerator for a screen. I watched the film for two days. What is amazing is that was 25 years ago and I am still running the exact same offense I started running the offense in 1987. What I am going to show you today is how the offense has evolved.

We still run a base wishbone but this is a combination of how the offense and my philosophy has evolved over the last 25 years. Each year we start out in the base wishbone. We learn how to run that offense before we do any of the things I am going to show you today. We do not progress past the wishbone offense until we can run it well. It is first and foremost that our players understand how to run the wishbone.

OFFENSIVE PHILOSOPHY

- **Can be effective at all levels**
- **Ability to use multiple formations**
- **Gives offensive linemen an advantage**
- **Difficult for other team to simulate**
- **Stretches the defense vertically and horizontally**
- **Develops toughness**

The wishbone can be effective at all levels. You can take a bunch of youth league players and run this offense. You cannot teach a more fundamental offense than the wishbone. Our kids start running it in the third grade. They do not run many plays but they can run our base play, which is the 15-16 option. They start in the third grade and run it through high school.

You have the ability to use multiple formations when you use this offense. We run the base wishbone but we use many formations with it. That is the luxury you have with this offense. You can get in a double wing, double slot, trips, and other formations but you are still running the base principle of the wishbone.

The wishbone gives offensive linemen an advantage. We do not ask our offensive linemen to line up head up with a defender and ask him to move the defender. We are like anyone else. We have small offensive linemen trying to block massive defenders. We are a down blocking team. We combination block and chip off the block for the linebackers at the next level. An eight year old can understand that concept.

This offense is hard for the opposing team to simulate when they practice against it. It is amusing to watch them in warm up trying to duplicate our offense. We are a high repetition offense because we run the same plays thousands of times over the course of a season. By the time our players are juniors in high school, they may have run the play ten thousand times.

This offense can stretch the defense vertically, and horizontal. I will show you how we do that later. We have to get over the top of the defense and get to the edges.

This offense develops toughness. Not only does the offensive line and offense get tough but the defense working against it gains toughness. We are a two-platoon football team. We do not put our first team against the second and third defenses. We go ones-on-ones. If your defense sees that daily, they get dag-gone tough. I am the head coach and I have the whistle. None of my assistants carries a whistle.

We get after each other. We do not go out and practice in shorts. We go in pads on Monday, Tuesday, and Wednesday. We may be in shorts on Thursday, but the rest of the time, we get after it. If you coach your players up right, they will not do stupid things. They will not clip anyone or take a cheap shot on the quarterback. We play hard, but we do not try to hurt our own players. We keep everything above the waist but our linemen are getting after it.

2012 CLINTON-MASSIE OFFENSIVE STATS

Rushing
Attempts = 600
Yards = 5,752
Average = 9.6
TD's = 88
Yards Per Game = 385.5

Passing
Completions = 41
Attempts = 70
Yards = 963
TD's = 16
Yards Per Game = 64.2

Scoring = 119 TD's
Kick PAT'S 104 - 2 Rushing PAT's
822 Points = *All time Ohio High School Scoring Record

We are the smallest school in our conference and we do not play against the Little Sisters of the Poor. We are playing against larger schools.

One of our goals this year was to score every five plays. We had a 15 games schedule and scored a touchdown every 5.4 plays. We scored a lot of points and we were able to move the ball, but we did not pass very much.

This is our base offense. It is not rocket science. It is just like any other offense you learned when you played peewee football. We number our backs 1-4. The quarterback is 1, fullback is 3, and the halfbacks are 2 and 4. (Diagram #1) The odd number play go to the left, and even number plays go to the right side. That is very basic and easy to remember. The number of plays you can run is only limited by your imagination.

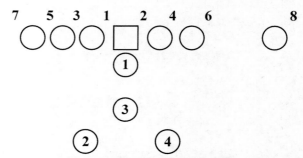

Diagram #1. Base Wishbone Set

When you run a wishbone offense the splits in the offensive line are tremendously important. If the splits are wrong, the mesh is wrong.

OFFENSIVE LINE SPLITS

Base Split
- **Split 2 feet between the center and guards.**
- **Splits between the guard and tackle, and the tackle and tight end are 3 feet.**

Alignment Calls
- **Norma (normal split)**
- **Tammy (Tight splits – cut splits down to 6 inches to 1 foot)**
- **Wilma (Wide split – expand as far as the defender will go)**

Alignment Rules
- **Off-tackle play (Norma)**
- **Inside play (Wilma)**
- **Outside play (Tammy)**

In 80 percent of our offense we want to be in a normal split. If we run inside, we want to expand our splits to give us wider gaps to run. If we are going to the outside, we want to tighten up the splits to bring the corner closer to the play. If we want to run a power pitch and get to the edge, we call "Tammy." That tightens down the splits and lets us get to the edge quicker. We can run the 6-hole veer play with the tight splits. When we run the veer, we delete the fullback out of the set and run split-back veer plays.

If we call Wilma, we want to increase the size of the split between the center and guard. When we do that we run the midline play and move the 3-technique further from the read. We are not too crazy on our guard-center splits. If we have a trap or any play coming inside the guard, we widen the splits.

RUNNING BACK ALIGNMENT:

- **Fullback** - 9-12 feet from the tip of the football depending on his speed.

- **Halfbacks** – 18 inches X 18 inches square off the heels of the fullback. If in the slot or wing position, the alignment is 3 X 3 feet off the tackle or tight end.

After running this offense for 25 years and watching other high school teams, I think the biggest mistake they make is setting the fullback too deep. This year we aligned our fullback at ten feet from the tip of the football. I do not know the last time I had a fullback setting at 12 feet.

If you have a slower, bigger, fullback, you need to move him up to 3 yards from the tip of the ball. If the fullback's depth is not exactly right, it will screw up the timing of the offense. The deeper the fullback, the deeper the halfbacks because they align off him. If our linebackers see a fullback deeper than 12 feet, they will beat him to the point of attack.

We set the halfbacks at 18 square inches off the heels of the fullback. The means from the outside of one halfback to the outside of the other halfback, the distance is six yards.

The first formation I want to show when we break the bone is the double slot. (Diagram #2)

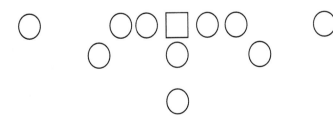

Diagram #2. Double Slot

I am going to show you how we scored all those points and how we got most of our yardage. We use the double slot when we run against and even defense. We want to spread them and create running lanes.

We see many teams that run the 33-stack or the "3-5" fronts. When we see this type of front we like to go to a tight double slot. (Diagram #3) They have three stacks and do all kinds of crazy stunting from that front. If you call the tight double slot formation, we get eight defender packed to the inside. It is not hard to figure out what to do. We run outside.

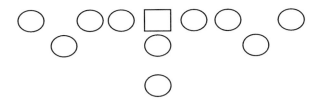

Diagram #3. Tight Double Slot

The next thing we do is run a formation we call "Roger/Louie." (Diagram #4) We use this formation to make the defense declare their strength. If you are an odd or even front team that stems to the strength of the formation by using this formation, we force the defense to declare their strength to one side or the other.

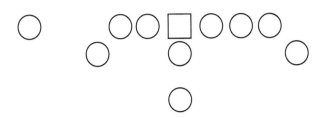

Diagram #4. Roger/Louie

The base play in our offense is 15/16 option. We must be able to run this play. All our players learn how to run this play at an early age. They develop and understand the play. You can get an 8-year-old kid to read all three phases of the option. I am not sure you can take a high school junior and teach him to run the play in two years. You must start your players early so the play becomes second-nature to them.

15/16 OPTION

- **Entire offense based off this play**
- **Must force defense to respect fullback**
-

COACHING POINTS:

- **Quarterback and fullback must recognize the 1-technique and 3-technique to alter the fullback's course. 1-technique aiming point is inside hip of the guard -- 3-technique outside hip of the guard.**
- **Junction Block – frontside halfback must get to the safety.**
- **All players need to recognize the head up defender outside number 1.**
- **Alabama Block – Junction block will now block the number 2 defender and the safety becomes the pitch read.**

If you have to play a player both ways do not make it the fullback. It is hard for this position player because he has to be the guy you go to on offense. He has to be the player that does all the dirty work. He is the player that makes the tough blocks, does the isolation blocks, pass blocks, and plays hard nose football. He has to be the player that sets the table and force teams to gang up on him.

The quarterback and fullback have to recognize the difference between the 1 and 3-technique defenders. Where these two defenders align alters the course the fullback takes. When we practice during the week, we set up a board on the precise angle we want the fullback running that week. Making him run the board shows him the crease you want him to use.

The coaching point in the first step is to step with the opposite foot as the first step. If the fullback goes to the right he does not step with his right foot as the lead step to his crease. We found it more difficult to teach the crease step with the onside foot. He steps with the left foot at the target. That may sound strange, but it works.

If there is a 1-technique or a nose defender, the fullback steps for the inside hip of the guard. He has to stay on the crease for three yards. Once he gets three yards beyond the line of scrimmage he can square his shoulders, be an athlete, and make a big play. We do not want him to deviate from the crease until he is three yards beyond the line of scrimmage.

The quarterback on the mesh opens at 2:00 o'clock to the right and 10:00 o'clock to the left. I do not want him to hop. He takes a good step at 2:00, extends the ball to the fullback, reads the number 1 defender, and rides to his belt buckle. If the fullback feels pressure from the quarterback's hand, he will not get the ball. When the quarterback's hand comes off his belly, he will get the ball. This is a high rep offense and our players run it hundreds of times.

The quarterback must understand who the number 1 defender is. In most cases, he is the defender over the offensive tackle. That is the read key. The number 2 defender is the pitch key. Usually he will be a second level player. He could be an inside or outside linebacker or someone out of the secondary.

I got the "Alabama Block" off the Darrell Royal instructional video a long time ago. Our

quarterbacks are like glass. We do not want anyone to smoke our quarterback. If the defense has a number 2 defender coming hard off the edge, the big guy (quarterback) calls "Bama, Bama," and the halfback blocks the number 2 defender or the pitch key. We block this often to keep the quarterback from taking a big hit.

When you teach your quarterback to pitch the ball, recognizing the technique of the pitch defender is part of the instructions. If the quarterback pitches the ball, he wants to fade away from the pitch key and gives ground off the line of scrimmage away from the defender.

The first defense I want to show you is the even front with a 3 and 1-techniques by defenders over the guard. (Diagram #5)

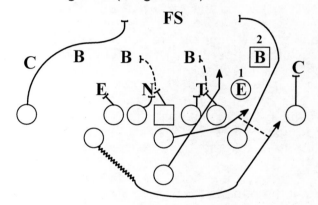

Diagram #5. 16-Option vs. 4-3 to the 3-technique side

The fullback runs to the crease on the outside cheek of the guard. The playside slot arcs and runs up for the free safety. The slot has the junction block on the free safety. If the number 2 defender walks up on the line of scrimmage, we give a "Bama" call and the slot junction blocks the number 2 defender. We do not block the free safety. We think we will be in good shape with the running back on the free safety. That is a good trade off for us. The backside slot comes in motion and is the pitch back on the play.

If we run the same play to the 1-technique, the fullback's path changes from the outside hip to the inside hip of the offensive guard. (Diagram #6) The tackle tries to release inside the 5-technique defender and get on the inside linebacker. The quarterback reads the 5-technique defender as his read key. The force player is the pitch key. The wide receiver blocks the corner and the slot goes up for the free safety. The playside guard blocks down on the 1-technique. Everyone else blocks back and the backside back does the same thing.

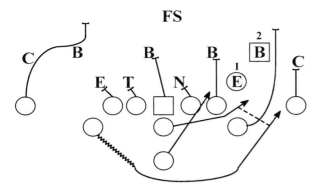

Diagram #6. 16-Option vs. 1-Technique

The big plays come to the split end side of the formation. Our wide receivers know we do not throw the ball much. They are not going to get many balls thrown their way so they may as well block. Our split end is a tough kid that will block. If the split end can block and catch the ball that skill is a big plus.

If the defense is an odd front with a nose guard, we double-team the nose guard to the backside linebacker. (Diagram #7)

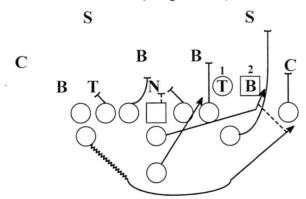

Diagram #7. 16-Option vs. 50-Front

The fullback's crease is the inside hip of the guard. The quarterback reads the 5-technique defender. The 9-technique linebacker is the pitch key. The offensive tackle blocks the playside linebacker.

We motion many times in this offense. A third grader could call our cadence. Our cadence is "Ready, Set, Hut." The backside halfback comes in motion on "Ready." He is going fast and his aiming point is the heels of the fullback. The big mistake the motion back makes is getting too deep on his motion. He has to make up the ground he loses if he goes too deep. We want him to come flat to the fullback's heels.

The reason we run the option is it is effective against any defense. In 25 years, I have seen many defenses. The second reason is we must make people respect the fullback. For the offense to be effective, the fullback must be a threat to the defense. The offense has to make the defense gang up on the fullback to stop him from gaining yardage.

If we feel the defense is rotating with the motion, we have options. (Diagram #8) We can run the motion as always but instead of running the play to the same side as the motion, we run the dive play to the side of the motion. The slot comes in motion, gets to the fullback's position, and we snap the ball. We run the dive to the side of the motion. The motion stops and reverses his action back to where he came from. We call this "dick'em" motion. He is still the pitch back.

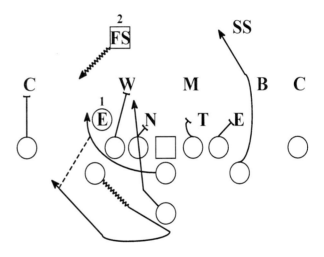

Diagram #8. 15-Option Reverse motion

We can get in a conventional I-back set and run the same play. The fullback's position and alignment does not change. The I-back does not give direction to the defense with any motion.

The teams we like to play are the ones that have the tubby players on the defensive line. The big players that do not move well do not play well against this offense.

Against a 33-stack, we cannot double the nose because we do not know what the middle linebacker is doing. (Diagram #9) We zone the middle stack with the playside guard, center, and backside guard. The playside tackle comes inside and blocks the playside outside linebacker. The fullback's crease is the inside hip of the playside guard. Everything else on the play is the same.

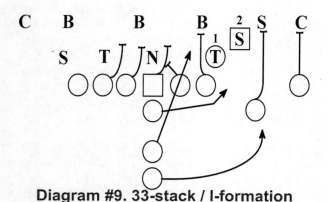

Diagram #9. 33-stack / I-formation

When we get into the red zone we like to get into the wishbone and run the ball. We need to get three and half yards to continue. We have four downs to get the first down when we get inside the 25-yard line. The quarterback in our offense this year ran a 5.0 forty time. He was no blazer but he got the job done. He was very smart and grew up running this offense. If we get into the red zone we will be in the bone. We want to go downhill and make yards.

In this offense, you can dictate the tempo of a game. To dictate tempo, set the huddle at three yards. Our play is in the game before the referee marks the ball ready for play. We can run a play every 10 seconds. You can control the tempo by setting the huddle at three yards. We like to run the twin set I-formation with the triple option. When you get into the twin set, the defense puts two defenders out to cover your receivers.

I think I can show you something here of interest. The "31-32 trap" is an explosive play. Our fullback this year ran for almost 1800 yards. Many of the 1800 yards came off this play.

31-32 TRAP

- **Played off the triple option and toss play.**
- **Call when linebacker is moving with motions or overplaying the option or toss.**

On this play, it is essential for the quarterback and running back to carry out their fakes. If they do not carry their fakes out the play will not work

COACHING POINTS

The guards must give an up or down call based on the defensive front. We use the down call against a 1-technique or true nose guard defender. We give the up call against the 3-technique defender on the playside. On the

up call the guard pulls outside to influence the 3-technique defender to widen or follow him outside. The fullback must hear up or down. The hole is wider on the down than on the up call.

The playside tackle must get to the front side linebacker. To do this he must take a very flat course. The halfback and quarterback always fake the option opposite the call. Example: 31 trap = 16-option.

When the pulling guard hears a down call, he knows the playside guard is blocking down on the 1-technique or nose guard defender. His trap block will be wider than normal. He probably will trap the 5-technique defender. If he hears the up call, he knows he is trapping the 3-technique defender. The fullback has to hear the call and know his path changes on the two calls. On a down call, the fullback gets flatter in his path. On the up call, the fullback takes a 45 degree step and goes at the inside hip of the playside guard.

The backside tackle has an important block on this play. If there is a backside 3-technique defender on the pulling guard, the backside tackle has to cut him. The backside 3-technique can run this play down from the backside. The backside offensive tackle takes a flat step down the line of scrimmage and uses a "superman" block. He steps inside and launches himself in a dive as if he were superman. He wants to cut the 3-technique down. It is a legal block

This play is "31-trap" against a playside 3-technique defender. (Diagram #10) The playside guard pulls and blocks the 9-tchnique end. The tight end blocks the Sam linebacker. The playside tackle blocks down on the Mike linebacker. The center blocks back on the 1-technique nose.

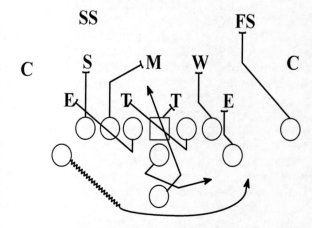

Diagram #10. 31 Trap vs. 3-Technique

The pulling guard pulls and traps the 3-technique defender. The backside-tackle steps through the B-gap and seals up on the backside linebacker. The fullback takes a 45 degree step to the backside and attacks at the inside hip of the playside guard. His path is tight and more vertical up the field. The quarterback and pitch back carry their fake out to the opposite side.

If there is a 1-technique to the playside, the guard gives a "down" call. He blocks down on the 1-technique defender. (Diagram #11) Everyone else applies their rule. The fullback knows the ball is going outside the 1-technique and must take a flatter path to the outside. He follows the pulling guard and cuts up behind the trap block.

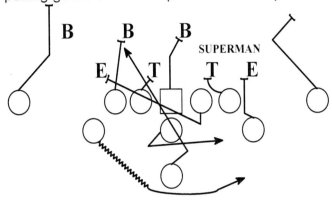

Diagram #11. 31 Trap vs. 1-Technique

The complimentary play with the 15-16 option is the "28/47 toss."

28/47 TOSS

- **Complimentary play to option.**
- **Used as a speed play to get the edge when the defense is committed to the fullback.**

COACHING POINTS

- **Do not block any defenders lining up on the playside tackle.**
- **Playside halfback sets the edge; he is responsible for first linebacker he sees.**
- **Playside tackle loops to block the safety or corner; he blocks the safety if he has a split end to his side of the formation. If he has a tight end to his side, he blocks the corner.**
- **Motion must be no deeper than the heels of the fullback and must be fast.**
- **Fullback always kicks out the opposite defensive end or linebacker.**

On the 28-toss the linemen step and block their playside gap. (Diagram #12) All they have to do is get across the face of the defender. If they can get across the face of a defender the defender will not make the play and they can get downfield and block someone else. The playside tackle has the tight end to his side. The tight end loops and blocks the safety. The playside tackle loops flatter to the line and blocks the corner. The wingback blocks down on the outside linebacker and sets the edge.

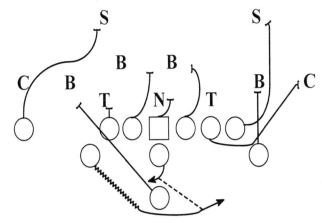

Diagram #12. 28-Toss

If we run the play to the split end, the tackle loops for the safety. The split end blocks the corner, and the slot seals the edge.

24/43 COUNTER

- **Play called off the toss play.**
- **Called when linebackers are moving with the motion or overplaying the toss. Look for the defensive line slanting with motion.**

COACHING POINTS

- **Offensive line blocks down just like power play.**
- **Fullback must have a good inside/out course to kick out end man on the line of scrimmage.**
- **Quarterback and halfback must sell the toss fake.**
- **Ball carrier must stay flat to the line and hit the hole tight to the linemen.**

The play has to look like the toss play. (Diagram #13) The offensive line blocks down and the fullback kicks out at the point of attack. The fullback gets his angle on the end man on the line of scrimmage. The coaching point is the slot back running the counter. He must stay tight to the line of scrimmage. He picks up the fullback and cut inside his block.

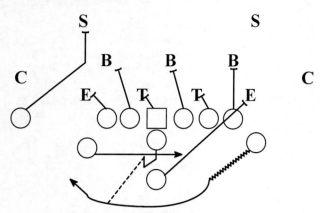

Diagram #13. 24-Counter

This is the last point I will cover. I want to show you two play action passes.

PLAY ACTION PASSES

- **Played off the toss play.**
- **Boot Pass – called when the safeties are rotating to motion.**
- **Seam Pass – called when the safeties are trying to run the lane to stop the toss play.**

COACHING POINTS - 27/48 BOOT PASS

- **Offensive line zooms to play and blocks the running play. No pass blocking.**
- **Fullback must hit EOL and then release to the flat at 3 yards.**
- **Backside receiver – one end stretches the field with a post or seam route. The other end runs a drag pattern.**
- **Split end has a post/corner or go route.**
- **Quarterback fakes toss and gets depth.**

When we run this play, the offensive line is firing off the line and blocking aggressive. They are not showing pass or any pass protection techniques. The fullback has to hit the end man on the line of scrimmage. If he misses him, he will sack the quarterback.

This set has a split end as part of the formation. (Diagram #14) We fake the 28 toss and run the boot play off the fake. The playside split end runs a post corner route. The backside split end runs a deep pattern through the middle of the field. The backside slot runs a drag route across the field, and the fullback hits the EOL and releases outside into the flat at three yards deep.

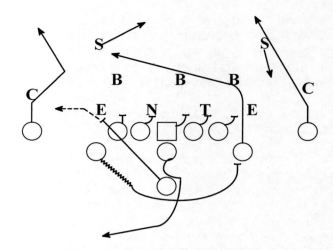

Diagram #14. 28 Boot Pass with Split Ends

COACHING POINTS FOR 27/27 SEAM PASS

- **Offensive line blocks aggressive run blocking.**
- **This is a 3-man route with a go in every third of the field.**
- **Halfback (slot) must read the safety. If the safety runs the lane, the halfback bends to the middle of the field. If the safety does not run the lane he will fade to the hash.**
- **Quarterback fakes the toss and sets up behind playside tackle. His read is the safety. If he has doubts he throws it away.**

This is not a long pass. (Diagram #15) We want to key the safety. If he gets one-step out of

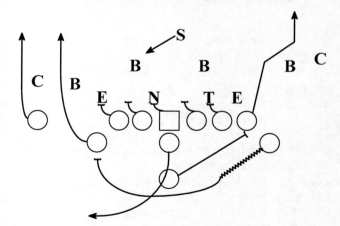

position, we have a big gainer.
Diagram #15. 47 Seam Pass

Shoot me an E-mail if you have questions. I will try to answer it. It is a privilege to be here and I thank you for your time.

Matt Ortega

Leadership And Competition In Your Program

Coatesville High School, Pennsylvania

Today I want to talk about Building Leadership and Competition in your Football Program. This is a subject I really believe in and I believe it enabled us to turn the corner for our program this past year. We implemented this program two years ago. I think we have added some things this year to make it even better than it was the year before.

I want to start out talking about leadership in America. Eighty percent of Americans believe the United States faces a leadership crisis. A couple of years ago I sat down with a Division-I coach and asked him what makes a good leader for a team. He told me he had not had a good leader in the past seven years. What I found to be ironic is this coach had been very successful. I asked him why he felt that way after having a great deal of success. He said kids today are just different. That conversation spoke volumes to me. You have to think out of the box today as coaches to build leadership on your football team.

According to a lot of 19th Century leadership theories, leadership was something you were born with and not developed. I can believe that when we look at some recent leaders like Tim Tebow and Ray Lewis. This kind of thinking dominated the field of leadership studies until the late 1940's and remains popular even in today's society. As coaches, we are constantly trying to find these types of players. I try to teach my own son that he should try to learn from others to leaders like them some of those players. This helped me realize not everybody is born as a leader. Those two guys are special cats. Hopefully as coaches we get to coach these types of guys.

Last year during our run we did not have a great individual leader. What we did have was group leadership. I want to explain how we developed it on our team.

There are two quotes that best describe our philosophy in leadership. The first one is from General George S. Patton.

"Don't tell people how to do things, tell them what to do and let them surprise you with their results."
General George S. Patton

The next quote is from Vince Lombardi.

"Individual commitment to a group effort – that is what makes a team work, a company work, a society work, a civilization work."
Vince Lombardi

Again, we are focused on a commitment to a team. Commitment is the biggest thing we try to get across to our team in our off season program. Everything we do is result based. Every time our kids come into the weight room they are going to compete, compete, and compete.

Coaches need to have certain things present to have good leadership.

MOTIVATION

1. **A good leader must demonstrate the ability to motivate.**

Coaches must be able to motivate players. That is common sense.

2. **It is human nature to lose interest in a cause if constant guidance and incentives are not set.**

This is the ONE thing that is different in today's society. Back in our day as players we had internal motivation to be successful. We were motivated each day in the off season to go into the weight room to get better. I hate to say it, but today's society is just not like that. You must have incentives with most kids these days. You have to give them something to shoot for. They have to be able to see it. It is not something that is internal. This is something you have to be conscious of when you are trying to develop leaders in today's society.

3. **Motivation should not be illustrated through fear because this only produces short term production.**

The old way of ruling with an iron fist cussing and getting in their face does not seem to work today with our kind of kids. That does not mean we have to be soft. We can ride our kids harder today than we could before we started this program. It took time to get to that point.

4. **New challenges are a great way to keep followers interested in the goals.**

As leaders, we have to understand we have to change things up. We have to put new challenges in front of them. We are building a new cross fit program outside for this year. This is our new challenge for our kids. We bust our kid's butts in the weight room every day through the week and they work hard. We are going to raise the level this year. In the end, they love the challenge because they have bought in and are motivated. If it is done the right way you can push them to a high level.

COMMUNICATION

1. **Communication is one of the most important key elements of leadership.**

We are always growing when it comes to our communication. I am not even close to where I should be as a good communicator. I know at times last year I did a terrible job of communicating want I expected from our kids. As a leader, we have to be conscious of this. We have to understand communication is a key and we have to grow each year. I made a conscious decision this year to make sure I communicate better with my staff and to my players.

2. **Good communication skills need to be learned to effectively become a good leader.**

I do not think we ever get to the point where our communication is perfect, but it is learned. Every year we try to get better. Not only do we as adults have to get better at it, but our kids have to get better as well. With social media like Twitter, Facebook, texting, and emails, I can tell you our kids are terrible at communicating.

I have been embarrassed when we have had recruiters come to visit some of our kids and how they carried themselves and communicated

with adults. We have to teach them the basics of even shaking hands and looking people in the eye. I know I have to talk to our kids about those things. With kids these days that is a lost art. Not only do we have to get better at it, we know our kids need to work on it. I talk to our guys about communication.

3. **Followers and subordinates need clarity in what goals the group is trying to achieve.**

In the past I do not feel I did a good job letting our guys know what our goals were. I wanted to have some type of plan to help our guys become better leaders. I quickly developed a plan and threw it out to them and did not know what to expect. But now I know I initially did a lot of things wrong. After making some changes I feel as if we have accomplished a lot of things now. We learned through trial and error.

INNOVATION

1. **A good leader must show innovation through various ways of dealing with problems and issues that face the group. Think out of the box.**

I am not one of those guys who think if things are going great, don't change them. I believe you can always find ways to get better. Analyze it and look at the situation. Are we getting the best and are we efficient at what we do?

Here is an example of thinking out of the box that worked well for us. I noticed when we took our kids away for camp they were like zombies in the morning. We would have them on the field early in the morning and work them throughout the day thinking they would be so tired at night they would go right to sleep. I was wrong. They were still up at 1 or 2 in the morning.

This year we started bringing in the kids at 1 p.m. for summer camp. I was explaining it to a new coach and he asked me why we practiced so late. I told him the kids are going to stay up late anyway. I told him I let them sleep in and get some breakfast or lunch and they are much more alert and ready to go at 1 p.m.

2. **There is not always a correct answer and there are different ways of dealing with situations.**

Again, we have to think out of the box. What works for me may not work for you. We have to constantly think of ways to be innovative in all areas in order to be a better leader.

3. Followers can give helpful feedback and generate new ideas for the group.

I learn the most when I talk to my coaches and when I talk to the kids. They are the ones putting the work in. They are there every day. I may think I know what is right but our kids have bought into our program so much, when I ask them for the positives and negatives feedback in our program, they give a very fair assessment. As a leader, we have to listen to the group and take into consideration how they feel about the program.

LEARN FROM YOUR MISTAKES

1. To be a good leader you have to take calculated risks and you will certainly make some mistakes along the way. Admit them and learn from them. Do not repeat them.

I am not afraid to admit it if I make a mistake. I made some mistakes early on in my career. I micro managed some of my staff. I reflected on it and thought I was never micro managed, why did I get this way? I think it had a lot to do with stress. I had to win and I had to have positive results. I started to act out of character. As a leader I was not afraid to admit I had made a mistake. Once I was able to admit it, we took off as a staff. There was a mutual respect both ways and that has made a big difference with our staff and our program.

2. The more a leader is able to continually evaluate others, the more the leader will be able to keep up with evolving times.

We are constantly trying to find ways to make us better. We are constantly trying to find ways to make the program more efficient. Evaluate your staff. Evaluate your kids. More importantly evaluate your actions. I look at myself in the mirror and try to make myself better every day.

Success comes from good decisions. Good decisions come from experience. Experience comes from bad decisions.

DO WHAT YOU SAY YOU ARE GOING TO DO

1. Accountability starts with you. That means you, as a leader, need to keep your promises. And if you are going to miss a deadline, communicate it.

I really can hang my hat on this one. The success we have in our program today is because of the attitude I have developed about following through on my promises. I know from talking and dealing with my kids they have had people in their lives that have promised to do certain things for them but never followed through. As a leader and as a coach this is one area I will always follow through with and do what I say I will do. I firmly believe the success we have had with our program is based on this concept.

2. It is not good enough to just apologize afterward. It comes down to showing respect for one another by doing what you say.

Now let me move into our program and tie everything together. For the last four years, this has been the goal of our football program.

HAVE A PLAN FOR SOME FORM OF HIGHER EDUCATION, MILITARY SERVICE, OR JOB IN THE WORKPLACE!

Every time I meet with our kids in January, this is the goal. I set the goal and if I am going to follow through on what I say, it better happen. If I set this goal and it does not happen, our kids are not going to buy into our program.

HIGHLIGHTS OF THE PROGRAM

- **100 Percent High School Graduation**
- **Over 70 Percent of Graduating Seniors on the Football Team attend College.**
- **1.2 Million Dollars in Football Scholarships in 4 years.**
- **90 Percent of our Division-I and II Scholarship Athletes qualified.**
- **Team GPA is 82.4 percent.**

This all comes from our kids believing in the goal. I get the same feeling when one of my kids signs a scholarship offer as I do playing in a championship game. Our school is in the bottom 15 percent academically of schools in Pennsylvania. Still most of our kids qualify. Why? It takes hard work, and we work at it. I am at a great school but we still have our challenges. We set the goal and I get my kids to buy into the program by our results. This is the proof of it as well.

WHAT IS THE GOAL FOR 2013?

Win the Ches-Mont Championship!
(This is our League Championship)

- **2009 was our first year. Our record was 3-3 which was fourth place.**
- **2010 our record was 5-1, good for second place.**
- **2011 again 5-1 and second place.**
- **2012 5-1, second place.**

We are going to raise the bar and get our kids to understand what it is all about.

In 2012 I set three goals for our program.

1. **We Need Leadership -** I did not know how I was going to do it or how it was going to happen, but it was a goal of ours.

2. **We Need Discipline -** Discipline had to be a major component of our program.

3. **We Need to Gain Weight and Strength.** - I had these goals but I did not understand how the program was going to work.

Going into 2013 we have identified areas for improvement.

1. **We have leadership, but we need more verbal leadership.**

Last year we started out 2-2. The rumor was we were going to have a new coach if we did not win game five. The reason we were able to turn it around was because of our leadership. Our guys were used to failing but they came in the next day and got right to work. We instilled an attitude to compete in everything we did. It does not matter if you win or lose, the next day you have to compete to get better. On that Monday we went straight to work and won eleven straight games from that point on and went to the state championship. This year we want more verbal leadership from our guys. We are starting to see some of it now.

2. **Discipline. Pay attention to details. Do the small things. There is a reason why we do things a certain way.**

I tell our guys this has to be done in all aspects of our program, in our lifts, our techniques, and everything we do. Listen because small things matter.

3. **Strength - Emphasis on Chest, Triceps, and Grip Strength. Emphasis on Technique.**

Let me get to our program. How have we as a group of coaches been able to improve leadership? We have done it through group leadership. We do not have a Tim Tebow or Ray Lewis. The group concept is what works for us right now.

GROUP LEADERSHIP

In contrast to individual leadership, group leadership allows more than one person to provide direction to the group as a whole. With group leadership the team member best able to handle any given phase of the competition becomes the temporary leader. Additionally, as each team member has the opportunity to experience the elevated level of empowerment, it energizes the team members and feeds the cycle of success for the team.

Group Leadership or Leadership Teams have specific characteristics.

CHARACTERISTICS OF A TEAM

1. **There must be an awareness of unity on the part of all of the team members.**

We group our guys into teams every day. We want them to practice competing as a team.

2. **Members must have a chance to contribute and learn from and work with others.**

Our guys have to work together. We cannot wait until August to start to work together. We have to work together in January and February, during those dark months. This group leadership concept makes that happen.

3. **The members must have the ability to act together toward a common goal.**

Every day we have a goal. Every week we compete. We have to understand this concept.

4. **Members proudly share a sense of why the team exists and are invested in accomplishing its mission and goals.**

Our guys are proud to wear their red jersey every day in the weight room. They are proud of their team. Now our guys talk trash back and forth every day. "Red team is better than the Black team." It is all done in the spirit of the team. It is a great environment and motivates our kids to be there every day.

5. Conflict is dealt with openly and is considered important to decision making and personal growth.

An example of that happened the other day. One of our teachers came to me and told me one of our players was cussing and acting up in class. I told the teacher I will take care of it. The next day in the weight room I told the red team that their teammate was acting up in class and acting out of character. He was a bad influence in the class and set a bad example of our program. That was minus 5 points for the red team. You should have seen his reaction and the players getting on him.

What is the goal this year? Verbal leadership is the answer, and we are starting to get it. Call your guys out. It is the one way to get your kids to respond. You know peer pressure means everything. Peer pressure is number one. If we can get our kids to verbalize to one another as to where they are falling short, or where they are making gains, it is going to go a long way.

6. Members know their roles in getting tasks done and when to allow a more skillful member to do a certain task.

When I group the teams, I make sure I have skilled guys in each group. I make sure I have linemen in each group. Depending on what the competition is, each group knows they can rely on certain members of their team to help compete in the given competition. It teaches the guys how to work together and to rely on each other when we compete. Each team has ten members with a mixture of seniors, and other classes on each group.

This past year we had five groups. In the past, I did not have coaches assigned to the teams. This year I have learned and I have assign an assistant coach to teams to help motivate, to give guidance, and to help watch over the group in general.

COMPETITION

Our daily competition in the off season helps us find players. We know who the studs are most of the time. Competition helps us find backups and our special teams players. It helps us find the undersized guys who are tough and hard nosed that we want to get on the field. By working them hard in the off season, we do not have to wait until August to find out who they are.

GROUP COMPETITION

1. Grades
2. Weight Gain
3. Strength Gain
4. On Time
5. Correct Uniform
6. Daily Effort
7. Group Competitions
8. Bonus Points
9. Loss of Points

Our guys compete in these areas. Our philosophy in group competition builds leadership, discipline, strength, and weight gain.

POINT SYSTEM

Grades
- **All Classes Increase in total percent.**
- **Overall Team Report Card Percentage.**

Example: Second grading period Red team averaged 81.2 percent. In the third grading period the Red team averaged 83.4 percent. This was an increase of 2.2 percent.

For every full percent of improvement, they get 25 points. The red team would earn 50 points. This provides motivation for them every day in the classroom. We can give bonus points based on an individual's performance if we see they have turned the corner in a certain subject or in each class they are enrolled in.

Weight Gain
- **Weigh in every 7 weeks**
- **Weight gain is Total Gain for Team**
- **If you are designed to lose weight, you will be put on same scale**

Example: Nutrition is important. Our parents are going to make sure their kids are going to get all the protein their kids need after a workout. I do not have that. I have to find a way to make it available for them every day. What I did was this. Gatorade has a great program where you can get a protein shake for 50 cents. That is dirt cheap. They have a pre workout with the chews and a post workout with the shake.

We are trying to get to where our guys are getting some nutrition. Some kids are at school all day with practice, class, and other school activity. I want those guys to have two shakes. I want to find a way for them to get their calories so they aren't breaking their bodies down.

Strength Gain
- **Max weight every 7 weeks**
- **Gain of Strength for each 7 weeks**

> Bench
> Squat
> Clean
> Push Press

Example:

Bench	Gain	Place	Points
Red	120 lbs.	1	30
Black	110 lbs.	2	25
Silver	100 lbs.	3	20
Gray	90 lbs.	4	15
Maroon	80 lbs.	5	10

You will notice there isn't a big difference in points between first and second place. This is by design because we want to keep the level of competition close. We want to keep them motivated. Even if they are in last place, they can make a difference in the next evaluation.

On Time
- **Points are given every day.**
- **1 Minute warning given by a coach.**
- **Players must be in weight room - 1:30 p.m.**
- **On Time = 1 point per day. (10 points)**

If a player is late, he will get progressive discipline from the Head Coach. If a player is late one point will be deducted. You may say, wait a minute. This is what they are supposed to do. Our kids have to have an incentive. They are not going to do it on their own. Kids are just not built that way. In the first year we must have had fifty times where players were penalized for being late. This year we only had two. We are making a difference with this program.

Correct Uniform
- **Points are given every day.**
- **Player must have a designated color of shirt on for each workout.**
- **Correct Shirt = 1 point per kid. (10 points)**

If a player does not have their shirt, he gets progressive discipline from the Head Coach. If a player has the wrong color shirt, one point is subtracted from their group.

I give the guys two shirts each year. I tell them to go buy another shirt of the same color. They better have the right color of shirt at workouts.

Year one, we probably had 80 offenses. This year we had three. That is a big difference.

Daily Effort
- **Points are given every day.**
- **Points are determined by total group effort each day.**
- **Each team can earn 10 points each workout.**

Each coach rates their team for that day. "Red team got 8 points today!" Then we explain to them why.

Competition
- **Competition TBD.**
- **Competition changes.**

We have a variety of competitions. One example may be capture the flag while on all fours in the mat room. It can get really physical. We like to keep it on all fours because we do not have to worry about knee issues. We mix it up.

Bonus Points
- **Group Report Card increase of 3 percent or more.**
- **Every member of Group on Honor Roll.**
- **Grade Percent of 85 or higher.**
- **Grade Percent of 90 or higher.**
- **Community Service Projects.**
- **Head Coach can reward points for a wide variety of reasons determined by him at any time.**

I want to always have a way for our kids to earn bonus points. I really feel like we need to do more with community service. I am making a commitment to that this year. I want them to organize it, not me. I am going to work on a couple of things but I want them to take the imitative in order to earn bonus points.

Minus Points
- **Determined by Head Coach.**
- **ISS, Character Ed, CSS, Write Ups, Detention.**

We deducted points if they get into trouble. Our guys know I am calling them out on this. When I call them out, I know our strength coach will call them out, and their teammates are going to call them out when they screw up.

Insubordination
- **3 Strikes - Removal by coach to alternative weight room.**

- **4 straight days of positive effort - back in program.**
- **3 Removals - Suspensions from Spring Ball and or Summer Activities.**

Fortunately we have not had guys screw up so I have not had to use this.

It is amazing to see that every single team member has bought into this program. That includes the worst player on the team who is never going to step onto the football field.

Let me give you an idea of what our weight schedule looks like.

Day	Time	Total Time
Monday	1:20 – 2:20	60 minutes
Tuesday	1:20 – 2:20	60 minutes
Wednesday	1:20 – 2:20	60 minutes
Thursday	1:20 – 2:20	60 minutes
Friday	1:20 – 2:00	40 minutes
2 times/month - Team Meeting		
2 times/month - Group Competition		

I know we may have it different than what you may have at your school. I have our guys the last period of the day for an hour.

Four days a week we have 40 minutes of a workout and then we have 20 minutes of core burnout at the end. That is what we do. We work the kids hard but they love it.

Two times a month we have a team meeting. The first year I thought I would teach them about leadership by talking to them and showing a real nice power point presentation. I showed film of Tim Tebow. I was trying to teach them about leadership, verbally. Guess what? It does not happen that way. I do not do this anymore.

I still meet with them two times a month. I am able to communicate our schedule and other important aspects about our program. This also provides a break from the weight room.

If a kid has a game in another sport, we start off by getting dressed in our appropriate team colors. We then go through a warm up period and then they are done. We keep in touch with them by having them for the short warm up period.

I do not have every single player for the last period of school. Some guys who are in an accelerated program may not be there. I have to make sure I have an alternative program. I make it a rule where they have to be there at least four days a week. We have set up Monday thru Thursday from 2:15 – 3:00 as an alternative schedule for those kids to get their workouts done.

Something I started this year was Orange shirts. These are for the guys who I do not feel have fully bought in to our program. Maybe they quit the year before, or it may be based on their past effort. I still put them on a team but I make them earn the shirt of their team.

I bring the entire group together and let them know that so and so is doing a great job and finally earned their shirt. Their whole team goes crazy for them when that happens. It really helps get the buy in we are looking for. "Show me you want to play." It worked really well for us this year.

As I said earlier, kids these days want incentives. This is what we gave as Team Incentives this year.

For the third grading period the overall team winner got a Nike Compression Shirt. We advertise it on posters throughout the weight room. The forth grading period they got Nike Combat Shorts. The Overall Team Winner before the summer break gets a plaque of the team on the weight room wall. I do not carry this on through the summer. I have too many guys and too many young guys in the weight room during the summer and it just would not work right. We carry the team concept all the way to the last day of school, when we have our final competition.

In the workouts, everything is on a timer. We place it in the weight room so they can see how much time they have. It is probably the best purchase we made all year. When the bell rings, we move. They stay with their team all during their workout. I make sure they see all of their point totals on the weight room boards so they see it every day they are in there. It is a lot of work for me but it is worth it because I believe in it. They can see just how far they are from the top spot and it gives them incentives to work harder for their team. Our kids love the competition of it and they have bought in.

The hardest part of this whole thing is picking the teams. We have kids that play spring sports and do not play football in the program. It is difficult to divide them into groups because I do not know that much about them if they are not in football. I believe in what we are doing and I think it has helped us move to the next level.

My time is up. Thanks guys.

Derek Pennington

Two-Backs Shotgun Spread Running Game

Zeeland High School, Michigan

This lecture is going to be about our "Two-back Shotgun Spread Running Game" and our 20 personnel package. I am going to talk about five minutes on philosophy and 45 minutes on plays we run. We did this talk at Indianapolis earlier this year and got some good feedback. This is an old version of the two-back spread offense. Rich Rodriguez is going to be here tomorrow. I stole most of this from him and his offensive line coach Rick Trickett.

We were fortunate in the last three years to go 29-4. We scored 1,323 points over those three years. We averaged 40 points a game in 2012. We are a spread team but we are not a finesse team. We play in Michigan and at the end of the season when the playoffs are going on the weather is terrible. There is no air raid offense or many screens run during that time of year. We are a physical running team out of the spread formation.

This year we had two players run for over a thousand yards. One of them averaged over 11 yards a carry. We did not play bad football teams. We played teams that had a significant amount of talent. We play several teams that are much bigger than we are. I do believe you can run the spread offense, and at the same time be physical and run the football. We patterned ourselves after Rick Rodriguez when he was at West Virginia.

We are in a two-back shotgun set with a 2 X 1 formation. Our primary personnel's grouping is 20 personnel. We do not play with a tight end. I get frustrated with one-back sets. I am an old I-formation coach that is more comfortable running with two backs in the backfield. I feel better running the counter-tray and solid plays. I like the physical downhill running game.

We are in the shotgun but we are a physical downhill running team. The first play I want to show you is a two-back zone stretch play. We have run this play a ton of times over the past three years. The years we ran the stretch play well, were the years we ran the ball well. If we tried to throw the ball and be a fineness team we did not run the stretch play well at all.

In the formation, I like the two backs side by side. The quarterback aligns at six yards deep and the backs are at five and half yards in the B-gaps. Some teams play with what they call an H-back and they offset him all over the backfield. The defense gets an idea about who will carry the ball because one of the players is a running back and the other is a fullback. We do some of that but I prefer to align them on opposite sides of the quarterback and at the same depth. I like that because it gives us a two-way-go to the right or the left.

We align in a balanced set in the backfield which allows us to go both ways. We double call plays in the huddle and automatic at the line of scrimmage in the direction we want to run the play. In the huddle, we call 48-49 stretch, with 48 being to the right and 49 to the left. Our quarterback will call the play based on what we talked about in our film session and scouting report.

The defense may be in an unbalanced defense and we want to run toward the fewest defenders. We may want to run the ball to the 1-technique side instead of the 3-technique side of the formation. It might be because the team we are going to play is a field defense. When you see us you will notice we run a ton of plays to the wide side of the field, but we also run the stretch into the boundary.

48-STRETCH RULES

PST: Zone step, base 1, and eat the armpit.
PSG: Zone step, spike arm, covered ricochet to 2.
CENTER: Zone step, uncovered eat the armpit.
BSG: Zone step, spike arm, covered ricochet to 2.

BST: Zone step, capture B-gap, possible cut.
LEAD BACK: Read 1, if hooked outside, not hooked inside.
BACK: Two steps pass QB read 1, go or bang.
QB: BS read, carry out fake hold DE.

When we run the 48-stretch play, the entire offensive linemen zone step to the right. We have terms we use to describe the technique we want them to use. We tell them to eat the armpit of the defenders. That means to get their heads across the defender and run. The offensive linemen like this play because they get to move.

The quarterback reads the backside defensive end. The lead back keys the number 1 defender over the playside tackle. The playside tackle base blocks the defensive end, which we call number 1. (Diagram #1) We tell him if he cannot hook the defender, to run him out of bounds. This play will not always get to the edge. It is a zone stretch but it is not a sweep. The thing I like about the play is it gets the linebackers running east and west. The hardest tackles for a linebacker to make are those types of situations with a cutback.

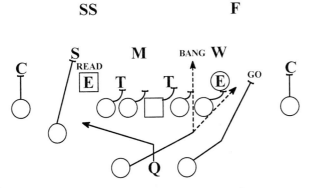

Diagram #1. 48-Stretch

I watch the running backs at West Virginia gaining 1000 yards running this play, so I decided to install it. I did one thing wrong when I taught the play. Our running backs were getting downhill too fast. I had to get some explanation about the technique of the running back getting the ball.

The alignment of the heels of the running back has to be on the toes of the quarterback. He goes foot to foot with the quarterback, rolls over the ball, and takes it. He goes two steps past the quarterback's midline and reads the butt of the lead back.

The lead back is reading the block of the playside tackle. The playside tackle hooks the

5-technique defender in three steps, or he is going to run him to the sidelines. The lead back reads the tackle's block. If the tackle hooks the 5-technique, the lead back goes to the outside. He blocks the next defender on an inside/out angle. If he does not hook him, he goes to the inside.

The running back reads the path of the lead back. He has two options. He bounces the ball to the outside, which we call "go" or he "bangs" the ball straight up the field.

If the defense plays with double leverage on the offensive tackle we have a problem. Double leverage is a defender aligned over the offensive tackle and another defender outside of him. If we get that situation, we have to use the H-back alignment I talked about earlier. That moves the lead back up toward the line of scrimmage so he can get on the overhang defender quickly. The offensive tackle base blocks on the number one defender on the line of scrimmage. If the number one defender slanted to the inside, the tackle blocks him.

I talked earlier about running plays off other plays. We are going to run the quarterback GT off the stretch play. The blocking for the play is a gap scheme.

QUARTERBACK GT

PST: Gap Scheme, B-gap, 3-technique.
PSG: Gap Scheme, A-gap, 3-technique possible head switch.
CENTER: Gap Scheme, BS A-gap BSG.
BSG: Counter Pull for DE.
BST: Tight Power Pull up to #2.
LEAD BACK: Carry out stretch fake.
BACK: Carry out stretch fake - block DE.
QB: Fake stretch play, track to A-gap.

We run the play to the two-receiver side. (Diagram #2) The running back fakes the stretch play. We want him to cheat a bit so he can get inside and cut off the 5-technique defender playing on the outside shoulder of the backside tackle. The tackle is going to pull. The running back has to cut off the backside defender to keep him from following the play. The center blocks back on the 1-technique defender to cut off for the pulling guard. If we double call this play, we want to run to the 3-technique defender because it is easier for the center to block back on a 1-technique that it is to block back on a 3-technique.

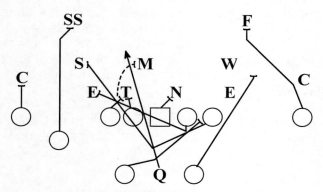

Diagram #2. Quarterback GT

The GT tagged on the play means the backside guard and tackle pull on this play. The playside guard has a 3-technique defender aligned on him. He is an A-gap blocker but must help the playside tackle secure his B-gap and get the Mike linebacker blocked. They block the 3-technique to the Mike linebacker. The backside guard pulls for the playside defensive end. The backside tackle pulls and follows the pulling guard. He wants to stay on the outside hip of the guard to stay out of his path, so if someone knocks the guard down, he does not fall. His block is inside the kick out block to the playside linebacker.

The quarterback fakes the stretch play, pulls the ball, and attacks the A-gap. He wants to follow the pulling tackle into the hole. The defender on the line of scrimmage with the most responsibility is the defensive ends. In our blocking schemes and play selections, we try to mess with their minds. We run the stretch outside of him. When he starts to jump outside, we trap him and run inside of him.

Some of the defensive ends get so far up the field the guard does not need to block him. We tell the guard if that happens to turn up the field and ignore him.

POWER

PST: Gap scheme, B-gap, 3-technique.
PSG: Gap Scheme, A-gap, 3-technique.
  possible head switch.
CENTER: Gap scheme, BS A-gap, possible call
  with BST.
BSG: Counter pull thru for number 2.
BST: Gap scheme capture B-gap, possible call
  with center.
LEAD BACK: Press B-gap; kick out DE with
  shoulder block.

BACK: Press A-gap track.
QB: Read BS DE, carry out fake and hold the
  DE.

The power play is a two-back running play. (Diagram #3) We kick out with the lead back on the defensive end, pull the backside guard, and turn through the hole to block the linebacker. The backside tackle has to capture the B-gap. However, he may need to help the center with his turn back block on the 1-technique.

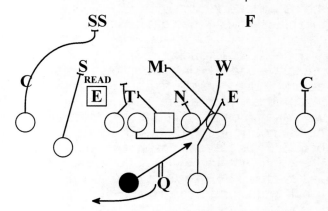

Diagram #3. Power

There are some coaching points that go with this play. The lead back's angle to the defensive end has to be up toward the B-gap and turning out at the defensive end. He has to get his body in the proper position to block an end. He is undersized to take on some of the defensive end we face. If he goes straight at the defensive end his angle is bad and he may not be able to kick him out. What we do to help him is not to call the power until we run the stretch at the defensive end first. When you get him to widen on the snap, it makes the block is easier for the lead back.

The pulling guard turns into the hole. If the defensive end is fighting inside the lead back's block, he puts him back on that block and wipes out the hole. His assignment is the linebacker. If the defensive front is an odd front, we block our gap scheme blocking.

The quarterback read the backside defensive end. We did not run our quarterback as much as we would like to run him. However, we did not have a proven backup ready to go. What we did to the backside instead of letting the quarterback run the ball off the read, we threw the bubble screen off the play. The play was a read for the quarterback. He left the ball with the running back and we ran the power play, or he pulled the ball and threw the bubble screen to the backside.

If teams want to play us with eight defenders in the box, we add our two tight end package. That way we add two more blocker to our package. That gives us two more down blockers on the power play. It is a gap scheme with everyone blocking down. The lead back kicks out and the backside guard wraps around for the linebacker. It is downhill running. The backs run with their pads down and driving hard. When we run this play, it goes in the A-gap. The angles are good and we get movement. If the defense blitzes the play, they will not make a play. The scheme is a gap scheme that accounts for every gap.

I showed you the quarterback GT. The only problem with that play is the quarterback has to carry the football. I do not like to run the quarterback. Instead of running the quarterback, we run the back on the GT. That play gives us a cross-buck type of action.

TWO-BACK GT

PST: Gap scheme, B-gap, 3-technique
PSG: Gap Scheme, A-gap, 3-technique
     possible head switch
CENTER: Gap scheme, BS A-gap,
BSG: Counter Pull Counter pull for DE
BST: Tight Power Pull up to 2 Track.
PSB: Carry out Stretch fake and block BS DE.
QB: Two fakes and carry out fake

We block the power running play with the backside pulling and kicking out the defensive end. (Diagram #4)

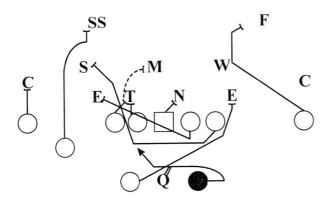

Diagram #4. Two-Back GT

The backside tackle pulls and turns up inside the guard block and blocks the number 2 linebacker. The playside is a gap scheme. We combo the 3-technique defender and come off for the Mike linebacker. The center blocks back for the pulling guard. The playside back runs his stretch play fake and cuts off the backside defensive end.

The backside back takes a counter step to the outside to time out the play and gives direction to the linebackers. After the playside back clears, he takes the handoff and gets on a tight B-gap track. The quarterback fakes to the playside back, gives the ball to the backside back, and carries out his fake to the outside.

The Washington Redskins ran this old counter trey play back in 1985. When we run this play, we describe it as a kick and wrap play. The guard kicks out and the tackle wraps around for the linebacker. Teams try to read our guards with their safeties and get down in the box. We tie the bubble screen to this play and it has been very effective against teams that try to involve their safeties into the run support.

We want to throw the bubble screen against teams that bring their safety down into the box. We set the number two-receiver to the backside of the play. We want the pullers going away from the bubble screen. That takes the safety on that side with the pullers.

The cross-buck action gets the linebackers to move. The thing that we emphasize with our back is not to bounce the ball. These plays are north and south plays. They need to stay inside and break after they are at linebacker depth. We ran this play about 57 times this year.

COUNTER

PST: Gap scheme, B-gap, 3-technique
PSG: Gap Scheme, A-gap, 3-technique
     possible head switch
CENTER: Gap scheme, BS A-gap, possible call
     to the BST
BSG: Counter Pull Counter pull for DE
BST: Gap scheme, Capture B-gap, possible call
     from center
LEAD BACK: Aligns in strong H-back position,
     power pulls up the 2 linebacker
BSB: Press the A-gap track
QB: BS read, carry out fake, hold DE

The counter is a power play blocking scheme except we exchange the blocking responsibility of the pulling guard and the lead back. (Diagram #5) The back aligns in a strong H-back position in the strong side B-gap. The quarterback and running backs are in their normal position. The playside blocks gap scheme blocking. The playside guard and tackle block the down defender and the Mike linebacker. The backside guard pulls and kicks out the defensive end to the play side. The lead back follows the guard, turns up inside his block, and blocks the linebacker.

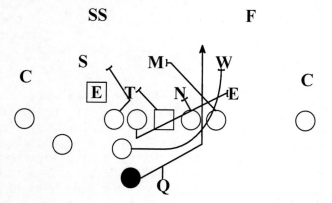

Diagram #5. Counter

The lead backs like this scheme more than the power scheme. In this scheme they block a linebacker instead of a defensive end.

We have an isolation play in this scheme.

LEAD

PST: Base block, Head in the hole
PSG: Base block head in the hold, Double team the 1-technique
CENTER: Base block, double team 1-technique
BSG: Base block, double team 3-technique
BST: Zone step, Capture B-gap
LEAD BACK: BOB up to the number 2 line backer
PSB: Tight track to B-gap
QB: BS Read, Carry out fake, hold DE

If we play a well-coached team and are having difficulty running our regular offense, we go to the lead play. We like the lead play because we are not pulling anyone. We are putting body-on-body and pushing. It is a physical play. We like the play better when we have big linemen. We did not have a big offensive line this year but we ran the play well.

When we run the lead, the offensive line gets into a base blocking scheme. We could have two double team blocks on the play. (Diagram #6) The playside tackle base blocks the defensive end. He wants to make sure he gets his head in the hole. He tries to drive the defender off the line and to the outside. The playside guard and

center double-teams the 1-technique defender off the line of scrimmage back into the Mike linebacker. If the Mike linebacker comes under the double team block, the center comes off and blocks him. The guard stays on the base block and drive on the 1-technique.

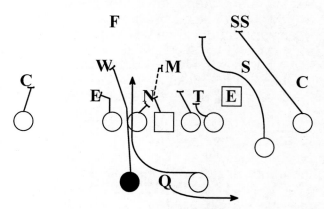

Diagram #6. Lead

The backside guard base blocks on the 3-technique defender. The backside tackle zone steps into the B-gap. He has to capture the B-gap. He blocks anything that comes into that gap. His block could end up in some kind of combination with the playside guard.

In the rules, the lead back's rule is "Bob." That stands for "back on backer." He comes through the B-gap and isolates the linebacker. The running back is on the opposite side of the lead block. He takes his stretch steps, plants, and read the hole. If he can take it into the B-gap, he runs downhill. If the defensive end slants inside, the tackle has to wash him inside. In that case, the back can bounce the ball to the outside.

This phase of our offense has been the core of our system for a long time. I appreciate your patients. Thank you very much.

John Rodenberg

Utilizing Cover-2 Versus Multiple Sets

Moeller High School, Ohio

Thank you very much. It is a pleasure to be here today. I am going to talk about the "Cover-2 Against Multiple Sets." The problem with cover-2 is carrying the slot receiver on verticals to the half safety players. We have to build confidence in the underneath players so they do not worry about losing a receiver. They know they have the safety over the top. That gives the defenders help. The defenders we must have confidence in are the linebackers. If they miss the collision on the receiver, he trails the receiver. That makes the launch point of the quarterback's ball go up in the air. The thing we want to stop on the vertical patterns is the quarterback throwing a straight shot to the receiver. We must convince the linebacker if he continues to trail the receiver, the quarterback will have to arc the ball to get it over him. That gives our safeties a chance to break on the ball.

It has been a good coverage for us. By being physical with the receivers we take them out of the game. I want to show you some things we believe as far as our defensive goals.

DEFENSIVE GOALS

- **Win!**
- **Allow 17 points or less.**
- **Hold opponents to 150 yards or less rushing.**
- **Hold opponents to 150 yards or less passing.**
- **Hold opponents to 300 yards or less of total offense.**
- **Never allow more than 10 consecutive plays.**
- **Never allow a run of 15 yards or longer.**
- **Force 3 turnovers per game.**
- **Less than 50 percent completion rate.**
- **Keep our opponents from scoring a touchdown after our offense has lost the ball on a turnover.**

We had to revise the goals somewhat because of the teams we play. The teams we play throw the football. We see 60 percent passing from our opponents. We very seldom see the I-formation from teams we play. We do not see that much I-formation even in the goal line situation.

Last year, we played Louisville Trinity and Louisville St. Xavier, and they threw the ball several times. St. Xavier was more traditional with a two-back set, but Trinity is a spread offense and they like to throw the ball. Against them, we had to play good zone defense.

I was an offensive coordinator for a long time. They told me if we were 60 percent throwing in a game, we would win the game. Since I moved to the other side of the ball, one of our goals is to hold the offense to 50 percent or less passing the ball. If we can do that, we have a better chance of winning a game.

As a defensive secondary coach, I try not to depend on the defensive line making a sack. That is why we play physical with our backs. We practice it in the summer and fall in our defensive progression.

We give our defensive players helmet awards for accomplishing certain goals. We give them skulls and crossbones. We give them awards for making interceptions, forcing a fumble or recover a fumble, making an individual open field tackle, or to scoring a touchdown. We give everyone on the defense an award for a team shutout. In addition, we can give special awards for exceptional coverage. The defensive backs get more skulls for great coverage than the other goals.

We play a cover-2 shell on defense. On most snaps, we are a quarter-quarter-half team. In this coverage, we can take away the boundary then flip the coverage and take away the field. When we get in long yardage situations we are in cover-2. It does not matter if we play cover-4 or cover-2, the corner has to know how to collision receivers. When we play against a 3 X 1 formation, we have three different ways we want to cover the formation.

COVER 2

- **Shell look to all coverage's for disguise.**
- **Control three-steps passing game.**
- **Re-route timing in the five-steps passing game.**
- **Being physical with wide receivers.**
- **Collide from soft, jam, and lock gives us great disguise.**

If we are in cover-2 or cover-4, the alignment has a two-deep safety look. We start with the two safeties 14 yards off the ball. By the end of summer, their alignment is 10 yards deep. The corners align five yards off the ball. They align in a head up position on the receiver.

We can play cover-2 three different ways. That difference relates to the flat defender. We want to be physical with our safeties in the run game. We know we will give up a big play in the play-action pass game, but we roll the safeties down into the box.

In this coverage, I want to take away the three-step pass game. I want to take away the hitch and out in the three-step passing game. I want the offense to throw the fade route. It is a hard throw and we work hard on getting the safety over the top of the fade route. We control the receivers on the three-step drop and reroute the receivers in the five-step drops.

We play the receiver using three techniques. The first technique is a "soft" technique. We align at 5 yards and head up the receiver.

The second position is a "jam" technique. We align in a press position head up on the receiver. There are times when we play the "jam" position, and we are in zone coverage. It looks like man coverage but we are in zone.

I have no problem with the corners getting back into the coverage because we reroute the receivers. We practice the "jam" technique from a press position as well as the soft alignment. You also have to teach the players what to do when they miss the jam.

The third technique is "lock." That is a man-to-man technique. If the corner is in a "jam" technique, he reroutes the receiver to the middle of the field safety. If we are in "lock," he runs them

to the sidelines. The technique means the corner **zone** turns in jam technique and **man** turns into lock coverage. We must practice that daily.

We practice within six minutes periods. We practice five periods of individual period or 30 minutes of individual practice through the eighth game of the season.

The big part of cover-2 is the collision on the receivers. When we collide with a receiver, we collide with the hips and feel with the hands. That keeps the defender from lunging into the receiver with his hands. When we drill this technique, the defender puts his hands behind his back and works with the hips only. This is like taking a charge in basketball. We want the defensive back in the receiver's way.

After we teach that technique, we bring the hands into the drill and punch the receiver. When we get good at punching him, we get low with the hips and grab the jersey around the belly area. We reroute the receiver with our hips. As soon as the receiver begins to break clear, we release the jersey.

The defensive vision is for the run fits. The defensive back coach stands behind the receiver so he can see the eyes of the defensive back. We want his eyes focused on his run responsibility. In his alignment, he wants to be on the outside shoulder of the receiver, so he can funnel the receiver into the safety.

Once he collisions the receiver, he backpedals into a zone, and turns headed for the numbers. After he does his zone turn to the numbers, he sinks in his coverage. We do not cover anything that threatens us in the flat. He plays the smash route and not the hitch route by the outside receiver. If we play a lock technique the defensive back takes an inside leverage position, makes a man-turn, and forces the receiver outside. We play the ball through the receiver's hands and we do not look back for the ball.

In the collision, it is a catching action using the hips and not a lunge at the receiver. When we practice this technique, we practice with the receiver on and off the line of scrimmage. It is a more difficult technique with the receiver off the line of scrimmage.

The safeties are 14 yards deep and one yard plus or minus on the hash marks. When we feel the backs are more accomplished, we move them up to 10 yards. At the snap of the ball, the safeties do not move back. The safeties squat and read the number 2 receiver. We do not cover something we do not need to cover.

In a 2 X 2 scheme, if the number 2 receiver goes outside, the number 1 receiver is coming inside. If the number 2 receiver goes vertical, the linebacker to that side collisions him and runs underneath him. The safety sits over the top of that pattern. The thing the safety must do is stay on his landmark the entire time. In our drill work, we practice many ball drills covering deep passes from hash to hash. The corners force the number 1 receiver into the safeties. The safeties read the number 2 receiver and do not back up at the snap of the ball. If they get a run read, they come down hard to the line of scrimmage. If the number 2 receiver does not threaten the safety, he does not backpedal.

The linebackers always have inside leverage to the receivers. They align with their outside shoulder on the receiver's inside shoulder. Once the linebacker gets the pass read, he drops into the receiver with his hips and feels with his hands. He does not drop and read. He drops to the receiver and collisions his hips. Our outside linebackers are good athletes that run well. The outside linebacker reads the number 2 receiver in the 2 X 2 formation. He collisions him and get into the trail position.

Disrupting linebackers will get nervous when they miss or lose the receiver. They forget they have a safety over the top. The main job is to make the quarterback throw the ball high so the safety has a chance to react to the ball. If the receiver runs vertical, the linebacker wants to collision and get as close as possible.

The first ten days of our summer camp we work on the following drills. We do the collision drills with or without pads. The slide hips and hands drill is almost like pass blocking hand placement. We want to get into the chest of the receivers with our elbows in and the thumbs up in the placement. The linebackers do not do any jam drill. We want them running and getting their hips in front of the receivers.

DRILLS

- **Slide hips during 10 day camp.**
- **'W' drill chest over toes short steps.**
- **Collide and get angle to the numbers with zone turn.**

- **Collide outside for man turn.**
- **Safety balls hash to hash.**
- **Stalk drill:**
  - Engage with outside arm free.
  - Press inside.
  - Never cross 10's keeping outside leverage.

When the corner works on his zone turn he does not work straight back. He angles toward the numbers and forces the receiver inside. We work the colliding drill on the receivers.

COLLIDING RECEIVERS

- **Collide with the hips.**
- **Feel the hands.**
- **Vision for run fits.**
- **Collide from soft, jam, and lock gives great disguise.**
- **Understanding coverage to determine man vs. zone turn and safety help.**
- **Corners are 5 yards head up to bump depth.**
- **Safeties play 10-14 yards deep, and 1 yard either side of hash.**
- **LB's are also responsible for colliding through their zone.**

We practice these things every day with our defensive backs. During our practice we have two opportunities to practice collision drills. We do it in individual drills and in inside-drills period. In addition to helping the corners in their technique, it helps our receiver in defeating that type of technique.

The other thing we work extremely hard on is the safeties off the hash. We do not want the safety keying through the number 1 receiver. We want the safety keying the number 2 receiver because he is the closest receiver to the quarterback. However, we want him to break on the ball. If the corner does a good job of staying underneath the number 1 receiver on the vertical, the safety can stay over the number 2 receiver and still break on the outside throw.

Because of the way we teach the collision, we do a great job against the stalk block by the wide receiver. We work the drill in an off position by the defensive back. We practice the stalk drill twice a week. On one day we work on the right hash and the next day we work from the left hash.

When we run the drill the coach gives a cadence and the defensive back goes into his backpedal. That puts distance between the receiver and back. The coach gives the command and the defensive back comes forward and attacks the outside shoulder of the blocker. He keeps his outside arm free and presses the receiver inside. The coaching point is the back is not responsible for making the tackle inside. The way they make the tackle is to squeeze the receiver inside. That way they get help from the linebacker and safety.

To me, the technique is a bad technique if the blocker gets any part of the corners outside shoulder. What I do not want to happen is the running back to get to the outside of the corner. The corner does not try to blow up the receiver. He wants to make contact, keep the outside arm free, and squeeze the receiver inside.

We are a "4-4" defense. (Diagram #1) However, when it all is said and done, 90 percent of the time we are in a "4-2-5 look." That happens because of our adjustments to the spread offense. The "R" in our scheme is a Rover linebacker. On run-downs, we play cover-5 in the secondary. The open side corner plays the half coverage to the backside. The Rover is down into the flat on action his way. The free safety and corner to the strong side play quarter coverage.

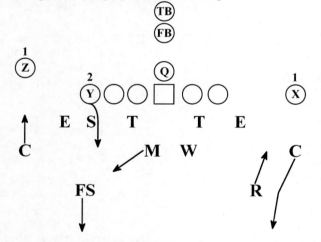

Diagram #1. Base Defense vs. Pro

In our alignment the defensive tackles align in 3-techniques to both sides. The Mike and Will linebackers align in 20-techniques on the offensive guards. The Sam linebacker is in a 6-technique head up the tight end. The defensive ends align in a wide 9-technique to the strong side and a wide 5-technique to the open side.

The Sam linebacker plays very physical on the tight end and forces him inside. If the Y-end

tries to run a vertical route the Mike linebacker is responsible for him.

In the 2 X 2 formation, we have the same principle. (Diagram #2) However, the Sam linebacker has a tougher job because the number 2 receiver is in the slot. He has inside leverage on him by alignment, but must funnel him inside to the Mike linebacker. The Mike linebacker takes the Y-receiver is he goes vertical. Our Mike linebacker is not that capable of a runner but he can do it. If the Y-receiver runs across the field, the linebackers pass him across. The Mike linebacker can pass him to the Will linebacker if he continues across the formation.

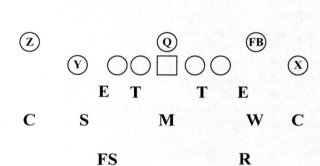

Diagram #2. Cover-2 vs. 2 X 2

The Sam linebacker does not carry the number 2 receiver vertical unless, the receiver gets outside of him. If that is the case, he runs with number 2 and the Mike linebacker takes his coverage in the flat area.

We see the 3 X 1 set many times. (Diagram #3)

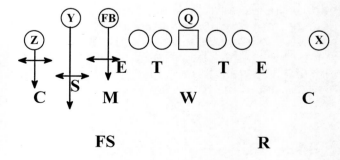

Diagram #3. Cover-2 vs. 3 X 1 Regular Verticals

We have three ways we can cover that set that gives the offense some different looks. To the backside the corner is the half player and the Rover is the flat defender and supports on the run.

We want the free safety and Rover involved in run control. The alignment for the four down linemen does not change. The Will linebacker becomes the middle linebacker. To the three-receiver side, the corner, Sam linebacker, and Mike linebacker align on the numbers 1, 2, and 3 receivers.

They are five yards off the line of scrimmage. At the snap of the ball, they read the action of the receivers. If all three receivers go vertical, the three defenders collision the receiver and get into a trail position on them. The free safety stays over the top of the receivers.

There are two types of coverage adjustments to play the 3 X 1 formation. If we play regular coverage, the free safety plays over the number 2 and 3 receivers on vertical route. The corner plays the number 1 receiver. If the number 1 receiver goes vertical, the corner collisions him and plays him man-to-man. If the number 1 receiver goes vertical, the corner plays a man technique and forces him outside to the sidelines. The free safety plays over the patterns of the number 2 and 3 receivers.

If the Y-receiver goes outside, the Sam linebacker works with the Mike linebacker and looks for the H-receiver coming outside. (Diagram #4)

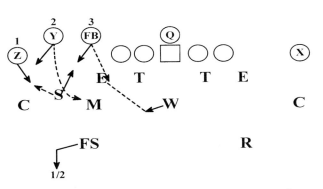

Diagram #4. Cover-2 vs. 3 X 1 Regular Under Patterns

If the Y-receiver goes to the inside, he works with the corner on the Z-receiver. The Mike linebacker keys the H-receiver. If the H-receiver

goes inside, the Mike linebacker drops into the shallow cross-area. If the H-receiver goes outside, the Mike linebacker looks for the Y-receiver coming inside.

In practice, we align the defenders opposite the receivers and they work all different types of packages against the defense. They read the receivers in a five-yard area.

If the offense is in a 3 X 1 formation, but we feel they are going to run the ball we play "Blue" coverage. (Diagram #5) That rolls the Rover into the flat area weak and puts the corner in the deep half of the field. We play this in a run situation. We can also play backside corner in a straight man-to-man coverage. To the 3 X 1 side we play regular cover-2 coverage.

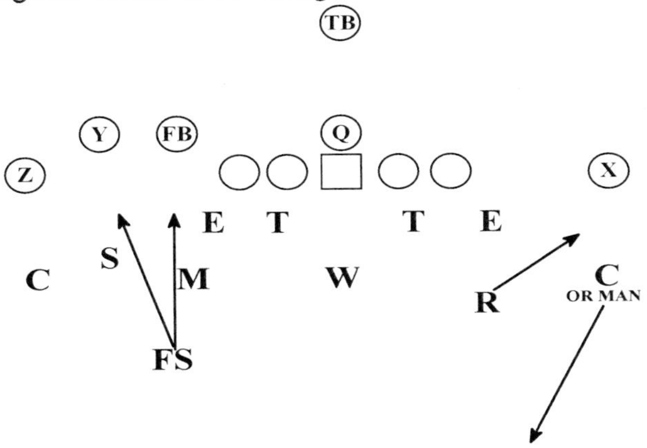

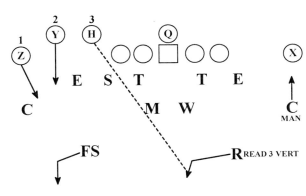

Diagram #5. Cover-2 Blue

When we play "Gold" coverage, we involve the Rover with the vertical patterns. (Diagram 6) When teams go to a 3 X 1 set the defense has to worry about vertical patterns.

Diagram #6. Cover-2 Gold

The offense tries to use the H-receiver to stretch the opposite hash vertically. They want to stretch the free safety. We get the Rover involved and he reads the number 3 receiver on the vertical route. On "Gold", the boundary corner plays a lock technique on the number 1 receiver. He plays him man-to-man.

This allows the free safety to play over the top of the numbers 1 and 2 receivers. The Rover plays over the top of the H-receiver. When we play regular, we play the free safety over the number 2 and 3 receivers, with the corner locked on the number 1 receiver vertical. On "Gold", the free safety plays over the top of the number 1 and 2 receivers and the Rover plays over the top of the H-receiver.

If the offense throws something in the flat or the smash route to the three-receiver side, we do not cover the short pattern and rally back for the tackle. We play physical with the receivers but we do not guard that space unless they threaten it.

We have two ways to play the "bunch" set. We cover with what we call "box" and "bull's eye." If we get a bunch set with man coverage as the call, we call it off and go to "box" coverage. (Diagram #7) This coverage has man and zone principles in it. We align the Sam linebacker in a jam alignment on the middle receiver in the bunch. He is not playing a jam technique. His job is to funnel the receiver to the inside. After he funnels him inside, he drops into the flat to play the out cuts of the formation.

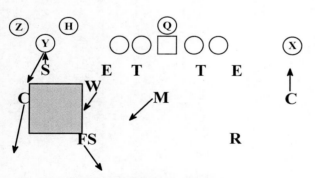

Diagram #7. Bunch Box

This is the only time he plays the technique this way. We want him to jam the outside shoulder of the receiver, force him inside, and get to the flat. One of the other receivers will go into the flat. The key on the box coverage is to make sure the Sam linebacker disrupts the Y-receiver. The corner drops into the outside quarter zone. The

free safety drops into the inside quarter zone. The Will linebacker drops into the hook/curl zone.

We play a box 5 yards off the line of scrimmage. We think that will take care of all the patterns. The Mike linebacker expands to the outside hook zone keying the tailback for a release. To the backside of the bunch set, we play any way we chose. We can play man on the X-receiver or some kind of half coverage with the Rover.

The problem with the box coverage is the Z or H receiver getting into the hook area in the middle of the box. To handle that, we play "bull's eye" coverage. (Diagram #8) The Sam linebacker instead of dropping into the flat settles into the soft hook zone. He is still physical with the Y-receiver, but does not drop to the flat. The corner rolls up into the flat area. However, if there is no threat in that area, he sinks into the outside quarter and gains depth. When the corner has a roll responsibility, he plays it as a sink technique until the receiver threatens him in the flat.

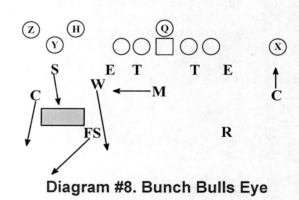

Diagram #8. Bunch Bulls Eye

Instead of putting the free safety in the deep zone, we send the Will linebacker into the deep zone and slide the Mike linebacker to the bunch side into the hook/curl area.

We play box coverage unless a team starts to hurt us in that area. If a team throws a ball into the hook area, we play bull's eye the next time to make sure they cannot use that area as a steady diet. The reason we do not play this as a rule is the difficulty of running the Will linebacker vertical.

The adjustment to handle that problem is to call "bull's eye-gold." That brings the Rover to cover the vertical route in the middle of the field. The Will linebacker goes back to playing the hook/curl zone and the Mike linebacker goes back to his normal drop. The corner on the backside plays the X-receiver man-to-man.

The problem with the "gold" coverage is the run support to the weakside. When we scout the opponent the first thing I want to know is how many time they run vertical out of the 3 X 1 formation. Most teams do not run vertical out of that set. They do not run the Y or H receivers vertical to the backside hash marks. In our defense, unless we have a "gold" coverage, the Rover is not playing too much technique to the backside hash.

We feel teams trying to play this type of coverage, gets the backside safety locked into the single receiver and does not play very well on the hash mark away from the trips set. We throw that vertical pattern into the middle and try to catch the ball over the center position.

These adjustments are scouting report automatics. If we get the bunch set, we automatically call box coverage. If they hit the hook in the box, we go to the "bull's eye." The adjustment to "bull's eye" is the "gold" coverage.

We practice all the adjustments in that 10 day period in the summer. We practice our hip techniques, collisions, and 3 X 1 looks. We want to stay regular as much as we can. If we have a jam call and the offense comes out in 3 X 1, we drop back and play soft coverage. We can play man coverage from the soft alignment but we do not do it that often. When we see the 3 X 1 formation, we want to drop to 5 yards and read the receivers.

If the Z-receiver runs a hitch or quick out, the corner has to see the pattern of the slot receiver. If the slot is running vertical, he has to sink on the corner route in the smash concept. We make the quarterback throw the hitch and rally back for the tackle. The hitch is not the route the quarterback wants to throw. You must practice the smash route many times when you are a collision corner. The corner has to develop a feel for the smash.

On the smash route, the slot receiver has no goal to get deep down the field. The route is a lazy route that the slot tries to work behind a rolled up corner. We want to sink under the route and make the quarterback throw the perfect pass to hit the corner route if he tries to go there. This allows the Sam linebacker to push the slot off the corner and start looking for the flat route by the fullback or third receiver to that side. The Sam linebacker has help and he knows he can push him off to the outside.

A coaching point for the corners on their collision technique is in the release of the receiver. If the receiver has a violent release straight up the field at the defender instead of slanting, or some kind of other break, we take the collision off. We do not need to reroute him because he is going where we want him to go. If he stems his pattern inside or outside, we reroute him and get under him.

To play this coverage you must learn how to collide with the receiver at the hips and play with the hands. We never lunge or tell the defender to destroy the receiver. We want to get in his way and move him off where he is going. We learn how to grab the jersey to give direction and let go when he breaks away from us. We teach the holding technique the same way you teach an offensive lineman. After the collision, they must learn the trail position and make the quarterback arc the ball on his throws.

I appreciate it. If I can do anything for you shoot me an E-mail and I will be glad to talk with you. Thank you very much.

Rick Stewart

Developing Team Building Concepts

Fresno High School, California

Last year I spoke at this clinic and I talked on defense and the Pistol wing-T Offense. I just mentioned a few remarks about Leadership and the Team Building part of it which we feel is the most important thing for the team. My coaching staff is here with me this weekend. I give the staff all the credit. If you can find me or one of the staff members we will be glad to talk about Team Building Concepts.

We have been luck to be able to turn three programs around. I believe this with every breath I breathe, and every sound of my being. There were four things we did to turn the four programs around. I am telling you that Team Building was the number one thing on the list. The weight room was number two.

W.I.N.

- **Play For Each Other**
  - Team Building
- **Strength And Conditioning**
- **Surround Players With Adults Who Love Them**
- **X & O's - 4th On My List**

You should surround yourself with people that love kids. This includes parents and coaches. This is very important. I hate to say this, but there is no silver bullet. The X's and O's are fourth on my list.

When I was a young coach I ended up with great plays. I was real happy with our Pistol wing-T offense, and our Gang Green Defense.

If you are in a program that is struggling, get the players to play for each other. This is big. You need to get some sort of a weight room and strength program going. At McFarland High School we did not have a weight room. We started a program where we were on the grass. We did pushups, pull ups, and other exercises. We did all of the isometric exercises. I got most of the things we did from the Marines Boot Camp.

There was not a weight room anywhere in that town of a couple of thousand people. We fit the bill, and we were strong and we were in good condition.

When I sit down to interview a new coach to hire, the X's and O's is my second part of the interview. When I talk to potential assistant coaches we are going to talk for an hour or two on "How are you going to treat the kids"? This is big. I am at the point of my career now where I can see the importance of this. I did not see it when I was a 28 year old with my first job as a head coach.

I want you to understand where we came from. To this date we still have not coached a Division-I player in the different schools we have coached. So the point is we did not turn these programs around with a group of Division-I players. Here are the points to view at the schools we turned around.

FIRST PROGRAM

- **1-19 Program to playoffs 2nd year**
  - **600 kids**
  - **16 out of 23 field workers**
  - **1st year finished with 13 players**
  - **No Weight Room**
  - **No Money**
  - **No Frosh**

We had mostly Hispanic kids. They were all field workers. It was a very small town. They are respectful and extremely hard working people. Very few of them had parents around. There was not a business office in the entire town. We did have a McDonalds, a Subway, and a Chevron Station. That was it. We had to figure out how to turn the program around.

SECOND PROGRAM

- **0-20 Program to undefeated league title in 2nd year**

- 700 kids
- Finished the Weight Room
- Monetary support
- Averaged 28 on the roster.
- Frosh played 5 games

In our second program we had a few more kids. We had to build a weight room from scratch. We took a sledge hammer and knocked all the walls down of an old shower stall. We were close to the State Prison. The prisoner Charles Manson donated all of his weight equipment to our school. We put the equipment in the old shower, and that was our weight program. In the second year we were undefeated league champs.

CURRENT PROGRAM

- 8-42 Program to?
  - 28 wins in three years
  - 1st playoff win in 117-year history
  - Back-2-Back Section Finalist
  - 1,700 kids
  - JV haven't lost a game in two years
  - Started a youth feeder program

We were able to go in and build a larger program. It was a rural school. It was a large school but it was at the Foothill Mountains where there is a lot of agriculture, and those types of jobs.

The school I am at now, is close to the same size, with over 2,000 kids, but it is an inner-city school. Every player on our Fresno High School team rides a city bus to and from school. Every day before practice I walk to the office and get a bag full of bus tokens because all of our kids get a free bus token because they are playing football.

At our team dinner, our coaches do the cooking because there are not any parents available. When we coached at Porterville High School we were really blessed. We had the best parents in the valley. They were phenomenal. I think that was because we embraced them.

I want to talk about our Team Building. This is the order in which I think you need to follow in building a program. You will see the X's and O's are last on my list. It did not used to be that way. I would go to Nike and Glazier Clinics and I was into the reverse plays, and the "Wrap around Sally" type of plays. I was all X's and O's. The X's and O's you use must be solid. You cannot take the field Friday night and not be technically sound. If you name any offense or any defense, we can find a team that is 10-0 that is running the offense or using the defense. Some team is 10-0 running the wing-T, the Double wing-T, the Spread Offense, the 3-4, or the 4-3 Defense.

When you go talk to those 10-0 coaches they will tell you this. "We are real proud of our X's and O's, but we won because of Team Building and in the Weight Room."

TEAM BUILDING

- **NOT JUST PLAYERS**
  - Coaches
  - Parents
  - Campus

It is not just the players. Porterville High School taught me this. When we got to Porterville High School we were big on Team Building with our Coaches, Parents, and with our Campus. Team Building is not just your players. You must build a program so your players are proud to be associated with it. When you build a team of parents, alumni, and campus people, the players will start to realize they are playing for something bigger than themselves. This is very important.

Everyone on this planet wants to be a part of something bigger than what he is. This is why so many people jump on the band wagon when a team is going to the Super Bowl. Kids want to be a part of something bigger than what they are. They will join gangs, and end up doing a life sentence in prison for that gang. They want to be a part of something special.

When you start including your parent, and not just your lynch mob, you will see a different attitude of the parents. You may not want to see them walk through that door, but you have to embrace your parents. When they get involved and they are part of the team, your players will see how big the program really is. They get that feeling they must show up at the weight room because they are playing for the community, campus, and their parents.

Your coaches must realize this fact. If you have a bad coach or a bad coordinator, you have to sit down in the offseason and have a talk. These clinics sessions are a great time to get together with the staff. You must make sure the coaches define who they are. It did not take long for us at Porterville. Once the assistant coaches learned what I was about, it was not hard for them to jump on board.

Once you find out how the coaches operate, and who they are, and how they define themselves, if they are not willing to change, you must cut ties with them in early January. They all want to coach on Friday night. They all want to show up once the season starts. Do they want to coach in January, or are they here with us this weekend? You know what I am talking about. That first year you have to cut bait. You just have to let some coaches go. You give them the whole year to show their interest and who they are.

SHIFT EMPHASIS

- **FROM X's and O's to PSYCHOLOGY**
  - **Start focusing on the player and not the playbook**
- **Not COACHING Players.**
- **You are TEACHING kids.**

When I interview a coach those are the points I am going to focus on.

When I go into a new program that first year I am the coordinator of everything. I am not going to turn over any coordinator responsibilities over to anyone until I have a chance to work with them for a year, unless I really know them from previous experiences. When I come in new, I am going to run everything until I find out about the staff.

When I shifted my focus from X's and O's it really showed up on the scoreboard. The reason it appeared on the scoreboard, was because I did not care about the scoreboard. John Wooden's chin up philosophy! OK!

FEAR VS. LOVE

- **Do you love the jersey number or the kid wearing the jersey?**
  - **What would he say?**
- **No sub for time. Earn trust!**
- **Never give up. It doesn't always happen on your schedule.**
- **Don't care how much you know as long as he knows you care.**

You have to see how the coaches feel about the season. We ask the coach this question. If I went to the school and talked to the players, what would they say about you? That is a hard question. I know I have some players that would not speak kindly of me after one year. I did not treat those players right? For every kid I have tried to save, I am only batting about 200 percent. It gets frustrating. You have to realize it is not going to happen on your schedule. We know we cannot give up trying.

I always have a one-on-one Post Season Interview with every coach. I think this is good for Team Building, Program Building, and the Trust factor. It is always in a nonthreatening environment. It may be over lunch, or having a cup of coffee. I have a form with a list of questions I ask them. I want them to do a lot of the talking. "Where do you see yourself next year? When do you see yourself in five years? If you were the head coach last year, what would you have changed? What was good and bad on our team last year?" You would be shocked at what you get.

COACHES

- **1 on 1 Post Season Interview.**
- **Saturday Night Dinners with Wives.**
- **Post Season Dinner.**
- **Coaches Retreat.**
- **Text Players in Student Tree Program once per week.**

We started a Post Season Dinner with the coaches at the end of the year. The first year I paid for the dinner. Later we had a fund raiser to pay for the dinner. The bill was between $400 and $500. It was a nice dinner and it included the coaches and all of wives. We were at the restaurant until 2:00 a.m. The wives were very appreciative of the dinner and had a lot of fun. Some of them admitted that Rick Stewart was not a bad guy. The next year we found our wives were sitting together at the football games. This made a big difference with the assistant coaches and their wives feeling a part of the team.

Once a month we go out to eat. The staff meets until a few hours before in the morning, and them we all go to dinner including our wives. We accomplished Team Building with this approach. So we do something once a month, and at the end of the year we do a big bash type dinner. When I am talking about Team Building, it is not just the players.

As a head coach you need to do some fun things with the staff. The Coaching Retreat can be a Coaching Clinic. For us, this clinic has always been an opportunity for our coaches to get together. We consider this clinic as a Team Builder for our staff. We may go to several other clinics in the offseason.

When you are losing and things are going wrong, and people are getting after you and the staff, you must circle the wagons, right? Coaches must have each other's back. The things you do in the offseason are really big. As the Head Coach you have a mandate. "If you are going to coach in this program, attendances to these functions are mandatory." If you are a paid coach in my program you must attend at least one clinic. I will give them a choice to pick one clinic from four clinics that I give them to chose from. They must attend one of these four clinics. The Coaches Retreat is non-negotiable, and they must attend that function.

One of our goals is for the players to take ownership in their program. It must be the player's team. They must feel like they are at the best school for them. They must feel we run the best offense in America, NS we run the best defense in America. They do not want to be anywhere else. That is our ultimate vision of Team Building.

T.E.A.M.

- **Teach**
- **Enforce**
- **Advocate**
- **Model**

THREE LEVELS OF TRUST

PLAYERS
- **Coaches Trust Player**
- **Player Trust Coach**

Most Important
- **Players - Trust - Players**

The kids think Trust means something like this. "Coach, I will not steal your wallet!" That is what they think Trust is. You must sit them down and explain to them what Trust really is.

Then you have to deal with the kids that will tell you this. "Coach, I am going to give it my all on Friday night." That is when I say to them, "Johnny, what players do not give it their best on Friday night?"

When we talk about Trust we are talking about these issues. When I walk out to take attendance, are you going to be there? When I get in my car at 6:00 a.m. going to school, can I Trust you are going to school as well? Can I Trust, when I put you in a game that you have paid attention during practice and were not in the

back talking with Jimmy? That is the type of Trust I am talking about.

At the Campfires we reverse the idea and have the kids ask the coaches why they should trust the coaches that work with them. "Can the players Trust the coaches?" We go through all the reasons the players can Trust us as a staff. This is all done at our Campfires and Team Building Activities.

We started winning a lot of games when we started building that Marine Corps mentality. "Do I want to be in a foxhole with you? I took this mentality to the football field and it became very powerful. All we talk about is: "Don't let each other down." When I discipline a kid, it is framed as the Team concept. "You let your team down." We always frame everything around the Team and Trust concept.

As far as Team Building you must make sure every player is important. Our linemen get special treatment. We want every player to feel like he is a part of the team.

SUB GROUPS

- **LINE: Special Treatment (water breaks, pre-game meals, articles, T-shirts, pride run, POY)**

- **ASSASSINS: (shirt, no condition)…kickoff**

- **GAME BREAKERS: Kickoff Return Score every time take the field**

- **DEFENSE:**
  Lights out - shirt, belt buckle, cookie, Drive stoppers - get a belt buckle to wear that week

We do not want the prim-donna on our team. Unintentionally we set them up to be heroes. We set them up to be a prim-donna.

SUPERSTARS

- **Program Kids: - Anyone can be a superstar!**
- **Friday Morning Circuits**
- **Summer Retreat**
- **Carry Flag Out On Friday**
- **Name On Jersey**

Do up have things in your program where every kid on the team can be rewarded? Do you have it set up in your program where a nonstarter can be a captain? At the rewards banquet can the nonstarters get some rewards? When you do the rewards logos on the helmets can your non-starters receive those logos? The players must fill if they bust their tails they should be part of the team. You need to think about some of the things you can do to make sure every player feels special.

On our Friday morning circuits when we are in the weight room we do a bunch of team stretching exercises. Everyone can be a part of that exercise. In the weight room everyone can set a record. Everyone can lead the team stretching exercises. The kids talk about "Come In or Quit." The kids all talk about that quote.

Everyone gets to go on the Summer Retreat. Everyone gets to go to our Campfires. When we do our Team Leadership set ups, we include a "Scout Player of the Week." We have five players that come out of the tunnel just before we kickoff for the toss of the coin. We pick these players on Thursday night. We pick an offensive player, defensive players, a special team player, a lineman, and a Scout Team Player. The Scout Team player is the middle man between those other four players and is our "Scout Player of the Week." He is the one that carries the flag out on Friday night. That is the last award we do on Thursday night. Every kid on the team knows they have a chance to lead the team out of the tunnel.

For kids to get their names on the back of their jersey is to show up for 90 percent of the time in the summer workouts. I had a parent take me to the School Board on this issue. "Coach, that is not promoting Team Building. California is a liberal state. You are going to hurt Johnny's feelings. What about the other kids that did not get their names on their jerseys? How do you think they feel? My son will have to go see Dr. Phil to get his self-esteem back?"

The school board was drilling me on this issue. We did have five or six kids that did not have their names on the back of their jerseys. This was how I responded to them. I told them they took attendance at schools. They have a deal where the students with perfect attendance are rewarded. Those students get to go to lunch first, and they get to go on a field trip to the Park.

I told them we were rewarding the kids that showed up for attending our voluntary workouts by having their names on their jerseys. That is how we get our kids to attend summer workouts.

In the spring if they show up 90 percent of the time they get to go to the Lake for the Team Retreat we do. It is a cool place to visit. But in the summer workouts, if they attend 90 percent of the sessions they get their names on the back of the jersey.

PRACTICE

- **Attendance Lines**
  - **Student Tree Program**
  - **Everyone Does Reminders for Absences/Tardies**
- **Warrior Reminders**
- **Brotherhood Circuit**
  - **Protect My Brother**
  - **Know My Role**

What do we do in practice to promote Leadership? I do a Student Tree Program. If you are a senior you pick five kids to be on your team. Also, we have a coach in charge of the senior leaders. The assistant coach collects all the Gold Cards, grade checks, and he has to interact with those senior leaders. I only have to deal with the assistant coach that is in charge of the senior leaders. I meet with the assistant coaches every Thursday morning. The assistant coaches provide me the feedback from their groups.

The senior leaders have junior and sophomores on their team. This forces the senior to interact with them during the day. He has to go see them to get their grades check form. He has to walk around the campus to find things out with his group.

We do an attendance check. I check with the assistant coaches to see if anyone is missing. If a player is absent from practice, the next day everyone in that players group stays after practice and does reminders together. What am I teaching in doing this? This lets the player that misses' practice knows that he has let his teammates down. The whole group does extra conditioning. "Don't Let Your Teammates Down."

The Warrior Reminders is the name of the exercises we do after practice. We do the Terrible Tens and Dirty Thirty's. We do not call out all of the exercises. We just call them Warrior Reminders. The word Reminders is important. If they screw up in practice we keep them after practice and they do the Warrior Reminders.

They are going to be reminded the way we want them to act. They are going to be reminded how important it is not to let the team down.

I give credit for this next point to Dennis Moody. He is one of the best coaches in the "Valley." One year we had just returned from summer camp and we were real weak and rundown. So in August we dedicated between ten and fifteen minutes to what we call the Brotherhood Circuit. We came up with five things the players had to do to be declared a member of the Brotherhood. We call it our Brotherhood Challenge.

BROTHERHOOD CHALLENGE

- **I Am A Warrior**
  - **Never Quit**
  - **Show No Mercy**
  - **Give A Little More**
  - **Know My Role**
  - **Protect My Brother**
- **I Must Live And Honor This Code**
- **Survive The Challenge And Be Rewarded With Strength And Courage**

It was their Creed. We did 20 days of this circuit. At the end of the three weeks we gave them a black T-shirt. The five points of being a Warrior was on the back of the shirt. It was a real neat thing. I am going to show the five items used to accomplish the feat of being a Warrior. We talk about the players and the fact they must honor the code.

NEVER QUIT – 1 player tries to score from 10 yards out. The other 4 players stop him with hand shields. (Diagram #1) The Running Back has to come through the four defenders to score. We are teaching the back to never quit trying to score. We are teaching the four defenders to never quite defending the goal.

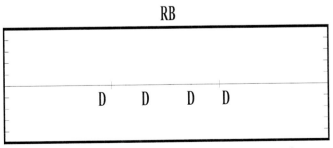

Diagram #1. NEVER QUIT – 4 on 1

The next drill is SHOW NO MERCY. The defender tries to tag the Running Back. (Diagram 2) We have blockers with the back and only one

defender. It is similar to the first drill. While the drill is in progress the teammates are yelling, "Show No Mercy! Never Give Up!" These sayings become ingrained in their head.

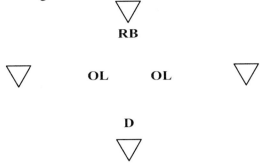

Diagram #2. NEVER GIVE UP – SHOW NO MERCY

Next is the Bear Crawl. We named it GIVE A LITTLE MORE. (Diagram #3) You need a ten yard square area for the drill. This drill last for 3 minutes. As the drill proceeds the players and coaches are yelling "GIVE A LITTLE MORE!"

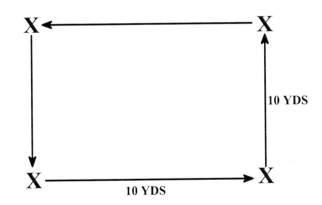

Diagram #3. GIVE A LITTLE MORE – BEAR CRAWL.

Our fourth drills is a Tire Flip. We call the drill Know My Role! The players flip a tire for 10 yards. The freshman push the 2-man Sled 10 yards.

KNOW MY ROLE – TIRE FLIP

The last drill is similar to the Bear Crawl but we add a CARRY to the drill. We want the players to carry a teammate a minimum of 10 yards. We call the drill PROTECT MY BROTHER. It is a partner carry drill. The players can use the Panther Brother Carry, Straddle Fireman Carry, or the Bear Crawl Carry.

PROTECT MY BROTHER – PARTNER CARRY!

After we added these drills after our Retreat we did them for 20 days. After the season I was with the seniors for pizza and this is what the seniors told me about the drills. One player told me, "Coach, I hated the drills in the Brotherhood Challenge. At first I thought they were stupid. But Coach, I can't tell you how many times in the fourth quarter when I was in the huddle those little sayings kept popping in my head." We tattooed the slogans on their brain. The idea is mental toughness and giving them some of the ideas we felt were important.

Our JV and Varsity teams practice together. I will never do it another way. I think this was the most important thing we did at Porterville High School. On one field we have offense and on another field we had the defense. We had offensive coaches and we had defensive coaches.

COMBINE JV AND VARSITY

- **Freshman Do Not Hit Seniors!**
- **Both Teams Do Offense**
- **Both Teams Do Defense**
    - **Indo's is easy**
    - **Be careful about Team 11 on 11.**
    - **Might have 40 kids combined - then it works**
    - **Eliminate a corner**

The JV Team goes on offense the first hour, and the Varsity Team goes on defense the first hour. We have a water break and then the Teams switch fields. The Teams and Not the players switch fields. Our Varsity players will never hit the JV players. They are never on the same field together. The JV coach goes with the JV's and I stay with the Varsity when we switch fields. Our kids get to know each other this way,

Here is what this promotes. It promotes three layers of trust including players trusting coaches. If it is a freshman moving up to the JV's he knows that defensive backs coach for four years. The important point is they come up to the varsity level trusting the coaches they have worked with. We do everything together including the Team Dinner. The practices end at the same time, and we go into the locker room together. Seniors and sophomores are always around each other.

With this system we never have a problem bringing up a JV player to the Varsity. The other good point is the JV parents get to know us as their sons' position coach. By the time the players are seniors the parents are some of my close

friends. Because we did everything together, parents get to know us and to trust us.

We can serve each team by combining some drills. The Indo's is a good example. The JV defensive backs may go over and work against the Varsity receivers on fade routes. The JV defensive backs may need work against the fade rout. So it is good practice for both squads.

As far as Team Building and Program Building, we are not just Team Building our Varsity Team. We are Team Building an entire program. On Saturday mornings our players come down to the Youth League Games and run the chains for us.

We do the Youth Camp with our Varsity and JV teams. We use our coaches and the players demonstrate how to run the drills. We pick Players of the Week in the Youth Program and they get to be the ball boys for the upcoming game on Friday night. We have three ball boys. We have one from the Peewees, Juniors, and Seniors. Team Building for the entire program is going on.

In the weight room everybody lifts together. The players do not do anything in the weight room on their own. They do not go get a drink on their own. We are lucky that we have Squat Racks all around the room. It was not always like that, but we have them now. There are five players at each squat rack. I would put our Weight Program up against anybody. We do mini-rotations. I am watching them. I am not on my laptop or cell phone. When they finish the squat they look at me. When they have all finished I call out "Rotate."

WEIGHT ROOM

- **Everybody Lifts Together**
- **Human Spotters**
- **Change Lifting Groups Up**
- **Plateau Busters**
    - **Sideline Basketball, Relays, Dodge ball**
    - **Wacky Baseball**
    - **Team Transport**

When the players rotate and get to the next station they all look at me. I call out one of the slogans on the back of their black T-shirts. "Lift To Win!" They all call out the slogan I used and then they attack the bar. We do not move to the next station until everyone has finished their reps at each station. If a player is having a problem completing his reps, the entire team is going to cheer for him to complete that last rep.

We use human spotters on our lifts. The players have each other's back. We all lift together. No one is cutting reps, and no one is sitting down. We start and we finish together on each rep. I think the Weight Room is a powerful Team Building tool.

On the Plateau Busters this is what we do. About every four weeks we do something fun. The kids love Sideline Basketball. The kids beg for that drill. There is a lot of contact. It is where you find your 11 defensive players.

We do relays. Our weight room is next to our basketball gym. I come in early and set up the weight stations I want the players to do in the relays that day. We have 10 teams of five players each. They have two or three exercises such as pushups that the do in the gym. Then they must run over to the weight room and do the lifts I set up earlier. After they do the reps on the lifts they have to run back to the gym and get back in line.

The team that finishes the drills first is the winner. It breaks up the monotony and it is fun. I usually have donuts for the winners. If you can think out of the box, you can get a lot of Team Building in your weight room.

We do not lift weights on Monday anymore. We lift in the summer on Tuesday, Wednesday, and Thursday for one hour and a half. I asked them if they wanted to go Monday through Thursday for one hour. The kids wanted to go three days for one hour and a half. So we take our Mondays off. What is cool about this is the fact when we are done on Thursday, we are done. The summer practice sessions can be a grind. This is what we do on Total Team Thursday.

We actually make out brackets for the entire team. Winners go to the right and losers go to the left. The players are paired into teams.

TOTAL TEAM THURSDAY

- **Iron Man Type Lifts**
- **Make Actual Brackets**
  - ○ **Winners And Losers**

We had sixteen teams in the brackets. The teams were evenly divided. We paired Team 1 against Team 2. The winner moved to the right side of the bracket and the losers move to the left

side of the bracket. After about fifteen minutes they advance to the next round. The first drill we called Framer's Walk. Here are some of the drills in the Farmers Walk. We had two 5 gallon paint buckets full of water as one drill. Each person had to walk a certain distance with the buckets of water. They could not spill the water or they were penalized.

We took a 25 pound weight and a 20 pound weight. We tied the weights to a handle and had the players walk with the weights that were uneven for them. We did a Keg Carry for a given distance. The players carry an empty keg a certain distance.

OTHER EVENTS

- **Truck Pull Or Push**
- **Bleacher Walk**
- **Wheel Barrow**
- **Partner Slides/Carry**
- **Group Dead Lift**
- **Tire Flips / Jackhammer**

The players love the truck Push or Pull. You are in teams of four players. You have 2 – F-150 Trucks at the Goal Line. There are three players in the back of the truck, and one player to push the truck for 25 yards. After the first 25 yards is completed, he stops and gets in the back of the truck, and a second player must push the truck 25 yards. They push the truck from one goal line to the other goal line. They love the drill. Think out of the box and do some fun things on Thursday.

If a kid stays with you for four years and all he knows is the walls of the weight room, it gets monotonous. Break it up a little on Thursday. Every Thursday we change the groups of five. We want the kids to interact with other kids.

ACTIVITIES

- **Car Wash**
- **Clean Up Locker/Weight Room**
- **Paintball, Madden Tourney**
- **Visit Other Teams**
- **Retreats**
  - ○ **Team – May, June, and August**
  - ○ **Seniors - April**

I hate Car Washes. But, it is a good Team Building activity. You must organize the players and how they are going to perform when washing the cars. It takes organization. Someone has to collect the tickets or money, someone has to wash the car, and someone has to rinse the soap off, and so on.

When I do an activity such as a Car Wash I want to make $5,000 or more. But we have done a Car Wash for $600. I watch the kids in action and I can see it if we are in a Building Team oriented activity. That is the reason I will do one Car Wash each year.

Before we come into practice in August, I have the team come in and clean the locker room. We paint the room and the lockers and put our logos up. We clean the showers and use bleach to make sure it is free of germs. The kids work together on this and that is a Team Builder.

Visit other teams to see how they practice. There is a lot of Team Building in getting organized to visit another team. After we visit the other team we stop to have something to eat. We sit there talking and the kids get to know me more than just their coach. We are interacting. It is like a road trip.

RETREATS

- **Position Groups In Charge**
  - **Meals, Activities**
- **Include Parents**
- **JV's Most of Time**
- **Frosh Do Their Own Thing**
  Bowling, Paintball, Swim Party

We do a lot of Retreats. We do a lot of camping. At Porterville High School we want on three camping trips per year. We went on these Retreats in May, June, and August. We always take the seniors somewhere in April. Every senior gets to go as long as they meet the criteria.

SENIOR RETREAT

- **Student Tree Draft**
- **Team Symbol**
- **Spirit Packs**
- **Team Expectancies**
- **Circle Of Compliments**
- **Commitment Cards**

When we have our May Retreat we have two nights of campfires. We have one on Friday night and one on Saturday night. You have to get the players talking when they stand up in front of the team. To do that we have coaches talk first on Friday night. The players get their turn on Saturday night.

MAY RETREAT

- **Call Out**
- **Commitment Cards**
  - **Accountability partner**
  - **Choices / Character Sticks**
  - **Player 1-On-1 Meetings**
    - **How Can I Motivate You?**
- **Adversity Role Play**
- **Telephone During Meals**

On Friday night the coaches talk about what we have decided to do at the campfire. You have to get the players talking, but you have to get the coaches to go first on Friday night. The coaches must be serious. We talk about the Circle of Trust. When we come back from these campfires, I have enrolled nine kids in drug rehab. We find out a great deal about players in these sessions.

Some of the stories the kids tell are amazing. One kid talked about seeing his father getting shot in the head when a drug deal went bad. Did I treat that kid different after that? You bet I did.

The players get up to talk on Saturday night and they can Call Out another kid and tell him he thinks he is soft. The kids call each other out and tell them how they feel.

I get the players in a circle and I ask them to tell us one thing we do not know about them. I do not expect them to say, "I play the flute." The players get emotional. If you have the coaches speak from the heart on Friday night at the campfire, then on Saturday night those players will be crying their eyes out with the stories they tell when they get up.

You may think the session would go from 9:00 p.m. to 11:00 p.m., but I can tell you it is going to last until 2:00 a.m. These kids love this and they need it. As men, we have the same problems. Kids do not get many opportunities to get their feelings out. When you get the players in this environment, they let 12 years of their lives come out. They want to get things off their chest. I would never have guessed some of the stories these players tell would ever come out.

AUGUST RETREAT

- **Blindfold Or Team Blob**
- **Call Out**
- **Roll Appreciation Cards**
- **Commitment Cards**
- **Who Has To Make You Cry**

When we get to August we go through "Hell Week." On a Friday we have a team scrimmage. We scrimmage early. We send some parents up to get the campfire ready for that night. It is a one night for the team. We have our dinner and we are up in the mountains at camp about 7:00 p.m.

We sit around the campfire talking about hell week, the scrimmage, and what we have coming up the next week. What the kids do not know is that we have bought them a T-shirt. I had a parent that made sure the love ones in each player's life got to sign that T-shirt. Everyone that loved that kid had to sign the T-shirt. They even shipped some of the T-shirts across the country to get relatives to sign the T-shirts. They had one grandmother sign a T-shirt from New York City. They sent the shirt back after they signed it. The notes and letters those loved ones wrote to the players were inspiring. The T-shirts are powerful.

We ask the players what got them through "Hell Week?" Who is in the stands cheering for you? Why did you decide to play football? I am trying to get them to understand they are not playing for a scoreboard. Then we tell them they have something in a packet outside of the campfire area. They are told to go find the packet and wait for the signal to return to the campfire area.

They all find their packet and come back to the campfire area. I ask them why we cry when we talk to our teammates. Then we ask them to open their packet. We go around the circle and each player reads the notes and names written on the T-shirt in the packet. The players are crying their eyes out. Everyone reads what is in his packet and what is on the T-shirt.

When the games start, each player wears that special T-shirt under their shoulder pads. They wear the T-shirt on every Friday night for the entire year. The whole thing is what we call "Why Do We Cry." That is our August thing.

I am getting a sign my time is up. I will go fast.

TEAM DINNERS

- **Monday Night Football**
- **Thursday Night**
  - **Sing 4 Your Wings**
  - **Cheerleaders (Water Buckets, Balloons)**
  - **Service Clubs**
- **Game Day Lift**
- **Game Day Lunches**

Monday night we take the linemen to pizza. Running backs do not get to go. I pay for the pizza and the players decide where to go. They get a chance to have some camaraderie together.

Our Thursday Night Team Dinners are a big deal. This is where we have them sing for their wings. The players have to do a skit about the coaches or sing a song. They have to be in groups of three or four. One year we said the group had to include one cheerleader and three players. Some kids want to go alone in this deal. We do not allow this. He must find other players to assist him. We do not allow large groups of 10 players. We film the skits and put them in the highlight film at the end of the year. Our Thursday Night Dinner is special. It is a Mini-Award Banquet. We make it a Big Deal.

We reach out to the community and a different group feeds us every Thursday night. That includes the Lions Club, Kiwanis Club, and the Police Department. Also, the list includes Teacher, FCA, and other community groups. Now our community feels as if they are a part of our family. That is Team Building.

Our players do not leave campus on Friday. We have them something to eat ready about 3:00 p.m., and then the players come to my office area and we have a chalk talk.

I see I am out of time. I will move around the corner and try to answer any questions.

The one thing I have learned about clinics. You cannot do everything we do. The ideal clinic is when you go home with two or three ideas from all of the speakers, and apply those things to your program. It has to be your program and you have to take ownership.

My book – ***WORST TO FIRST – Building A Championship Program*** is available at Championship Productions website. www.championshipproductions.com

Two people that were good resources for me were Jeff Janssen and Greg Dale. If you want to contact me I am leaving my website and e-mail. I have the book for sale on my website as well. Thanks for your attention.

559-723-1211
www.footballcoachessite.com
rick@wingtcoaching.com

James Vint

Pistol Precepts And Zone Insights

Coronado High School, Texas

I love to talk about the pistol offense. I spent the better part of nineteen years of coaching as an offensive coordinator. We fell into the pistol by accident. We started to figure some things out with the offense and by the 2005-2006 we were into the offense full time. We were a Power-I team with two tight ends. On occasion, we put a wide receiver in the game and told him to run down field. We never threw him the ball. The head coach wanted to pack everything in the box and run the ball.

We had to sit down and think about some things. We talked to the head coach and figured out we might be able to run some option football. We became an I-formation team running the midline, load veer, isolation, toss sweep, and trap. On occasion, we ran some Power plays and threw the ball 5 or 6 times a game. One year we opened it up and threw the ball eleven times in a game. We had some success and went to the playoffs for the first time in school history.

The problem was when we got to the playoffs, we got spanked. We could not stand up physically with the team we played. We started playing with the spread in the earlier 2000. Art Briles was running the zone read at Stephenville High School in Texas before anyone ever heard of it. Jerry Campbell came up and helped us install the zone read in our offense. We had success with the zone read but defenses start to play games with the location of our running back. Whichever side you set him on they ran games to that side. We decided since people were keying where we set the back, we would put him behind the quarterback. In 2006, we got into the pistol full time.

WHAT IS THE PISTOL?

- **The pistol puts the tailback, fullback or any other back directly behind the quarterback in the shogun.**
- **We can also put a back next to the quarterback.**

- **We can put a second back in the backfield next to the quarterback.**
- **We can put two backs next to the quarterback with the third back behind the quarterback.**

The offense can be whatever you want it to be. For us the pistol is a back behind the quarterback in the shotgun set. We can align any number of backs in the backfield at any position. That kept defenses from reading the set back and calling their defense.

In the shotgun, everything seemed to go east and west instead of north and south. We thought we could get in the I-formation with the quarterback under the center and get the downhill type of running we felt we needed. However, when we put the quarterback under the center, everyone knew what we were going to do. We were going to run power, isolation, and the toss.

When we were in the shotgun, we ran zone read and speed option plays. We thought we had a multiple offense and would be hard to defend. When I talked to our defensive coordinator he told me we were not that hard to defend. If we were in the I-formation they played us one way, when we went to the spread, they played us another way.

WHY THE PISTOL?

- **Teams could no longer game our zone read.**
- **We could run our downhill run plays.**
- **We did not have to jump under center then back into the gun.**
- **Consistency of performance.**
- **Ability to be diverse on offense.**
- **Simple concepts that could be run multiple ways.**

When we got in the shotgun with the pistol the defense did not know what type of play we were going to run. Now the quarterback could take the snap and hand it off to the tailback as he did in the I-formation. Another thing it did was to help us in the passing game. I coach the quarterbacks and it is easier to teach a three-step drop than it is to teach a five-step drop. If we already have some depth in the passing game, it was going to help us be more diverse.

When we go into the pistol we were still a run first team. However, we could effectively throw the ball 25-30 times a game. You can be effective in the quick passing game even if you do not have a good quarterback.

In the I-formation, the tailback is seven yards from the line of scrimmage. When we were under center in an I-formation, the defense loaded the box and the safety played seven yards off the line of scrimmage. When we went to the pistol, that same team played a five and half defender box. Now we can run the football better.

We are going through a deal now to create our formations. I have always wanted it to be simple when we used multiple formations. We have five formations. We designate them by using R and L words to mean right and left.

FORMATIONS

- **Rip/Liz:** that gives us a Y-receiver with his hand on the ground (tight end).
- **Ron/Lou:** Y aligns in a twin set.
- **R/L:** Y-receiver aligns in a wing one yard outside the offensive tackle and one yard off the line of scrimmage.
- **Rex/Lex:** Bunch set.
- **Randy/Larry:** Twins closed.

The words in the formation tell the Y-receiver where to align. The Y does not have to be a tight end. It could be your third back or third receiver. We call our personnel and they go on the field. We may call 21, 30, or 10. When we get on the field with 30 personnel, we have three running backs on the field with no tight end.

We align the fullback by using numbers. The even numbers go to the right and the odd numbers go to the left. They are the same positions on difference sides of the ball. The 0/1 position is the same position. The 0 is to the right and 1 is to the left. The 0/1 position is a sniffer position 1 yard off the line in the guard-tackle gap.

The 2/3 position is the halfback position at the quarterback depth. The 4/5 position is a wing set

1 X 1 off the end man on the line of scrimmage. The 6/7 is the slot position splitting the distance between the tackle and wide receiver. The 8/9 aligns the fullback as the widest receiver. (Diagram#1)

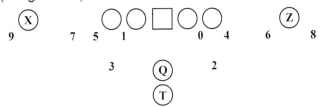

Diagram #1. Fullback Alignment

Our base formation is Ron-7. Ron is the twins-formation with the Y-receiver in the right slot position splitting the difference between the tackle and Z-receiver. The number 7 tells the fullback to align in the number 7 position, which is the slot position to the left side. He splits the difference between the tackle and the X-receiver to the left. The fullback in our offense is not a traditional fullback. He is a hybrid player, which makes him part fullback and part receiver. We call that position the H-back.

The only formation that needs an explanation is the bone-set. (Diagram #2) If we call Ron-3, the formation has a small adjustment. Ron-3 is a twin formation with the H-back set in the halfback position to the left of the quarterback. The word "bone" brings the Y-receiver into the halfback position to the right of the quarterback. That gives us a three-back look with the quarterback in the shotgun and the pistol behind him.

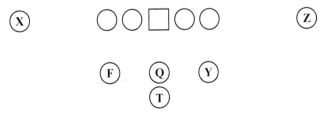

Diagram #2. Ron-3 Bone

Our motion concept is simple. We have an AP, IP, or OP to signify our motion. The letters mean the type of motion. The "A" is across the formation, "I" is into the formation, and "O" is outside the formation. AP motion goes across the formation. IP motion goes into the formation, and OP motion goes outside the formation. To get the right player running the motion we put the first letter of the position on the motion. Yip-motion is the Y-receiver using motion into the ball. If we want to move the tailback, we use "motel" and "motor." Motel means motion to the left and motor means motion to the right.

The thing I like about this is you can run anything you want to run in the pistol. We are a zone read team but we do many other things out of the pistol. Our base plays are our inside and outside zone reads. When we went to the pistol, we started with what we knew. We started with the midline, veer, isolation, toss, and trap. We wanted to run a power play so we used the counter trey. The first year we installed the pistol, we put in more than we needed.

Since then we narrowed it down. We run the inside and outside zone, jet sweep, and rocket toss. We run the power play with 15 variations with one blocking scheme. The last play we run is the midline. We run the plays repeatedly and it looks like a ton of different plays.

The first year we got into the zone read, not many people were running it. Everyone is running that play now and I am glad because it is good stuff. When we went to the pistol, defenses stop playing games to our read side. With the back behind the quarterback they did not know which side was the read side.

I am not going to waste a lot of time with our blocking scheme but we are a count team. (Diagram #3) We use zone blocking, which means we block an area rather than a man, but we still count the defenders. We number from the center to the outside 0, 1, 2, and 3. If the center comes to the line of scrimmage and a defender is aligned on his nose that defender is 0.

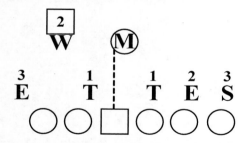

Diagram #3. Count System

If no one aligns on the center's nose, he calls out the linebacker as the 0 defender. From the linebacker to the outside they number the defenders 1, 2, and 3. We number the defenders going both ways from the center.

We run the zone and zone read with the same blocking scheme. The difference between the zone and zone read is the zone is a give to the tailback and the quarterback runs a boot fake. On the zone read the quarterback reads a defender, and gives or pulls the ball off the reaction of his read.

The reason we have two plays from this one play is the play of the defense. If you have a zone read play only, the defense will force the quarterback to pull the ball every time because they do not want the tailback carrying the ball. We run the zone play and give the ball to the tailback regardless of what the defensive end does. Our goal is to get our best player the football.

On the zone play, we work a covered/uncovered concept. The offensive linemen work in tandem on two defenders. If the play is an inside zone play, the covered linemen's landmark is the playside number on the jersey of the defender. When we talk about a landmark that is where the offensive blocker has to get his back knee. We do not teach putting the helmet to the landmark. We feel if we teach that all the linemen will do is to lean into the defender. If they get the inside knee to the landmark, the feet will be in position to block.

We want them to keep the shoulders as square as possible. We do not want the shoulders at a 45 degree angle. Their shoulders should be at a 20 degree angle. That means the shoulders are almost parallel to the line of scrimmage.

An ace call is a tandem block between the center and playside guard. The center's rule is A-gap. He steps into his A-gap and keys the 3-technique defender. If the 3-technique defender is moving away, his rule is to climb to the linebacker. The coaching point is for the center not to vacate the line of scrimmage too quickly. If he climbs to the linebacker immediately and the ball folds into the hole, the 3-technique will fall back into the hole and make the tackle. The center wants to step and punch the 3-technique onto the guard's block. He does not have to worry about the linebacker.

That linebacker will come into the A-gap. If the linebacker does not fill, the ball will hit home free. He cannot get in a hurry to climb.

The quarterback takes the snap, opens at a 45 degree angle, rolls back, and gives the ball to the tailback. We do it that way because we want the quarterback with his back to the line of scrimmage when he hands the ball off. He has the ball in two hands, and rolls back, and with one hand places the ball into the tailback's pocket.

The tailback is three yards behind the quarterback. On the snap of the ball he takes a zone step to let the quarterback catch the ball. He crosses over, takes the ball, and is downhill to the line of scrimmage. If you do not get another thing from this lecture, listen to what I say about the pocket of the tailback.

The tailback places his thumb against the sternum of his chest with the palm almost under his chin. That gives the quarterback a deep soft pocket to place the ball. It is the quarterback's responsibility to put the ball in the pocket. If the tailback pins his thumb against his sternum, the elbow is up and out of the way. (Diagram #4)

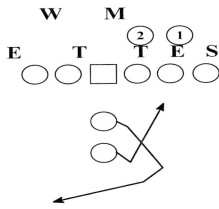

Diagram #4. Tailback Read

The tailback reads the first down lineman to the second down lineman. If the first down defender is in, the tailback is out looking at the second defender. If the first down defender is out, the tailback is in. We have a running back now that is not a big fan of the 1 to 2 read. He says, "Coach, if there isn't a defender there that is where I'm running it." That is a simple way to put it. I think we overcomplicate things.

There is no perfect football play. I went through our tapes looking at every play we blocked perfect this year. I am still looking for it.

In our offense we use a bunch of tags. When we run the zone play without the read, we have to find a way to secure the backside C-gap. (Diagram #5) That keeps the backside end from running the play down from behind. We use the H-back to block back on the defensive end. His rule is to seal the backside. We can align him in any number of places. Most of the time we motion the H-back into position to block the defensive

end. We can align him in the backfield and send him across the mesh to block the end. We can align him to the defensive ends side, motion him away, and bring him back in return motion.

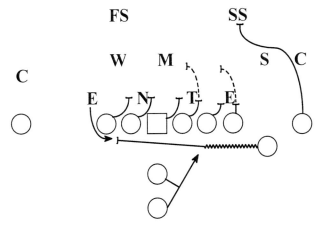

Diagram #5. Backside Seal

The coaching point for the backside seal is for the blocker to hug the line of scrimmage. He has to take on the defensive end with an inside/out block. If he does not get tight to the line of scrimmage, he cannot make the block. We can run the play without sealing the backside and get away with it. We can also run a bootleg or reverse without blocking the crashing end. There are a number of ways to keep him honest but the defense wants to crash the end more than keep him home.

We can call the inside zone play with a "bend" tag. (Diagram #6) The bend play means the H-back is going to block the backside inside linebacker. We chart the people that make tackles during a game. If the backside linebacker is making tackles on the inside zone play, we call "bend." The playside linemen block the inside zone play. The backside blocks solid. They are blocking man-to-man on their defenders.

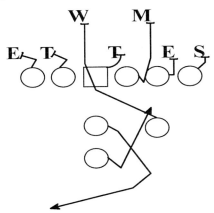

Diagram #6. Inside Bend

They are not stepping into gaps and area blocking. If the backside guard has a 3-technique, he turns him out. The backside tackle turns out on the backside defensive end. The H-back leads up on the backside linebacker and the tailback bends the ball to him. The tailback must sell the play going downhill to the playside.

In our zone read concepts, we have three blocking tags that give us some options. (Diagram #7) We call Boss, Bob, and Bison. We can run the inside zone many different ways. It takes us three days to get the inside zone package installed. Once we get that in, we have the entire offense installed essentially. The "Boss" call is the H-back on the strong safety. That is the fourth defender to one side. The "Bob" call is back on backer, which is the isolation play. The "Bison" call is backside isolation play.

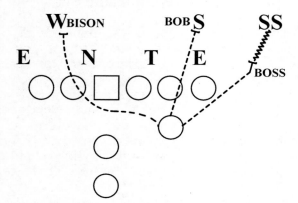

Diagram #7. Boss, Bob, Bison

The H-back does not need to align as shown in the diagram. He can come from any place in the formation. We can use motion and get him anywhere we choose. We like to run the "Bob" call against the 3-3 stack defense. We widen the splits in the offensive line to spread the stacks and run the isolation on the outside linebacker.

Another thing we do to keep the backside end at home is to run a fake reverse. We set the formation and run "Zip" motion into the formation. It is like jet sweep motion. He has no other responsibility. If the defensive end runs upfield, we do not block him.

The companion play of the inside zone play is the inside zone read. (Diagram #8) This is where the fun begins because I am an option coach. I would rather read a defender than block him. The play is inside zone to the right. The quarterback reads the left defensive end. The offensive line blocks inside zone right. The quarterback steps

with his right foot and pushes off the midline to 4:30 on the clock face. He steps back at a 45 degree angle with his left foot. We do not want the back running straight downhill.

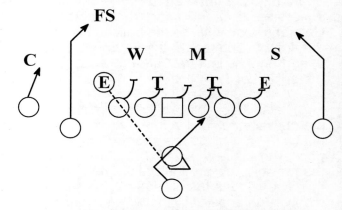

Diagram #8. Inside Zone Read

Since we are reading the left defensive end, the tailback's first step is with his left foot. He takes three steps and pivots at a 45 degree angle to align to the hole. The quarterback reads the defensive end and pulls the ball or leaves it and we run the inside zone.

The quarterback will have questions about when to pull the ball. The quarterback has to understand the differences between squeeze and chase. If the defense closes to the inside in the C-gap, that is not a chase. If he squeezes down the line, that is not a chase. For the quarterback to pull the ball, the defensive end has to turn his shoulder to the inside and run to the tailback. If the defensive end does that, the quarterback pulls the ball and runs out the backside. We tell the quarterback, if the defensive end takes three steps to the inside, he pulls the ball. If he thinks the defensive end can tackle the back, he pulls the ball.

Defenses scheme to force the pull and play the quarterback with a scraping linebacker. (Diagram #9)

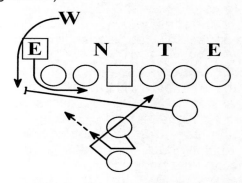

Diagram #9. Deuce Scheme

They tell the defensive end to key the offensive tackle. If the offensive tackle goes inside, the defensive end runs the heel line of the offensive tackle. The defense tells the Will linebacker to scrap off the butt of the defensive end and take the quarterback. We run what we call a "deuce" scheme. We send a second blocker for the weakside linebacker.

The deuce blocker can be a flexed tight end or an offset H-back. The deuce blocker cross the face of the inside zone mesh and keys the defensive end. He reads the same thing the quarterback reads. If the defensive end comes up the field, the quarterback gives the ball to the tailback on the inside zone. The deuce blocker goes inside of the defensive end and up the field to block the Will linebacker, or he may get all the way to the safety. If the defensive end chases the tailback, the quarterback pulls the ball. The deuce blocker wraps around the defensive end and blocks the Will linebacker.

The key to the play is the deuce blocker has to understand leverage and landmarks. The deuce blocker hugs the line of scrimmage and reads the defensive end. If the defensive end squeezes, the deuce block is outside. If the defensive end is outside, the deuce blocker is inside. It looks simple but you must drill it repeatedly to get the deuce under the mesh and in a position to wrap up on the linebacker. This is something you can teach without a ball in the weight room.

The other thing we can do with the deuce block is make a "deuce-triple" call. (Diagram #10)

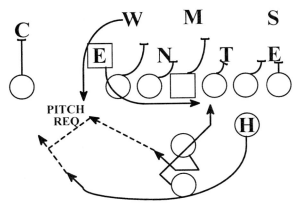

Diagram #10. Deuce-Triple

On this call, the deuce blocker takes a drop step, comes outside the mesh of the quarterback and tailback, and becomes the pitch-back on the option. The quarterback reads the defensive end. If he comes up field, the quarterback gives the ball on the inside zone. If the defensive end chases the tailback, the quarterback pulls the ball, and options the Will backer as his pitch key.

A variation on the same play is the "cowboy" call. The number 2 receiver to the read side becomes the pitch back on the option. The quarterback reads the defensive end. If he chases the tailback, the quarterback pulls the ball and option off the Will backer. His pitch-back is the slot receiver. The slot receiver backpedals inside, plants, and gets into the pitch relationship with the quarterback. It takes time to get it right but do not over coach this technique. Let them be athletes. This is just one more thing the defense has to defend.

We have ways to read the 1-technique, 3-technique defender, or a linebacker. We use a tag on the play. If we say "tuna", we read the defensive tackle. We call "Bama" and read the linebacker. If the defender playing one of those positions is whipping our tail, we read him. If a backer is making the plays we call "Bama", read him, and run away from him. We run it off the trap series. We pull the guard and read the backer.

The offensive tackle uses a solid block on the defensive end. If the linebacker follows the pulling guard to the playside, the quarterback pulls the ball and runs where the linebacker left. We can do the same thing with the "tuna" call.

This is a better call. The 3-technique aligns on the offensive guard. When the guard pulls toward the center, they coach the 3-technique defender to get in his hip pocket and follow him. If he does, the quarterback pulls the ball and run inside where the 3-technique vacated.

Some teams like to crash the end and attack the mesh of the quarterback and tailback. When they attack the quarterback in the mesh area, we give the ball to the tailback. He will not tackle the back because he is too far up the field.

My favorite play is the power play. There are many different ways to run it. The offensive line does not block the end man on the line of scrimmage. We kick him out or read him. We run one-back, two-back, or three-back power plays.

The first one is the two-back power. (Diagram #11) We do not get under the center. We keep the quarterback at four and half yards and do not move him toward the line. He takes the football, rolls back, and gives the ball to the tailback.

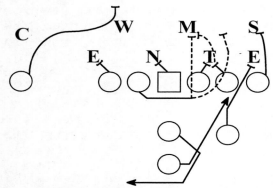

Diagram #11. Two-Back Power

The offensive line blocks a gap scheme. The backside guard is pulling for the Mike linebacker. He wraps through the first playside window. The offset back kicks out the outside linebacker.

When we run the power, we like to read the backside tackle. (Diagram #12) The quarterback takes his read steps for a backside read. The tailback takes his read steps to get in position to take the ball. The quarterback reads the defender playing the backside B-gap.

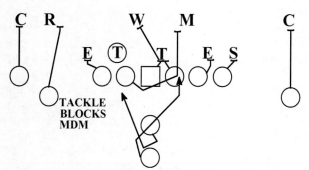

Diagram #12. Power BS Tackle Read

If he gets in the hip pocket of the pulling guard, the quarterback pulls the ball and runs into the B-gap. The backside tackle turns out on the backside 5-technique defender.

We can also read the frontside of the power. (Diagram #13) The line blocks the power play. We tag the plays to get the action we want from the backs and the quarterback. The quarterback reads the end man on the line of scrimmage. He shuffles on his ride of the tailback.

If the defender widens the quarterback gives the ball to the tailback. If he squeezes inside, the quarterback pulls the ball and the fullback leads him around the corner. We tell the quarterback in

any read situation, if he gets confused, pull the ball and make something happen.

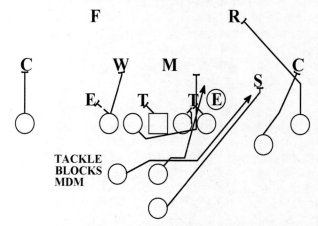

Diagram #13. Power Read Frontside

I want to show you the midline. (Diagram #14) We run so much wide zone we must have something up the middle. In the odd front defense, the quarterback reads the 5-technique defender. If the defender reaction is squeeze and chase, the quarterback pulls and replaces. The quarterback pushes off the midline and steps at 6:00. The tailback is directly up the center's butt. From the pistol, the back can break the ball almost anywhere. If the tailback stays on path, the play can flip out the back door.

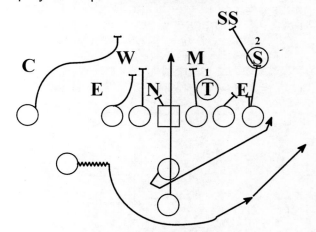

Diagram #14. Midline

The playside guard takes his best release. If he has a 3 or 5-technique defender, he releases inside to the linebacker. If he has a 2 or 2i-technique, he releases outside the defender. Against a 2i-technique, the quarterback thinks pull, but he still reads the play. The 2i-technique can always play outside into the guard.

I see my time is up. Thank you very much.

Geoff Walters

Crossing Routes Versus Man Coverage

Evangelical Christian High School, Tennessee

I think coaches belong to a big fraternity and we all learn from each other. I always want to start these clinics off with a little scripture that I would like to share with you. I think this speaks to coaches as much as anyone. "Anyone who walks with wise people grows wise, though companion of the foolish people suffers harm." You can take that for what it is worth. We are here, in a fraternity of coaches, and learning from each other.

I never came up with anything original and I have borrowed or stole from many people. This is an accumulation of 25 years of coaching. I coached in eight different schools in those 25 years. I was a head coach, janitor, daddy, mommy, or whatever role the coach had to be.

The topic of my lecture today is "defeating man coverage with crossing routes." We are not a big physical team. We are a spread team and we want to distribute the ball around to our backs and receivers. We want to have as much balanced as we can. Our goal is to be 50-50 in our run to pass games. Our quarterback is going to Mississippi State on a baseball scholarship. He will be hard to replace.

When teams try to stop our offense, one of the first things they do is press our wide receivers. If the defense can align man-on-man and defeat the receivers, we need some answers. One of the first answers we have is our **fast screens**. All we do is try to get the ball on the perimeter as fast as we can. If we can get the ball on the perimeter, we do not have to beat 10 defenders. We want to get our best player on the defense's worst player.

From Wednesday morning, until we play on Friday night, the only thing I concentrate on is personnel. Your players are just like my players. You have some weak links. If we play you, I will try from Wednesday morning until game time to locate your three weakest players on both sides of the ball. I hope our schemes are already in place to attack those players.

I do not want to beat your best players. I want to beat your worst players with my best players. It is easier for the offense to put their best players on the defense's worst. The defense does not know where the offense is going to motion. If I can find the weak link, it will be a long afternoon for him.

I am not going to talk a lot about the fast screen, but I do want to touch on it. They are as simple as they can be. We call the fast screen "loop and loop." (Diagram #1) We have a simple signal we give to the quarterback. We run the screen to the right and the left and the quarterback chooses where to throw the ball. You have to train the quarterback how to pick the right receiver to throw to. If the defense is in man-to-man coverage, we always have a bubble route that we can throw the fast screen pass to.

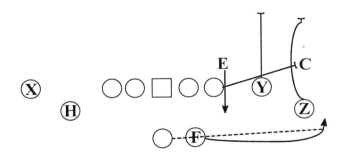

Diagram #1. Fast Screen

The fast screen invites the defensive contain defender to attack the quarterback. The back releases outside and the quarterback dumps the ball to him, if the tackle or guard to that side is the personnel protector for the back. This play is good against man coverage. The tackle blocks the defender assigned to the running back.

If we get straight man coverage, we isolate our best receiver on the worst corner. (Diagram #2) We split him to one side or the other, rise up, and throw him the ball. We generally send a tackle to that side as a blocker. There is some coaching to get that done. The quarterback has to deliver the ball quickly. The receiver has to catch the ball and get vertically up the field. You must teach the tackle how to get into the screen and block the corner. He kicks him out if he rolls and stalks him if he hangs deep.

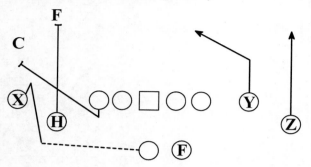

Diagram #2. Wide Receiver Screen

The tackle has to come straight down the line of scrimmage to the outside. All he wants to do is to get his pads on the defensive back. We want him to get in the defensive back's way. We tell them to be a speed bump.

The next answer is the **speed option**. We use the speed option to eliminate one of their best players. We run the speed option at their best defensive end. We do that so we do not have to block him. If he attacks the quarterback, we pitch the ball. If he works away from the quarterback, the quarterback runs the ball. If they are better than we are on the perimeter we have to block them.

If they are better than we are, blocking is not always the best option. It is an answer but it may not be the best one. It will help if we can do it. What does the defense do in man-coverage? They get in man-coverage because they are going to blitz.

There will come a time where the opponent is better than you are. He will lock you down in man coverage and you can do nothing about it. The best way to attack the defense is by running the crossing patterns. The scheme I am going to go through is the shallow dig concept.

SHALLOW / DIG

- Progression Reads
- Pre-snap go outside
- Hot
- 1-shallow
- 2-Dig
- 3-Back

When I first started coaching the quarterback, I gave him too much to handle. I told him if the defense was in a 3 deep, to throw a certain pattern. If they were in a 2 deep, we throw a different pattern. You cannot give him "if's" when you talk to him about coverage. You cannot do that because he has 1.7 seconds to make a decision.

We want to give him a group of plays that do not change regardless of the defensive alignment. The defense will not affect the way he reads the defense. Our quarterback knows his read progression is hot, shallow, 3 dig and 3 back. It does not matter if the defense is in a 3 deep, 2 deep, or man coverage. His reads do not change.

In this scheme, the outside receivers have outside go-routes. This is a pre-snap read. The quarterback knows before the snap of the ball, he is going deep, or he knows he is not going deep. When he is an experienced quarterback, he can delay that read. However, if he is a young quarterback, he cannot. If he cannot go deep, he has to throw the hot route against the blitz. If the blitz is coming from the right, he throws the hot to the right.

If the defender on the receiver blitzes as the quarterback catches the ball, he throws to that receiver. We do not care if it is a zone blitz. We do not feel they can blitz off the receiver, drop a defensive lineman, and get into that coverage before we the ball there.

The first read after the hot throw is the shallow. There are different ways to run that pattern to be successful. The quarterbacks read progression is hot, shallow, dig, and the back. The Y-shallow is the first read we have. (Diagram #3)

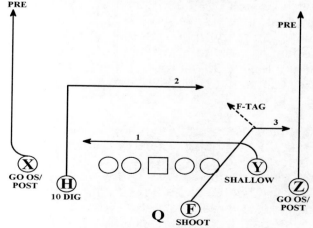

Diagram #3. Shallow Cross

In the 2 X 2 set (Ace), the tight end flexes and runs the shallow route. The outside receivers run a "go" pattern. The slot receiver runs the 10 yard dig pattern and the running back runs a shoot flat pattern.

We have a number of coaching points in running this pattern.

COACHING POINTS

- **Go Outside routes must be outside of corner.**
- **Shallow route: no false steps, depth is heels of the D.L., after catch stay outside numbers.**
- **Dig route: alignment must be 10 yd. minimum from tackle, must release outside of OLB, after cut stay flat across at 10 yards.**
- **Check Shoot route: must get to the numbers, unless tag angle. (if MLB taking out shallow)**
- **Tags: F-angle, Post over top of dig if Safety hanging on dig.**

You can print the routes on a wristband and know what to do. We used the wristbands at one time but got away from them because the pace of the game. I did not realize the theory of the wristbands until I started using them. We did this in 2003 and that was before Tony Franklin got into it at his clinics. All this came out of Hal Mumme, Mike Leach, and Chris Hatcher, when they were all at the University of Kentucky. I was at Ball State at the time.

The first thing we talk about is the patterns of the outside receivers. They must take an outside release as they run vertical up field. The wide receivers are X and Z, and must release outside of the defenders that covers them regardless of what defender it is. The reason to get outside of him is to get his back turned to the ball.

The "go outside" takes the corner out of the coverage. If he does not run with the receiver deep, he is sitting in the area where the shallow is coming. He can blow up the tight end.

If we know the defense has a weak corner and we get him against a fast receiver, we can tag the play. We tag the play and throw the outside vertical route exploiting the mismatch. That is a pre-snap adjustment. After we snap the ball, the vertical is not an option. The first read is the "hot."

The tight end runs the shallow at the depth of the heels of the defensive line. The quarterback reads the area over the ball. If there is no defender in that area, he delivers the ball to the Y-cross pattern. The defense tries to stop the shallow with the 0-technique linebacker. It does not matter what the defense does. The quarterback reads 1, 2, and 3. If there is a linebacker in that area, he goes to his 2nd read.

When we have a perimeter drill, the Mike linebacker shields the crosser every time. When we have a scrimmage and run play action, he never finds the shallow pattern. Coaches instruct their receiver to catch the ball and go north and south immediately. We want the Y-receiver to get to the numbers of the field. We want him to go up the outside of the numbers.

The second read is the "dig" coming across the formation from the other side of the formation. The first thing he must do is align at a minimum width of 10 yards outside the defensive tackle. If he does not it constricts the play. That is a huge point in our instruction.

We run the dig route at a minimum depth of 10 yards. When the receiver releases, he has to stay outside the outside linebacker. We want the linebacker to tilt toward him so he does not see the shallow coming from the backside. When the receiver reaches his depth, he breaks into the middle and comes straight across the field. He stays flat and does not drift in his pattern.

If the linebacker plays a good wall technique on the H-receiver, he may have to dip under the linebacker. He plants and rips across the inside hip of the linebacker. He must stay flat as he runs the dig across the field. He cannot go 11 yards or nine yards and he cannot round off his cut. If the coverage is zone coverage he can shut the pattern down in a window.

The third option is the running back running a shoot pattern to the flat. He runs his pattern at a depth of three yards, looks for the ball, and wants the pattern to get to the numbers. The biggest problem we have with this route is the back not getting to the numbers. In practice, if you have someone throwing him the ball, do not throw him the ball until he gets to the numbers. If you throw the ball too soon, they will develop bad habits and not get wide enough.

We can tag the shoot pattern with F-angle." The back takes his shoot pattern for six steps, plants and angles back into the middle of the field. This is a great adjustment because the Mike linebacker has coverage on that receiver coming out of the backfield.

The back is the third receiver out and sees a match up zone or man coverage, the Mike linebacker has the coverage. He is running hard out of the middle to get to the route. The running back plants and has the middle of the field open until he sees the safety.

Our goal for this play is 100 percent completion. We do not expect 96 percent. We think you should complete this pass every time. Our fifth grade team runs this play. They all can complete it. They always hit the shallow route.

The thing the coach does not want to do is get too creative too fast. For several weeks only run the play to one side. Let him get used to doing the reads to one side only. If the quarterback understands the concept of the play, they can read it properly.

The good thing about the wristbands is the perception the players have. If you have a receiver who thinks he is all that and more, it keeps him playing hard. If he does not get the ball thrown to him, he will not work hard. On the band, it tells the wide receiver to outside release. That does not tell him if he is the primary receiver or just a decoy. Wristbands you can install quickly.

I want to repeat this. If you train your quarterback to run this play, only do it one-way until he is comfortable running it. I do not believe in teaching the whole system. I coach this play as a stand-alone play. This can be the man-beater play.

You can switch the patterns to different receiver in a different formation but you must have the shallow from a tight position in the formation. That pattern has to happen fast. You cannot have the shallow run by a wide receiver in a slot position because it takes too long for him to get across the field. The shallow has to happen immediately. The quarterback has to understand the play and know it must be to a player on the line or near the tight end position. He has to be comfortable with the pass.

We call this play "Creek." We tell the running back to stay out of the creek. He has to run his pattern opposite the shallow route. If we call "creek-right", the running back runs his pattern

left. That is an adjustment you do not need to make with your quarterback until he gets comfortable running the pattern.

Our goal is to snap the football within five seconds after the referee marks it ready for play. We got a delay of game penalty because we snapped it too quickly. We like to run the shallow play from some kind of play action. We do not run the cross-zone running play, but we run the play action pass.

We call the "hot" pressure valves. He has to know where his pressure valves are. If the quarterback gets internal pressure, he goes to his valve right now and the read is gone. If he gets external pressure, he tries to step up and read the play. The running back does not block anyone. He has a free release. We have had more success throwing to the back than leaving him in to block. His rule is release to the flat.

If you have motion as part of your scheme, this is the perfect play to get the wide receiver involved in your shallow route. (Diagram #4) From the same formation, the H-receiver comes in motion toward the ball. The quarterback fakes the read play to the running back and he continues to run the shoot pattern.

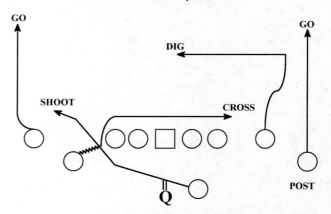

Diagram #4. H-Shallow

The Y-end stems outside the linebacker to his side and runs the dig route at 10 yards. The H-receiver runs the shallow and the wide receivers run the "go" routes. Nothing changes with the quarterback's reads. He reads, hot, shallow, dig, and back.

The play to set up the shallow is to bring the H-back in motion and seal the edge for an outside play. He comes inside and knocks the water out of somebody. That sets him up to run the shallow and linebackers will never see him.

The answer for the safety dropping down on the dig pattern is to run the post over the top by a wide receiver. We add a tag to the play. If the safety cheats down the quarterback reads him. We run a post to the inside and behind the safety.

If we have a good tight end, we like to exchange the patterns of the Z-receiver and the tight end. (Diagram #5) This pattern is good against a two-high safety look. The Z-receiver comes in motion back to the ball and runs the shallow pattern. The tight end stems outside and deep on the safety to his side. He can undercut the safety and get into the middle of the field. The other safety is working to the wide receiver on the other side of the formation. If you have a good tight end, this gives you a chance for a big play.

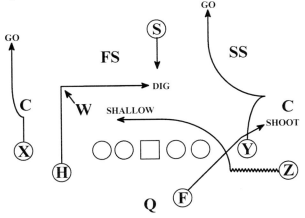

Diagram #5. Z-Shallow, Y-Post

The next play is "Y-mesh." You buy into this play or you do not. It is a five-read play. It takes time to run this play. It is the best man-beater plays there is. It is a great red-zone play. The quarterback has to be smart to run this play.

Y-MESH

Progression reads
- 1. Y-Corner
- 2. Corner side mesh
- 3. Corner side Back
- 4. Backside mesh
- 5. Backside Back

If you run this play, you must work on it. It is like the screen. If you are going to be any good at running the screen, you must have a screen period in practice every day or you will not be any good at it. If you are going to run this play, you must develop a "mesh period" as part of your practice. It is not just for the receivers. It is for the entire offense. Central Florida runs this play and they work with half of their offensive line in the drill. Working with half an offensive line is a safer way to work.

The good thing about a half line in the drill is the conditioning aspect of the drill. After the quarterback throws the ball, the lines have to run down the field.

When I talk about the progressions, the first progress is Y-corner. That is the inside receiver. It does not have to be the tight end.

The corner read on the mesh is immediate. We call this Y-Mesh, but it could be another receiver. I do not want to get into quarterback mechanics but we do not crossover step with our quarterback. He takes one big step and two shuffle steps to get to his throwing position. We do the same thing in the three-step drop. The reason we do it this way is to be able to get the ball when he needs to. If he needs to throw the ball in the middle of a crossover step, he cannot do it. If he is taking shuffle steps, he can. In this play, there are three mesh areas.

COACHING POINTS

- **Corner 6 steps (plant and nod) burst to pylon, 25 yd line and closer = back pylon, 26 yd line and out front pylon.**
- **Always throw corner route to grass not the man.**
- **Mesh routes: right side sets depth 6 yds, left side adjust, Buzz the umpire (gives aiming points and helps prevent holding calls.**
- **Mesh routes read man or zone on the run, Zone settle after cross, Man keep running gaining depth to numbers.**
- **Check swing Right: get to numbers.**
- **Check Swing Left: get to numbers.**
- **Tags Y-Post or COP vs wide Safeties, Mesh return if opponent running pattern match man.**

You can run the play from a 2 X 2 formation with the twin receiver to each side in a stack position. (Diagram #6) You can put both backs in the backfield and run the pattern from there. The Y-tight end flexes from his tackle and runs a corner route. He is the first read on the play.

The Z-receiver aligns in an outside position one yard outside the Y-tight end and two-yards off the line of scrimmage. On the snap, the

Z-receiver releases behind the tight end and aims for the umpire position over the ball.

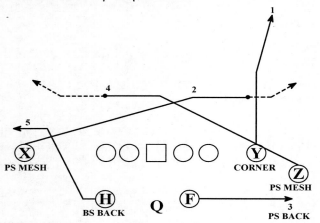

Diagram #6. Y-Mesh

On the corner pattern, the Y-tight end takes six steps, plants his foot, and nods his head to fake the defender. He breaks to the corner. For two steps, he does not look for the ball. In those two steps he gets his eyes on his target. If we are at the 25 yard line or closer, his target is the back pylon of the end zone. When you train this route, make the receiver run the route without a throw. That makes them look at their target. If the ball is at the 26 yard line or further out, the target is the front pylon of the end zone.

The quarterback is not throwing the ball to a man. He is throwing the ball to the target. He throws the ball to the pylon and it does not move. He is not throwing to a moving target. If they try to throw to the tight end on the corner route, the ball will be long every time. That is the first read and they throw it on their first gather step.

If the corner route is not available, the 2nd read is the playside mesh pattern to the X-receiver. The F-back is the third read. We run this pattern to the numbers. If we get inside pressure, he becomes the pressure valve. We free release the front side of the play and check release the backside. If the defense tries to run a linebacker out to cover the swing pattern by the F-back, the X-receiver is wide open.

The pattern by the F-back is the same pattern he runs on a fast screen right. The hardest thing the back has to do is keep from turning his body to look for the ball. When he turns his body, he slows down. He takes an open step and a crossover step. He cannot look for the ball until after the third step. If I am standing by the quarterback, I never want to see his front numbers on his jersey.

He can catch the ball over his shoulder as easy as he can by turning his body to the quarterback. The different is he cannot run as fast. If he turns his shoulders to the quarterback, he will never get to the numbers. If he does not get width, it does not help.

The backside H-back has a blocking assignment. He has to check for the blitz before he releases. He shuffles over and takes his time getting out of the backfield. If the coverage is man-coverage he releases quicker. The H-back releases right now against man coverage. In man coverage the quarterback reads the playside mesh to the backside back.

In a game situation, the corner sees the Z-receiver take a hard inside release. The Y-tight end comes wide open on occasion. The backside mesh runner (Z-receiver) sets the depth of the mesh of the Z and X receivers on the inside. The Playside mesh receiver's job is to avoid running into the Z-receiver. The Z-receiver goes on top and the X-receiver is underneath as they mesh.

When we run this play, we never get a holding call from the umpire. The receivers are buzzing around him and he is trying to avoid being hit.

We tell the Z-receiver to brush the butt of the umpire. We want the X-receiver to brush his belly. We want to mesh in the middle wherever the umpire aligns. If he is at four-yards, we mesh at four yards. If he is at six yards, we run the mesh at six yards. In our drill work I stand where the umpire would be. As they pass, I hold out my hands and they slap them.

If you plan to run this play make, sure you give the practice time the play needs. In spring practice and the 10 days before the season starts is not enough time to get good at this play. You need to spend 10 minutes a day working on the timing of the play. When the receivers run the mesh in the middle off the umpire, they gain depth as they run toward the numbers. They should be at a minimum of 10 yards when they reach the numbers.

We rarely throw to the backside back because it is the last read. We very seldom get to him unless it is man coverage and they are doing a good job of covering. The quarterback does not get to the fifth read before he throws the ball.

On the corner route the sixth step of the tight end should put him on his inside foot. Make sure the quarterback throws the corner route to grass and not the man. Train the quarterback early. Make him throw to a barrel or hula-hoop. Do not let him throw to a receiver for at least two days. Make him throw to grass. The same thing is true of the route runner. Make him run the pattern without throwing the ball.

The mesh receivers in the middle need to recognize whether the coverage is man coverage or zone coverage. They need to look and see if anyone is following them. If they have a defender following them, they continue to run through the mesh area. If it is zone coverage, they may sit down in the windows of the zone.

Our pass protections are simple. If we play a "4-3" defense, the five offensive linemen are responsible for the four down defenders and the Mike linebacker. In the "3-4" defense, the offensive line has the down three defenders and the two inside linebackers. We have one fire zone protection. We call it "fire-drill." If the quarterback is not sure, he calls "fire." The offensive line uses a slide protection to the left. The back has the right edge. If the quarterback releases the back, he is responsible for the blitz coming off the right edge.

Teams will play hard cover-2 against this pattern. (Diagram #7) They play their corner down hard and send their safeties wide. We tag the play and get a "top" route from the tight end. He runs the corner as he always does except, he runs two steps to the corner, plants, and runs the post cut into the middle of the field.

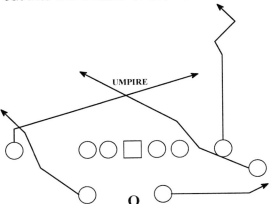

Diagram #7. Y-Mesh Top

The other adjustment we make is a "Slugo" call to the Z-receiver. (Diagram #8) The pattern is the same for everyone except the Z-receiver. On this pattern, the Z-receiver comes underneath the tight end and runs a "Slugo" pattern down the

middle of the field. Slugo is a slant and go route. He runs the six-yard mesh pattern, plants, and takes it deep up the middle of the football field.

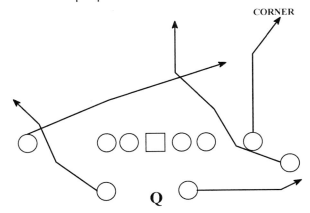

Diagram #8. Y-Mesh Slugo

If we have this called, the quarterback knows if there are two safeties in the middle, he throws the "Slugo." If there is one safety in the middle, he throws the playside back pattern.

The mesh concept takes time to develop. It is more complicated and has more reads to it. If you want to throw the shallow concept, you can add it tomorrow and run it well. Thank you for your attention.

Mark Wechter

Evolving Stunts In The Defense

Washington Township High School, New Jersey

I am not going to talk a lot about philosophy but I think it is important you understand what got us to where we are today. Is there anyone in here from New Jersey? I am going to give you everything I have and more. I got the chance to go back to my high school and work for my head coach when I played there. I had the opportunity at that time to go to clinics like this one. That is where I started listening and learning about this great game.

From 1991-2007, I went to every clinic you can imagine. Every spring we went to a different college to try to find things to work into our program. In 2008, I was burnt out with the clinic scene. At that time, we were a wing-T team and had been for 20 years. We only threw the ball about three times the entire season.

We needed to get back to throwing the football. In 2010, we had our worst year in 25 years. I had to evaluate myself as a head coach. I needed to get away from the X's and O's and get back to what was important. I was burning myself out. I was burning my staff out and I was burning the team out with too much information. It became too much like a job.

We took a new approach to our off-season. We shorten the time spent on a weekly basis. The players were fresher and paid more attention to the coaches. That was a big risk on our part coming off a 3-7 record and the worst season in 25 years. In 2011, we went 7-4 and made the second round of the state playoffs. In 2012, we were 7-3 and got into the first round of the playoffs. That was two good seasons for us with the players we had. It was fun.

It is great to get out of our area and see some new faces. We have many clinics in the Atlantic City area. This is refreshing for our staff.

Throughout the 1990's and into the early 2000's we were a heavy blitz team. However, as we all know, you live by the blitz and die by the blitz. During those years we spent most of our practice time going through the traditional "fronts and stunts" periods on air.

The time we used for those periods took time away from working on fundamentals. With limited practice time our fundamentals suffered greatly. Especially our defensive run fits. We found that teams were preparing for our blitzes and were able to beat our stunts/blitzes with sound run schemes. We found ourselves "guessing" and being out of position. When we played "base", we were not very successful.

Around 2006, we began to spend a lot more time on fundamentals and run fits. However, we had very little time to practice our stunt/blitz schemes. Therefore, we got away from using a lot of stunts and blitzes and found ourselves playing a lot of base defense. There is nothing wrong with that. We were successful. Our players were very good at lining up and playing sound defensive football. Unfortunately, we have become physically smaller over the course of those years.

We are now at the point where we need to be able to stunt/blitz due to our physical size. However, we need to be able to be good at playing "base" and strong in our run fits. However, once again practice time is limited. It became very clear to me what we needed was to learn by watching our offense.

We are a no-huddle offense. We verbally call in the plays to all of the players from the sideline. We use a wristband system. We are also a no-huddle defense and have been since 2004. However, we would signal in the defense. It is difficult to signal in stunts/blitz by using the body. You simply run out of limb motions you can use. Now our defense uses the same wristband system as our offense. On one single wristband, we have up to 126 defensive plays. The wristband shows each player his responsibility on each play. This allows us to eliminate the need for the player to memorize stunt schemes, the names of those schemes, and the signals for those schemes.

What we do teach is the paths they must take when stunting/blitzing. We teach A-gap, B-gap, C-gap, and D-gap blitzes. Players must get good at their paths, depths, and angles. They must know how to contain and "blitz peel". They maintain good pad level while running through their assigned gaps. They must know how to run to daylight and change direction if need be. We practice these techniques in pre-season and reinforce them throughout the season.

Defensively we are an 8-man front team. We are "4-4" or "3-5" stack team. Sometimes we change personnel to go from the four-front to the three-front and sometimes we drop a linebacker down or stand him up, depending on the defense. In the secondary, we show a cover-2 shell but we also play cover-1 and cover-0. If you are a "4-3" or "3-4" team, you could take what we do and incorporate it into your scheme.

I want to cover how we call our defenses and how we blitz. On our wristband we can call 126 blitz combinations from the "3-5" and the "4-4" defense. You must build your toolbox with the stunt package you want. The wristband is our toolbox. Once you put together the wristbands, you do not need to do it every week.

As a defensive staff, you must know the scheme. The problem is to get your players to know what that scheme is and how to run it. If you have a linebacker who is tough, fast, and physical, but cannot play that way because he is always thinking where to go, the staff has to build a playbook for him.

This past year we played more of the "3-5" defense because of personnel. We did not have defensive linemen but we had five butt kickers for linebackers. They were small but they could run and tackle. My starting Mike linebacker was a three-year starter. He is going to West Point and wants to play football and become a ranger. Besides being a good football player, he was ranked 17th academically in a class of 650. I have smart players but we chose to be simple in our scheme. He knew the scheme.

Next year, I have hard-nosed players that will fight anybody, but they are a little smaller and slower than in the past. If I can minimize the thinking, they can play faster. Defense is about

speed. If you have to think before every snap, it slows your body down.

I took our playbook, and typed out combinations of stunts. I wanted to figure out what combinations worked together to make all the blitzes come true. I wanted to figure out what I could run to make us gap sound in all the blitzes. When you do your scouting, you know the blitzes you will be running in a particular game.

STRONG SIDE STUNT – RED

LIGHTING
- DE: Base
- DE: Base
- DT: WK = A/Base
- DT: ST = B/Base
- ILBER: ST = A/Base
- ILBER: ST = A/Base
- OBER: Base
- OBER: Base

STING
- DE: ST = C/Base
- DE: ST = C/Base
- DT: ST = C/Base
- DT: ST = C/Base
- ILBER: ST = A/Base
- ILBER: ST = A/Base
- OBER: Base
- OBER: Base

SPEAR
- DE: Base
- DE: Base
- DT: Base
- DT: Base
- ILBER: ST = A/Base
- ILBER: ST = A/Base
- OBER: Base
- OBER: Base

STORM
- DE: ST = C/Base
- DE: ST = C/Base
- DT: Base
- DT: Base
- ILBER: Base
- ILBER: Base
- OBER: ST = A/Base
- OBER: ST = A/Base

STORM – SWITCH
- DE: Base
- DE: Base
- DT: ST = C/Base

- DT: ST = C/Base
- ILBER: Base
- ILBER: Base
- OBER: ST = A/Base
- OBER: ST = A/Base

In our defense the tackles and nose guard work in tandem with the inside linebackers. The defensive ends and outside linebacker work in tandem together. All they need to know is what gaps they go in.

We simply call in a color and number combination. For example; if we call in "Blue 12", they look for the blue colored cell that is #12. If the crowd is loud, we can signal in the color and number very easily. This system allows us to spend more time on techniques and less on schemes. Players do not care about schemes. They just want us to teach them how to make plays. If a player has great defensive technique (fundamentals), they will be better playmakers.

The linebackers give a strength call to give the blitzes direction. (Diagram #1) We designate our blitzes with strong and weak calls. If you look at the "Sting" stunt on the form, the strong side defensive end runs a stunt into the C-gap or plays base. Since he is on the strong side, he runs the C-gap stunt. The weakside defensive-end plays his base technique. The strong side defensive tackle stunts into the A-gap. The weakside defensive tackle plays his base call. The strong side inside linebacker blitzes the B-gap and the weakside inside linebacker plays a base technique. Both outside linebackers play base technique.

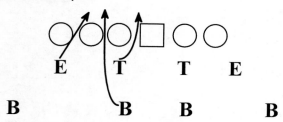

Diagram #1. Sting

To the strong side of the formation, we have a three-man stunt with the defensive end, tackle, and inside linebacker. Everyone else in the defense plays base technique. They play their base technique with their run fits and pass rush if it is a pass play.

On the wristband in addition to the strong side stunts, we have weakside stunts, double inside, and double outside stunts. The chart is an example of our strong side stunts. We do the same thing with the other categories of stunts.

WEAK STUNT (BLUE)

Wave
- DE: WK = B/Base
- DE: WK = B/Base
- DT: Base
- DT: Base
- ILBER: Base
- ILBER: Base
- OLBER: WK = C/Base
- OLBER: WK = C/Base

Each stunt has an assigned number so they can readily find each stunt. If we run a "Red-1", the stunt would be "Lightning." They find the color and look for the numbered stunt.

This is an example of a weakside stunt. (Diagram #2) The defensive end to the weakside of the formation runs a stunt into the B-gap. The strong side-end plays base. The inside linebackers and defensive tackles play a base technique call. The outside linebackers run a C-gap stunt. If there is no tight end, they blitz off the edge of the offensive tackle.

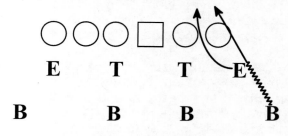

Diagram #2. Wave

We can run a combination of the two stunts. (Diagram #3) If we want to combine any two stunts, you can have multiple blitz packages. We print them on the wristbands and color-code them. We run the "sting" stunt to the strong side and the "wave" stunt to the weakside of the formation.

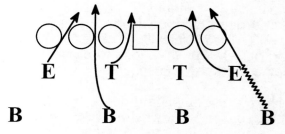

Diagram #3. Sting/Wave

The average high school football player does not worry about the defensive scheme. They do not want to watch film. They want to play the game. On my staff right now, I have five former players that played for me. They all told me that. The players do not want to study the opponent they want to make plays.

For each game, I have a master call sheet. The stunts on the call sheet are color-coded. The blue color stunts are our "4-4" defensive calls. The Red stunts are the "3-5" defensive calls. I condense the call sheet and eliminate the stunts I do not want to run. That way I am not looking at too many stunts. That is the worst feeling in the world. You know what you want to run, but cannot find it on the call sheet.

On the call sheet, I have the stunts broken down into five and six-man pressure stunts. If we bring a five-man pressure, it is generally a single outside or inside blitzer. The six-man pressures are double stunts inside or double outside stunts. I also have six-man pressure coming from the strong side inside and outside as well as the weakside inside and outside.

What I am showing you today I did on vacation in a matter of two hours. You know what you want to do with your defense. All you need is a computer and an Excel file. That gives us every possible sound blitz we can run out of the "4-4" and stack defenses.

The secondary coverages are included on the wristbands. We will call the coverages from the sidelines depending on the blitz combination we run. Our cover-0 is a true man-to-man with no free safety. The safety walks down and covers the number 2 receiver.

Another advantage with our defense is we are balanced in both the "4-4" and the "3-5" defense. Therefore, we do not need a strong or weak call. We can call left, right, or middle stunts with no reference to strength of the offensive formation. On occasion, we slide the four-front to the tight end side. We slide the tackle to the tight end side to a 3-technique and the backside tackle to a 1-technique.

In the "4-4" and "3-5" sets if you split the defense down the middle we have a balanced defense. If the linebackers, line, and backs know where the slant comes from before I call the play, it will make it that much easier. We call the strength of the offense by the alignment of

the tight end. When we call strength, we use a "Roger" and "Lucy."

We send the call into the game. As an example, we call "Purple-13." The defenders look their wristband and sees "Weak-B/Base." To keep him from getting confused as to the alignment of the strength call, we took that thought out. In our thinking, "right" was automatic strength and "left" was automatic weak. If the defender played on the right side of the defense, the only key he looked for was strong.

We do not flip-flop our defensive line. If the left defensive end aligned in his technique, he knows he is the weakside defensive end. He looks for weak keys only. If we call "Red-20", he looks at the wristband. It says, "Strong-B/Base", he plays the base call. Before we break the huddle, he knows he does not need to look for a strength call. He does not have to think where he is going. He is playing base football.

If the call is "Red-22", he looks at his wristband in the Red plays. Number 22 tells him, "Weak-C/base", he knows he is stunting into the C-gap. We minimize the thought process so he can perform his technique. He applies what we have taught him about slanting and blitzing. He works on the proper angle and getting into the proper gap.

We can read the double rules on the wristbands and sometimes we have to do it that way. When you find teams that have tendencies, you want to stunt to those tendencies. In that case, we want to bring the blitz from the weakside and not necessarily from the left. If the call is "Red-22", and the wristband reads "Weak-C/base" he must listen for the strength call. If he gets a "Lucy" call, he runs a C-gap slant. If he gets a "Roger" call, he plays base. For the last two years our defense has played fast and we have used the wristbands.

Our linebackers are no different from the defensive line. They need to know where they fit on running plays. With the balanced defense, we have four defenders on each side of the ball. In the "3-5", we split the nose stack and count them on both sides. The left and right rules hold the same for the linebackers in the predetermined call. The right inside linebacker is the strong linebacker and the left inside linebacker is the weak linebacker. The outside linebackers have the same predetermined call. Left is weak and Right is strong in all our calls. The predetermined strength calls make it easier for the linebackers to play fast.

When we bring six-man pressure, we send one from the inside and one from the outside. I do not like to blow both inside linebackers. I like to send inside and outside combinations from different sides. If we bring six-man pressure and play cover-3, we give up a flat area in that scheme.

If we play a good passing quarterback that reads well, we do not want to give him the quick throw to the flat so we must play cover-0. (Diagram #4) That means we are man-to-man across the board and walking down the free safety to cover the number 2 receiver. The free safety has to know where the number 2 receiver is going to be. If we run the "Storm/Lightning" combination stunt, "Storm" is the inside blitz and "Lightning" is the outside blitz from the strong side. He knows that right is strong and rolls down to the right slot receiver.

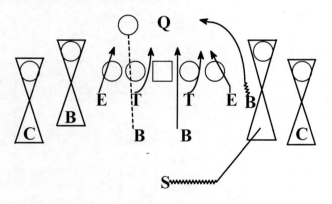

Diagram #4. Storm/Lightning Cover-0

With the secondary, I have two student coaches. One of them gives the coverages and the other one gives a body language signal. I yell the coverages to the field, which are dummy calls. I tell the coaches to give the correct signals. Any signal given above the waist is cover-3. If he gives anything below the waist with a whirling motion with his hand means we are in cover-0. After the whirling motion he gives a strong or weak signal with his right or left hand. The safety knows if he gets the strong signal, he is going to the right side. If he gets the weak signal, he goes the opposite side. He knows where he is going and can disguise his alignment to the quarterback. He can walk "left and right", and "up and back." As soon as we break the huddle, he knows which side he is covering down.

If we double call a color, it means we are sending a 7 man rush. (Diagram 5) If we call "Red-15, Yellow-19", yellow is the six-man blitz, and red is the single blitz call. The linebackers read the band. They read the "Red" band first. If they do not have a blitz on the red band, they read the "Yellow" band. It was hard to fit the 7 man blitz so we had to double-call the color.

If it is a loud night or the opponent is trying to steal our signals, we go to our body language signals. In our bands, we have six colors, which are red, green, purple, silver, blue and yellow. The first three colors are red, green, and yellow. The next three are purple, silver, and blue. We signal the colors with body language signals. Red is the back of the neck (redneck). For blue, the coaches points to the sky. If he points to the ground, that is "green." "Silver" is the strong arm to the hips for foot soldier. Purple is the balls. For Yellow we form a banana.

After he signals the color, he has to signal the numbers. The top of the head with either hand is zero. The right side of the body is odd and the left side is even numbers. The right ear is 1. The right shoulder is 3, the elbow is 5, the hand is 7, and the thumb is 9. On the left side of the body, the left ear is 2, left shoulder is 4, elbow is 6, and the hand is 8. When we signal off the sideline, we continue to signal until the offense comes to the line of scrimmage.

If the call is "Red-14", he touches the back of his nick, right ear, left shoulder and repeats the sequence. He does not stop until the offense is in position.

Now that I have thrown all this information at you, go back and do it the way that best fits what you do. There are not that many combinations when you sit down and put them all together. The important thing is not to confuse the players. Make sure they understand what you want to do. The defensive wristbands have not changed in two years. Our offensive coaches change their bands every other week.

When we make calls on the field, we may be making dummy calls. We have six colors. If the defense is yelling "Black-12" or "East-West-9", they are for the quarterback and the offensive line on the other side. The defense looks at the bands every down. They want to convince the offense there is a blitz coming on every down. There are times in a game where we blitz every down.

If teams try to play hurry up tactics with us, we have the same game plan they do. In a hurry up, the offense runs few plays from few formations. They want to catch the defense in a situation, where they cannot change defenses and must play base. We have a hurry up call sheet just like the offense. I have four or five blitzes we go to when the offense tries to hurry up the game. We scrip them and run them just as the offense does. In a four down series, the offense will see four different blitzes that will go against anything they run.

This system allows you to do many different things fast. The way we run the defense is a thought process. The players are not confused and are able to play freer and without hesitation.

If we have to go from a four-front to a "3-5" front, we substitute a linebacker for a defensive lineman. If we want to do that, we signal from the sidelines and the lineman comes running off as the linebacker comes running on the field. We make personnel changes without any problem.

You should spend time in practice making the players better at their techniques. The fundamentals of football are the most overlooked aspect of the game. What we teach in practice is general alignment and techniques of running slants and blitzes. We do not spend time running the blitzes in practice at the expense of individual work.

How many coaches in the room started on the defensive side of the ball? My hat is off to you people. Most defensive coaches start on the offensive side of the ball. If you coached offense before you coached defense, you understand the offensive mind. You know what they try to do to defenses. Look at your defense, and see what you are doing. Evaluate yourself and see what you can do to simplify what you are doing to make it easier for the players to learn. You can simplify your blitz schemes and teach them to the players in an orderly fashion. The faster they play the better you are defensively.

There is no substitute for fundamentals in the game of football. When things start to go sour, go back to the fundamentals of the game. Players play the game. The faster they play the better you are. Do not restrict their ability by making it so complicated they cannot turn loose and play. Football is blocking and tackling. What you want on your team is a bunch of blue-collar players that are fundamentally sound. Defense is about speed, lack of thought, and reaction. Make it fun.

I appreciate you being here and I hope you got something from this. Thanks for coming.

Rich Wellbrock

Coaching Today's Athlete

Goodyear Desert Edge High School, Arizona

Thanks to the Nike Coach of the Year Clinics for allowing me to speak today. I also want to thank my staff for all they do for our program. I would not be standing before you if it were not for our football players.

I am going to talk about our program and how it has evolved and how I have evolved. I started out as an offensive line coach at Cactus High School. I was there for six years and then went to Glendale Community College. I never did play in the offensive line as I was a wide receiver. The first guy I coached with said I could move up to the varsity level if I agreed to coach the offensive line. It was the best thing I ever did.

We have 1,500 students at Desert Edge. We are a Title I school with 50 percent plus of our students on free or reduced lunches. We have 150 to 160 students in the football program at all three levels.

We promote and encourage our students to be multi-sport athletes because we only have 1,500 students. It works out well for us. We are in the Sweet 16 in our state high school basketball tournament today. Eight of the ten basketball players are also football players. We encourage our students to play multiple sports. We want to make sure our kids are exposed to as many people as possible who can influence them to do the right things.

Desert Edge had a record of 18-41 through 2009. We came into the program in 2010. Our record has been 31-7 in the past three years and we have been in the playoffs each of those three years. We were in the championship game this year and lost in the final twelve seconds. I have four freshman coaches and six varsity/JV coaches. We two platoon our coaches. Our varsity and JV teams practice together. It allows our kids to be on the same page at all levels. This system has worked well for us. The freshman practice is on the field next to us so I can watch all practices from where I stand.

I am the CEO of our program. We treat it very much like a college program. I do not call the offense or the defense. That does not mean I am not involved in every situation. I was a head coach in the past and called every play on offense, defense and special teams. The best thing I did when I first came to Desert Edge was to turn those things over to people I have a great deal of trust and confidence in at a very high level. This allows me to deal with today's student athletes and their needs. We are a two platoon team except for special packages. We run a pistol spread offense and the 3-4 defense.

We are past Generation X coaches and we have moved on to Generation Y athletes. It is the new thing. These kid's lives are full of distractions. Just as soon as they get to school, they are on their phones. Our school allows phones on campus and even in some classes to participate in certain projects. These kids have X-box, the internet, and they are stimulation junkies. They have to have something in their hand. I even notice it with the younger coaches on my staff. My younger coaches are always on their phones.

We want to make sure we create as much stimulation for our kids as possible, whether it is in meetings, in practice, or in games. We do not want them to have anything else they are thinking about when it is time to get down to business. We keep them on the move constantly. We throw little clips from YouTube or wherever we can get them, into our film sessions to keep players alert.

The Generation Y athlete has been told they are Special their entire life. Mommy and daddy have told them how great they are because of self-esteem. They had to make sure their self-esteem was taken care of. We have many of those kids in our program. These kids have been sheltered and need constant attention.

They are confident to a fault at times. Some of our corners think they can line up at six yards because they see it in the NFL on Sundays. They think they can cover any wide receiver at six yards deep because they saw it on TV with the pros. They believe they are better than they are because of what they see on TV and they think they can line up wherever they want.

When we took over at Desert Edge it was in the middle of May in 2010. We did not have a spring practice together with our kids. Coach Baker came up with our "Grab an Oar" philosophy. What that meant was we did not have time for a lot of questions. We had to jump into a passing league and start our lifting program right away. We told our kids we were short on time and we were not going to go through a lot of back and forth stuff. We told them to "Grab an Oar" and if everybody is rowing we can make great things happen. Now, we all know that stuff works really well if you win games. We sold it throughout the off season and we won the first game. It has just continued from there.

Some of the kids like to know why, which is not surprising with Generation Y athletes. In the end, with us if you are asking a lot of why questions you are not moving fast enough and you are going to get past up.

We have high expectations on a low budget. What I mean by that is we do not ask a lot from the kids. They have to pay $100 to play football. If they are on the free or reduced lunch program, they have to pay $20. I do not ask a lot from the parents. Our kids are not going to walk out in all matching shorts or they may not have the best looking hats, but I can tell you, I do not have a lot of parent problems. Our kids do not have a lot. In today's economic times, it is difficult for some of our families. A single parent family has a lot to deal with and we have a lot of players in that category. We do not ask a lot from the families and they trust us to take care of their kids.

I make all personnel decisions at all three levels. Parents or kids do not have to go to any of our assistant coaches. They come to me. If they do not like their playing time, it sits right with me. I let our freshman coach know who our freshman quarterback is and who the tailback is. I take the coaches input and in the end it is going to be based on what they decide, but I am responsible for all of those decisions. I do not want any of our coaches to worry about kids or parents questioning them. Mommies and daddies can come to me with their questions. I handle all of the discipline problems. If a kid is in trouble in the school office, I take care of all three levels in that area.

We want to create an atmosphere where our kids want to play football at Desert Edge. It is very competitive in our area. We have two private schools in our area so we want to create the type of environment where our kids want to play for us and be a part of something special.

After the run we made this past year, we sat down as a staff and decided we needed to put as much money as possible into new uniforms. Why did we do that? Our kids love their uniforms. The kids complained about their uniforms all year and at the time it went in one ear and out the other. Once the season was over and we took a look at it and we decided that is what the kids wanted.

We had old baggy uniforms and we were playing against teams with nice form fitting uniforms. Again, going back to generation Y, they wanted new uniforms. We got with our athletic director and he did a great job for us in getting the new uniforms.

What does our atmosphere sound like? Every place you go that involves Desert Edge football, music will be involved, period. It will not be my music, it will not be my staff's music, but it will be the kid's music. We create a play list of 75 songs and put it on an iPod. We have two different sound systems that go along with it. If we go to practice, if we go to meetings, if we go on the road, when we get off the bus, it will be their music, period.

Now, the only issue you have with that is finding the PG rated version of all their songs. That is what I get to do. Our booster club takes care of iTunes cards and I go through and get the non-explicit version of all their songs. They get to change it up three times each year. You would be surprised how big this is. It is by far one of the biggest things for them. I may get a text at 2:00 am from a kid in the summer asking me to add a new song. It is very important to them. That is the type of atmosphere we have created.

I was at a previous clinic and heard a coach say they play oldies and a variety of music. We do not do that! We play what our kids want to hear all of the time. There is a certain song our kids like to hear when they get off the bus. Our coaches do not like it all of the time but our coaches have learned to deal with it. Coaches try to get away from the sound as much as possible.

We want to create an environment where the student-athletes are the decision makers. Are we going to direct them to the decision we want? Absolutely! In the end they believe they made the decision. I meet with the key stakeholders at least once a week. They can be a junior or a senior, whoever the kids select. We all know who those kids are in our programs. We do not just have senior leaders. I may have position coaches involved and sometimes it is just me dealing with them. The players are going to make decisions on everything. What uniforms to wear, what to wear on Thursdays, what to wear on Friday night, what music to hear, etc. They are going to be involved in the decision making.

At practice our coaches are working their tails off as they always do. I am writing notes on little cards I carry around to remind me of issues that my coaches or I need to take care of later.

If we have a problem with a kid in practice or they are not doing what they are supposed to be doing, they are sent to me. Practice keeps on going with the next man up. The thing is it allows me to meet with these kids. When we had 20 minutes of scheduled defense, I got to meet with our quarterback for 20 minutes. I got to find out what was going on in his world. It helped us progress as the season went on. Our middle linebacker was having some problems during the year. During offensive practice I was able to get him away from the group and talk to him.

By me giving up the offense and defense, it helped our kids. Our kids have more going on in their lives than just football and we tend to forget that sometimes. There are just a very few of those kids where football is more important to them than it is to us. Football is pretty important to us and we put a lot of long hours into it. There are very few kids that it means that much too anymore. We have to remember that.

We have a set criteria for evaluation and participation. We do not have a set list of 50 rules to go through. Everything falls under this rule criteria in order to be a football player at Desert Edge.

CRITERIA - EVALUATION / PARTICIPATION

- **Respectful to all Members of the Desert Edge Staff and Community.**
- **Respectful to Your Teammates.**
- **Play With a High Level of Effort.**
- **Produce.**

That is how you participate and how you get on the field. Everything falls under that. It is very important how they treat our support staff on campus. It is important how they act and are seen in the community. Our secretaries, janitors, support staff, and faculty, spends countless hours doing things to support our kids. Our players must be respectful and understand that fact.

Being respectful of their teammates is very important these days. They have so many opportunities to talk about each other with Facebook and Twitter. We did not have that when I was playing.

They have to give a high level of effort and that is a key for us. In the end, they have to produce. Our quarterback was a tough and speedy type quarterback. One of our coaches said he ran a 5.0 in the 40. He may not have been able to run a 5.2. We run the pistol spread offense and the kid looks like he is running in quicksand. However, the kid flat out produced. He produced 3,600 yards for us and he wanted to play defense the whole time. He produced and that is what is important. He is a great kid and he made it work.

Let me talk about the staff and how they relate to today's athlete. I will put my staff up against anybody in Arizona. The time, energy, and effort they put out 365 days a year cannot be measured. They understand when they become part of our staff, we are the player's parents. Of our top ten or twelve athletes we are only talking to a single mom. Dad is not anywhere to be found. That is just the way it is. We are going to spend more time with a lot of these kids than their parents do.

I let the coordinators make the pre-game speeches. That is their baby. Sometimes I get to hear them, sometimes I don't. One of the reasons I do not give the pre-game speech is I do not want it to go onto deaf ears. When it is time to crack the whip during the game, I am up and down the sideline going crazy and yelling for three hours.

We were down 21-3 at halftime of our quarter final playoff game and everybody's hair was on fire. We could not do anything and the kids were going crazy. I sat down in front of everyone and told them to relax and that everything was going to be fine. If I was talking to them every single minute of every single day, they would not get it and they would turn a deaf ear.

They came out and stayed calm the whole second half and we were able to come back and win the game. Sometimes if we keep hammering on kids, they are going to turn us off. I do not want the kids to turn us off. It is important to me that the staff and the kids keep listening at all times.

The staff has to be prepared at all times. The kids will notice everything we do. The kids notice every little thing if you are not ready for practice and they know it from day one. I want our coaches to look for to make us a better team. I tell our kids to look for things to make us better. We look for something to do that will make everybody else's job easier.

Let me move on to today's technology. Our players think I have pictures of every pretty girl you can think of and I use them to befriend our football players so I can check out their Facebook pages. It is of legend proportions at our school. I know they believe this because a basketball player told me so. As coaches, you should know there is stuff on their Facebook that should not be on their Facebook pages. You just don't know? It is important to know what is on their Facebook page.

If we do allow Twitter, we have someone from our staff sign up to follow them on their Twitter account. We do not allow any of our football material to be posted on YouTube. I check You-Tube three times a week. I just type in Desert Edge, Desert Edge Football, or any combination of words that would allow me to see anything posted on YouTube.

We do not even allow our kids to post their highlight videos. If they want highlight videos, we send them out for them. It is very important that we know what is on their Facebook pages, their Twitter account, and on YouTube. We talk to our kids at least once a week about not doing anything that would take them away from the experience they are having. Those types of things you cannot take back. Facebook, Twitter, and texting you cannot take back and we have to talk about it to our kids constantly.

We talk about the "Village" at Desert Edge. Our administration has been really good to us at Desert Edge. I think it is important to get as many on campus coaches as possible. I am fortunate to have five or six on campus coaches. We make sure our teachers and our special education kids are wearing jerseys every Friday. We find as many old jerseys as we can and hand them out to our teachers. You would be surprised how that affects the moral of the teachers toward our football program. We also make sure the special education kids are included. We want to bring the village in and make sure they feel they are a part of our program.

We have a counselor we utilize as a football academic advisor. It is listed on her card. She is dressed in team gear during games and looks better than our team does. That is important to us. Players may have a teacher on campus that has a reputation of not getting along with football players. We wanted an advisor who could help us with those types of teachers if they show up.

We talk about our community constantly. About six years ago when Boise State beat Oklahoma I heard a lot of talk about the Bronco nation. We call ours "Scorpion" nation. We want our kids and the people in our area to talk about Scorpion football. We want it on the tip of their tongue. We want to rule the market in our area. We want the people throughout Scorpion nation to send their kids to Desert Edge High.

Let me talk about how we practice because of today's athlete. We never go any longer than 2 hours and 15 minutes in practice. Why? Because of the kids attention span will not allow us to go much longer. Their attention span is not very long. Sometimes the coaches' attention span isn't very long, either.

We talked about the kids before in that they are stimulation junkies. We want them to have a life outside of football. Sometimes in the summer we give the kids a week off. They may need to recharge their battery. Everybody needs to recharge their batteries at some point. If you go any longer than 2 hours and 15 minutes, wives and girlfriends start to question whether our coaches should really be coaching football. I have only lost one coach I wanted to keep in the past three years with this problem. I want to keep coaches. Winning does not hurt but I think a lot of it is how much time we are away from our loved ones.

We rarely condition, but we practice at a very fast tempo. All we ever talk about is transitions. If you cannot run and hit at Desert Edge, do not bother showing up. We want them moving constantly. Since I do not have to worry about calling plays on offense or defense, I can spend my time making sure they are moving at a rapid pace. We have a clock set at five minutes. If I see a coach that might be going a little over on a drill, I am going to talking to him.

Drill structure is very important to us. I do not want to see a line of twelve defensive backs. I want to see four lines of three players. I want to see a lot of reps. Our sports medicine group makes sure there is water with every group and they follow the groups. We do not stop for team water breaks. If a kid needs water we want him to go get it. If you do not have a sports medicine group, find a kid even if he is the lowest kid on the totem pole in your program. This speeds things up drastically. We make sure it happens so we can practice at a very high tempo.

We do not team stretch, even in pre-game. That is the biggest waste of time I have ever found. Here is why. We want to steal time for talking to the kids. We start on defense every single day and our kids are at their position groups. The kids stretch within their group. In the end, all we want out of stretch time is that they are stretched and that they do not pull muscles. This allows our coaches to steal a few minutes to talk to their kids about their day. We want to take an opportunity to find out what makes them tick and what is going on in their lives. They have plenty of other time to cheer during the game. We are going to get it done in position groups and it has really helped us with tempo in practice.

The heat in Arizona is nasty. Three years ago people were talking about having to modify practice to where we could not go out on certain days because of the heat. So, on Tuesday after our first game, we decided to go out in shells, just helmet, shoulder pads, and shorts. We won game one and then we wanted to keep our kids legs fresh. We had just been with them going at it for three months straight. What we started to noticed was on Friday nights, our kids were fresh and running around looking for somebody to hit.

We still form tackled three days a week. We still get after it in practice. Sure, we could be better in some positions, but we are going to fly around and hit you. We now do it all of the time. It saves our kids legs and it makes them absolutely hungry come Friday night. They are ready to clean somebody's plow. Those of you who have been coaching for a long time, and hitting and tackling every single day, if it works for you, then good.

We do not have a lot of depth. If we lose our 6'2" 220 pound tailback, I don't have another one that size. We have to watch our depth. Our coaches know if we get a kid hurt in practice, they better have a good darn reason. This is

how we do it. We are going to form tackle three times each week at stations organized by position groups. We do not have to worry about fresh legs. We do not have to worry about modifying our practice because of the hot weather because we have addressed that situation already.

In our form tackling we do not take anybody to the ground. Again, it started out because of our depth issues. It keeps us moving faster in practice because it allows us to get more reps without having to wait for kids to get off the ground. I run the whistle on all live drills. We talk to our kids from day one about staying up. Most of the injuries that occur happen when you take players to the ground.

The other issue is this. Changes are on their way. After talking to our team doctor and trainer, they think some of the tackling may be coming down in the next five years because of concussions. We are under attack as football coaches but we believe we are ahead of the curve at Desert Edge. Our kids know when the whistle blows they are to stop. If they don't, they know we will find somebody that will. We have only had two concussions in the past three years. Both were on the hands kickoff teams where the kids got blown up waiting to catch the ball.

We sell the mentality of "we will take on anybody, anytime, and anywhere." The kids really bought into this. I am not sure we were really as good as our kids thought we were. I think sometimes they were disappointed the Arizona Cardinals weren't showing up against them on a Friday night. They came out and they played like it was their last game. They played with a chip on their shoulder. Our kids are going to run around and hit people, and we are selling the "we will take on anyone anytime" mentality all the time.

Another thing we do is to keep a pulse on the flow of practice. You have to be creative. If the flow of practice is not going well and you are not getting what you want, switch it up. We will put some juice into it. It is not scripted but we will get two kids and circle up and go at it. Again, no one is going to the ground. We draw the line to see who is going to win. That is good stuff. Boom! We change it up and get the tempo going a little faster. If we are missing two or three reps of an inside drill period, that is okay. If the practice is flat, it does not matter. Change it up!

I do not know about your program, but at our program, the kids are always dancing. Or at least they think they can dance. One day this year practice was not going very well so we circled up and called kids out to dance. The only dancing we saw was two offensive linemen got in the middle and slow danced. That was the only thing that happened. They did not want to get out there and dance in front of everybody. The other thing we have done is freestyle rap.

One of the things the kids love is when we pull out popsicles in the middle of practice. We pull them out in a Gatorade bucket and it looks just like another water bucket. We pop the cooler open, start cutting with scissors and throw them Otter Pops. You might ask why we would do that. This is football. We do it because we want to change things up. It keeps their attention.

Sometimes you tell them they deserved something special, and sometimes you don't. Sometimes you just throw them at them, and it gets their attention right away. It cost you maybe six dollars. We are trying to get the most out of these kids. This is supposed to be fun. If you throw two Otter Pops to a kid in 107 degree heat, I guarantee you this. It becomes fun for them at that point. They are standing outside in the heat during football practice eating Otter Pops. You have to make it fun sometimes.

We do run a scripted practice. We may change it up toward the end of the season around game eight or nine. We usually go with four to seven minute segments, or we go for a certain amount of positive reps. If we get four good reps and the coordinator is good with it, we may move on to the next segment.

It allows us to fly through practice. The kids and coaches are flying around from segment to segment making sure they have good reps, for what? So they can go home. If you are doing it right, why continue to do it just to do it, we are going to move fast. It really invigorates the staff and they are trying to get the kids to transition as fast as they can to stay one step ahead. The pace is fast but you still get to everything. It is very similar to what some coaches do on Thursday, except we just do it every day.

This is how we get prepared on game days. Different kids get ready for a game in different ways. If you tell some kids they have to be quit and serious for a few hours before the game, they are not going to be ready for the game. We create a separate environment for those types of kids. We create a separate environment for those kids who cannot have any sound around them.

We also have a training room environment where they can hang out and talk with other people. We want to create an environment so that every kid feels ready. The coaches move around and watch to make sure each kid is in their place to get the optimal output they can give on a Friday night.

The game is supposed to be fun. We come out in pre-game just in our jerseys until game time. We come out in pre-game in all of the bands and illegal stuff the kids want to wear. They come out with everything on their arms and legs. You cannot get a penalty for it in pre-game. The referee will come up to me and tell me the players cannot wear this and that. I say, I know. When we take the field and hit the sideline our kids know they cannot have that stuff on. We did not have one penalty because of it this year. It is the best thing I have done for the kids.

For games we come out with the drummers in the school band leading us to take the field. If you have problems with the band director, tell him you want part of the band to lead the team on the field just before the kickoff. If you walk out with the drummers and they put a little flavor into their entrance, it will get the kids excited. Our kids love it, the administration loves it, and the band parents love it. Everybody is happy. It is awesome.

If you have any questions drop me a note. My email is: rwellbro@aquafria.org. We would love to talk with those that are interested, especially coaches from out of the state to exchange ideas and information. We can do it by email, hudl, or however you want to communicate. We want to learn as much as possible. Thank you.

Joey Wiles

Defending Trips Formations

St. Augustine High School, Florida

First I want to say something special about the football coaching profession. Wherever you coach, be loyal to the people that hired you. I love the school where I coach. I love the St. Augustine community.

What I am going to talk about today is nothing original. The coaches that were instrumental in helping me develop the defense we run are names that most football coaches know as defensive coaches. I can trace everything we do to Bob Stoops, Bo Pelini, Tom Bradley, Greg Mattison, Ron Vanderlinden, and Chuck Bresnahan just to mention a few.

We are a 4-3/3-4 quarter cover team. We play a two-deep concept and cover-4 in the secondary. When you get to the trips formation, it is an entirely different concept.

I do want go through some of my philosophy so you will know where we are coming from. I am not a full time football coach as some schools have. When I get to school in the mornings, I have three anatomy classes waiting for me. All my coordinators and most of the other staff are full time teachers. Those coaches have many things going on in their lives and we try to make what we do in football simple.

JACKET DEFENSIVE PHILOSOPHY

1. **Stop the run (Load the box)**
   - **Movements for undersized kids**
   - **Division 1 (29 – 1, when opponent under 100 yards)**
2. **Simple = Success (Dungy)**
3. **Must Be Fixable (Stand the test of time)**
4. **Win Turnover Battle**
   - **NFL Study: 82 percent Win**
5. **Must Be Able to Play Some Form of Man**
6. **Have Two Answers For Each Set**
7. **Must Be Able To Pressure (Fire Zone/ Silver)**
8. **One Rep Every 25 Seconds**
   - **2 scout groups for Skeleton/Inside**
9. **Do not Give Up the Big Play**
10. **Take Away opponent's "Bread and Butter**

The first thing we must do on defense is to make sure we are gap sound and have all the fits in the running game covered. Stopping the run is the number one goal over everything we do. Tony Dungy is a respected football coach and his main thought about football was to keep it simple. The coaches have a tendency to want to do too much. You must keep the defensive scheme simple so your players can execute what you want them to do. That has caused me to look at what we were doing and try not to do too much.

When you defend the trips set, you must be able to play some form of man coverage. When you install a defense or coverage, you must know how to fix anything that goes wrong in the coverage. You need answers when the offense presents a problem. Going into a game we want to have two answers for each set we see. We are seeing the trips more and more.

You must condition your defensive backs, particularly against an offense that likes to send receivers deep. Teams will try to fatigue defensive back by running a number of fresh receivers at him on successive plays. When we have our skeleton pass coverage drills, we have two groups of receivers work against our secondary. We run one group at the secondary. As they are coming back from the first group of receivers, the second group is lining up to run the next pattern. We want to get one rep every 25 seconds.

Today there are so many teams playing up-tempo offenses. They depend on the defense misaligning or getting tired and making a mistake. When we scout a team, we want to take away their bread and butter plays. We want to take away six runs and passes that they depend on running. When it comes down to what is important, you must stop the run, be simple, and win the turnover battle. If you do that, you have a great chance of winning.

There are many different trips sets. The tight end with two detached receivers outside of him is a "Trey" set. The set with three detached receivers to the same side is another set you must cover. You need to know why they are running the trips set. Is it part of their offensive scheme or are they running it to get a mismatch with their best player? We need to know if they are an "X Game" team.

Do they like the perimeter screen game? If they are prone to do that, we must defend that differently. You need to know if they are a big weak side run team or do they like strong side perimeter runs. You need to know if they play with more 10 or 11 personnel. Some teams get into the spread to run inside. Anytime you play a trips team you need to know if the quarterback is a run threat. These are things we must game plan in playing the trips formation teams.

Everything we do comes from a two-high shell. The protection schemes and run blocking has to be simple for the offense. We want to have movements and games from the front. We have more sacks when we run twists and games than when we bring linebacker blitzes. We run games with the two inside down linemen and twists with the tackles and ends.

When we rush, we want to come with five-man pressure with fire coverage. We can bring six-defenders on a blitz with Silver coverage behind it. However, when we bring six rushers, we are in trouble and need to sack the quarterback. You cannot play the corner the same way every time. You must change his technique to confuse the quarterback. You can press the corners, play press and bail, or play off the receiver.

If you try to play the same coverage every time, the offense will find ways to beat it. You need two to three coverages to change up the looks. When you play the nickel and dime package, they must do a good job of disguising what they do. We give them a line to walk so they disguise what they are doing.

Our base coverage is "palms." Our rules tell us how to handle the trips set. We play quarter coverage to the trips side. Everything works fine with the rules until the number 3 receiver run the vertical route. In the base coverage, the Mike linebacker walls the number 3 receiver out

of the middle and has to take him deep if he goes vertical. That becomes the issue with this coverage. This could create a mismatch in some cases, but it also takes him out of the run box.

PALMS

(This is not a check, it is a call.)

Play Side Responsibilities
- **Sam: Wall #2**
  - **Take #3 to the Flat (Carry Wheel)**
- **F/S: Read #2**
  - **Play #2 Vertical**
  - **#2 Flat, Look to #1**
- **Corner: Read #2**
  - **Play #1 Vertical**
  - **React to #2 in the Flat**
- **Mike: Carry #3 vertical**

The coverage we play in this set is "**palms**" coverage. (Diagram #1) The corner and free safety read the number 2 receiver. The corner aligns on the number 1 receiver and reads the number 2 receiver. The free safety aligns on the number 2 receiver and reads his release. If the number 2 receiver goes vertical, the free safety has him. If he goes to the flat, the free safety releases him and looks for the number 1 receiver. He plays over the top of the number 1 receiver. If the number 2 receiver goes to the flat, the corner rolls and takes him.

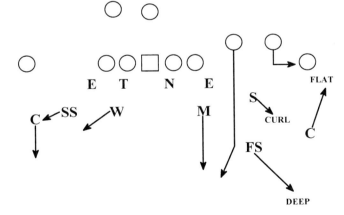

Diagram #1. Palms (Quarters)

I want to give you a brief overview of what we do in our trips checks. When we talk about trio coverage, we take three defenders to handle the 3 vertical routes. With three deep threats to the same side, we have to bring someone from the weakside to cover one of them. We handle the outside and slot receivers with the corner and strong safety. What you must decide is who covers the third receiver to that side if he goes vertical. That is what the checks do in the trips formation. That is what the trio coverage does.

TRIO

- **Handles 4 vertical, weak on bubble screens**
- **Our first check if we have a solid backside corner; Safety plays poach technique**
- **This allows playside Sam/Corner/Safety to play quarters**

MINI

- **Handles bubble screen; Much flexibility backside**
- **Sam/Safety read #3, Corner is man-coverage**

CURLY

- **Takes stress off Corner; Sam buzzes flat; Free Safety read #2; Backside safety poaches**

The first check we use is a "Trio" adjustment. On this check, we use the strong safety to cover the number 3 receiver to the trips side on the vertical.

TRIO

(Regular quarters With S/S Carrying #3 Vertical)

Play Side Responsibilities
- **Sam: Split the difference between 2 and 3 (End of LOS)**
  - **Drop to Inside Shoulder of #2**
    - **Wall #2**
    - **Take #3 to the Flat (Carry Wheel)**
- **F/S: Align outside of #2**
  - **Read #2**
    - **Play #2 Vertical**
    - **#2 Flat, Look to #1**
- **Corner: Align outside of #1**
  - **Read #2**
    - **Play #1 Vertical**
    - **React to #2 in the Flat**
- **Mike: Align towards trips**
  - **Wall #3**
- **S/S: Align 2 x 10 off ghost TE**
  - **Poach #3**

In Trio, the strong safety handles the number 3 receiver if he comes vertical. (Diagram #2) If

number 3 goes to the flat, the Sam linebacker plays him. If the number 3 receiver releases inside the Mike linebacker walls him out of the middle, and plays him in the hook area up to 12 yards deep. If number 2 goes to the flat and number 1 releases vertical, the free safety turns and looks to the number 1 receiver. When he breaks to the post, the free safety picks up his pattern. The corner sinks into his area and looks for number 3 receiver running the wheel.

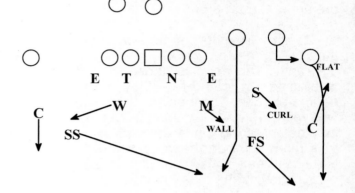

Diagram #2. Trio

The Sam linebacker plays trio as he did in quarter coverage. He aligns splitting the difference between number 2 and 3 receivers. He opens to number 2 and carries him for 10 yards in zone coverage. He is playing 2 to 3. He aligns on number 2 but keys the pattern of number 3. The only thing that will take him to the flat is number 3 going to the flat. The corner and free safety play the number 1 and 2 receivers as they did in their regular "palms" (quarters) coverage. Nothing changes for them.

The Mike linebacker plays "palms" coverage. He tells the strong safety, he cannot take the number 3 receiver vertical and still be a box player on the run. The strong safety aligns on the ghost tight end to the single receiver side at a depth of 10 yards. He is an alley player on a run to him. On a speed option, he plays the pitch.

He is going to poach the number 3 receiver to the trips side if he goes deep. On pass, he opens to the number 3 receiver and has him deep. However, the Mike linebacker is going to wall the number 3 receiver up to 12 yards deep.

That helps him with the distance he has to cover. If the strong safety flies into his coverage, it can be dangerous. In his haste to get to the receiver, he could overrun the pattern and let the number 3 receiver inside him down the middle.

That is why we are not in a big hurry to get to him. The Mike linebacker holds him off and the strong safety keeps his inside leverage on him.

The strength of the Trio is it can handle the 4 verticals. If the offense runs the speed option to the weakside, we have no problems. We can play the inside runs well because we are sound inside with two linebackers. The corner and free safety can play quarters and nothing changes for them. In the run game, we are gap sound with all gaps covered.

The problems occur to the backside with the coverage on the X-receiver. We end up in man coverage on the X-receiver and the Will linebacker has to man up on the running back. That could present a problem with match ups. The Will linebacker cannot allow the back to out-leverage him. He may have to adjust his alignment slightly to the outside.

To the trips side we could have some problems with the bubble screen and the jet sweep. It has to do with the leverage position of the Sam linebacker. The number 2 receiver has a crack alignment on him, which could present a problem with the bubble screen. The same thing is true with the jet sweep.

If the number 3 receiver does not go vertical, the strong safety has to help the corner to his side on the spacing patterns. (Diagram #3) On the spacing pattern, the number 3 receiver goes to the flat and the Sam linebacker plays him. The number 2 receiver runs the corner route and draws double coverage from the free safety and the corner because the number 1 receiver went to the inside.

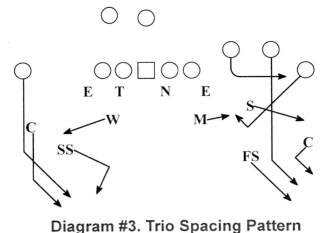

Diagram #3. Trio Spacing Pattern

The Mike linebacker drops into his hook/curl area and plays the number 1 receiver. The strong safety drops to the backside and helps the corner on the post route of the number 1 receiver from the backside.

The strong safety in the run game on flow to the formation side is the cut back player as he is in the cover-4 scheme. If you have a good corner, play him in press position on the number 1 receiver to the trips side. That discourages the bubble screen and allows him to play the smash route.

When we play **"Mini"** to the trips side it gives us a change up. This goes back to the "palms" concept in our quarter coverage. The free safety and Sam linebacker play palms coverage on the number 2 and 3 receiver. We lock up the number 1 receiver with man coverage from the corner. We play quarter coverage as if the number 1 receiver was not in the formation.

MINI

(Man #1 and Play Regular Palms (1/4) to #2 and #3)

Play Side Responsibilities
- **Sam: Align outside of #2**
  - **Read #3**
    - **Play #2 Vertical**
    - **React to #3 to the Flat**
- **F/S: Align Outside of #3**
  - **Read #3**
    - **Play #3 Vertical**
    - **#3 away, Play #2 Vertical**
- **Corner:**
  - **Man #1 (except shallow cross)**
- **Mike: Hip the end towards Trips**

The free safety and Sam linebacker read the release of the number 3 receiver and apply their rules. (Diagram #4)

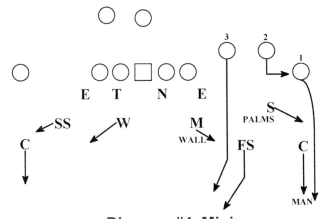

Diagram #4. Mini

If number 3 goes to the flat, the Sam linebacker rolls to the flat and covers him. The free safety reads number 3 to the flat and looks to the number 2 receiver. The Mike linebacker walls the number 3 receiver out of the middle. If both number 2 and 3 receivers run vertical, the free safety has the number 3 receiver and the Sam linebacker has the number 2 receiver.

If the number 3 receiver goes to the flat and up the sidelines, the Sam linebacker has to take him. If the number 2 receiver runs any type of outside breaking pattern, the Sam linebacker has him. If he runs the wheel route, he belongs to the Sam linebacker. The Mike linebacker walls the number 3 receiver out of the middle and plays the hook/curl zone to the formation side. He could end up playing coverage on anything breaking into his zone.

We will run the "Mini" adjustments against teams that run the bubble screen to the trips side. It is good against the X-receiver because it allows help coverage from the strong safety. We can play the outside run both strong and weak equally well. The pattern that hurts us in the "Mini" is the smash and flood route because it isolates the Sam linebacker on the slot to the corner route or sideline cut.

Our huddle call is "Slide-Palms-Mini." The "Slide" is the front call. We slide into an over front. The "Palms" is the coverage call. We play palms against any set with the exception of the trips set. If the formation is a trips set, we play "Mini."

The Sam linebacker aligns one yard outside of the number 2 receiver at six yards. He reads the release of the number 3 receiver. If number 3 goes to the flat, he takes him there. If the number 2 receiver comes up the field, he plays inside with a "scooch" technique. That is not backpedaling. He plays a foot replacement technique and shuffles back.

We play this against teams that want to exploit the defense with the X-receiver to the backside. You can play any kind of two-man coverage you want. The corner can press with the strong safety over the top. You can invert the strong safety underneath and play the corner over the top. There are endless ways to take him out of the game.

If you want to protect the Mike linebacker in the play action pass scheme, we use a tango call.

(Diagram #5) This protects the Mike linebacker on his fill in the B-gap. It allows him to work to his pass coverage on his run fit. The defensive end slants into the B-gap and the Mike linebacker has the C-gap on run his way. If the play is a pass, we wrap the nose to the outside on a twist. The end comes into the B-gap and the nose wraps to the outside for contain.

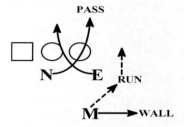

Diagram #5. Tango

We call the third way to play the trips set, "Curly." It is a bit different.

CURLY

(S/S Buzzes flat with FS playing CURL)

Play Side Responsibilities
- **Sam: Buzz the flat**
  - **Carry Wheel routes**
- **F/S: Read #2**
  - **Play #2 Vertical**
  - **#2 Flat, Look to #1**
- **Corner: Play 1/3 Tech**
  - **Play #1 vertical.**
  - **Play heavy inside, defend the post**
- **Mike: Wall #3**

The reason we run "Curly" is to take the stress off the corner. The corner bails out and plays deep on this coverage. (Diagram #6) The Sam linebacker buzzes to the flat and play that zone for all patterns. The free safety reads the number 2 receiver.

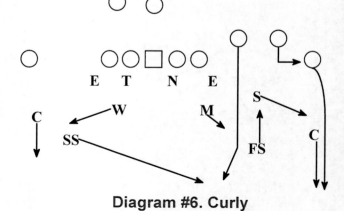

Diagram #6. Curly

If he comes vertical, he takes him. If he goes to the outside, the free safety rolls into the curl area in the immediate zone. The strong safety has the number 3 receiver on vertical routes as he did on the "Trio" coverage. The technique for the Mike linebacker and strong safety are the same as they were in "Trio."

This allows the Sam linebacker to play the flat and the free safety plays the smash route by the number 2 receiver. (Diagram #7) That puts the free safety on the corner route with the corner dropping deep into the deep third. The Sam linebacker buzzes the flat and covers the hitch by the number 1 receiver.

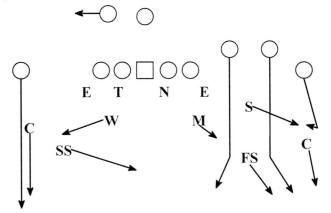

Diagram #7. Curly vs. Smash

If the offense runs the number 2 receiver to the flat and curls the number 1 receiver, the free safety robs the curl by the number 1 receiver. The Mike linebacker plays the number 3 receiver if he goes vertical. He walls him out of the middle and carries him for 12 yards. The strong safety poaches from his weakside position to cover number 3 on the vertical.

The good thing about "Curly" is it handles four verticals. It is good against speed option to the trips side of the formation. It takes the pressure off the corner by allowing him to drop into the deep third and not worry about patterns thrown in front of him. "Curly" also is good against flood patterns. (Diagram #8) It allows you to cover the three levels of the flood route.

The weakness of "Curly" is the same weaknesses of the trio check. Since the strong safety poaches to the trips side, the corner has the X-receiver man-to-man. It puts the Will linebacker in man coverage on the running back. He has to make the same adjustments in his alignment as he did on the "Trio." He cannot allow the running back to out-leverage him.

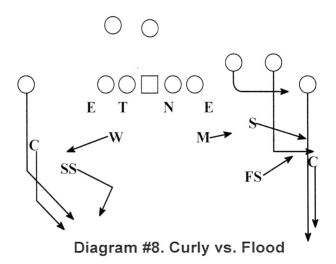

Diagram #8. Curly vs. Flood

"Curly" has the same adjust for the strong safety if the number 3 receiver does not go vertical. If the strong safety starts to poach to the trips side and sees the number 3 receiver not coming vertical, he reverses his path and folds back to help the boundary corner on the post cut by the single receiver.

The trips formation is a unique formation that presents challenges in covering the number 3 receiver on the vertical. However, you can remain sound in your running game. When you play teams that run the trips set you have to decide what they are trying to do. If it is a part of their offensive scheme, you need to have checks and adjustments to cover it.

If they are aligning in the set to spread the defense and get a running quarterback on a lesser defender, you can play less pass coverage and more run cover. If they have an athlete at the single wide receiver side and work to him that is where you need to concentrate the coverage. Do not let the offense beat you with their best receiver because you are scheming to take away their fourth best receiver. Decide what the offense wants to do and prepare accordingly.

I hope you got something that you can use. These coverages are not difficult to run, but you must communicate within the defense. I appreciate your attention. Thank you very much.

NOTES

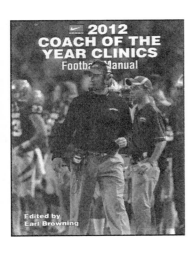

2013
COACH OF THE YEAR CLINICS MANUAL & NOTES

Featuring lectures from some of America's most renowned coaches at the 2012 Nike Coach of the Year Clinics.

Clinic Manual (College Coaches) - $35.00
Clinic Notes (High School Coaches) - $34.00
U.S. Shipping & Handling included

CLINIC MANUALS
2013 Clinic Manual - $35.00
2012 Clinic Manual - $25.00
2011 Clinic Manual - $20.00
2002 - 2010 Manuals - $15.00 each
1969 - 2001 available on DVD

CLINIC NOTES
2013 Clinic Notes - $34.00
2012 Clinic Notes - $24.00
2011 Clinic Notes - $20.00
2004 - 2010 Notes - $15.00 each
Table of contents on our website

nikecoyfootball.net
Go to our website for all Telecoach, Inc. Publications
including Manuals, Notes, C.O.O.L. Clinic Manuals, E-books, and Coaching DVD's
Telecoach: The More We Tell, The More We Sell

Title	Price	Qty	Total
Kentucky residents must include tax form 51A-126 or pay 6% sales tax. **Plus**	KY Tax 6%	→	
Shipping & Handling included in cost for orders within the USA **Plus**	Shipping	→	
Canada add $9.50 for each Clinic Manual to Canada;	Total	→	
International add $15.00 for each Clinic Manual to an International Address			

Name: _____ Organization/School: _____

Address: _____

City: _____ State: _____ Zip: _____ Phone: _____

Method of Payment: Card (___) Check (___) Check #: _____ Purchase Order (___) PO #: _____

Card Number: /____/____/____/____/____/____/____/____/____/____/____/____/____/____/____/____/

Expiration Date: /____/____/____/____/   CVC Number: /____/____/____/____/

Signature: _____ Email Address: _____

Mail Check or Credit Card Information to: Earl Browning, Telecoach, Inc. 3512 Foxglove Lane Louisville, KY 40241	Checks Payable to: Telecoach, Inc. Website: nikecoyfootball.net Email: telecoach@insightbb.com